Research Methods
in Social Work

D. C. Heath and Company

Lexington, Massachusetts   Toronto

Research Methods in Social Work

An Introduction

Charles R. Atherton
David L. Klemmack
University of Alabama

For Andrew
and for Petra, Britta, Joel, and John

Preface

During World War II, author C. S. Lewis published a series of satirical letters that were eventually collected in a book entitled *The Screwtape Letters*. These letters were purportedly written by Screwtape, one of hell's more important demons, to his nephew and apprentice, Wormwood. The letters contained Screwtape's advice on how Wormwood should go about corrupting the human being who had been chosen as his first "patient." Lewis, a serious Christian, found himself under considerable tension while writing these letters. In order to get the effect that he wanted, he thought that it was necessary to write from the point of view of a demon. Lewis described his uncomfortable experience as being "all dust, grit, thirst, and itch."

Unfortunately, this is the way that many social work students feel about research. Although it is going too far to suggest that social work students feel that they are working a bit close to demons, it is not an exaggeration to observe that they do seem to feel that their activities are accompanied by a considerable amount of torment.

It is impossible to remove all the dust, grit, thirst, and itch from research. In *Research Methods in Social Work: An Introduction,* we have tried to discuss the various research tasks in some detail and to show that each research operation is a series of related steps. A great many examples from social work have been provided in order to be as concrete as possible. The chapters on statistics have been written with the nonmathematician in mind. Although the various formulas are given in the text, the actual problems are worked out in steps, rather like a recipe. We believe that we have included enough detail to enable the patient reader to follow the discussion.

Research Methods in Social Work: An Introduction was written to be used in the first course in research methods for social work students. It can be used by undergraduates or by first-year graduate students. The book is organized into four units. Part I is a basic orientation to the research process. This material is generally shared by all social science and is not exclusive to any one field. We have focused on the basic philosophy of research, the principles of measurement, and the design of research. Part II first discusses the various tasks involved in data collection. The emphasis of the book then shifts, in the remainder of Part II, to focus on the kinds of data-collection instruments that are useful in social work research. Part III addresses the use of statistics in social work research.

This material will not totally substitute for a full course in statistics, but it will show the social work student how statistics can be used in social work applications. Instructors in programs that do not include a separate statistics course may need to slow the pace when this unit is taught. Part IV deals with the actual practice of research and examines some issues that are currently important in social work research.

At the end of each chapter, the reader will find a list of the important terms that have been introduced in the chapter, some questions for discussion, a series of projects or exercises, and some suggestions for further reading. Because many of the readings are more advanced than the material in the text, each bibliographic item includes a brief annotation that will help students and instructors to make appropriate choices.

This book has several distinctive features. First, it differs from the standard practice usually followed in research texts of discussing in an early chapter how one gets started in research. We have deferred this discussion until Chapter 13, because we believe that one is better prepared to select a research question and to do research after the earlier content has been mastered. However, this chapter can be assigned at the beginning of the course, also. In fact, because all of the chapters are relatively self-contained, their order can be varied with little difficulty.

A second distinctive feature of this book is that it emphasizes the ethics of research. We have chosen to discuss ethical questions in the chapters on data collection (Chapters 5, 6, 7, and 8). This decision was made in order to put the ethical questions in the context of the encounters between researcher and subject. Each method of collecting data has ethical considerations peculiar to that method. Therefore, it seemed logical to us to organize the material in this way.

A third feature is the inclusion, in the last chapter, of discussions of a number of current issues in social work research. We chose to discuss these issues in a separate chapter in order to emphasize them.

For the most part, we have used examples that have some connection with human behavior, social policy, or social work practice. In some cases, particularly early in the book, the examples are from everyday experience. What we have tried to do is to lead the student from a general orientation to research into a specific social work frame of reference.

A number of examples used in this text are drawn from research projects funded by the National Retired Teachers Association–American Association for Retired Persons Andrus Foundation and the Research Grants Committee of the University of Alabama. We gratefully acknowledge permission to use these data.

We are grateful to the Literary Executor of the late Sir Ronald Fisher, F.R.S., to Dr. Frank Yates, F.R.S., and to Longman Group Ltd., London, for permission to reprint tables from their book *Statistical*

Tables for Biological, Agricultural and Medical Research, 6th edition (1974). (See Tables B-2, B-3, and B-6 in Appendix B.)

We would also like to thank Professors John H. Behling and Bruce S. Jansson for their careful reading of the entire manuscript and their helpful comments. Professor Lucinda Roff also read portions of the manuscript and made a number of pertinent and helpful suggestions.

Finally, we also want to thank Linda Oakley and Zoe Atherton for typing various drafts of the manuscript.

C. R. A.
D. L. K.

Contents

13 Statistical Inference and Hypothesis Testing   257

PART IV   289

14 Doing Social Work Research   291

Research Methods
in Social Work

PART I

Part I discusses the basic nature of research in social work and the social sciences. The content is not exclusive to social work but is shared with psychology, sociology, social psychology, political science, and education. Chapter 1 explores the relationship of science to knowledge building. Chapter 2 discusses the basic issues in measurement. Chapter 3 describes the kind of research that is done to explore new ideas and to describe the characteristics and attributes of individuals, groups, and institutions. Chapter 4 looks at the kinds of research designs used in experimental and evaluational research. This Part presents the basic building blocks in the research process.

1

Introduction

What Is Research?

Research is the use of a rational set of activities that enables one to accumulate dependable knowledge. As Dame Agatha Christie's clever detective, Hercule Poirot, might have put it, research is the use of "order and method" in the task of understanding the world and what goes on in it. This approach is commonly known as the scientific method of knowing. Although social workers are not primarily scientists, they use the products of science in their practice and, on occasion, add to the body of orderly knowledge that is considered to be scientific.

Science in our time gets mixed reviews from its critics. Some view science as a diabolical force that has produced industrial pollution, chemically adulterated food, and plastic gadgets. Others regard science as a kind of magic that is expected to save the world from hunger, illness, and drudgery. Although most people would reject these extreme views, there is a lingering tendency to invest science with a certain awesome authority. Some advertisers certainly seem to believe in the power of scientific image. We are encouraged to buy a variety of health-related products on the grounds that they are the fruits of scientific research. On television, an authoritative man or woman wearing a starched laboratory coat holds up an official-looking document, prominently imprinted with the words *Scientific Report,* and urges the consumer to purchase the product described in that report. The consumer is not told about the similarities among products—only that three out of four doctors who make a recommendation suggest this product. Advertisers seem to regard science as a powerful source of persuasion. At least they continue to invest in commercials of this type.

Surely science is a mysterious, powerful phenomenon that is remote from the minds of ordinary people! After all, something done by men and women in laboratory coats using "fragile philosophical instruments" must be beyond the understanding of ordinary citizens!

Actually, science is not as remote as all that. In fact, the scientific approach is often very pedestrian and even dull. The procedures of science are *not* sacred rites. They are simply methods that have been devised over time as dependable means of getting some answers to certain kinds of questions. Although social workers are not limited to scientific knowledge (because they also may depend on intuitive judgments and insight), they can benefit from the application of scientific ways of thinking. The methods of science provide ways of testing and verifying professional experience and practice wisdom.

It is important to emphasize that science is not an absolute. All that can be claimed for the scientific method is that the information gained is more likely to be verifiable than information obtained by most other approaches to knowledge building. Scientific activity, no matter how well done, does not give absolute answers. Neither the physical nor the social sciences expect final answers, anyway. Most scientists agree that the products of science are simply the best answers available at the time. Answers are subject to change as new evidence is integrated into the knowledge base of any science. Scientific methods themselves are not static but are subject to changes over time. Science is, at bottom, primarily a model-building enterprise. Science devises models, which are basically conceptual frameworks, to explain the past and present or to predict the future. The most scientific model is usually the one that explains the most. As new facts emerge, even the best models change to reflect an enlarged understanding.

If science is not a source of absolute knowledge, then why use it? It is the best means that human beings have devised for providing factual and dependable answers to questions requiring factual and dependable answers. Science is superior to the various alternatives available. A recent textbook considers tradition as an alternative to science:

> Each of us inherits a culture made up, in part, of firmly accepted knowledge about the workings of the world. We may learn from others that planting corn in the spring will gain the greatest assistance from the gods, that sugar from too much candy will decay our teeth, that the circumference of a circle is approximately twenty-two sevenths of its radius, or that masturbation will make us blind. We may or may not test these "truths" on our own, but we simply accept the great majority of them. These are the things that everybody knows.[1]

Tradition is an important source of wisdom, values, and sentiments, but it is not always a dependable source of factual knowledge unless support is forthcoming from other sources. For example, for many years, the role of women in society was determined by tradition. This tradition was based on faulty information and untested assumptions and has led to a great many totally erroneous generalizations. "Everybody knows," for example, that women cannot be doctors because they are not strong enough. They can, however, be nurses because they are strong enough for that! Tradition is not immune from illogical and inconsistent positions.

Another source of knowledge that is often considered is "authority." Often, when we want to know, we seek out an expert who is supposed to know. This course may be dependable in many cases, but it is not certain. It has been noted that an authority can make a mistake, especially when speaking outside of his or her realm of expertise.[2] One of the authors of this text knows of a physician who is often asked for his opinion on the purchase of farm land. The physician always gives a confident opinion on whether or not the proposed purchase is a sound one. The problem is that the physician knows very little about farm land, but he cannot resist giving an authoritative opinion when asked for it. It is a fairly common experience when consulting experts to find that they disagree, are not understandable, or are simply wrong.

A third source of knowledge is "common sense." The trouble with common sense is that it is very uncommon. Further, one person's common sense is another person's foolish opinion. Far too often common sense appears to be unrefined individual bias, which may be mixed with some tradition, based on the limited experience of just one person. Although there is a great deal to be said about the worth of shared experiences, the experience of one person may be so highly subjective that it is misleading when used as the basis for generalizing.

What Is the Scientific Approach?

The first paragraph of this chapter stated that science as an approach to knowing is characterized by a central focus on "order and method." Although all sciences depend on these characteristics, the philosopher Abraham Kaplan doubts if it is possible to isolate any single method that is used by every science. He argues that one "could as well speak of 'the method' of baseball." [3] Kaplan's point is that science is too complex to be confined to a narrow list of techniques. Ultimately Kaplan is probably correct. However, there is a general pattern to science that gives coherence to the activity of scientists. The use of "order and method" in science follows common patterns derived from the school of philosophy known as *empiricism*. Briefly, this philosophical approach assumes that the world as it is perceived through experience is real. This is to be contrasted with classical Greek philosophies, which held that the only true reality existed in the realm of pure ideas, independent of human knowledge. To the empiricist, reality is knowable through the senses. Whatever cannot be comprehended by some kind of sense experience is not real to the empiricist. To put it another way, to the empiricist, everything real can be seen, tasted, smelled, heard, or touched. If some kind of "hands on" experience is not possible, then a phenomenon cannot be scientifically analyzed. In essence, then, for a thing to be considered empirically real, we must have some way of apprehending it through sense experience—some kind of measurement process that describes the dimensions of the thing to be understood.

This discussion is not intended to deny the worth of systems of morals or religion. The point is simply that science proceeds on an empirical view of reality. If you are thinking scientifically, you are acting (if only temporarily) as an empiricist. A longer discussion of the nature of science as a value system would be out of place here. The reader who wishes to pursue this point will find some suggestions for further reading at the end of this chapter. It is sufficient to point out that the scientific approach to knowledge building need not be seen as a competitor to theology or any other value system that is concerned with questions that transcend perceivable reality. Science is a rational approach to knowledge building and can be understood only in a pragmatic and rational framework that deals with perceivable reality.

Granting the earlier point made by Kaplan, there are certain practical characteristics that all science shares:

1. *Science is interested in regularities.* This holds true in both physical and social science. Unique exceptions may be of great curiosity; but basically the scientist wants to explain events in some systematic way. It might be interesting, for example, if one child became withdrawn as a consequence of parental neglect in the year 1647. One case of this sort would stand as a matter of great curiosity. It would not, however, be very useful to children in general. Far more important is the observation that neglect is generally harmful to children.

2. *Science is rational.* The scientist operates on the belief that events have reasonable and verifiable causes. There is no magic if one really understands what is happening. If a rock goes up instead of down, a person who believes in magic might think in terms of levitation, whereas the scientist would probably look for a source of propulsion.

3. *Science is parsimonious.* The scientist wants to be able to explain things in the simplest, most economical way. Given two equally true explanations of a given phenomenon, the scientist will choose the one that explains the greatest number of events with the least amount of complication. Amusing literary examples of parsimony can be found in Joyce Porter's stories about Inspector Dover of Scotland Yard. The real explanation of the crime is usually fairly complicated. Dover invariably suspects the criminal for the simplest, crudest reasons (shifty eyes, mean disposi-

tion), and yet he always gets the right man or woman. Porter's skill always carries these stories off very well. The good scientist looks for the simplest explanation, but unlike Inspector Dover, the scientist wants to be correct for the right reason.

4. *Science measures objectively.* The scientist tries to devise objective measuring devices that will yield similar results under similar conditions. A ruler is a good example of an objective measuring device. A full-grown person who stands 5'10" tall today should also measure 5'10" next week. If a person who was 5'10" yesterday is 5'6" today, we would certainly question the objectivity of the measuring device. The idea in scientific measuring is to use or invent a measuring instrument that is free of bias. This aim is not always achieved, but it is always desirable in good scientific practice.

5. *Science is orderly.* The scientist should specify in advance what he or she is looking for and how the result is to be identified when it occurs (or does not occur). It is true that many scientific discoveries are the results of accidents. Further, some useful ideas and inventions were once regarded as useless by-products. Even "accidental" discoveries, however, are based on some amount of orderly knowledge. Chemists do not go into a laboratory and randomly mix chemicals in the hope that a new drug will perhaps be developed. Rather, experiments will proceed with some regard for known properties of the materials and procedures involved. Surprising uses are now being made of waste products. An agricultural chemist recently told one of the authors of this book that five hundred products are now made from corn cobs. Corn cobs are now too valuable to throw away or burn in the wood stove. These uses did not occur by chance; they are the result of a deliberate search for uses of agricultural by-products.

6. *Science is cumulative.* Because scientists record what they do, others who follow them can know what has and has not been done. There is no need to reinvent the wheel, because the properties of the wheel are known and an enormous amount of data is already available. Even unsuccessful studies are useful, if for no other reason than to serve as cautionary examples to those currently interested in a problem. Of course, scientific knowledge does not accumulate in an unsystematic way. A certain amount of selection and weeding out must be done by each generation of scientists. All conclusions are open to challenge by new knowledge, and no bit of scientific knowledge is wholly absolute.

The Role of Theory

The term *theory* may be defined as "a generalization or a series of generalizations by which we attempt to explain some phenomena in some systematic manner." [4] Theories are not just hunches or intuitive guesses. A theory can be constructed only from evidence, in two ways. A theorist may start from a single observation (or a set of related observations) and build a logical framework that can be tested for its explanatory power. This is known as the *inductive* approach. A theorist may also start with a framework that has already been built and reason in the direction of new testable statements (hypotheses) that, when supported by evidence, will fill gaps and either extend the framework or challenge its usefulness. This approach is called the *deductive* approach.

Generally science acquires knowledge through one or the other of these two broad approaches. Sherlock Holmes, though not a scientist, often used the inductive method. In *A Study in Scarlet,* Holmes drew an accurate picture of a murderer from the observations he made about the length of the killer's stride, the height of some writing on a wall, some scratches, a bit of cigar ash, and a quantity of blood. Despite the tendency to think of this kind of exercise as deduction, it is induction—organizing pieces of data into a meaningful generalization on the basis of evidence. Holmes did use deduction on occasion. In the short story "The Speckled Band," Holmes and Watson spent an uncomfortable night in Helen Stoner's room (while Helen spent the night at an inn), waiting for a poisonous snake to come through a ventilator grill. Holmes's theoretical framework, derived from prior observation, required that some kind of poisonous creature appear. When the snake entered the room, Holmes's hypothesis was supported.

In the first example, Holmes used inductive reasoning to move from particular facts (the clues) to a general conclusion (the description of the killer). In the second example, Holmes had already formed a fairly clear picture of what was going on from Helen Stoner's story. He then used this general understanding as the basis for predicting a particular event.

A social work example of the relationship between induction and deduction may help to differentiate them. In taking a social history, a social worker elicits a number of pieces of information from a client, usually in a fairly random way. By themselves, these pieces of information may not mean very much. However, as the social worker reflects on what she learns from the client, she begins to put the pieces together in an orderly way. If the social worker can establish connections among the various facts, she can formulate a tentative explanation for the client's behavior. This is an inductive process analogous to building a theory. Once she has established a general understanding of the client's behavior, the social worker may use the explanation as a source of suppositions about other behaviors or thoughts of the client. This is a deductive process analogous to using a general theory to predict new facts.

Can Scientific Research Answer All Questions?

No. The question to be answered has to be answerable according to certain rules of the game. We cannot answer philosophical or religious questions with scientific techniques. Philosophers and theologians have their own techniques and approaches for answering questions appropriate to those ways of thinking. For example, the question, "Is it more moral to use encounter groups rather than psychosocial therapy when dealing with neurotic marital interaction?" cannot be answered by scientific methods. Of course a researcher could determine which of the two techniques was more effective in a given situation. Or the researcher could find out whether or not participants thought one method better than the other. But whether or not something is moral remains an ethical question, not a scientific one. Science can deal only in things that are susceptible to empirical proof.

Should Scientific Research Be "Pure" or "Applied"?

Although this question still arises from time to time, it is not very important. Supposedly, the "pure" scientist is objectively interested in knowledge for knowledge's sake, whereas the "applied" scientist has only a practical motivation. These two approaches to research have not remained neatly separated in the real world. It has turned out that doing "pure" research has led scientists into applied areas. Practical scientists who start out to solve a pragmatic problem may end up making a contribution to a body of theory. For example, a scientist may be working on an interesting problem in friction and discover a way to make soap lather better. Conversely, an industrial chemist trying to make soap that produces more lather may discover an important principle of friction! The point is that each kind of research usually has some implications for the other. Because social work is a professional field with treatment decisions to make and program planning to do, most social workers would probably identify themselves with applied research. At the same time, social workers have made contributions to theory, as later pages will show.

Why Should Social Workers Study Research?

Even if we grant that somebody needs to do research, it still does not necessarily follow that social workers should study it. In fact, social workers do very little research in comparison with psychologists, sociologists, social psychologists, and political scientists.

There are arguments for more inolvement in research by social workers. Here are four:

1. Social workers who are knowledgeable about research would use research techniques for analyzing and processing data, which could lead to better practice and policy decisions.
2. Social workers who have developed some sophistication in research would be less likely to be deceived by poorly done research.
3. Social workers with research skills would be in a better position to evaluate the usefulness of research from other disciplines.
4. Social workers who can participate in research can demonstrate their accountability to their various constituencies—boards, legislators, and citizens, especially clients. Most service professions are in a better position than social work when it comes to assuring clients that their techniques have a demonstrable effect.

Although these arguments may not be wholly convincing, they have influenced the decisions of social work educators to include research in the social work curriculum.

What Is the Role of Statistics in Social Research?

Students occasionally quote Disraeli's famous remark, "There are three kinds of lies: lies, damned lies, and statistics!" Some years ago, Darrell Huff entertainingly showed how statistics are misused in the book *How to Lie with Statistics.*[5] Although it is true that people are often exposed to distorted data, this is not an exclusive property of the field of statistics. Tools can always be misused by those who are bent on misusing them. Statistics as a discipline includes procedures that allow the processing and analyzing of quantitative data in a logical and coherent fashion. The object of using these procedures is to present quantitative data to a consumer in a form that promotes the understanding of phenomena. The consumer should be able to perceive something of the nature of a phenomenon by knowing its quantitative dimensions. Of course, not everything of importance can be reduced to numbers. When used legitimately, quantitative data can assist understanding. Statisticians do not usually deal in certainties. Statistical data at best allow a researcher to make some statements about reality with some degree of confidence under certain conditions.

In this text, statistical procedures have been inserted into the discussion of research methods at appropriate points. This book's treatment of statistics is no substitute for a course in statistics. We have included this material in order to show how statistics can be used in social work research and to make the research process and the role of statistics more intelligible.

Social Work Research or Social Research?

This text is addressed primarily to the social work student. It must be understood, however, that no specific body of knowledge relating to research belongs exclusively to social work. This book is about research as it applies to social work, but the techniques are shared with other social and behavioral sciences. It is our conviction that the knowledgeable social work practitioner and researcher must be aware of general social science research methods in order to understand when to make applications that are useful to social work purposes.

Key Terms

research	theory
science	induction
parsimony	deduction
empiricism	

References

1. Earl R. Babbie, *The Practice of Social Research,* 2nd ed. (Belmont, Calif.: Wadsworth Publishing Company, 1979), p. 8.
2. Babbie, op. cit., p. 9.
3. Abraham Kaplan, *The Conduct of Inquiry* (Scranton, Pennsylvania: Chandler Publishing Company, 1964), p. 27.
4. William Wiersma, *Research Methods in Education* (Philadelphia: J. B. Lippincott, 1969), p. 11.
5. Darrell Huff, *How to Lie with Statistics* (New York: W. W. Norton, 1954).

Questions for Discussion

1. Is science bad? good?
2. Do unscientific methods result in dependable knowledge?
3. Is there any room for intuition in the knowledge-building process?
4. Can science really be objective and rational? After all, scientists are people and are subject to human limitations.
5. Are theories really necessary to the scientific enterprise?

6. Can clinical social workers depend on those whose professional roles are primarily in research to provide clear, dependable information?
7. Why should social work students know something about statistics? Math is not really related to clinical concerns.

Exercise

Write five questions that can be answered in a scientific way. Remember that your questions should be answerable in an empirical framework and should not deal with questions of value.

For Further Reading

William J. Goode and Paul K. Hatt. *Methods in Social Research.* New York: McGraw-Hill, 1952. Although this book was published twenty-five years ago, it is still quite useful. Chapters 2, 3, and 4 are helpful on the roles of science, values, and theory.

Darrell Huff, *How to Lie with Statistics.* New York: W. W. Norton, 1954. This is an entertaining look at the way statistical data has been manipulated in the public media.

Fred N. Kerlinger. *Foundations of Behavioral Research,* 2nd ed. New York: Holt, Rinehart and Winston, 1973. Chapter 1 contains a very sophisticated discussion of the scientific method and its applications to social science.

Claire Selltiz, Lawrence S. Wrightsman, and Stuart W. Cook. *Research Methods in Social Relations,* 3rd ed. New York: Holt, Rinehart and Winston, 1976. Chapter 1 in the new edition has a good introductory discussion of the functions and use of research.

Tony Tripodi. *Uses and Abuses of Social Research in Social Work.* New York: Columbia University Press, 1974. Written by a prominent social work educator, this book is an important contribution to the discussion of the role of research in social work and its relation to both policy and practice.

2

Basic Concepts
of Measurement

The scientific approach assumes that things can be described in ways that permit some kind of measurement. If a phenomenon cannot be measured, then it is not susceptible to scientific analysis, although it could perhaps be understood in some other frame of reference. The term *measurement* must be understood in its broadest context. Although it is sometimes possible to measure things with a good deal of precision, in other instances the researcher is doing well just to be able to say that a characteristic is either present or absent.

In many everyday cases, measurement is a readily understood process. Everyone is familiar with measures of weight, height, time, and speed. The notion of measurement gets more difficult when it is extended to include abstractions—for example, affection, anxiety, or marital commitment. Selltiz and her colleagues suggest that measurement "consists of a technique for collecting data plus a set of rules for using these data." [1] If this is understood, some of the mystique of the scientific approach falls away, leaving a fairly straightforward principle. We can measure virtually anything empirical *if* we can develop a technique and can set forth clear rules for using it.

Data collected from the subjects of research are expressed as *variables*. A variable is an attribute or characteristic of a phenomenon that can take different numeric or symbolic values. In order for measurement to take place, a range of values must be possible for any given variable. For example, one could not measure marital status as a variable if all human beings were single. Measurement requires that there be at least two different values for any given variable.

There are two basic kinds of numerical values: discrete and continuous. A *discrete* variable can take only the value of a whole number. For instance, a questionnaire item may ask, "How many children do you have?" A person answering the questionnaire (a respondent) can answer only with a whole number. No one has one and a half children. (Of course, it is possible for a group of people to *average* one and a half children each, but that does not affect this particular point.) A *continuous* variable may take any value for which a numerical scheme exists—for example, decimals or fractions. The assumption behind the concept of a continuous variable is that the characteristic being measured can take any value on a continuum from zero to infinity. In practice, obviously, there has to be a way of expressing the value in some kind of rational numbering scheme. Length measures are good examples of continuous variables. Regardless of the length measure being used (feet, meters, rods), it is possible to measure a given object with great precision, because scientists have assumed continuity in devising measuring systems and have developed complex numerical ways of expressing the units of these systems. One could measure the height of a human being in millionths of an inch, if anyone wanted to go to the trouble of doing it.

It is possible to express attributes in nonnumerical ways, but when words are used to express the values of a given variable (the use of *small, medium,* and *large* to denote size, for example), measurement becomes much more imprecise.

Usually the researcher wants to know something about a population rather than about a single individual. There are exceptions to this policy, as we will see in Chapter 9, but it is still a useful generalization. A population (some writers prefer the word *universe*) is simply the set of people or things that is the focus of study. It is up to the researcher to define exactly what is meant by the population in any given study. Sometimes the researcher will be interested in a large population—for example, all fourth-grade children in the United States. At other times, the focus of study may be quite small—for example, the persons holding doctoral degrees in astrophysics who live in the Great Plains states.

When the researcher has identified the population under study, he or she can collect data from some or all of the individuals (subjects) in that population. Such data are collected on *scales.* A scale is simply a measuring device that allows one to make comparisons. A collection of several scales used as parts of a larger measuring effort is usually referred to as an *instrument.*

Types of Scales

Scientists use four basic types of scale, as outlined below. Later chapters will cover specific applications to data gathering.

The Nominal Scale

The simplest way in which data can be collected is a scale that allows the researcher to sort subjects or characteristics of subjects into mutually exclusive categories. These scales are called nominal scales, because the scale categories are simply names of things. Order is neither implied nor expressed in the way in which the categories are stated. For example, if a researcher wants to show the sex composition of a group of research subjects, he or she would record whether each person was male or female. As simple as this sounds, this device is a scale that measures the sex composition of a group. Obviously the nominal scale is not a very complex measuring procedure. There is a definite limit to the kinds of data processing and analysis that can be done with a scale that makes only very crude distinctions. However, if what one wants to do is to show differences between one thing and another, the nominal scale has its value.

Actually, a good deal of the data that is collected by social work researchers (and other social researchers) is nominal in character. For instance, a researcher might be engaged in a study of the differences between urban and rural life-styles. It would be necessary, in carrying out such a study, to sort rural people from urban people. The researcher would provide a definition of what was meant by the terms *urban* and *rural* so that a decision could be reached about where a subject would be placed on a simple nominal scale of "urbanness" or "ruralness."

Other examples of the use of nominal scales include sorting client problems into diagnostic categories and certain demographic characteristics of subjects—for example, marital status (single, married, divorced, separated, and widowed). In these examples, no particular order of categories is involved. The categories are different, but no ranking is implied.

The Ordinal Scale

Researchers who are able to construct a scale that allows the ordering of characteristics or attributes of subjects in some meaningful but still imprecise way use ordinal scaling. The simplest kind of an ordinal scale involves gross differences—for example, "small," "medium," and "large." There is no mathematical relationship of one scale category to another in an ordinal scale even when numbers are used. That is, medium is not twice as large as small, nor is large three times the size of small. This is true even if one numbers the categories as, for example, 1 = small, 2 = medium, and 3 = large. Using the numbers only allows a kind of commonsense ranking, but the numbers themselves have no real meaning. Obviously, in using ordinal scaling, human judgments are important. When is a thing so big that it is graded medium instead of small? The more guidance that the scale categories provide for the user, the more accurate the judgments that can be made and the more useful the scale.

There are a number of applications of the ordinal scaling technique. Perhaps the most common everyday use with which you will be familiar occurs when a friend asks, "On a scale of 1 to 10, what did you think of the movie you saw last night?" Although the research applications of the ordinal scale are usually more sophisticated than this example, the principle is the same.

Another common example of the ordinal scale is the scoring of certain types of athletic competition. Whereas many sports are scored through accumulation of points for making a goal or scoring a run, others are scored on the basis of style points assigned by judges. In assigning a score for high diving, for example, the judges have to take into account certain elements that have been agreed upon as marks of a good performance. Whether or not the diver's feet are together, the position of the hands, and the "cleanness" of the entry into the water are all important factors. A television viewer who watches Olympic diving will notice that the judges are not far apart on their evaluations. This is contrary to ordinary experience in which one moviegoer's 4 is another's 8. The reasons for the consistency of judgments are a clear definition of what constitutes good performance, training in making judgments, and plenty of practice. These three factors enhance the effectiveness of the measurement process.

Increasingly, social work researchers use ordinal scales in evaluating programs and in measuring client improvement in treatment. For example, a social worker might record whether clients are "much improved," "somewhat improved," or "not improved." Although these measurements lack a certain precision, they do allow some degree of measurement. Later in this book, we will discuss the technique of goal-attainment scaling, a fairly sophisticated ordinal scale.

The Interval Scale

An interval scale has all the properties of the less complicated scales plus a distinctive feature of its own. That is, an interval scale allows one to sort responses into categories as does the nominal scale; and it allows one to order those responses as does the ordinal scale. In addition, the interval scale has meaningful intervals. The zero point on the scale, however, is arbitrary. A simple example of the interval scale is the thermometer. Consider the familiar Fahrenheit thermometer, which is used to measure the temperature of the air. Generally these instruments are calibrated from 50° below zero to 120° above. Such thermometers provide us with useful and important information and allow us to make comparisons. The information, however, is not quite as precise as the neatly calibrated scale would suggest. The zero point in the Fahrenheit scale really has no particular reference to anything in the experience of ordinary people. Although the intervals on the scale are equal, and intricate calculations can be made with them, their ratios are meaningless. Although 80 is twice as much as 40, 80 degrees is not really twice as warm as 40 degrees. The interval scale, then, is useful and often can be interpreted in a way that is understood; but it is quite arbitrary in its starting point. Consequently, the interval scale has meaning only in some context that provides a conventional interpretation that is of practical use.

The Ratio Scale

This scale has all the properties of the interval scale plus one additional feature. It has a true zero point. The phrase *true zero point* means that if a subject had a score of zero for some attribute on a ratio scale, then the attribute did not in fact exist in an empirical quantity. For example, the measure of wealth that we commonly use is the dollar. Actually, dollars are not intrinsically worth anything. The only thing a dollar is good for *of itself* is starting fires (unless it is a silver dollar). The dollar is worth something extrinsically simply because society has agreed that the paper note inscribed "one dollar" is a scale on which one can measure wealth. If you were to measure someone's wealth in dollars and find that person had zero dollars, then you could truthfully say that the person was in fact "broke." To use another simple example, if a person were zero inches in height, he or she would not exist. Height is measured on a ratio scale.

We measure many things in ratio scales. Height, weight, and wealth are all easily understood examples. In social work, a limited number of ratio scales are relevant. Most of the occasions on which they would be used involve simple measurable characteristics like wealth (or income), age, or a count of the number of behavioral events—for example, the frequency of psychotic episodes per person per month.

Types of Data-Collection Procedures

The beginning researcher often thinks only in terms of the questionnaire. It is true that questionnaires are used extensively by social science researchers in both theoretical and applied fields. However, there are more ways of collecting data. The major approaches are summarized in the following short paragraphs. Later chapters will provide more detail about their construction and use.

1. *Observations.* A good deal of research involves data gathered through direct observation of the subjects. This approach best lends itself to research in specific behaviors. Generally one is either looking at the

frequency or meaning of behaviors or rating some kind of performance on a scale.

2. *Questionnaires.* A questionnaire, as nearly everyone knows, is a series of questions to which the respondent gives his or her answers directly on the paper containing the questions or on a separate answer sheet developed for the purpose.

3. *Interview guides.* An interview guide is a list of questions that are read by an interviewer to a respondent. The interviewer records the answers. The questionnaire and the interview guide are very nearly alike. The chief difference lies in who actually writes the answers. Both have advantages and disadvantages, as you will see in later chapters.

4. *Projective tests.* A projective test is a procedure in which the subject is given some test materials. The person giving the test observes what the subject does with the test materials and infers meaning from the subject's creative use of the materials.

5. *The study of records.* A fair amount of research is done by studying the records of an agency or institution. Of course, this is not just a random reading of any records but a deliberate search for specific kinds of content.

6. *The study of a case or cases of a certain type.* Frequently researchers interested in the development of clinical understandings study a single case over time and in great detail. Again, not everything about the case is relevant; the researcher looks for specific things.

7. *Nonreactive research.* A limited amount of research is done in ways that do not intrude upon the subjects. Therefore the subjects cannot react to being subjects, because they do not know it. This approach can raise some ethical problems, because research subjects do have certain rights to privacy. When no ethical difficulties are involved, this can be a novel way of gathering data. A simple example of this kind of research would be an attempt to learn about the life-style of a neighborhood by studying the residents' garbage. Unpleasant as this may sound, this kind of study has been carried out more than once.

8. *Situational tests.* One way to discover whether or not people possess a skill is to put them in a simulated situation in which they are called upon to demonstrate that skill. In other words, it is possible to test subjects by placing them in a situation that is lifelike but still under control, so that the subjects are protected from danger.

Most of these approaches involve the use of one of the four kinds of scales that were discussed in the preceding section. Each approach has its use; some have long histories, others are relatively new. The good researcher selects the proper approach for the specific job in hand. Selecting the proper data-collection approach is not the end of the researcher's problems. The researcher must face certain difficulties in the measuring process rather straightforwardly.

Difficulties in Measurement

Even if one has worked very hard to select or devise a good scale, measurement remains a tricky business. Naturally a good researcher wants to be accurate, and intends that any differences measured between one person and another (or between two measurements of the same person taken at different times) represent true differences. However, measurement is done in a world in which conditions can affect the measurement process. For this reason, researchers try to control as many conditions as possible. Absolute control, which is possible for some physical sciences in the laboratory, is impossible for the social work researcher. A number of factors can be threats to accuracy.

Personal factors may cause differences. A subject may score differently from one time to another because of fatigue or illness. Factors in the measurement situation may affect scores. The presence of other people, noisy conditions, or differences in the way measurements are done may make a difference. The scale itself may be poorly constructed and may not measure what the researcher thinks it measures. The questions may be unclear, or the researcher may not ask the right questions. Further, the researcher may simply use the wrong kind of measuring device for the kind of information desired.

Evaluating the answers can also be problematic. Subjects may be evaluated, for example, on their appearance rather than their performance. Researchers are not necessarily free of biases of a racial, class, economic, or sexual nature.

Moreover, the subjects (or respondents) may constitute their own source of error. Some people may misrepresent themselves on questionnaires or may try harder in experimental situations than they would normally do. People are amazingly cooperative with researchers and will often try to give the unwary researcher what he or she wants. The researcher must be aware of these sources of bias in the measurement process and try to avoid their effect. In order to make dependable measurements that minimize these difficulties, researchers aim to use scales that are valid and reliable.

Validity

To be valid, a scale must measure what it is supposed to measure and not something else. For example, one would not use a thermometer to measure length. A yardstick or a meter stick would be a valid measure of length, but a thermometer would not. Different measuring tasks raise different validity issues. Cronbach[2] distinguishes four different types of validity: criterion-oriented (or predictive), concurrent, content, and construct. Each concept of validity relates to a specific type of scale.

Criterion-Oriented Validity. In some cases, the researcher wants to devise a scale that will measure a future potential. For instance, suppose someone wanted to be able to predict how effective a therapist a student would be after completing training. The normal procedure would be for the researcher to devise some kind of scale (or perhaps an instrument that included a number of scales) that would measure certain skills that are considered important to effective therapy. The measuring device would then be used to assess the skills of a fairly large number of people already judged to be successful in the field, in order to secure norms for comparison. The instrument would then be given to students. Students who possessed the skills associated with successful performance could then be predicted to be successful. In effect, one would say that the students met the criterion that had been established for successful performance and therefore would be good therapists at some future point. The real test of whether or not a measuring device can be said to have criterion-oriented validity is in its value as a predictor. Thus criterion-oriented validity is best judged over time. Obviously, if an instrument did not predict very well, it would not be valid.

Concurrent Validity. Sometimes a researcher wants to know whether or not a new measuring device works as well as one that is already in use. Generally this concern occurs because the new measure is simpler, cheaper, and more convenient than the one with established validity. Suppose that a researcher has devised a means of testing casework skill that has proved to have criterion-oriented validity. Suppose further that this testing procedure takes three days and can be done only in Chicago. The procedure has validity, but it is expensive and time-consuming. Now suppose that another researcher devises a much simpler test that involves filling out a short questionnaire that takes only ten minutes to complete. The question is whether the new procedure measures the same thing the older, more expensive procedure did. If, after comparing the results, the new procedure yields the same results for the same people, it would be said to have concurrent validity. This would mean that both tests measure casework skill although they are, in fact, quite different devices.

Content Validity. When a researcher wants to accurately measure knowledge of some specific content, he or she is interested in the test's content validity. An instructor who wants to measure whether or not students are learning the appropriate information in a course on human behavior is faced with this kind of a validity problem. The usual way to show content

validity is to have the test inspected and evaluated by experts in the knowledge area that the test is supposed to measure.

Construct Validity.   On many occasions, the researcher is interested in
measuring whether or not a certain construct is characteristic of a group
of subjects. A *construct* is an abstration that is used to put some theoretical concept into words. A good example of a construct is the term *anxiety*.
Because anxiety is not an empirically real thing (in that one cannot go
out and buy a pound of it), one has to measure it indirectly by looking at
some characteristic or attribute that can be agreed upon to be the thing
that is meant by the term *anxiety*. The research question, then, becomes
whether the measuring device really measures the thing called anxiety and
not something else. Construct validity is very hard to establish. Frankly,
it appears that whether or not a given procedure measures a construct is
determined by the judgment of those assumed to be knowledgeable in a
given field. Because the things that are measured by such tests are not real
in the same sense that weight, height, and distance are said to be real, it
is extremely difficult to say that one is actually measuring it. For example,
over the years it has come to be accepted that anxiety can be measured by
an increase in the galvanic skin response. Therefore, many accept a high
galvanometer reading as evidence of anxiety. It may be possible for a person to be highly anxious without increasing the electrical conductivity of
the surface of the skin. It is possible that anxiety is not really being measured. Because the measurement of constructs is always indirect, researchers must take great care in interpreting such tests.

Face Validity.   Some writers have argued that it is possible for a measuring device to be considered valid "on its face." That is, if an instrument
looks like it asks the right questions or makes the right measurements,
then it may be considered valid. In some very clear instances (a questionnaire item that asks if one is male or female, for example), no problem
arises. However, if a complex variable is being measured, it can be very
risky to assume that a measure is valid on its face. It is better to consider
valid only those instruments in which practicality indicates some justification for it.

Reliability

Not only should a measuring device be valid, but it should also be reliable. The *reliability* of an instrument refers to its consistency in measurement. If one were to measure the length of a table with a ruler and find
that the table was six feet long, he or she could reasonably expect that
when the table is measured again with the same ruler, it will still measure
six feet. Admittedly, there is an assumption here that the table does not

change between measurements. The point is that if a measure is reliable, it will give similar results under similar conditions. If one continued to measure the table with the same ruler and got different lengths each time, the ruler would certainly be regarded as unreliable.

In social work and in other social sciences, we need to be sure that the measuring devices we use yield results that can be depended on to show changes only when changes occur. Unfortunately, the kinds of measuring instruments that are used are not as simple as rulers. Therefore, reliability is sometimes difficult to establish. There are four generally (but not universally) applicable methods for approaching the problem of demonstrating reliability.

The Test-Retest Method.   Suppose that a researcher devises a scale that measures a characteristic that will be called "professionalism." Assume further that the scale has been found to be valid. The question now is whether or not the scale is reliable. The scale consists of 100 multiple-choice items. In order to test the reliability of the scale, the researcher might administer it to a set of 200 professionals. Thirty days later, the researcher would administer the test to the same 200 people. If the same people scored about the same on the second test, the test would have reliability. This, of course, assumes that the people have not become more (or less) professional between tests. Testing the reliability of a scale by any of the means listed here depends on the assumption of stability of the group being used to test the scale. Once the reliability of the scale has been established, it then can be used to measure changes. This is analogous to the problem of any scale maker. Once a person determines that a ruler reliably measures length, he or she can use it to measure things of different lengths and can have confidence in the reliability of measurement.

Reliability of a scale is usually tested by correlating the scores obtained in the two trials. The nature of correlation is addressed in Chapter 11. It is enough for now to say that correlation is a process by which two sets of scores can be compared to see how similar they are.

The test-retest method's usefulness is not confined to paper-and-pencil tests. One could also check out the reliability of a performance test or a rating scale in much the same way.

The Alternate-Form Method.   In this approach to establishing reliability, the researcher constructs two forms of the same test. The test of professionalism that was used as an example in the previous section could be checked this way just as well. The problem is that one would have to have two hundred-item tests that were very much alike. Sometimes it is difficult to write enough items to make two similar scales. Assuming that it is possible to construct two versions of the same measuring instrument, one could give them to the trial group one after the other. The advantage to this approach is that one would not have to wait for time to elapse before comparing the two. A number of commercially available tests have alternate forms that yield virtually identical results. The Miller Analogies Test, which is used by many graduate schools as part of their admissions process, has four alternate versions. Effectively, these tests are equivalent but not identical.

The alternate-form approach is also not limited to paper-and-pencil tests, although they are the most common examples. Nothing would preclude the alternate-form approach from being used with rating scales, performance tests, or interview guides. Bear in mind that alternate forms of a measuring instrument must have the same general format. If one uses entirely different kinds of measuring devices as alternate forms (for example, a questionnaire and a performance test), the question of validity arises, and the researcher must be prepared to demonstrate that two entirely different things are measuring the same characteristic. This would not be a reliability problem; instead the researcher would be faced with establishing concurrent validity.

The Split-Half Method.   Sometimes it is neither possible nor convenient to have two complete versions of a given instrument. It may not be practical to use a test-retest approach. Under either of these conditions, one may choose to use the split-half method. A researcher with a 100-item questionnaire would record the scores on the even-numbered items and the scores on the odd-numbered items. Then he or she would compare the two halves of the test using a correlation formula. If the two halves can be highly correlated with each other, the test is assumed to be reliable. After all, there would be no reason to suppose that the even-numbered items were any different from the odd-numbered ones. If a subject measured high on the even-numbered items, he or she would also be high on the odd-numbered ones. If this is not the case, then the reliability of measurement device is suspect.

Internal Consistency.   It is possible to test a measuring instrument for its internal consistency. That is, we can perform some calculations (see Chapter 5) that will allow us to estimate the reliability of the test by demonstrating that the items are consistent with each other. These calculations provide a kind of shortcut estimate of reliability without requiring the trouble of splitting the test. Although such tests of internal consistency are not quite the same thing as genuine reliability tests, they are a reasonable, if somewhat more computationally complex, substitute. Several formulas for these estimates can be found in advanced works on measurement. It is enough for the present introductory purpose to note that there are ways to deal with this problem.

Observer Agreement. Another reliability question arises when observation is the data-collection process. The researcher would like to know that the observations are accurately recorded. Ordinarily one ensures such accuracy by using several observers. The reliability estimate is simply the degree to which the observers agree.

Validity and reliability are complex concepts. They are not generally easy to establish. The researcher's goal is to get the greatest degree of validity and reliability possible. In general, it is not possible to achieve perfection, but the researcher can usually know to what degree the goal has been attained and the limitations of the research.

Key Terms

measurement	scale
variable	instrument
discrete variable	nominal scale
continuous variable	ordinal scale
population	interval scale
validity	ratio scale
criterion-oriented validity	reliability
concurrent validity	test-retest method
content validity	alternate-form method
construct validity	split-half method
observer agreement	internal consistency

References

1. Claire Selltiz, Lawrence S. Wrightsman, and Stuart W. Cook, *Research Methods in Social Relations,* 3rd ed. (New York: Holt, Rinehart and Winston, 1976), p. 161.
2. Lee J. Cronbach, *Essentials of Psychological Testing,* 3rd ed. (New York: Harper & Row, 1970), pp. 121–123.

Questions for Discussion

1. How trustworthy is measurement of nonempirical realities?
2. Are the differences between ratio and interval scales important?
3. How can ordinal scales be made more accurate?

4. What kind of scales are most appropriate to nonreactive research? to observations?
5. Discuss the difference between concurrent validity and reliability.
6. Can a test be reliable without being valid? Can it be valid without being reliable?

Exercises

1. Devise a nominal scale that measures some human attribute.

2. Devise and test an ordinal scale that measures the quality of the chili in the student union's cafeteria.

3. List as many interval and ratio scales that apply to human beings as you can.

4. Check out a commercial test from your college library. The reference librarian will help you, if you do not know where to start. Obtain the test manual, and look for the way in which reliability and validity were established.

For Further Reading

Lee J. Cronbach. *Essentials of Psychological Testing,* 3rd ed. New York: Harper & Row, 1970. This is a highly technical book written by one of the most respected authorities in the field of psychological tests. Chapters 5 and 6 discuss in detail the questions of validity and reliability.

Marty J. Schmidt. *Understanding and Using Statistics,* 2nd ed. Lexington, Mass.: D. C. Heath, 1979. Chapter 1 contains a highly readable and understandable technical discussion of measurement.

3

The Design of Exploratory and Descriptive Research

Science is differentiated from other means of knowing by the formal deliberateness with which knowledge building is carried out. Deliberateness is relative, of course. The typical picture of a white-coated scientist who coolly sets up a highly complex experiment in a search for absolute truth is a false one. In an extremely cogent discussion of this point, Meehan[1] argued that very few physical scientists followed strictly the formal kind of scientific process that philosophers of science say that they do. Most scientists are very pragmatic. They have developed a way of working that is practical and useful, but it is not as rigidly formal as one might think. Further, useful knowledge has been discovered by many scientists by accident or as a by-product of something else.

Despite the reservations noted above, we can still say that the scientific approach is more disciplined than other means of knowledge building. Deliberate design is, or should be, apparent from the beginning of the research effort, because research is a planned activity. Selltiz and her colleagues[2] offer the following definition of the research design:

> A research design is the arrangement of conditions for collection and analysis of data in a manner that aims to combine relevance to the research task with economy in procedure.

Selltiz lists four purposes for research in the social sciences. One does research:

1. to gain familiarity with a problem, to gain insights, or to develop a clear hypothesis for future research.
2. to describe a phenomenon or a set of phenomena.
3. to determine the frequency with which something occurs or to determine a degree of association between two or more variables.
4. to test a causal relationship between variables.[3]

Researchers and practitioners, especially in social work, may also have a fifth purpose: to evaluate the effectiveness of a program or technique.

The Basic Research Process

The actual type of social research performed will depend on which of the above purposes is to be served. However, a basic process occurs in all types of research done in the various sciences. In its simplest form, this process involves the following:

1. a statement of the problem.
2. a review of the work of others on the problem.
3. a clear description of the work to be performed in the present research.
4. a presentation of the findings.
5. a conclusion based on the findings that relates them back to previous work and points out the direction for future work.

It may be hard to reconcile these simple statements with the complexities of published research articles. Nevertheless, no matter how complicated the results sound, this pattern should be at the bottom of all orderly research.

Types of Social Research

The purposes of social research in general can be accomplished by four basic research types: exploratory (sometimes called formulative), descriptive, experimental, and evaluative. This simple typology will also serve social work research. Some authorities argue that evaluative research is descriptive, whereas others say that it is a special type of experimental research. Its current importance and the adjustments required in the research process justify our treatment of evaluation as a separate category. This chapter focuses on exploratory and descriptive research. Chapter 4 contains discussions of experimental and evaluative research designs.

Exploratory Research

As the term suggests, exploratory research is used to explore a phenomenon or problem area in which clear knowledge or usable ideas are scarce. Selltiz and her colleagues have said:

> Many exploratory studies have the purpose of formulating a problem for more precise investigation or of developing hypotheses. An exploratory study may, however, have other functions: increasing investigators' familiarity with the phenomenon they wish to investigate in a subsequent, more highly structured study, or with the setting in which they plan to carry out

such a study; clarifying concepts; establishing priorities for further research; gathering information about practical possibilities for carrying out research in real-life settings; providing a census of problems regarded as urgent by people working in a given field of social relations.[4]

Ordinarily the sociologist or social psychologist will use the exploratory approach with a view toward the formulation of an explanatory hypothesis—that is, a statement that can be tested for its explanatory power. (See *hypothesis* below.) The social work researcher will not usually be interested in this use of the exploratory study but will more likely be interested in the other purposes of such research.

What Forms Does Exploratory Research Take?   Generally, exploratory research is carried out in a simple, uncomplicated way. Because of its preliminary and tentative character, exploratory research does not demand the same rigor that more complicated studies do. The researcher may literally start with a simple question or statement. The exploratory process could take one of the following forms:[5]

1. *The literature survey.* A social worker interested in tightening up the definition of a term might consult the professional literature on the subject. For example, you might be interested in the different meanings that various writers have given to the term. As a piece of exploratory research, you would probably read and take notes on articles concerned with the idea in which you are interested. After you read some of the more prominent definitions, you would prepare a report or summary based on your readings. This report would not be regarded as definitive or final. It would, however, provide the basis for a more systematic definition later on.

2. *The experience survey.* A researcher might do some exploratory research by gathering information from people who work frequently with a given problem area. At this level of research, these conversations would be unstructured and unsystematic in nature. They might involve very simple questions—or even no set questions at all. The researcher might just ask people to share what they know, think, or simply guess about in a given problem or question.

3. *The study of selected examples.* A researcher might study case records of a certain type, looking for generalizations. The cases do not have to be as carefully chosen as they would for more complex types of research. It would be all right for exploratory purposes to ask colleagues for their most unusual or most recent cases of a certain type.

4. *Interviews with individuals with different viewpoints.* These interviews would be conducted with people who one thinks are knowledgeable about the problem area. This could mean clients, members of the public with an interest in the problem area, or critics of the agency and its program. Because the researcher is simply seeking ideas at this level of research, it will not be crucial if the persons interviewed are not representative of all possible data sources.

5. *A careful review of one's experience.* It is legitimate for an investigator in the exploratory stage to distill his or her own experiences into a more or less orderly whole. Researchers must take care with this approach, however, because it is not uncommon for people to romanticize their own experiences. Such an introspective study—even if written up in a formal report—is, of course, not conclusive. It can, however, be a sound exploratory beginning to more complicated research at a higher level of organization.

The following are examples of the kind of research questions that a social work researcher might select as topics for exploratory research:

1. Has the use of the term *anxiety* changed in the last ten years?
2. How do agencies deal with the problem of the waiting list of clients who cannot be seen immediately?
3. Are there common factors in today's child-abuse cases?
4. How do clients view the agency's current intake policy?
5. What insights can be identified about the effect of the termination process on the client?

Descriptive Research

As the name suggests, descriptive research has to do with the description of a phenomenon or the description of the relationship between two or more phenomena. Generally, descriptive research uses the survey techniques described in Chapter 6. A great amount of sociological, social psychological, and social work research is of this type. Descriptive research includes:[6]

1. *Studies that describe some characteristic of a community.* A study that described the distribution of aged persons and their needs would be a good example.

2. *Studies that describe the use of a community facility.* A study that answered the question: "Who uses the mental health clinic, and what are their characteristics?" would be a descriptive study.

3. *Studies that solicit the views of a group of people on an issue*. If an agency undertook a study of the views of the community on poverty and the role of the public welfare agency, it would be doing a piece of descriptive research.

4. *Political surveys*. Generally social workers would not do straight political surveys. However, if social workers were to ask people "political" questions—for example, "If the referendum were held today, would you vote 'yes' or 'no' on the question of increasing taxes to enlarge the mental health clinic?"—they would be doing something analogous to political research. It is important to recognize that this kind of research is descriptive because it tries to describe the state of mind of the electorate at a given date. It is not experimental despite its use in predicting election outcomes.

5. *Studies of association*. If a social work researcher asked the question, "Do children who are spanked earn higher grades in school?" then he or she would be doing a study of association. The researcher would be trying to find out whether there was a mathematical relationship between the frequency of spanking and children's grades. Notice that the question does not go so far as to say that spanking causes higher grades. If the question were stated that way, the researcher would have moved into experimental research, in which the design provides for the testing of causal statements.

The Characteristics of Descriptive Research.   There are several important differences between exploratory and descriptive research. The rules are more precise for descriptive research. This is not because descriptive research is morally better than exploratory research, but because its purpose is more distinct. Exploratory research is by its nature a formative stage in the knowledge-building process. A person does exploratory research because he or she is looking for the right questions to ask. When someone has explored a problem, we can assume that he or she now knows more precisely what to describe and what the right questions are. Consequently, descriptive research differs from exploratory research in that descriptive research involves:

1. more attention to securing a representative sample of the population under study.
2. more precise data-gathering techniques or procedures.
3. a clearer statement of the problem.

The person doing exploratory research may operate under fewer restrictions in selecting a sample. He or she may use samples that are conveniently at hand. The person doing descriptive research ought to widen the scope. Further, the person doing exploratory research is permitted to gather data more informally, because he or she is searching for the right questions or the important variables. Later chapters are devoted to the more formal data-gathering procedures used in descriptive research and the more technical aspects of sampling. This chapter will address the matter of the statement of the problem—the research question.

In descriptive research, the question to be investigated is stated in a much sharper and more economical way than is true in exploratory research. As an example, consider the question, "Are there common factors in today's child abuse cases?" which was suggested as an appropriate subject for exploratory research. When the researcher gets to the level of descriptive research, he or she should be able to identify specific elements of importance. The question would then be restated, focusing on those elements.

For instance, an exploratory study might suggest that parents reported for child abuse displayed very little anxiety. They also seemed to show little concern for whether or not their children got to school. The descriptive study would then focus on anxiety and truancy for the purpose of describing the frequency of their occurrence. The researcher will be looking specifically at these two elements. Other elements that might be present would not be examined at this point, because they did not seem to have much promise during the exploratory study.

Formal and Operational Definitions of Concepts.   A new element in the statement of the subject for research must be introduced. Two terms have been used above that must be explained to be intelligible: they are *anxiety* and *truancy*. These terms are called *concepts*. A concept is an expression that stands for the phenomenon that is studied.

> We use concepts as symbols of the phenomena we are studying, and it is really these underlying phenomena which we are relating to one another.[7]

Usually a concept is an abstraction. It is always a symbol. Goode and Hatt warn against treating concepts as anything other than symbolic representations of reality:

> It is sometimes forgotten that concepts are logical constructs created from sense impressions, percepts, or even fairly complex experiences. The tendency to assume that concepts actually exist as phenomena leads to many errors. The concept is not the phenomenon itself; that is, such logical constructs do not exist outside the stated frame of reference. The failure to recognize this is termed the fallacy of reification, that is, *treating abstractions as if they were actual phenomena.*[8]

"Anxiety" and "truancy" do not exist as things. These words are concepts. One cannot go out and buy a ton of "anxiety"! Strictly speaking, as Goode and Hatt point out, these terms refer to certain identifiable aspects of phenomena that we get from impressions, perceptions, and experiences. As a result of experience with the reality of a phenomenon, the researcher tries to give it a name so that the thing itself can be referred to in communication with other people.

The first task for the researcher in this stage of study, then, is to devise a set of useful concepts that represent real phenomena and to define them. If the researcher wants others to know what is meant by the word *anxiety*, it must be defined so that it can be differentiated from everything that is *not* anxiety. Generally the definition of concepts takes two forms.

1. The researcher needs to arrive at a *formal* (sometimes called a *nominal*) *definition*. The researcher must find a clear and unambiguous way of defining the concept to be explored in words that communicate the meaning of the underlying phenomenon being studied. This definition should be as simple yet complete as possible. It should set apart the phenomenon under study from any other phenomenon. If you are studying a tiger, your definition should not be one that could as easily fit a lion, a panther, or a pussycat.

2. The researcher needs to write another definition for each key concept. This time, the researcher must specify what concrete operations must be performed to arrive at the recognition of the phenomena in measurement terms. This definition is called the *operational definition*. Although this definition still involves the symbolic identification of the phenomenon under study, the symbols that are of interest are different. Now the researcher must specify the measurements that are used to delimit the phenomenon.

In the example, consider the term *anxiety*. A formal definition might say, "For the purpose of this study, 'anxiety' means an excited state in which the subject reports a feeling of a sense of dread, fear, and uncertainty." It is not necessary for everyone to accept this definition. It *is* necessary for everyone to understand what the researcher means.

The researcher might then move to define anxiety operationally by saying, "Operationally, anxiety in this study will be measured by a score on the Taylor Manifest Anxiety Scale." This scale is a commonly used way of measuring anxiety, and studies of many groups of people can be used for comparison. A score on the scale defines or identifies in actual operations what the term *anxiety* means for the purposes of this piece of research.

You can see that investigators have to develop a more formal approach to data collection when doing descriptive research. They must also take precautions against bias. This involves more care in the construction of data-collection instruments (see Chapter 5), the selection of subjects (see Chapter 9), and the rigor of the design.

The Hypothesis in Descriptive Research.   Part of the additional rigor of descriptive research lies in the use of a hypothesis. A *hypothesis* is a statement that can be tested in an empirical way.

Good practice in descriptive research requires the question being investigated to be stated in a concrete and explicit way. In addition to being concerned about the way concepts are defined, the researcher must also worry about the statement that relates the concepts. The hypothesis, then, is a statement that defines the relationship of one or more concepts so that the relationship can be tested.

In descriptive research, the hypothesis often takes one of the following forms:

1. *X* has a certain characteristic. For instance, if one were to hypothesize that "parents who neglect their children were themselves neglected," one would be using a descriptive hypothesis of this type. It is important to notice that the hypothesis says nothing about cause and effect; it merely states that neglectful parents have a certain characteristic—that they themselves were neglected. Obviously, if this proved true in a number of descriptive studies, then causality might be suspected, but more work would be necessary to demonstrate it.

2. *X* occurs more frequently than *Y* in a given population. An example might be, "Low income occurs more frequently than lack of formal education in parents who neglect their children." Notice that there is no causative intention here. The researcher is still hypothesizing descriptive elements.

3. *X* is associated with *Y* in some important way. In this format, the hypothesis suggests that there is a statistically important association between two variables. Such a hypothesis might say, "The higher the amount of deprivation of parents, the higher the number of abusive incidents with their children." Of course, it would be necessary to be able to express "parental deprivation" in numerical terms. The point of this hypothesis is that the researcher would expect that as the parental deprivation score went up, so would the number of abusive incidents. The relationship might be tested by a statistical procedure that would show the degree of association.

By showing the relationship between the concepts to be studied, the hypothesis provides a relatively clear guide to what is being researched and to what the outcome will mean.

Obviously, things are not always neat. Investigation will only rarely show that a descriptive hypothesis is true in all cases. A researcher would more likely find that the statement to be tested was true in a certain percentage of cases. If a statement were to be true in a large number of cases, one might reason that some degree of cause and effect might be present. This situation would require additional research that would effectively deal with causal relations.

Of course, not all descriptive studies use highly formalized hypotheses. A number of descriptive studies have as an implicit hypothesis a simple question, as do those used as examples earlier in the chapter—for example, "How are aged persons distributed in the community, and what are their needs?" or "What are the views of the community on the need for a new outpatient facility?" These are really informal versions of the hypothesis, "X has a certain characteristic." The sentence has been restated as the question, "What characteristic does X have?"

A great deal of the descriptive research that is done in social work has as its purpose the accumulation of knowledge about client groups, the attitudes of various important consumer and constituent groups, and the operation of social agencies. This research is an important contribution to the understanding of people, their problems, and the ways in which social agencies function.

Key Terms

research design	operational definition
exploratory research	concept
descriptive research	reification
formal definition	hypothesis

References

1. Eugene Meehan, *Explanation in Social Science* (Homewood, Illinois: Dorsey Press, 1968).
2. From *Research Methods in Social Relations*, 3rd ed., p. 90, by Claire Selltiz, Lawrence S. Wrightsman, and Stuart W. Cook. Copyright © 1976 by Holt, Rinehart and Winston. Copyright © 1951, © 1959 by Holt, Rinehart and Winston, Inc. Reprinted by permission of Holt, Rinehart and Winston.
3. *Ibid.*
4. *Ibid.*, p. 91.
5. *Ibid.*, pp. 91–101.

6. *Ibid.,* pp. 101–103.
7. William J. Goode and Paul Hatt, *Methods of Social Research* (New York: McGraw-Hill Book Company, 1952), p. 41.
8. *Ibid.,* p. 42.

Questions for Discussion

1. Are there other tasks for research that you would add to those mentioned in the chapter?
2. Discuss the value of exploratory research in social work.
3. Under what circumstances would a review of one's own experience be a useful exploratory study?
4. In what ways would descriptive research influence policy and practice decisions?
5. Do social workers tend to reify concepts? Consider concepts like "superego," "subconscious," and "defense mechanisms."

Exercises

1. Select topics for the following exploratory studies:
   a. a literature survey.
   b. an experience survey.
   c. a study of case examples.
   d. a study in which differing viewpoints are important.

2. Write a simple hypothesis, and define the critical terms for a descriptive study, following the three hypotheses given in the chapter:
   a. X has a certain characteristic.
   b. X occurs more frequently than Y in a given population.
   c. X is associated with Y in some way.
   Be sure to write both formal and operational definitions.

For Further Reading

Claire Selltiz, Lawrence S. Wrightsman, and Stuart W. Cook. *Research Methods in Social Relations,* 3rd ed. New York: Holt, Rinehart and Winston, Inc., 1976. Chapter 4 is an expanded discussion of exploratory and descriptive research.

Julian L. Simon. *Basic Research Methods in Social Sciences,* 2nd ed. New York: Random House, 1978. Chapter 4, pp. 41–55, covers the same ground using a more sophisticated descriptive classification than is used in this book. Simon sorts exploratory and descriptive research into categories he calls "case study descriptive research," "classification research," "measurement and estimation," "comparison problems," and "research that tries to find relationships."

Earl R. Babbie. *The Practice of Social Research,* 2nd ed. Belmont, California: Wadsworth Publishing Company, 1979. Chapter 4 is a chatty, informal approach to the design of research. This chapter also discusses the time dimension to research: cross-sectional, longitudinal, and cohort studies.

4

The Design of Experimental and Evaluative Research

As we stated earlier in this book, the ultimate purpose of all research is explanation. Exploratory research, despite its tentative character, looks for insights and directions that are preliminary to more complex searches for explanation. Descriptive research is explanatory to the extent that it enables a consumer to understand the nature of what is being described. This chapter takes explanation one step further, highlighting the logic of experimentation as the highest form of explanation. We will discuss simple experimental designs, in order to show the basic pattern of the experimental approach to explanation. The chapter will also introduce the subject of evaluative research. We place an introductory discussion of evaluation here because the designs used are closely related to those used in experimentation. Later chapters will elaborate on the basic ideas presented here and will show applications in discussions of data collection and statistical techniques.

Experimental Research

Experiments are, theoretically, the purest way of dealing with the problems of cause and effect, insofar as this is possible. Therefore, the experiment is the most sophisticated way of getting at the problem of explanation. Ideally, the researcher would like to be able to show that X causes Y. If this can be shown, then X can be said to explain Y.

However, in science (even the "hard" sciences), the state of the art seldom makes possible clear-cut, causative statements. In order to show that X causes Y, the researcher would have to demonstrate that X was both a necessary and a sufficient cause of Y. That is, the researcher would have to show that X must occur in order for Y to follow and that Y is the result of X and of nothing else. Suppose that a researcher wants to explain the occurrence of child abuse. He or she may suspect that a certain type of personality pattern in the parent is responsible. In fact, the researcher may have done some exploratory research that resulted in the strong suggestion that those with a compulsive personality pattern are frequently found among child abusers. In order to explain child abuse as a function of compulsive personality in the parent, the researcher would have to show that *whenever* a parent has a compulsive personality, he or she abuses children and that all abused children have compulsive parents and *no other kind.* The requirement that a cause be both necessary and sufficient before it can be said to fully explain an effect is a formidable problem. Because necessary and sufficient causes are very hard to identify, researchers usually are left with less-certain hypotheses to explore.

These less-certain hypotheses generally take one of three forms.[1] A variable may be *contributory* when X increases the likelihood of Y but is only one of a number of factors. For example, suppose that a researcher were exploring the influence of rational-emotive therapy on hallucinatory behavior in a group of patients. The researcher would not seriously hypothesize that RET completely cures hallucinatory behavior, but he or she might test the assertion that RET contributes to the *reduction* of hallucinatory behavior, recognizing that other factors in the treatment situation may have an effect (drugs, being away from one's ordinary social relationships, and so forth).

A second hypothesis type is the *contingent* hypothesis. A condition may have a causative influence when X increases the likelihood of Y under certain circumstances or in certain contingencies. For example, a researcher who theorizes that a job-locating service that may be a provision of a public welfare law will only decrease welfare case loads when work is readily available would be using a contingent hypothesis.

Whether either X or Z (another variable with promise) increases the likelihood of Y, then X and Z are said to be *alternative* conditions. Suppose that a researcher hypothesized that either of two conditions would produce about the same effect. As an example, a researcher might investigate whether or not a decrease in child abuse would occur if X (a change in parental behavior) or Z (a change in the child's behavior) took place. The researcher might find that one could reduce the incidence of child abuse equally well by pursuing either of two equally effective courses of action.

Independent and Dependent Variables

These hypotheses employ the idea that a change in X is somehow causally related to a change in Y. To put it another way, a hypothesis tests the theory that in some way any change in Y depends on a change in X. For this reason, researchers refer to variables in the Y position in the hypothesis as *dependent* variables. The variable in the X position is called the *independent* variable. In laboratory experiments, the researcher will manipulate X (the independent variable) in some way in order to measure any change that occurs in Y (the dependent variable). For instance, a researcher interested in studying the effect of a certain type of counseling (independent variable) on marital discord (dependent variable) might vary the amount of counseling, the intensity of the therapy, or the length of the sessions. If counseling has a calming effect on marital discord, then it should reduce the number or intensity of hostile encounters.

In a "naturally occurring" experiment, the researcher usually cannot manipulate the independent variable. The best that may be possible is for the researcher to note whether or not varying degrees of the independent variable that occur naturally have an observable effect on the dependent variable.

A study that looks for a statistical association between X and Y is a *descriptive* study. In an *experimental* study, a researcher has reason to anticipate causality, as well as association. We will discuss this distinction again in Chapter 11 in connection with our examination of the concept of correlation.

You can see that explanatory hypotheses of the types described are far less satisfying than a neat "X causes Y." In most cases, though, they are the best that can be done.

The Classical Experiment

Ideally, causation or explanation is established by a classical experiment. This design is theoretically useful when applied to laboratory conditions in which the occurrence of the experimental (independent) variable is regulated by an experimenter. It is also useful in naturally occurring experiments outside the laboratory. In this type of experiment, manipulation by the experimenter is replaced by some variable that occurs more or less in the normal course of things. However, naturally occurring experiments are obviously very hard to control.

In the classical design, the experimenter starts with two groups that are exactly equivalent to each other. Group A, the experimental group, receives the experimental treatment. (Note that *treatment* in research terminology means anything done by an experimenter. This might be a teaching technique, a therapy, or the bombardment of a substance with radioisotopes.) Group B, the control group, does not receive the treatment and may or may not receive a placebo, depending on the nature of the experiment. A *placebo* is an ineffectual substitute given to the control group so that subjects don't know who is experimental and who is control.

A naturally occurring experiment would differ only in that Group A would experience whatever would have occurred in the normal course of things, whereas Group B would not.

At the end of the experimental period, the researcher takes measurements on both groups and ascribes any differences that have occurred to the treatment. This design is as follows:

Beginning of Experiment	Initial Test	Experimental Condition	Follow-Up Test
A	O_1	X	O_2
B	O_1	P (or no X)	O_2

In the above representation, A and B are two groups of subjects who are equal in all relevant ways, X is the experimental procedure, P is a placebo, and O_1 and O_2 are observations or measurements given at the same time to both groups.

The success of the classical experimental design rests on the experimenter's ability to assure that the two groups used in the experiment are equivalent in all important respects. Although this is possible with fruit flies, English peas, and most varieties of beans, it is virtually impossible with human beings. One can make the case that access to a large number of identical twins would allow the researcher to form equivalent groups by placing one twin of each set in Group A and the other in Group B. In fact, some studies on intelligence have been done this way. The problem, of course, is that there simply are not enough sets of identical twins to go around. Even if there were, it is not certain that twins are identical in every important way.

Some researchers have tried to deal with the problem of equivalence by using matched groups. That is, if Group A contains a forty-year-old white female with a college degree in history who is 5′4″ tall and weighs 130 pounds, then Group B must contain someone whose characteristics match. This sounds like a reasonable approach. The trouble is that one can never be sure that the persons are matched on all the characteristics relevant to the experiment. Human beings are so complex and relationships so intricate that researchers cannot be certain that they know which characteristics should be matched.

In 1925, Sir Ronald Fisher found a solution to the equivalence problem:[2] assign subjects to either treatment or control group by chance. By assigning subjects to a group by chance, any differences between them in *entering behavior* (behavior at the beginning of the experiment) can occur only by chance and cannot be a factor in the selection process itself. In effect, the experimenter assumes that any differences between groups A and B are cancelled out unless there is some evidence to the contrary. This approach, called *random assignment,* has proven to be more effective than the attempt to match groups. Consequently, the use of matched groups is generally limited to natural-occurring studies in which randomization is impractical or impossible.

To illustrate how random, or chance, assignment works, consider a simple example: Suppose there are thirty people in a classroom. If you want five subjects for an experiment, you could make your selection in a number of ways. However, in the random approach, you would write the names of all thirty people on slips of paper and draw five out of a hat. Every possible combination would have an equal chance of being selected. It is conceivable that by chance you might draw the persons with the most extreme attributes in the room, but it is easy to see that the odds against doing so are enormous. It is more likely that you would draw a mix. A sufficiently large set of samples drawn randomly is as dependable a substitute for equivalence as is humanly possible. Chapter 9 will discuss this point further.

As stated earlier, the researcher's ideal is the classical experimental design. Unfortunately, this kind of control over experimental conditions is not often possible. Researchers usually have to settle for less. However, some forms of "settling for less" should be avoided unless there is no other way to try to explain the phenomenon under study. Of course, the exploratory study is an exception to this rule, because an exploratory study is a "fishing expedition."

The problem is extensively discussed in Campbell and Stanley's *Experimental and Quasi-Experimental Designs for Research.*[3] The following discussion summarizes some of the key ideas from this book.

One of the major difficulties in research design is the problem of being able to say that the research effort yields valid answers. This problem is analogous to the concern for the validity of a measuring instrument. In the case of an instrument, the validity question is, "Does the instrument measure what it is supposed to measure?" In the case of a design, the question is, "Is the design effective in demonstrating the effect that it is supposed to show?" Campbell and Stanley make a distinction between the internal validity and the external validity of the design:

> *Internal validity* is the basic minimum without which any experiment is uninterpretable: Did the experimental treatments in fact make a difference in this specific experimental instance? *External validity* asks the question of generalizability: To what populations, settings, treatment variables, and measurement variables can this effect be generalized?[4]

Campbell and Stanley list several kinds of variables that are threats to either internal or external validity. We will discuss some of these in the context of the designs that they affect most.

Three types of research (called *preexperimental* by Campbell and Stanley) are often found in the social work literature. One can argue that they are not wholly inappropriate as exploratory study designs, but they cannot be used in studies that seek causal explanations. Although other ways of classifying research designs exist, the Campbell and Stanley approach has become quite widely known, and it will be followed here.

The One-Shot Case Study

This is not properly a design at all, but Campbell and Stanley use it as a baseline from which to start. In this approach, the researcher measures a group of subjects following some kind of experimental or natural occurrence. In some books and articles, this is called the "after-only" approach. Diagrammed, it looks like this:

$$X \qquad O$$

As an example, consider a study of unmarried mothers, with pregnancy and delivery serving as a naturally occurring X. A caseworker interviews the women in a maternity ward, takes the measurement O, and rates the emotional maturity of the group. The women who are interviewed are selected as subjects simply because they are the women who happen to be in the ward during the current month. On the basis of this series of interviews, the worker writes an article describing the unmarried mother as an extremely immature person, because that is the way these women appear to be.

Because this caseworker makes no comparison with anything, such a piece of research is useless in scientific knowledge building beyond the purely exploratory stage. There is absolutely no control of any kind over the findings. Nor can the writer know anything of the effects of a number of factors that we discuss more fully in connection with the two designs that follow. The one-shot case study not only has almost every fault of the next two designs but also lacks a basis for comparisons of any kind.

The One-Group Pretest/Posttest

The pictorial representation looks like this:

$$O_1 \qquad X \qquad O_2$$

In this design, a group of subjects are given a pretest, exposed to an experimental variable, and then measured a second time. Changes are attributed to the effect of X.

As an example, consider a study in which a social worker devises a therapeutic scheme to alleviate anxiety in clients who have to wait for services in a clinic. The worker gains the cooperation of some clients and asks them to fill out the Taylor Manifest Anxiety Scale, a paper-and-pencil test that reveals the amount of anxiety one will admit. These clients are then offered the anxiety-reduction therapy that the worker has devised. After the treatment, the worker asks the clients to fill out the TMAS again. The second test shows a big reduction in anxiety scores, which is attributed to the procedure. The clinic decides to use this scheme as a way of improving overall working relationships with its clientele.

This process may sound very carefully done. Actually, it would be a very slender reed on which to rest a case for the efficacy of the treatment used. The effects of the following threats to *internal* validity may have affected the outcome:

1. *History.* This approach does not have any control for events occurring simultaneously to the treatment that might also have had a calming effect on waiting clients. Such things can occur. One could not know whether the treatment or something else had worked—for example, a more pleasant receptionist, new chairs in the waiting room, or a change in the weather!

2. *Maturation.* The clients might have become less anxious simply because they had matured a little. Everybody continues to grow and adapt to some degree, and the clients may have simply gotten used to waiting or become accustomed to the routine, and therefore felt comfortable in the waiting room.

3. *Testing.* Although the pretest makes the design look impressive, it constitutes a problem in itself. The testing process itself has an effect on people. It tells the subjects that they are special. Most subjects want to help out researchers. (People are amazingly cooperative with social research even when they are in very difficult personal circumstances.) Thus *anything* the researcher does may have a positive effect on the subject. Although some recent studies cast doubt on how important the effect may be, it is nevertheless a possibility that this design fails to consider.

4. *Instrument decay.* This design is susceptible to confounding from yet another source. Suppose the social worker used judges to evaluate the effect of the treatment, did the experiment, and then had the judges rate the clients again. The problem is that some changes might have occurred in the judges during the time covered by the experiment that would cause them to judge differently. This is analogous to the wearing out of a spring

in a laboratory scale: the instrument that is used to measure change is it-self liable to change. Of course, in our example using the TMAS, this problem does not arise, because this is a paper-and-pencil test. The point is that instrument decay is a possibility, depending on the kind of instrument.

5. *Regression to the mean.* Another problem inherent in this design is that the social worker might have taken his or her initial measurements on an especially high-anxiety day. The "improvement" may not be a result of treatment at all but simply a consequence of taking the second measurement on a day on which the anxiety of the clientele was closer to its average level. Most people tend to perform near their average most of the time, although on occasional days their performance will be very high or very low. If your average golf score is 95, as a rule you will post scores somewhere between 90 and 100. You will have an occasional glorious 85 and an infrequent disastrous 110. But most of the time, your scores will tend to regress (or cluster) close to the average score. This phenomenon is also true of scores or ratings of subjects in experiments. An experimenter may catch the subjects on their best day, their worst day, or an average day. This design offers no control for this potential problem.

The five design problems listed above are all threats to internal validity. That is, they all call into question the possibility of knowing whether the experimental variable made any difference in the experimental group. There are also two threats to *external* validity inherent in this design:

1. The possibility of the *interaction of the pretest with the experimental procedure.* This threat is, in Campbell and Stanley's terms, very similar to the threat of test effects to internal validity. Suppose that a social worker has devised an educational program designed to change the attitude of the public toward clients of Aid to Families of Dependent Children. The social worker might secure a couples' club from a nearby church as subjects. Prior to the educational treatment, the social worker devises and administers an "attitude toward AFDC recipients" test. Because the subjects know that a social worker is doing the program, and because the test obviously concerns their attitude toward recipients, how does one separate whatever changes in attitude that might occur because of the nature of the *test,* from changes that occur as the result of instruction? The answer is that one cannot make this separation. Therefore, one could not generalize that the instruction was valid for all people unless they, too, had been pretested. In other words, the pretest can easily become an inseparable part of the treatment. The two together may have an effect, but the treatment alone might not be effective.

2. The probability of an *interaction of subject selection with the experimental variable*. This means that the nature of the subjects selected might affect the result. In the above example, it is possible that the couples' club of Church A brings to the educational situation a different attitude than would subjects from Church B. Therefore, instruction that would appear to be effective in Church A would not necessarily be effective when used with another group. The point is that research with intact groups (a school class, a single ward, or clients from a case load in a given agency) may not allow the researcher to generalize to all such groups.

The Static-Group Comparison

This design looks like this:

$$X \qquad O$$
$$O$$

The idea here is that a group that has had some kind of exposure to an experimental variable is compared to a group that has not. Many naturally occurring experiments are of this type. In social work, for instance, one might read of the effect of group counseling on a number of young married couples compared to a group of similar couples who have not had counseling.

In addition to the problem listed for the previous design, Campbell and Stanley identify two additional problems:

1. There can be no confidence that the two groups were not different in ways that had nothing to do with being counseled.
2. There is a problem called *mortality*. This does not mean the death rate of the subjects but rather the dropping out of subjects from the experimental situation. Suppose that a researcher did want to look for differences between young married couples who had received counseling and other similar pairs. He or she might compare in some way the couples that had been counseled with a set of married couples recruited voluntarily from a local civic club. The comparison group would all be recruited *at the point of the comparison*. The experimental couples would all have been in a counseling group for a period of time. Some dropouts would probably occur as people move out of town, become discouraged and quit the group, or separate. At the point at which the comparisons are made, differences would be attributed to counseling. Actually, the differences might just as easily depend on the respective characteristics of the people who remain in the sample and those who drop out. Because the comparison group is

recruited for one time only (the day when the comparison is made), it has no dropouts.

Useful and More Valid Designs

A number of useful designs minimize the threats to validity that exist in the designs described above. We will examine three experimental designs here, following Campbell and Stanley's discussion.

The Pretest/Posttest Control-Group Design

This design is very close to the classical design. It looks like this:

$$R \qquad O \qquad X \qquad O$$
$$R \qquad O \qquad\qquad\quad O$$

The difference between this and the classical design is that the subjects are randomly chosen (R means "random sample") for assignment to the experimental and control groups. As in the classical design, both groups are pretested. The purpose of the pretest is to determine a baseline of entering behavior, attitude, or state of being prior to the introduction of the experimental treatment. By comparing pretest data, the experimenter can ascertain any gross differences between the two groups prior to the experiment. Even though the groups are selected by chance, differences can exist. If the pretest reveals important preexperimental differences in variables crucial to the experiment, the experimenter has two choices. The experimenter can either discard both groups and start over or compensate for the differences during the statistical analysis using procedures developed for that purpose.

Following the pretest, one group is subjected to the experimental treatment. The control receives either no treatment or a placebo. Then both groups are tested again. The differences between pretest and posttest scores are calculated and compared. If the experimental group changes significantly more in the desired direction than the control, then it is believed that the experimental treatment works.

Because random subjects comprise the control group, the researcher can make a comparison with a group that differs only by chance. The researcher also controls the effect of history, because both experimental and control groups will be exposed to the same events outside the experimental situation. Both groups mature during the experimental period, and we have no reason to believe that either group develops any advantage over the other because of experience. Because both groups are tested, any effects that testing may have are going to affect both groups. We avoid the problem of instrument change (if instruments that can change are used), because the instruments (judges, for instance) would change for both groups. Regression of performance to the mean is not a problem. If the researcher draws both experimental and control groups from the same pool, both would regress. There is no reason that any regression would be different for one group than for the other, because both are selected randomly. The problem of mortality is minimized, because dropouts would occur from both groups for probably the same reasons.

The above are Campbell and Stanley's solutions to the problems of internal validity. This design does not totally solve the threats to external validity, however. It is still impossible to separate the effects of an interaction of the pretest with the treatment.

The Posttest-Only Control-Group Design

One way of eliminating the threat to external validity posed by the possible interaction of the pretest with the treatment is to eliminate the pretest. Campbell and Stanley call this alternative the Posttest-Only Control-Group Design:

$$R \qquad X \qquad O$$
$$R \qquad \qquad O$$

The experimenter chooses two random samples from the population under study. One group receives the experimental treatment, the other does not. (The control group may be given a placebo experience in appropriate cases.) The experimenter measures both groups at the end of the experimental period. Because no pretest is administered, no interaction of pretest with treatment can occur.

This design almost sounds too simple to be true. Nevertheless, it is quite valid when it is clear that the experimenter is using naive subjects. Perhaps an extreme example will help. Suppose that an educator has devised a revolutionary way of teaching organic chemistry. This approach is supposed to be effective even on subjects who have had no previous background in chemistry. In order to test the teaching technique, the educator draws two random samples of social work students. By inspection of their transcripts, the educator determines that none of the subjects has ever had a course in chemistry, either in college or high school. In this case, and in others like it, it is quite proper to use this design and eliminate the pretest. Given naive subjects (in this sense, *naive* means knowing nothing about the experimental variable), a pretest would be of very little value, because the subjects could only guess at the answers. The pretest would only show random test behaviors.

Technically, the use of this design is not limited to use with naive subjects. Campbell and Stanley argue that researchers cling to pretesting for psychological reasons when they should utilize randomization:

> While the pretest is a concept deeply embedded in the thinking of research workers in education and psychology, it is not actually essential to true experimental designs. For psychological reasons, it is difficult to give up "knowing for sure" that the experimental and control groups were "equal" before the differential experimental treatment. Nonetheless, the most adequate all-purpose assurance of lack of initial biases between groups is randomization. Within the limits of confidence stated by the tests of significance, randomization can suffice without the pretest.[5]

Lin[6] takes the same position, and he adds two more reasons: This design saves the researcher time and money, and the calculations are simpler.

Despite the well-known and authoritative views of Campbell and Stanley, as well as Lin's sophisticated technical analysis (which is more complicated than the reference above suggests), we are reluctant to endorse the total elimination of pretesting, especially when the researcher has a logical or evidentiary reason to suspect that there are differences between the groups on the experimental variable. Clearly, though, it does seem that the pretest can be eliminated in experiments involving provably naive subjects.

The Solomon Four-Group Design

Another approach deals effectively with the interaction of a pretest with the experimental variable. This is the Solomon Four-Group Design, which some regard as the ultimate in "covering one's bets":

R	O	X	O
R	O		O
R		X	O
R			O

Notice that the first two groups are the same as in the Pretest/Posttest Control-Group Design. The additional groups allow the researcher to factor out the test effects and the interaction of testing and the experimental procedure. Group 3 gets the X but not the pretest, whereas Group 4 gets only the posttest. The experimenter can then separate the effects of testing from the effects of X.

Although this design is elaborate and theoretically sound, it is not used extensively. It is usually not possible to find enough subjects for four groups; and, of course, the expense of additional testing and the need to have two experimental groups put this elaborate design out of reach of all but the most well-funded researchers.

Quasi-Experimental Designs

A few quasi-experimental (experimentlike) designs are being used widely, primarily in situations in which the researcher might like to do a natural-occurring experiment but cannot do so, either because control subjects are unavailable or because randomization is impractical. A quasi-experimental approach might be used, for example, in studies of the effects of a new treatment technique on a hospital ward or the effects of a novel administrative procedure on a caseload in an office. In situations of these sorts, randomization is usually not possible. Subjects in these circumstances are usually referred to as *captive* groups, not because they are locked up, but because they are a set of people who are held together for some purpose not related to research.

The Time-Series Quasi-Experimental Design

Probably the most commonly encountered quasi-experimental design is the Time-Series:

$$O_1 \quad O_2 \quad O_3 \quad O_4 \quad X \quad O_5 \quad O_6 \quad O_7 \quad O_8$$

In this design, several measurements (not necessarily limited to four but at least three) are taken at regular intervals prior to the introduction of the experimental treatment X. A similar number of measurements are taken after X is in place or has been completed. A difference appearing consistently at measurements 5, 6, 7, and 8 supports the idea that X has some effect. For example, suppose that an agency wishes to know the effect of a change in policy on the attitudes of clients toward agency services. The agency would need to measure the attitudes of a number of clients several times before the introduction of the policy and then several times after. It is not necessary—and usually not possible—to use random samples. This approach can be used with captive groups—for example, patients on a ward or the current caseload.

This design has some of the problems of the before-after study in that no comparisons outside the treatment group are possible. Obviously, this design does not control every source of trouble. For example, it does not entirely control the effect of history. However, events external to the experiment would have to exert a powerful long-term effect on order to confound the effect of the treatment. The control of the interaction of testing and the experimental variable is also questionable, because the frequent testing of the subjects certainly reveals to them that something is going on outside of the usual run of events.

The Multiple Time-Series Design

In order to provide a comparison outside the treatment group, some experimenters have used a first cousin to the Time-Series Design:

$$O \qquad O \qquad O \qquad O \qquad X \qquad O \qquad O \qquad O \qquad O$$
$$O \qquad O \qquad O \qquad O \qquad\qquad O \qquad O \qquad O \qquad O$$

In this design, another similar group of subjects (for example, a similar ward in a neighboring hospital) is chosen as a contrast group. The contrast group is measured simultaneously with the subjects who are treated, but they do not receive X.

These quasi-experimental designs and others that have been devised are not as conclusive as are the genuine experimental designs. They are, however, much better for producing evidence explaining the effect of X than are the three nonexperimental approaches discussed earlier in the chapter.

The experimental approaches outlined here (and variations based on the same principles) are the most effective ways of obtaining dependable knowledge. However, they often impose practical constraints on the researcher. For instance, researchers cannot always select random groups of subjects from the significant population for control purposes, or they may be able to work with only one sample. In response to these and other constraints, Campbell and Stanley list sixteen quasi-experimental designs that represent reasonable compromises that avoid the gross inadequacies of the preexperimental approaches. It is outside the scope of this chapter to review all these alternative designs. You may want to pursue the full discussion in Campbell and Stanley's book.

The Single-Case Study

In recent years, there has been a great deal of interest in the study of phenomena through looking intensively at a single case rather than a number of cases. This approach follows Skinner's now-famous suggestion that more can be learned from studying one rat for a thousand hours than can be learned from studying a thousand rats for one hour.

The current interest might lead one to believe that single-case research was something new. Actually, it has been used in science for many years. Most of Freud's insights came from the study of individual cases. Pavlov conducted his work on conditioning on a single-case basis. These early uses of the single-case approach did not have the rigor of the present-day practitioners of the approach. The behavioristic psychologists, following Watson and Skinner, have probably developed single-case methodology to its highest state.

Despite its long history, single-case research is controversial. Herson and Barlow, two behavioristically oriented clinical psychologists, present an appealing argument for the single-case study.[7] Starting from the premise that the individual is the basic concern of the clinician, they argue that early single-case research was productive and led to many useful general theories about the human condition. They believe that the study of individuals fell out of general favor chiefly through the influence of Sir Ronald A. Fisher's work in statistics. Fisher, a mathematician whose field of interest was agronomy, was concerned with the problem of increasing yields from farmland. Because of this, he did not consider the individual plant important. He was more interested in what happened in a whole field. Further, Fisher faced the problem of inference. That is, if some factor affected the yield of a given field, how could one be certain that this factor was important in all fields? This problem should sound familiar. It is inherent in the questions of internal and external validity, which were discussed earlier in this chapter. That is, how does one know that something happened in the experiment; and, if something did, can the results be generalized to the population that was not part of the experiment? Fisher's work attracted the attention of psychologists and sociologists. Social scientists, in following Fisher, lost track of the importance of individual differences in their search for generalizability.

Studying large numbers at the same time, Herson and Barlow go on to say, raises some real difficulties. Some clinicians feel that the use of an untreated control group deprives people of treatment that could benefit them. Even though these treatments are unproven, most clinicians hesitate to refrain from doing something for people in pain. Further, it is difficult to get a large enough group of subjects at any one time.

A more important point made by Herson and Barlow is that when data are collected from groups of subjects, the individual differences are obscured. Some patients may have done well on the experimental treatment, while others may have grown worse. Both of these outcomes are lost when the results are presented as an average.

Finally, Herson and Barlow argue that findings that are based on group performance may not be translatable to the concerns of an individual patient. Something may well be *generally* true but not true in a specific case.

These arguments are convincing to many researchers. However, others argue in favor of using a number of subjects as the focus of attention, for the following reasons:

1. *All individuals are different.* In fact, because there is so much variability in humans (and in most organisms more complicated than the English pea or the fruit fly), the study of a single case may produce material so idiosyncratic that one cannot generalize from it. Because science is primarily interested in regularities, data that may be true only in a

single case does not add much to the store of scientific knowledge. A drug that cured only one person would not be of general importance, although it may well have been crucial for the one person that it helped.

2. *Some researchers have used a faulty design.* They have measured the subject, carried out the treatment, and then measured again. This is recognizable as a simple before-after study with an N of one. Single-case studies carried out in this way have all the problems of the before-after study with a group. For example, a person seeking casework help with a personal problem might appear to improve between the intake interview and a subsequent measuring point because of the effect of history, maturation, or any of the other factors that confound before-after studies.

The best use of the single-case approach is made when a time-series design is used. You will recall that the time-series can be depicted like this:

$$O \quad O \quad O \quad O \quad X \quad O \quad O \quad O \quad O$$

That is, the researcher makes a series of observations before treatment and another series after treatment. Although this is not a totally controlled design, it is good enough for most purposes. The collection of baseline data (or *entering behavior,* to use another term) needs to be stretched over some period of time to minimize the problems that occur with a before-after design.

Data can be gathered in several ways. If one is interested in behavior, one can count behavioral incidents during the observational periods. Standardized tests are also useful, but these may be less than satisfactory. The researcher may not be able to develop a test or set of tests that can be used eight times! There is also the question of selecting appropriate intervals between measurements. Should the measurements be a month apart? a week? The interval depends on the nature of the research, so no definite rule can be used.

In social work, as in clinical psychology, practitioners often use this technique as a way of measuring gains in treatment rather than as a pure research design. Often, if there is no specific behavior involved, the measurement will be by a rating scale of some kind. One of the simplest ways of doing this is to use a crude goal-attainment scale. The researcher rates the client initially—say over the first four interviews—on a scale of one to five. Intensive treatment is then applied and ratings are made in follow-up interviews. Usually, the practitioner sets a goal figure prior to treatment. The problem is that it is hardly ever possible to avoid some treatment during the exploratory phase. The baseline ratings may shift in such a way that the general trend of treatment cannot be separated from a spontaneous remission. For example, suppose that the diagram in Figure 4-1

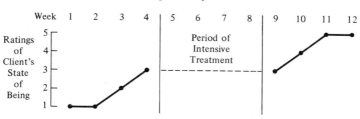

Figure 4-1   Treatment record showing a deceptive result

represents the course of treatment; it is not possible to say that treatment made a difference, simply because the general direction of the case was toward improvement even before treatment. What one hopes for is a nice, clear-cut result like that shown in Figure 4-2. In this example, the treatment appears to be working because the improvement in rating clearly follows the period of intensive treatment. Another problem inherent in the use of rating scales in the single-case study is that the practitioner is, in a sense, rating his or her own skills. Few practitioners will be able to rate objectively, particularly as the relationship develops. It is better, therefore, to have outsiders who are not carrying the case do the ratings.

The statistics that can be used to compare the later scores or ratings with the early ones are, frankly, quite complex. A work that claims to deal with elementary techniques is included in the For Further Reading section of this chapter. Despite the use of the word *elementary* in the title, the beginning student will find the procedures quite complex.

As long as the measurements are done objectively, either by a reliable instrument or by reliable judges, the single-case study may be a reasonably good way of showing client progress. It should be clear, however, that one case does not validate a treatment approach. Only through the collection

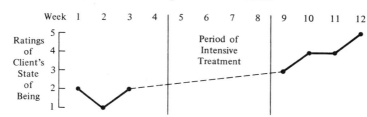

Figure 4-2   Treatment record showing a successful result

of a large number of single-case studies could this be done. Of course, when one accumulates a lot of single-case studies, he or she is, in effect, dealing with grouped data. Therefore, the single-case study often becomes merely one operation in a study of many subjects. If the data collected are to be used in research, the usual rules of informed consent and protection from social harm clearly apply.

Evaluative Research

Social workers have become increasingly involved in evaluative research. As social programs have become more important to society, their sponsors have been asked to demonstrate their accountability to taxpayers, contributors, and clientele. Schools of social work are adding preparation in evaluative research to curricula in order to meet these expectations.

Carol Weiss has stated the purpose of evaluative research this way:

> The purpose of evaluation research is to measure the effects of a program against the goals it set out to accomplish as a means of contributing to subsequent decision making about the program and improving future programming.[8]

The essence of evaluative research can be reduced to three basic questions:

1. *How effective is the program* (or agency, procedure, or administrative structure)? A program tries to accomplish certain goals. Usually, goals are very broad kinds of things—for example, "to provide quality mental health services to Woodland County" or "to provide a family counseling service that will prevent family breakdown in Hometown." These broad goals translate into specific measurable objectives—for example, "the reduction of hospitalization rates by 25 percent," or "the reduction of symptomatic behavior to a level of 50 percent of its present rate." Although some objectives are quite complex, the ideal is to work with expected outcomes that lend themselves to measures of performance that are as unequivocal as possible. The kinds of measuring instruments used to gather this data are the same as those used in other kinds of research. Usually, the designs of good effectiveness studies most resemble experimental or quasi-experimental designs, but a few are purely descriptive. Weiss summarizes the process by saying:

> The tools of research are pressed into service to make the judging process more accurate and objective. In its research guise, evaluation establishes clear and specific criteria for success. It collects evidence systematically from a representative sample of the units of concern. It usually translates the

evidence into quantitative terms (23 percent of the audience, grades of 85 or better), and compares it with the criteria that were set. It then draws conclusions about the effectiveness, the merit, the success, of the phenomenon under study.[9]

2. *How efficient is the program?* This raises the question of cost-benefit, or cost-effectiveness. What the researcher usually wants to know is: What is the cost per patient or per client of the activities under study, and is it as expensive as an equally effective alternative? For example, if one studied the cost of a new method of doing adoption studies and found that the same number of successful adoptions cost several hundred dollars less per case, the rational decision would be to adopt the new approach.

3. *Should the activity be continued* (or attempted, if this activity is being examined in a small pilot study)? A given program may be effective and efficient but still not be sound on moral or legal grounds. A competent evaluator will not ignore the value problems presented. One might argue that capital punishment is effective in stopping recidivism in robbery. It is also efficient, in that executions cost less than incarceration and rehabilitation attempts. But is execution the best answer from a legal and moral point of view? The evaluator can and should raise such questions in the report.

Weiss suggests that evaluation research has not been a major input to policy or program decision making. The evaluator's opinion is only one factor, and most policy and program decisions are made on a political basis. She says:

> Those who look to evaluation to take the politics out of decision making are bound to be disappointed. Within every organization, decisions are reached through negotiation and accommodation, through politics.... Evaluative facts have an impact on collective decisions only to the extent that program effectiveness is perceived as valuable. And, program effectiveness— inevitably and justifiably—competes for influence on decisions with considerations of acceptability, feasibility, and ideology.[10]

We must grant Weiss's point. In fact, research input of all kinds is sorely lacking in social work decisions. However, there seems to be a fresh wind blowing in the human-service field. The need for accountability has awakened social work interest in good research of all kinds. Now that useful designs are becoming better known and a stronger literature is being developed, social workers can do a better job of showing the validity of what they do. It is to be hoped that the increased interest in research will lead to more scientific rationality in both treatment and program decisions.

Key Terms

experimental research	instrument decay
evaluative research	regression to the mean
necessary cause	static-group comparison
sufficient cause	one-group pretest/posttest
contributory conditions	mortality
contingent conditions	pretest-posttest control group design
alternative conditions	posttest-only control group design
placebo	Solomon four-group design
naturally-occurring experiment	quasi-experimental
internal validity	time-series design
external validity	random assignment
one-shot case study	captive groups
history	single-case study
maturation	entering behavior
testing	

References

1. Claire Selltiz, Marie Jahoda, Morton Deutsch, and Stuart W. Cook, *Research Methods in Social Relations,* rev. ed. (New York: Holt, Rinehart and Winston, 1959), pp. 82–83.
2. Sir Ronald A. Fisher, *Statistical Methods for Research Workers* (London: Oliver and Boyd, 1925).
3. Donald T. Campbell and Julian C. Stanley, *Experimental and Quasi-Experimental Designs for Research* (Chicago: Rand McNally and Company, 1963).
4. *Ibid.,* p. 5.
5. *Ibid.,* p. 25.
6. Nan Lin, *Foundations of Social Research* (New York: McGraw-Hill, 1976), pp. 256–257.
7. Michel Herson and David H. Barlow, *Single Case Experimental Designs* (New York: Pergamon Press, 1976), pp. 1–30.
8. Carol H. Weiss, *Evaluation Research* (Englewood Cliffs, New Jersey: Prentice-Hall, 1972), p. 4.
9. *Ibid.,* pp. 1–2.
10. *Ibid.,* p. 4.

Questions for Discussion

1. What are the differences between a naturally-occurring experiment and one that might be done in a laboratory?

2. In what way do experiments "explain"?
3. Can you think of a way to match people for experimental purposes?
4. What is the difference between an experimental design and a quasi-experimental design?
5. Give examples of instrument decay, regression to the mean, and test effect that differ from those in the chapter.
6. Discuss the notion that social work interventions cannot be evaluated because social work is basically an art.
7. Discuss the pros and cons of the single-case study.

Exercises

1. Write a causative hypothesis (one in which you hypothesize that X causes Y). Share it with the class for their comments.

2. Write three hypotheses—one contributory, one contingent, and one alternative—and submit them to the class for comments.

3. Design an experiment that has relevance for social work.

4. Find examples of the one-shot case study, the before-after design, and the static-group comparison in the social work literature. Remember that these approaches are acceptable for an exploratory study, but it is not valid to base explanations on them.

5. Design a single-case study for the treatment of an alcoholic. Describe how you would collect baseline data and measure improvement.

6. Locate an evaluative study in social work. Are all three evaluative questions answered?

For Further Reading

Charles R. Atherton. "Acting Decisively in Foster Care." *Social Work,* vol. 19, no. 6 (November 1974). This before-after study shows the pitfalls of this approach.

Phillip Fellin, Tony Tripodi, and Henry J. Meyer. *Exemplars of Social Research.* Itasca, Illinois: F. E. Peacock, 1969. This book contains a number of examples of social work research.

Monica McGoldrick Organdis. "Children's Use of Humor in Psychotherapy." *Social Casework,* vol. 53, no. 3 (March 1972). A one-shot case study used correctly as an exploratory study that could form the basis for more definitive work. Organdis does *not* suggest that this is a definitive study.

Stephen M. Stillman. "Increasing Black Client Participation in an Agency." *Social Work,* vol. 21, no. 4 (July 1976). A static-group comparison that is well done and suggests a useful direction for future research.

Donald T. Campbell and Julian Stanley. *Experimental and Quasi-Experimental Designs for Research.* Chicago: Rand McNally and Company, 1963. This rather small book has become a classic in research design. Students will benefit from reading the early parts but may find the book hard going as it progresses.

Fred N. Kerlinger. *Foundations of Behavioral Research,* 2nd ed. New York: Holt, Rinehart and Winston, 1973. Chapters 2 and 3 address most of the material covered in this chapter but on a much more sophisticated level.

Janet Morsund. *Evaluation: An Introduction to Research Design.* Monterey, California: Brooks/Cole Publishing Company, 1973. Although this book does introduce the student to evaluation, it is broad enough to serve as a good primer on research design in general.

Claire Selltiz, Lawrence S. Wrightsman, and Stuart W. Cook. *Research Methods in Social Relations,* 3rd ed. New York: Holt, Rinehart and Winston, 1976. Chapters 4 and 5 in the new edition will provide additional background in research design for interested students.

Michel Herson and David H. Barlow. *Single Case Experimental Designs.* New York: Pergamon Press, 1976. This is a sophisticated discussion of the single-case study. Despite its high technical level, much of the discussion is understandable to the beginning researcher.

Walter W. Hudson. "Elementary Techniques for Assessing Single-Client/Single-Worker Interventions." *Social Service Review,* vol. 51, no. 2 (June 1977). Despite the title, this may be pretty heavy going for the beginner. Nevertheless, it is a useful reference for those who are serious about single-case research.

Carol H. Weiss. *Evaluation Research.* Englewood Cliffs, New Jersey: Prentice-Hall, 1972. This is a knowledgeable and well-written book on the evaluation process.

PART II

As we indicated in Part I, research involves making systematic observations. We develop this theme further in this Part, which focuses on the tasks involved in data collection.

Systematic observation implies that the researcher can describe in detail (1) what is to be observed, (2) how the observations are to be made, and (3) who or what will be observed. The chapters in this Part describe some of the procedures that researchers use in addressing these issues. It is important to note, however, that these issues are interrelated. Who is going to be observed influences how observations will be made and what will be observed.

Chapter 5, "Indexes and Scales," discusses how researchers usually proceed in constructing indexes and scales. It continues the discussion begun in Chapter 2, "Measurement," and illustrates one way of answering the question of what is to be observed. It gives primary attention to procedures used when the researcher is developing measures and testing hypotheses simultaneously. This is because the researcher rarely has the luxury of conducting a study whose sole purpose is the development of measures. The materials on assessing how well a measure has worked (for example, how valid and reliable a measure is) are somewhat technical. Also, they cannot be applied until after the researcher has gathered data. In social work programs that do not have a separate statistics course, instructors may want to defer these materials until they have completed the chapter on measures of association (Chapter 12). Students who have had a course in statistics, however, should be able to master this material in the present order.

Chapter 6, "Survey Research," describes an approach to the question of how observations are to be made. It begins with a discussion of how the materials in Chapter 2 and Chapter 5 may be combined to form a survey instrument. Next, it describes two of the most common ways of conducting a survey—the mailed questionnaire and the personal interview. The chapter concludes with a discussion of the relative merits of different types of surveys.

Although surveys are commonly associated with descriptive research (see Chapter 3), they may also be used with experimental and evaluative research designs (see Chapter 4). For example, a researcher interested in whether social workers vary in their treatment recommendations depending on the sex of the client could develop two mock case histories that are identical except for the sex of the client. Following the experimental design, the case histories could be administered to two randomly selected groups of social workers. The method of data collection, however, could be one of the survey techniques described in Chapter 6. The independent variable (the variable being manipulated) is sex of the client, and the dependent variable is the recommendation the social workers give.

Chapter 7, "Observational Methods," illustrates a second approach to the issues of what is to be observed and how observations are to be made. It focuses on different methods of making *direct observations* of behavior. As is the case with surveys, the approaches to gathering data described in this chapter can be used with descriptive or experimental and evaluative research designs.

Chapter 8, "Specialized Data Gathering Procedures," includes descriptions of data-collection techniques that are less commonly used in social work research than those described in Chapters 6 and 7. They are included both to stimulate creativity in approaches to data collection and to illustrate how alternative measurement procedures can often provide better information than more traditional techniques.

Chapter 9, "Sampling," addresses the final issue in systematic observation, that of who or what should be observed. The chapter begins with a discussion of how the researcher identifies who or what should be observed. Next, the issues of whether the researcher should sample and, if so, how large the sample should be are addressed. The chapter concludes with descriptions of a wide variety of sampling procedures and their relative merits.

5

Indexes and Scales

With the exception of sociodemographic characteristics like sex and age, which are usually measured by asking a simple direct question, most concepts are measured using a multiple-item approach. This strategy for measurement has wide acceptance, because it represents the simplest method for developing adequate measures of concepts. More specifically, most of the concepts employed in research are multifaceted. For example, self-esteem probably involves a sense of pride, a sense of accomplishment, a positive attitude toward self, and satisfaction with one's self as well as other similar attributes or characteristics. Because it is difficult to conceive of a single question that would generate information on all of these different aspects of what is typically meant by self-esteem, the researcher would probably adopt a multiple-item approach to the measurement of this concept.

The researcher, in developing a multiple-item measure, faces two major questions:

1. *How many and which items should the measure include?* Obviously, because the intent of the process is to develop a single summary or composite score that reflects how an individual rates on self-esteem, the items should all be measures of the same concept.
2. *How should the researcher combine the items?* The two most common procedures for item combination are index construction and scale construction. They are described in detail later in this chapter. The first of these simply involves adding item scores together to form a composite score, whereas the second approach requires an examination of the specific pattern of responses an individual makes on the items to be combined.

Another issue that the researcher must bear in mind is that the primary purpose of measurement is to differentiate among respondents. For example, the researcher who wishes to test the hypothesis that people who have more positive self-images are happier with life than those who have less positive self-images cannot test the hypothesis on subjects who all have a positive self-image. A measure that fails to differentiate among respondents, although it may be useful for some purposes, is of almost no utility in hypothesis testing. Consequently, a final criterion by which most measures are assessed is the degree to which subjects vary in their scores on the measure.

This chapter is divided into four sections. The first section discusses how researchers typically proceed to develop a set of items that form the basis for a multiple-item measure. The second and third sections describe the procedures researchers use in index and scale construction. In each case, we describe the measurement model, outline the procedures for assessing the adequacy of the model for describing how people respond to items, and provide an example of how the researcher applies these principles in constructing a measure. The fourth section describes some of the other measurement tools that are occasionally used in research. We devote particular attention to the more common methods that researchers use in obtaining a rank ordering of a set of objects.

Developing an Item Pool

Developing an index or a scale involves three basic steps:

1. *Define the concept to be measured as carefully and completely as possible.* It is extremely difficult to develop a good measure of a concept without a clear understanding of the concept to be measured. Furthermore, because many of the concepts employed in social work are used in somewhat different ways, it is important to be as precise as possible in the working definition of the concept to be measured.

2. *Develop an initial set of questions.* This process of generating an initial item pool is similar to brainstorming. The process is facilitated by a thorough understanding of the concept to be measured and by a knowledge of the professional literature that relates to the concept. The major idea at this point is to list as many items as possible.

3. *Organize the items.* For example, the researcher attempting to develop a measure of perceived powerlessness (that is, people's perception that they cannot control outcomes of events that are important to them) might note that he or she has included items focusing on different social

institutions (for example, government and education) and different levels of social organization (for example, local, regional, and national). Such an organizational strategy might suggest the addition of further items to complete coverage of the concept from this organizational framework. It might also suggest the elimination of items that are too similar to others included within the item pool. Sometimes scrutinizing items helps to round out the definition of the concept. That is, one may encounter an item that raises a point that the researcher wishes to include in the definition of the concept. On the other hand, the researcher may also find that an item actually measures something different from what is intended. If this happens, the researcher discards the item.

Good items not only accurately reflect the concept that they are to measure but also are easily understood by the respondents who are expected to answer them. This usually means that items must be clearly written. Often, individuals who have extensive experience with the target population can be helpful in this phase of the development of a measure. They can help to identify how questions that appear to be straightforward to the researcher might be misinterpreted by members of the population to be studied. Further, many researchers who ask others to review preliminary versions of measures are startled to discover how many assumptions, obvious omissions, and other crucial errors someone not so closely involved with the project can note.

Three problems in writing items are so common that they deserve special mention:

1. *The double-barreled item.* A double-barreled item includes two separate thoughts. The item "You still love your mother, don't you?" is not only double-barreled but also includes a conclusion on the part of the researcher. Tacking the "don't you" onto the end of the statement suggests that the researcher expects a "yes" answer to this question. A better format for this question is simply, "Do you love your mother?" This probably comes as close as possible to measuring what the researcher intended with the first question.

2. Asking a question of *fact* when the intent is to ask a question of *opinion*. For example, the question, "Do you believe most men prefer male to female supervisors?" asks for the respondent's perception about a fact. A yes response to this question could reflect an accurate belief on the part of the respondent that the statement is generally true, or it could reflect a sexual bias on the part of the respondent. Without further information from the respondent, it is difficult to ascertain which of these two interpretations of the response is correct. If the intent is to measure the degree to which respondents perceive that males are sexually biased, the question

is probably valid, provided that it is preceded by instructions that explain the purpose of the questions. If the intent is to measure the degree to which the respondent is sexually biased, a more appropriate format for the question might be, "Would you prefer a male to a female supervisor?"

3. *Halo error*. Respondents, like all of us, develop habits. A respondent answering a long set of similar questions might stop thinking about the questions and simply answer all of them with the same answer. To combat this tendency, the researcher usually attempts to word some of the questions negatively and others positively. This helps to maintain the attention of the respondent.

Many times in the construction of a measure, the researcher provides answer categories for the respondent to use in answering the questions. In doing this, the researcher must remember certain points:

1. Most obviously, the categories provided must *relate to the question asked.*

2. The categories provided should be *exhaustive.* There should be a category provided for every possible response. Respondents often find it frustrating to be unable to answer the question in the way that they would like, given the response categories provided. With nominal variables like religious affiliation, the researcher often accomplishes this end by including a residual category labelled Other. Thus, in asking about a respondent's religion, the researcher might provide the categories Protestant, Catholic, Jewish, and Other. For ordinal and interval variables, the researcher usually uses open-ended categories at the extremes. For example, in asking about a respondent's family income, the researcher might provide the following categories: less than $5,000, $5,000–$9,999, $10,000–$14,999, $15,000–$19,999, $20,000–$24,999, $25,000–$29,999, $30,000–$34,999, and $35,000 or more. The addition of the income categories "less than $5,000" and "$35,000 or more" makes the entire set of categories exhaustive.

3. The categories the researcher provides should be *mutually exclusive.* This simply means that a respondent's answer should fit into one and only one response category. The income categories in the previous example are mutually exclusive.

4. The categories must not have a too-high *level of complexity.* Most researchers, unless they are using visual aids, limit the number of choices from which the respondent must select to between five and seven. This is about the limit of the number of things that a respondent can remember

at a single time. If the response categories are statements, three or four choices are often the limit. If the researcher desires to include a broader range of response categories (and achieve finer discrimination among respondents), the categories are usually presented in terms of a system. For example, rather than presenting a respondent with one hundred choices, the researcher might ask, "On a scale from 0 to 100, on which 0 means strongly disagree and 100 means strongly agree, where would you rate this statement?" The researcher would then present an attitude statement, such as "The primary problem in this country is the high rate of inflation."

The Additive Model of Combining Items

Perhaps the simplest and most common method of combining item scores to obtain a single score is to add item scores together. The total score that results from this process is known as an *index* score. This approach to item combination is appropriate whenever (1) the items measure the same concept, (2) the items are viewed as equivalent to one another in measuring the concept, and (3) the items are measured at the interval level.

Assumptions

The importance of the assumption of unidimensionality among the items (that is, the items all measure the same concept) cannot be stressed too much. Because the item scores are to be combined to form a single measure, this measure must have some basis for interpretation. If the items that are combined measure different things, then it would be difficult to decide what the composite score measures. The following illustration may make this point clearer.

Suppose that a researcher asked clients of a community services agency two questions:

	Yes	*No*
Do you think you would *like help* in paying your heating bills?	1	0
Do you think you *need help* in paying your heating bills?	1	0

The first item appears to measure preference for energy assistance, whereas the second appears to measure self-assessed need for assistance. A composite index created by adding the scores on these two item together, on the other hand, measures an uncertain mixture of both preference and need. Although the distinction here between the items is relatively small, the point is valid. If, after examining the items, the researcher cannot determine what an index is measuring, he or she should not combine the items.[1]

The second assumption underlying index construction (that items are equivalent to one another in measuring a concept) is important both mathematically and from the perspective of the interpretation of scores. Again, an illustration best demonstrates the importance of this assumption. Suppose that a researcher, in an effort to obtain a measure of desire for help in paying energy bills, asked clients of a community service agency the following two questions:

	Yes	No
Do you think you would *like help* in paying your home *heating* bills?	1	0
Do you think you would *like help* in paying your home *cooling* bills?	1	0

The possible index scores are 0 (no to both of the questions), 1 (yes to only one of the questions), and 2 (yes to both of the questions). The assumption that the items are equivalent is important in this case, because the respondent will receive a score of 1 whether he or she answers yes to the first or yes to the second question. Because it is not possible to differentiate between these two cases on the basis of the total score, it is important that the items measure desire for help in paying energy bills to the same degree. It is only under this circumstance that a score of 1 on the index will have an interpretation.

The explanation of the final assumption underlying the construction of an index (that the items to be combined are measured at the interval level) is relatively technical. It is not appropriate to add nominal or ordinal scores together, because as was pointed out in Chapter 2, the numbers have no mathematical meaning. Because the process of constructing an index involves adding item scores, it follows that the items should be measured at the interval or ratio level.

Although each of the assumptions underlying index construction is important, each is often violated in practice. Of the three, the question of dimensionality appears to be most important. Usually, when the assumption that the items measure a single dimension is violated, the resulting index is neither reliable nor valid. Except in very unusual circumstances, violating the assumption that items are equivalent to one another appears to have very little effect on the study outcome. Furthermore, if the items are measured on the ordinal rather than the interval or ratio level, the additive model of item combination appears to work rather well. It is only when items are measured at the nominal level that the researcher needs to find another method for combining item scores.

Practice

The actual practice of scoring an index is simple. The researcher need only add together the respondent's scores on the items. In adding the item scores, it is important to be sure that a high (or low) score on each item means the same thing. If, for example, some of the items that make up the index are worded negatively and others positively to avoid a response set on the part of the respondents, the researcher must remember to revise the scoring system for one set. To avoid confusion in the analysis phase of the project, it is generally a good idea to design the coding so that a high score means a high amount of the attribute or characteristic being measured. Thus, for example, a high score on a measure of self-esteem should mean that the individual has high self-esteem.

One problem that the researcher frequently encounters when constructing an index is missing data. Respondents occasionally refuse to answer or inadvertently omit a question. Interviewers can, for any of a variety of reasons, fail to ask a question. The chances of this occurring increase as the number of items in the index increases. Thus, a researcher with a twenty-item index might discover that as many as 20 percent or 30 percent of the respondents have failed to answer at least one question. Most researchers are extremely reluctant to exclude subjects from the study because of their failure to answer one or two questions. At the same time, to calculate a total score on only those items that the respondent answered means that the respondents who have failed to answer one question will, on the average, have lower scores than those who have not omitted any items. To correct for this problem, the researcher has one of two choices. If most of the respondents who failed to answer one question omitted the same item, probably the item was a poor one. In this case, the best strategy is to base the index score on the remaining items, excluding the one that most respondents failed to answer. On the other hand, there may be no pattern to the failure to respond. If the nonresponse appears to be random, then the researcher usually substitutes the arithmetic mean of the items in the index that the respondent *did* answer for the items that were omitted. Often, when this approach is used, the researcher will include a case only if the respondent has answered a certain percentage, such as at least 80 percent, of the questions. This practice ensures that only respondents who have answered a majority of the questions in the index are assigned a score.

Evaluation

If the items in the index all measure the same concept to the same degree, then the size of the correlation coefficient between any pair of items should be approximately equal to that for any other pair of items, and all of the correlation coefficients should be greater than zero. This expectation forms the basis for a series of statistical tests to determine whether the additive model is an appropriate way to combine items. We will describe two of these in this section: the item-to-total correlation coefficient and the index of internal consistency.

An *item-to-total correlation coefficient* is simply a Pearson correlation coefficient (see Chapter 12) between the scores on a single item and the sum of the scores on the remaining items included in the index. A separate item-to-total coefficient is computed for each item (see Table 5-1). If, as the researcher hypothesizes when creating an index, the items are equivalent to one another, then the item-to-total correlations should be positive and of approximately the same magnitude. Because we can assume that a set of items is a better measure of the concept than a single item is, an item whose correlation with the sum of the remaining items is substantially below that obtained for the remaining items is usually excluded from the index. This system for *item* analysis was first proposed by Likert, a psychologist interested in measurement theory. It is probably the most common method of determining whether a set of items forms an index. Table 5-1 presents an example of item analysis.

Assessment

The item-to-total correlations in Table 5-1 are fairly uniform, although that for item 4 is somewhat low. Examination of this item suggests that its content may be somewhat different from that of the remaining five items. At the same time, removal of this item would reduce the reliability of the index. For this reason, the researcher probably would not exclude item 4 from the index.

A second statistic that is usually calculated when constructing an index is the *index of internal consistency,* also known as coefficient alpha. This method of assessing the reliability of an index is conceptually similar to the alternate- or parallel-test method mentioned in Chapter 2. In the alternate-test method of assessing reliability, the researcher develops two equivalent forms of a test and administers them to a set of individuals. The reliability of the tests is measured by the size of the correlation coefficient between the scores on the two forms of the test. Because the items that comprise an index are supposed to be separate measures of a single concept, it follows from the alternate-test method that the correlation between any pair of items is a reliability estimate. Because the number of different reliability estimates obtained in this fashion can be very large,[2] some method of summarizing them would be helpful. The index of internal consistency is such a summary statistic.

Although the statistical theory underlying the index of internal consistency is beyond the scope of this text, the computation formula is relatively simple. The simplest form is:

$$\text{coefficient alpha} = \frac{K\bar{r}}{1 + (K - 1)\bar{r}}$$

in which K is the number of items in the index and $\bar{r}$ is the arithmetic average of the correlation coefficients among the items in the index. Thus,

Table 5-1   Item analysis for an index of level of support for government expenditures on older people

	Item Mean	Item-to-Total Correlation	Alpha If Item Deleted
1. Government should help older people by making sure they have enough income to live comfortably.	3.85	.65	.72
2. Government should help older people by paying the bills for necessities like food and medical care.	3.42	.57	.75
3. If it weren't for special programs for older people, the elderly wouldn't get their fair share of the country's resources.	3.53	.50	.76
4. As the cost of living increases, Social Security payments to retired people should increase also.	4.20	.43	.77
5. Government should help support older people with taxes collected from all citizens.	3.69	.57	.74
6. The government spends too much money on older people.	3.90	.50	.76

K. the number of items in the index, is 6.

$\bar{r}$, the arithmetic average of the correlations between items, is .378.

$$\text{Coefficient alpha} = \frac{K\bar{r}}{1 + (K-1)\bar{r}} = \frac{6 \times .378}{1 + 5 \times .378} = .785.$$

Notes: 1. Item statistics are based on responses from a probability sample of 918 adult residents of Alabama. Funds for data collection were provided by a grant from the NRTA-AARP Andrus Foundation.

2. Except as noted, items were scored as follows: Strongly agree $= 5$, Agree $= 4$, Neutral $= 3$, Disagree $= 2$, Strongly disagree $= 1$.

3. Item 6 was reverse coded.

the internal consistency or reliability of an index is a function of both the number of items in the index and the average correlation among them.

The index of internal consistency is itself a correlation coefficient and should be interpreted as such. One of the scores for this correlation coefficient is simply the individual's score on the index. The second score is somewhat more complicated; it is a hypothetical score that represents the score the individual would receive if the measure were perfectly reliable. Thus, the value of the index of internal consistency is the correlation between the score the individual has on the index and the score that he or she would receive if the index were perfectly reliable.

Although researchers desire an index to be as reliable as possible, they can rarely attain such an ideal state. Because the development of highly reliable measures can be a difficult, expensive process, most researchers are willing to accept lower reliability values in exploratory research. Most, however, consider .6 to be the minimum acceptable value for the reliability coefficient. If coefficient alpha is not at least of this magnitude, the items should not be combined to form an index. Naturally, if the individual's score on an index is used for diagnostic purposes (for example, determining eligibility for benefits or specification of a treatment regimen), the reliability of the instrument should be substantially higher. A coefficient of internal consistency of .9 or .95 is not unusual in these circumstances.

The Likert Index

Perhaps the most common application of the additive model, at least in terms of attitude measurement, is the Likert index. It is named in honor of Rensis Likert, who first suggested that the additive model be used in the measurement of attitudes.[3] In fact, we base the description of the additive model in this text, particularly that part focusing on the assessment of the adequacy of the model, on Likert's proposals.

To construct a Likert index, the researcher develops a set of attitude statements on the topic of concern. Respondents are given the statements and asked the degree to which they agree with each. Usually, the respondents are given five choices ranging from strongly agree to strongly disagree, as is illustrated in the following example:

Below is a set of statements about poor people. Please indicate the degree to which you agree with each of these statements by checking the response category that comes closest to your opinion.

1. The reason people are poor is that they are lazy.

Strongly Agree	Agree	Uncertain	Disagree	Strongly Disagree
(1)	(2)	(3)	(4)	(5)

2. Poor people are a burden to the rest of us.

Strongly Agree	Agree	Uncertain	Disagree	Strongly Disagree
(1)	(2)	(3)	(4)	(5)

The researcher adds together the scores for each of the items (1 for strongly agree to 5 for strongly disagree in this illustration) to obtain a total score for each respondent. The values associated with each response usually do not appear on the form given to the respondent. They are presented here simply to illustrate how an item is scored.

Although many researchers tend to think of a Likert index as composed of items similar to those in the above illustration, this is simply an arbitrary convention. According to Likert, the important thing is not the "strongly agree"-to-"strongly disagree," five-point scale associated with his name. Instead, he emphasizes the following points:

1. *Statements should be statements of attitude, not fact.* Thus, depending on the nature of the statements involved, responses could range from "strongly approve" to "strongly disapprove" or from "very good idea" to "very bad idea."
2. *Responses should lie along a single continuum.* Furthermore, the number of choices available need not be five. Although the number of choices (response categories) should probably be the same for each item in the index, the number of choices presented is arbitrary.
3. *Item analysis is necessary.*[4] Most importantly (according to Likert), the researcher must conduct an item analysis using the procedures outlined in the evaluation section on the additive model. Specifically, items that reduce the internal consistency of the index or that have low item-to-total correlations should not be included in the measure.

The Scaling Model of Combining Items

A second approach to combining item scores to obtain a single value that reflects the amount of a characteristic that an individual possesses is *scalogram analysis.* The application of this procedure to a data set results in the development of a *Guttman scale,* named in honor of the originator of the procedure. Although this approach to item combination is not limited to dichotomous items, most Guttman scales are based on items of this format. Furthermore, unlike an index, which results in an interval-level measure, a Guttman scale attains only an ordinal level of measurement (see Chapter 2).

Models

Guttman scales, unlike indexes, involve the ordering of items in addition to the ordering of responses. The assumption underlying a Guttman scale is that items differ in their importance or intensity. For example, a researcher interested in how severe a problem must be before a social worker will recommend developmental disability assessment for a child might pose the following theoretical case:

> Suppose that one of your clients expresses concern about his or her six-year-old child. You speak with the child. Would you recommend speech assessment for the child if:

	Recommend	
1. the child has no speech?	Yes	No
2. the child speaks but not in sentences?	Yes	No
3. the child speaks in sentences but has a limited vocabulary?	Yes	No

These items appear to be ordered in terms of the presenting problem from most severe (no speech) to least severe (limited vocabulary). The difference in intensity among the items can be represented pictorially, as in Figure 5-1. Thus, individuals who have no speech would be perceived to have a more severe problem than those who speak but do not use sentences. Similarly, those who do not yet use sentences would be perceived to have a more severe problem than those who have a limited vocabulary.

In addition to the assumption concerning ordering of variables, scalogram analysis involves a hypothesis concerning the patterning of the respondents' answers to the questions. Specifically, respondents are assumed to behave in a consistent fashion. Thus, for example, a social worker who recommends speech assessment for a six-year-old child who uses sentences but has a limited vocabulary would also be expected to recommend speech assessment for a six-year-old child who has no speech. Also, a social worker who does not recommend speech assessment for the child with no speech would not be expected to recommend it in the other two cases.

The expectations concerning different response patterns that are consistent with the ordering of the items are often summarized in tabular form (see Table 5-2) as *scalograms,* which specify each pattern of responses that is consistent with the ordering of the items. Note the triangular pattern of "yes" and "no" responses in the table. This is characteristic of all

---

Figure 5-1   Level of severity of speech problem of three items

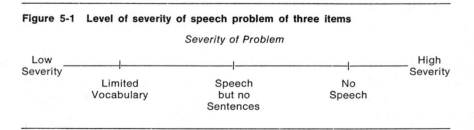

Table 5-2 Scalogram of social worker recommendations for speech assessment for children with different problems

Pattern	Expected Response Patterns		
	No Speech	No Sentences	Limited Vocabulary
1	No	No	No
2	Yes	No	No
3	Yes	Yes	No
4	Yes	Yes	Yes

scalograms. Note also that each response pattern consists of three responses, one for each of the three questions in this example. Unlike in indexes, the response pattern (that is, which questions are answered "yes" and which are answered "no") is important in scalogram analysis.

One of the strengths of the Guttman scale model is that knowing an individual's score on the measure allows a researcher to reproduce exactly how that individual scored on each of the items. In the example, the researcher is attempting to measure how willing social workers are to recommend a child for speech assessment. Following the rule for indexes that a high score should mean a high amount of the characteristic in question, the researcher would base this score on the number of "yes" responses the individual gives. The scores would vary from 0 ("no" to all of the questions) to 3 ("yes" to all of the questions). If the respondent behaves consistently, however, a score of 2 would not mean simply that the respondent answered "yes" to two questions, but rather it would mean that the respondent said "yes" to the first two questions and "no" to the last question (see Table 5-2). This is the only consistent response pattern that involves two "yes" responses.

Evaluation

Thus far, we have described the Guttman scale model and how respondents are expected to respond under this model. However, respondents do not always respond as expected. The focal point of Guttman scale analysis is a comparison between how respondents are *expected* to answer questions and how they *actually* answer. A set of items is said to constitute a Guttman scale if and only if the Guttman scale model does an accurate job of describing how individuals actually respond to the questions.

The primary tool for assessing the adequacy of the Guttman scale is the *coefficient of reproducibility*. It is important to note that the coefficient of reproducibility is based on the number of *responses,* not the number of *respondents.* We can think of the Guttman scale model as involving a set of predictions, one for each item in the scale. If 100 individuals each answer three questions, a total of 300 responses (and 300 predictions) are made. If 10 of these 100 individuals each gave one inconsistent response, the proportion of individuals with consistent patterns would be .9 (90/100); but the proportion of consistent responses would be .97 (290/300). Assessment of the adequacy of the Guttman scale is based on the latter figure.

Determining how many responses are consistent with the Guttman scale model is a multistage process. The usual method is to determine the number of inconsistent responses and subtract this number from the total number of responses to obtain the number of consistent responses. The total number of responses, as we indicated earlier, is the product of the number of items to be combined and the number of respondents. Thus, for example, if 300 respondents answer 5 questions each, the total number of responses is 1,500. The coefficient of reproducibility (CR), expressed in these terms, is:

$$CR = \frac{N \times K - I}{N \times K} = 1 - \frac{I}{N \times K}$$

in which N is the number of subjects, K is the number of items, and I is the number of inconsistent responses.

The final task in calculating the coefficient of reproducibility is to determine the number of inconsistent responses. Usually the researcher begins this process by listing each of the different response patterns that are possible (see Table 5-3 for an example). Next, the researcher examines each of the inconsistent patterns to determine the number of changes that must be made to convert them to consistent patterns. Four inconsistent patterns are possible with the example presented in Table 5-3 (that is, patterns 5–8). In each case, it is possible to convert the inconsistent pattern to one that is consistent by changing a single response. In this example, two of the three responses involved in each pattern are consistent, and one of the three responses involved in each pattern is inconsistent. Finally, to determine the number of inconsistent responses, the researcher multiplies the number of changes needed to make a pattern consistent by the number of respondents answering with that pattern. If, for example, three changes were required to make a pattern consistent, and eleven people responded with that pattern, the number of inconsistent responses associated with that pattern is 33 ($3 \times 11 = 33$). The researcher then adds together the number of inconsistent responses associated with each inconsistent pattern to obtain the total number of inconsistent responses.

A second tool used in assessing the adequacy of the Guttman scale model for describing responses to a set of items is the *item coefficient of*

Table 5-3   Consistent and inconsistent response patterns and changes needed to make inconsistent patterns consistent

		Possible Response Patterns					
	Pattern Number	No Speech	No Sentences	Limited Vocabulary	Changes Needed	Item Changed	Pattern Method
Consistent	1	D	D	D	0	–	1
	2	A	D	D	0	–	2
	3	A	A	D	0	–	3
	4	A	A	A	0	–	4
Inconsistent	5	D	D	A	1	3	1
	6	D	A	D	1	1 or 2	3 or 1
	7	D	A	A	1	1	4
	8	A	D	A	1	2 or 3	4 or 2

reproducibility. This coefficient is defined in the same fashion as the coefficient of reproducibility except that there is a separate coefficient for each item. Because each subject gives only one response to each item, the total number of responses for the item coefficient of reproducibility is equal to the number of respondents. Unlike the coefficient of reproducibility, which simply requires that the researcher determine the *number* of changes needed to make an inconsistent pattern consistent, however, the item coefficient of reproducibility requires that the researcher specify *where* to make those changes.

The researcher, in deciding where changes in an inconsistent pattern should be made to convert it to a consistent pattern, typically uses one of two rules:

1. *Minimize the number of changes.* For example, the only way to convert pattern 5 (DDA) in Table 5-3 to a consistent pattern with a single change is to change item 3 from agree to disagree and match pattern 1 (DDD). Because this is the only single-change option available with this pattern, the researcher would typically consider the response to item 3 to be the one that was inconsistent.

2. *Distribute the errors as evenly as possible across both the patterns that are matched and the items that are changed.* On occasion, the researcher will have a choice about how to convert an inconsistent pattern to one that is consistent. For example, pattern 6 (DAD) in Table 5-3 can be converted to a consistent pattern by changing either the response to the first item and matching pattern 3 (AAD) or the response to the second

item and matching pattern 1 (DDD). Depending on the choice made, the researcher will count inconsistent responses under item 1 or item 2.

One of the ways that the researcher could apply these guidelines to the inconsistent patterns shown in Table 5-3 is:

Pattern	to	Pattern	Item Changed
5 (DDA)		1 (DDD)	3
6 (DAD)		3 (AAD)	1
7 (DAA)		4 (AAA)	1
8 (ADA)		2 (ADD)	3

To obtain the number of inconsistent responses for an item, the researcher simply counts the number of subjects that respond with inconsistent patterns (for example, the number of people responding with pattern 6 and pattern 7 for item 1 here). Note also that the item coefficient of reproducibility for item 2, with the choices made in this example, will be 1.00.

The third statistical tool used in assessing the adequacy of the Guttman scale is the *coefficient of scalability*. The coefficient of scalability is a measure of the proportion of improvement of the coefficient of reproducibility actually obtained, over that expected by chance factors alone. The score on the coefficient of scalability provides a basis for interpreting the adequacy of the coefficient of reproducibility obtained in a given data set.

The coefficient of reproducibility is always greater than 0 and, in some cases, may be substantially above 0. Suppose, for example, that by chance alone an equal number of subjects responded with each of the response patterns in Table 5-3. Although the subjects are responding at random, the researcher would only note four errors for every twenty-four responses. The subjects that responded with consistent patterns (patterns 1–4) would receive no errors, and those that responded with inconsistent patterns (patterns 5–8) would receive one error each. Thus, the minimum value of the coefficient of reproducibility when subjects are responding randomly would be .83. In fact, because the largest number of errors recorded for an inconsistent pattern is one in the three-item case (see Table 5-3), the minimum value for the coefficient of reproducibility if all subjects responded with inconsistent patterns would be .67. (That is, two out of three responses are defined as consistent for each inconsistent pattern.) Obviously, without some estimate of the expected value of the coefficient of reproducibility under chance conditions, the interpretation of the coefficient as a measure of the adequacy of the Guttman scale model for describing how responses occur is difficult.

Although there are other methods of obtaining an estimate of the minimum expected coefficient of reproducibility, the most commonly used figure is the *minimum marginal reproducibility*. The minimum marginal reproducibility is the minimum value the coefficient of reproducibility can be, given how individuals responded to the questions. This measure is based on the assumption that the most frequent response to an item will be defined as a consistent response. It is calculated by adding the number of subjects in the most frequent response category for each item together and dividing the total by the total number of responses. For example, if 100 individuals took a two-item test, and 90 agreed with the first item but disagreed with the second, the minimum marginal reproducibility would be .90:

$$\frac{90 + 90}{2 \times 100} = \frac{180}{200} = .90.$$

The coefficient of scalability is defined by the formula:

$$CS = \frac{CR - MMR}{MMR}$$

in which CS is the coefficient of scalability, MMR is the minimum marginal reproducibility, and CR is the coefficient of reproducibility. Its interpretation is the proportion of improvement in the coefficient of reproducibility actually obtained over that which would be expected on the basis of how subjects responded to items. If the value of this coefficient is small, then the value of the coefficient of reproducibility is close to what would be expected if respondents were answering at random. If the value of the coefficient of scalability is high, however, then respondents are patterning their responses according to the Guttman-scale model predictions.

Practice

The process of constructing a Guttman scale is guided by rules of thumb that most researchers accept:

1. Although items can be ordered in intensity by theory a priori, most researchers order items after the fact by the percentage endorsing each position. For example, suppose that a researcher were interested in public support for government's providing energy assistance to special categories of persons. The researcher could attempt to develop a Guttman scale based on the priority that the respondents give to different categories of people. Rather than developing a theory to predict how categories of people would be ordered in terms of preferences, the researcher could simply order items by their popularity. This is the approach adopted in Table 5-4.

Table 5-4 A Guttman scale analysis of public willingness to have government help pay the energy bills of selected categories of individuals

Item Distributions

Category	Agree %	Agree (N)	Disagree %	Disagree (N)	Item Coefficient of Reproducibility	Scale Coefficients
Disabled	77.7	(335)	22.3	(96)	$1 - \dfrac{18}{431} = .958$	$MMR = \dfrac{335 + 223 + 302}{3 \times 431} = .665$
Low income	48.3	(208)	51.7	(223)	$1 - \dfrac{0}{431} = 1.000$	$CR = 1 - \dfrac{25}{3 \times 431} = .981$
Unemployed	29.9	(129)	70.1	(302)	$1 - \dfrac{7}{431} = .984$	$CS = \dfrac{.981 - .665}{.665} = .475$

Error Assessment

Possible Response Patterns

Disabled	Low Income	Unemployed	Item Changed	Number of Errors	Frequency	Total Errors
D	D	D	–	–	77	0
A	D	D	–	–	139	0
A	A	D	–	–	72	0
A	A	A	–	–	118	0
D	D	A	3	1	1	1
D	A	D	1	1	14	14
D	A	A	1	1	4	4
A	D	A	3	1	6	6
				Total	431	25

Source: Data are based on a random sample of customers of Alabama Power Company. Funds for data collection were provided by a grant from, and this material is used with the permission of, the Research Grants Committee, The University of Alabama.

2. A series of guidelines determines how large the values of the statistics associated with a Guttman scale should be before the items are said to constitute a scale. Most researchers expect the coefficient of reproducibility to be at least .90—that is, 90 percent of the responses are consistent with the Guttman scale-model predictions. Furthermore, most researchers expect the item coefficients of reproducibility to be at least .85—that is, no more than 15 percent of the responses to a single item are inconsistent with the Guttman scale-model predictions. Finally, most expect the coefficient of scalability to be at least .60—that is, the coefficient of reproducibility actually obtained is at least 60 percent larger than the minimum marginal reproducibility.

The example of a Guttman scale in Table 5-4 performs well on two out of three of these criteria. The item coefficients of reproducibility range from .958 to 1.000 and thus exceed the recommended minimum of .85. The scale coefficient of reproducibility is .981, considerably higher than the recommended .90. The coefficient of scalability, however, is only .475, suggesting that chance factors account for much of the ordering of the items.

3. A series of guidelines concerns items and item characteristics. Usually, a Guttman scale consists of at least five items, although many prefer the scale to be based on at least ten items. This guideline ensures that the proportion of responses that fit a perfect pattern by chance alone is small. For example, we noted with a three-item measure that four of the eight possible patterns are consistent. Thus, in this case, one would expect that at least half of the respondents would fit a perfect pattern by chance alone. With a ten-item scale, on the other hand, only 11 of 1,024 possible patterns are consistent. Thus, only about 1 percent of the number of respondents would fit a perfect pattern by chance factors alone.

Most researchers also exclude items on which more than 80 percent of the respondents either agree or disagree. Because, as we indicated earlier, the primary purpose of measurement is to differentiate among respondents, items with a very high proportion either agreeing or disagreeing are of little utility. If, for example, 95 percent of the respondents agreed with an item, the item could differentiate only between the 5 percent fringe and the 95 percent majority. Such an item would serve only to increase the value of the minimum marginal reproducibility and to decrease the coefficient of scalability.

4. Some guidelines help the researcher assign scores to individuals who respond inconsistently. The first strategy is simply to count the number of "agrees" and give the individual a score based on this sum. Thus, for example, the individual with the response pattern DAD would receive a score of 1. This is the most common approach for assigning scores

to inconsistent individuals. The second strategy is to assign the inconsistent individual the score that he or she would receive when the researcher decides how to convert the pattern to a consistent one. For example, the individual with the response pattern DAD would receive a score of 0 if the pattern matched was DDD, but a score of 2 if the pattern matched was AAD. Neither of these strategies is very desirable, because the score assigned to an inconsistent individual will be misleading in either case. The third strategy—excluding all inconsistent individuals from further analysis—is usually considered to be even less attractive and is rarely used.

Other Measurement Techniques

The two most common types of measures in social research today are indexes and scales. There are, however, many other measurement models. Some of these are of particular utility for certain types of problems. This section will review briefly some of the other types of measures that are used in social research.

The Semantic Differential

Occasionally, the researcher is interested in attempting to measure the image of some attitude object. Osgood and his associates proposed a method for doing this called the *semantic differential*.[5] In this approach, respondents are given an attitude object and asked to rate it on a series of bipolar adjective pairs. (See Figure 5-2.) Osgood notes that the adjective pairs can often be grouped into three sets: those measuring evaluation (for example, good-bad, fair-unfair); those measuring potency (for example, healthy-unhealthy, weak-strong); and those measuring activity (for example, decisive-indecisive, productive-unproductive). The researcher, after determining the dimensions on which to assess the object, uses the additive model to create composite measures.

Ranking Techniques

Often the researcher would like the respondent to rank a set of objects in order of preference. In addition to the direct approach of simply asking the respondent to rank in order of preference, researchers can use any of three other strategies. These are (1) the method of constant sum, (2) the method of alternating extremes, and (3) the method of ipsatizing responses.

Constant sum. In this method, the researcher asks the respondent to allocate a fixed number of points, usually 100, among different categories. The more points the respondent assigns to a category, the more supportive

Figure 5-2   A semantic differential for the object "nursing home"

Below are twenty-nine pairs of words that can be used to describe nursing homes in general. For each pair of words, we would like you to circle the number that comes closest to *your feelings* about nursing homes. For example, if you feel that nursing homes are more good than bad, circle a number closer to good. The *closer the number you circle is to good, the more good and less bad you feel nursing homes in general to be.* Continue with each pair.

GOOD	1	2	3	4	5	6	7	BAD
BEAUTIFUL	1	2	3	4	5	6	7	UGLY
RIGID	1	2	3	4	5	6	7	FLEXIBLE
DECISIVE	1	2	3	4	5	6	7	INDECISIVE
FAIR	1	2	3	4	5	6	7	UNFAIR
DIRTY	1	2	3	4	5	6	7	CLEAN
EXPENSIVE	1	2	3	4	5	6	7	INEXPENSIVE
HEALTHY	1	2	3	4	5	6	7	UNHEALTHY
HAPPY	1	2	3	4	5	6	7	SAD
PLEASANT	1	2	3	4	5	6	7	UNPLEASANT
UNPRODUCTIVE	1	2	3	4	5	6	7	PRODUCTIVE
WEAK	1	2	3	4	5	6	7	STRONG
ORGANIZED	1	2	3	4	5	6	7	DISORGANIZED
ACTIVE	1	2	3	4	5	6	7	PASSIVE
SELF-SEEKING	1	2	3	4	5	6	7	PUBLIC-MINDED
UNCERTAIN	1	2	3	4	5	6	7	CERTAIN

he or she is toward that category. Because the total number of points to be assigned is fixed, the more points the respondent assigns to one category or option, the fewer points he or she has available to assign to the other categories or options. (See the last column of Figure 5-3.) The obvious advantage of this approach is that the data obtained can be interpreted at the ratio level. Thus, rather than simply indicating that an option is rated first, the researcher can indicate how much more popular one category or option is than another (for example, twice as much support for category A as for category B). The limitations of this approach are that (1) the task is difficult for some respondents to complete, (2) the number of categories to be rated must be small (ten or fewer), and (3) the number of points to assign should be easily divisible by the number of categories.

Alternating extremes.   The researcher might consider this method when the number of objects to be ranked is large. In this approach, the researcher asks the respondent to select the most and least favored alternatives from the set to be ranked. After this is done, the researcher asks the respondent to select the most and least favored alternatives from those that remain. The process is repeated until all of the objects in the set have been ranked. This approach to ranking a set of alternatives is the least time-consuming and easiest for respondents to understand. If the number of alternatives to be ranked is extremely large, however, the task still can be quite time-consuming.

Ipsatizing data. In this third approach to ranking, the researcher, rather than the respondent, generates the ranks. Using this method, respondents are simply asked to rate a series of statements on a continuum, much as they do when a researcher constructs an index using the additive model. For example, in addition to giving a constant-sum response, subjects rate how good an idea they believe it is for government to provide energy assistance to the five different categories of individuals in Figure 5-3. To ipsatize the data, *the researcher obtains the arithmetic mean for the responses of the individual to the items in the set to be ranked and then divides the item scores by this mean.* The resulting score reflects the placement of each category relative to the mean and thus reflects a type of

---

Figure 5-3   An example of a constant-sum measure

Congress, in response to rising energy costs, passed legislation that provides money to certain groups of people to help them pay their energy bills. Below is a list of five groups of people that could be eligible for such assistance. I have two different questions to ask you about this list. First, I would like to know whether you think it is a good idea to use our tax money to help pay the energy costs for each of these groups. Second, I would like to know how much help you think each of these groups should get. *To answer the first question,* please put a check under the category that comes closest to what you think. *To answer the second question,* how much help you think each group should get, you are given 100 points. The more points you give to a group, the more money you think it should receive compared with the other four groups. If you feel all five groups should get the same amount of money, give each 20 points. If you feel one or more groups should get no money, give them 0 points. If you think one group should get all the money, give it all 100 points. Remember, there are no right or wrong answers. I am interested in your opinions only.

> VG: Very good idea to help this group with energy costs
> G: Good idea to help this group with energy costs
> U: Uncertain whether it is a good or a bad idea
> B: Bad idea to help this group with energy costs
> VB: Very bad idea to help this group with energy costs

	VG	G	U	B	VB	Points
1. People in poor health.	[ ]	[ ]	[ ]	[ ]	[ ]	_____
2. People who are disabled.	[ ]	[ ]	[ ]	[ ]	[ ]	_____
3. People with low incomes.	[ ]	[ ]	[ ]	[ ]	[ ]	_____
4. People who are elderly.	[ ]	[ ]	[ ]	[ ]	[ ]	_____
5. People who are unemployed.	[ ]	[ ]	[ ]	[ ]	[ ]	_____
					Total	100

ordering of categories for the respondent. The primary advantage to this method of ranking is that the task for the respondent is simple. It is probably the only viable approach to ranking if the number of statements to be ranked is large (over twenty). The major limitation of this approach is that the researcher does not seek any direct information from the respondent on how categories should be ordered.

Using Measures Developed by Others

As should be apparent, the development of a measure can be a time-consuming process. The researcher can invest substantial time and effort in designing a measure and gathering data only to discover that the measure is not internally consistent or has a low coefficient of reproducibility. An alternative strategy is to use measures that have been developed by others to the extent that this is possible. This approach has several advantages:

1. When a researcher uses measures developed by others, he or she can directly compare the results of the study to those of others. This builds continuity into the research enterprise and facilitates the codification of information.
2. This strategy substantially reduces the time required to develop a measure. The time thus saved can be allocated to other phases of the research process, thereby enhancing the overall quality of the project.
3. The researcher has a priori evidence concerning the internal consistency or scalability of the measure. Although the researcher will reverify these for his or her own project, it is comforting to know that others have found that the measures work.

The Survey Research Center of the Institute for Social Research has published compendiums of measures along with information on their validity and reliability. This set of works is an excellent place to begin a search for a measure of a concept.[6] Delbert Miller, in his *Handbook of Research Design and Social Measurement,* describes many measures.[7] Finally, when the researcher searches the literature to develop the statement of a problem, he or she occasionally discovers measures others have used that can be adapted to the project at hand.

Thurstone Scales

The focus of this chapter thus far has been on measurement strategies the researcher can use when the primary purpose of a research project is to test hypotheses. Thurstone scales represent a departure from this approach in that the researcher must gather substantial data simply to develop the scale. The first step in constructing a Thurstone scale is to have a number of judges (usually a minimum of ten) rate a large number of statements in terms of the degree to which each measures a particular concept. For example, a researcher who wants to construct a Thurstone scale of prejudice against individuals who receive Aid for Dependent Children payments would begin by developing a series of statements (usually at least fifty) about this category of individual. Judges would then be asked to rate how much prejudice is demonstrated by agreement with each statement, usually on a scale from 1 (agreeing with the statement means low prejudice) to 11 (agreeing with the statement means high prejudice). Note that the judges are not asked how much they personally agree with each statement, only how prejudiced someone who does agree with the statement is. Items on which there is substantial disagreement among judges are excluded as ambiguous. The remaining items (which, according to the judges' evaluations, are ordered in a fashion similar to that of a Guttman scale) are then given weights to reflect the degree to which agreement with each implies prejudice.

Once a Thurstone scale has been developed, the researcher presents respondents with the Thurstone items and asks them whether they agree or disagree with each. The researcher obtains a total score for each respondent by adding together the weights for each item with which the respondent agreed. For example, a respondent who agreed with the first and third items in the following Thurstone scale would receive a score of 8.6 (1.2 + 7.4 = 8.6).

1. AFDC recipients deserve a good life.   1.2
2. AFDC recipients shouldn't have to work.   1.9
3. AFDC recipients don't accept work when it is   7.4
   offered to them.
4. AFDC recipients don't deserve a penny of the   9.8
   taxpayers' money.

As should be apparent, the development of a Thurstone scale involves substantial effort on the part of the researcher. Furthermore, judges' evaluations of items tend to reflect their backgrounds and biases and thus are somewhat suspect. For these reasons, among others, the Thurstone scale is no longer widely used in research.

Key Terms

double-barreled question	coefficient of reproducibility
halo error	coefficient of scalability
additive model	minimum marginal reproducibility
Guttman model	coefficient alpha
index	item-to-total correlation
scale	semantic differential

ipsatizing data   constant-sum scale

Thurstone scale   method of alternating extremes

References

1. On occasion, respondents make distinctions among items that the
   researcher would not. In this case, the items should not be combined
   because the respondents use different dimensions in answering the
   questions. There are a variety of statistical tools available to test for
   this phenomenon. However, they are beyond the scope of this text.
2. The number of different correlation coefficients is given by $N \times
   (N - 1)/2$, in which N is the number of items in the index. The num-
   ber of different correlations for a five-item index is ten, whereas for a
   ten-item index it is forty-five.
3. R. Likert, "A Technique for the Measurement of Attitudes." *Archives
   of Psychology*, no. 140 (1932), pp. 44–53.
4. See also J. C. Nunnally, *Psychometric Theory* (New York: McGraw-
   Hill, 1967).
5. C. E. Osgood, G. J. Suci, and P. H. Tannenbaum, *The Measurement
   of Meaning* (Chicago: University of Illinois Press, 1957).
6. See, for example, J. P. Robinson and P. R. Shaver, *Measures of Social
   Psychological Attitudes* (Ann Arbor, Michigan: The Institute for
   Social Research, 1973).
7. D. C. Miller, *Handbook of Research Design and Social Measurements*
   (New York: David McKay Company, 1977).

Questions for Discussion

1. Some researchers argue that slang should never be used in questions.
   Why do you think they make this argument? What do you think about
   this issue?
2. How might a researcher establish that a measure is valid?
3. The additive model for constructing a composite measure is used more
   frequently than is the Guttman scale model. Why do you think this is
   the case?

Exercises

1. With the instructor's cooperation, divide the class into small working
   groups. Ask each group to generate some items that might be used to

measure the concept *hostility* (or some other complex characteristic). Share the items among the class members and ask that they be critiqued on the basis of clarity, relevance to the concept, exhaustiveness, and mutual exclusivity. Look out for double-barreled items, items that force a conclusion, and items that ask a question of fact when opinion is intended.

2. Using some of the items developed in Exercise 1, construct a simple Likert-type index of no more than ten items. Administer the index to a small group of people and then analyze the items following the procedure described in the chapter.

3. Devise a simple Guttman-type scale that measures empathy. Administer it to a number of subjects and assess the adequacy of the scale using one of the methods described in the chapter.

4. Devise a semantic differential for the object "AFDC Program" and administer it to a group of social work students and a group of students in some other field. Which group is the more positive toward the program?

For Further Reading

Warren S. Torgerson. *Theory and Methods of Scaling.* New York: John Wiley, 1958. Chapter 12 provides a thorough discussion of Guttman scaling and the Guttman scale model.

Claire Selltiz, Lawrence S. Wrightsman, and Stuart W. Cook. *Research Methods in Social Relations,* 3rd ed. New York: Holt, Rinehart and Winston, 1976. Chapter 12 and Appendix B, Part II, describe item construction and scaling.

6

Survey Research

The survey is the most common method of data collection in social research. In survey research, the researcher asks a selected set of individuals a specific set of questions. Intake interviews at a social service agency and classroom examinations are surveys. Intake interviews involve a survey of the problems and backgrounds of clients new to the agency, whereas an examination is a survey of the knowledge or skill level of the students in a class. The point is that the survey is a flexible method of gathering data that can be employed to obtain useful information in almost any situation.

This chapter is divided into three sections. The first section focuses on the principles involved in developing a survey-research instrument (either a questionnaire or an interview schedule). Topics included in this section range from the ordering of topics to the format for questions. The second section deals with methods of administering a survey instrument. These are divided into two general types: the self-administered instrument, which includes the mailed questionnaire, and the researcher-administered instrument, which includes the personal interview. We also consider variants of these two basic data-collection methods—for example, the hand-delivered questionnaire and the telephone interview. The final section of the chapter examines the factors to be considered when selecting a data-collection method. These include the complexity of the questions to be asked, the sensitivity of the materials, the resources available, and the response rates.

Survey-Research Instruments

Developing a good survey instrument is a long process that is as much an art as a skill. The researcher, in designing the instrument, must always bear in mind to whom and for what purpose the questions will be asked. In addition, the researcher must consider the order for general topics and for specific questions. Further, the wise researcher considers how the survey instrument relates to analysis, giving some attention to how the data will be coded and analyzed (see Chapter 10). It is not at all unusual for researchers to devote more time to the development of the survey instrument than they do to data collection and analysis combined.

In survey research, the objective is to gather data from a set of individuals in a systematic fashion. The tool that is used is called the *survey instrument*. It may be either a *questionnaire* (intended to be self-administered) or an *interview schedule* (intended to be administered to respondents by someone else). In either case, the survey instrument is a mechanism for systematizing data collection. As such, the instrument serves to structure the conversation between the researcher (who desires information) and the respondent (who has agreed to give information). In fact, if the researcher is not able to view gathering the desired information from the perspective of a structured conversation, he or she is usually well advised to select some other method for data collection.

The researcher must always remember that an *individual is never under any obligation to participate* in a research project. In fact, the researcher's first obligation is to make clear to the potential respondent that participation in the research project is strictly voluntary. This is particularly critical with research conducted using clients or potential clients of a social service agency. They must be told explicitly that participation or nonparticipation will in no way alter their eligibility for services and will not affect the manner in which services are delivered. (See Appendix A, Protection of the Rights of Human Subjects in Research, for further information on these points.) Further, so that potential respondents can make an informed decision about whether they wish to participate, the researcher has an ethical and a legal responsibility to explain the project prior to gathering any information. Normally, he or she will present such information in a cover letter accompanying a questionnaire or in introductory comments prior to beginning an interview.

Although the consent process may be implicit in many cases, only those who actually agree to participate in the study should receive the instrument. In the case of a questionnaire, those who agree to participate reflect this agreement by completing the questionnaire and returning it to the researcher. In the case of an interview, the potential respondent must indicate some willingness to answer questions prior to their being asked. In either case, respondents retain the right to change their minds and decide they no longer wish to participate in the study. Thus, it is important that the survey instrument be carefully structured so as not to offend the sensibilities of respondents. Often, this means that the researcher will make an effort to include interesting, easy-to-answer questions at the beginning of the instrument. Questions that are difficult to answer or that focus on sensitive issues usually occur later, after the respondent has developed some investment in the project.

The conclusion of the gathering of data from a respondent is as important as the beginning. Because the respondent has done the researcher a favor, acknowledgment of this is always suitable. With questionnaires, it is also important to include clear instructions about how the respondent should return the instrument to the researcher. With interviews, a more extensive acknowledgment of appreciation than a simple "thank you" is often appropriate. Frequently, the researcher can prepare the respondent for the conclusion of the instrument. This gives the respondent a sense of accomplishment and helps to avoid any surprise when there are no more questions to be asked. The objective is to leave respondents feeling satisfied about their participation in the research project.

Cover Letters and Introductions

Although the cover letter or introduction is the first exposure that a potential respondent has to a research project, it is usually the last part of the research instrument to be completed. Because the cover letter or introduction is the means by which the researcher obtains the respondent's informed consent to participate in the study, he or she must exercise great care in its development. This statement must include, as a minimum, the following types of information:

1. Who is doing the study.
2. Why the study is being done.
3. A brief description of the study.
4. How long it will take to complete the instrument.
5. What subjects the study is concerned with.

Further, the researcher has an obligation to communicate the voluntary nature of participation in the project. Of course, the researcher, in writing the cover letters, is attempting to convince respondents of the value of their participation in the research project. A poorly designed cover letter or introduction serves only to alienate potential respondents and to reduce the chances that they will agree to participate in the study.

Figure 6-1 reproduces a cover letter used with a mailed questionnaire in a study conducted by the junior author of this text and others in Alabama. The letter illustrates one approach to meeting the requirements set forth in the preceding paragraph. The first paragraph of the letter briefly describes the general purpose of the study (to determine citizens' preferences concerning the priorities for government expenditures) and one of

Figure 6-1 A sample cover letter for a mailed questionnaire

THE UNIVERSITY OF ALABAMA

Office for Research and Public Service   July 25, 1979

Dear Alabamian:

Today, with inflation as high as it is and with government trying to balance its budget, the question of how much emphasis should be given to different government sponsored programs is increasingly important. Your assistance in completing this questionnaire will go a long way toward helping us to provide decision makers with insights into what Alabama citizens would like government to do.

To make the questionnaire easier to answer, we have divided it into four parts. Part A deals with how you feel about life in general and about the government in particular. Part B concerns how government should allocate your tax money. Part C focuses on how you feel about older people and what you think about growing older. The final section seeks descriptive information about you and your family.

The questionnaire can be completed in about 35 minutes, but most people take somewhat longer to do so. Although we cannot afford to pay you for your time, we have included a quarter as a token of our appreciation for your cooperation. Even though you may not wish to return the questionnaire, you need not return the quarter to us. This is simply our way of thanking you in advance for your time.

You need not complete the questionnaire yourself. We are only asking that you or one of the other adults in your home (18 or older) do so. Naturally, these answers will be confidential; and the results will be reported in such a way that no one will be able to associate your name with the answers given. Also, at the end of the questionnaire, there are instructions on how you can return the completed questionnaire to us without any cost to you.

We would very much appreciate your help. If you have any questions, please do not hesitate to contact us.

Sincerely yours,

David L. Klemmack

Lucinda Lee Roff

the uses of the data to be collected (to inform decision-makers about these preferences). Because the questionnaire was relatively long (fourteen pages), the second paragraph expands on the initial description of the study.

The third paragraph describes how long it will take to complete the questionnaire and emphasizes the voluntary nature of participation in the study. Although the pretest results indicated that the median time required to complete the questionnaire was thirty-five minutes, the testing conditions were optimum (no telephone calls or children needing attention), and the respondents were well motivated. This suggested that, although the instrument could be completed in thirty-five minutes, it would probably take most respondents somewhat longer. Presenting respondents with the average rather than the minimum time to complete a task substantially reduces the possibility of respondent hostility. Thus, the letter indicated that it would probably take respondents more than thirty-five minutes to complete the instrument.

The researchers included a quarter with each questionnaire in an effort to increase the response rate. (See the section of this chapter devoted to mailed questionnaires for further information on this technique.) Because the quarter was a gift from the researchers to the potential respondents, it was necessary to indicate that accepting the quarter in no way obligated the individual to respond to the questionnaire. The third paragraph included a statement to this effect, to guarantee that all potential respondents recognized that participation in the research project was strictly voluntary.

The final paragraphs explained who was to complete the questionnaire and how the completed questionnaire could be returned. The letter informed respondents that the questionnaires would be treated as confidential communications to the research team. The issue of who was conducting the study was solved by using letterhead paper with the signatures of the investigators at the bottom.

The cover letter presented in Figure 6-1 is not intended to demonstrate the ideal letter. Rather, it is an example of the type of letter that is frequently used with questionnaires. At the same time, the researchers invested considerable thought and time into the construction of this letter. Nevertheless, it is probably too complicated, and it is certainly too long, to be considered ideal.

Creating a Survey-Research Instrument

There is no one "right way" to develop a survey-research instrument. The outline presented in Figure 6-2 is only one approach to this task. It does, however, represent an approach that we have found useful in our own research efforts. As you gain experience in research, it is entirely likely that you will develop alternative strategies for constructing survey-research instruments.

The Limits of the Instrument

There are several factors that affect the design and content of a survey-research instrument:

1. *The general parameters of the instrument to be developed.* The most important parameter for a questionnaire or interview schedule is the list of topics to be covered. Obviously, this list is related to the research problem and includes all of the concepts to be measured. Such a list is an essential tool for reviewing the instrument upon its completion and helps

---

Figure 6-2   Steps in creating a survey-research instrument

I. Limits of the instrument
   A. Topics to be covered
   B. Potential respondents
   C. Method of administration
   D. Length limitations
II. Content of the instrument
   A. Measures to be included
   B. Decision on using existing measure or creating new instrument
   C. Item format
III. Draft of the instrument
   A. Outline of instrument
      1. Similarity of content grouping
      2. Similarity of format grouping
   B. Draft
      1. Instructions
      2. Transitions
      3. Items
IV. Review Draft
   A. Completeness
   B. Clarity
   C. Difficulty
   D. Length
   E. Appearance
   F. Flow
V. Pretest Draft
   A. Time to complete
   B. Ambiguity
   C. Affect

---

the researcher avoid the embarrassment of having a research instrument that fails to include one of the central variables of the proposed study.

2. *The nature of the subject.* An interview schedule designed to be used with eight-year-old children is usually quite different from one designed to be used with college seniors. Although it is good practice never to use a vocabulary more complicated than is necessary, the range of acceptable words varies as a function of the experience and education of the potential respondents. Concepts such as "process recording," "psycho-social functioning," and "instrumental leader" have special meanings for social workers but no meaning at all for those who do not have a background in social work. The point is that survey-research instruments are designed to facilitate communication with particular audiences. If the researcher does not know who the intended audience is, it is almost impossible for him or her to design an appropriate questionnaire or interview schedule.

Although the same instrument often can be used as both a questionnaire and an interview schedule, occasionally there will be differences between the two. The need to repeat instructions, for example, is more characteristic of an interview schedule than of a questionnaire. In a questionnaire, the instructions on how to respond are always available to the respondent; this might not be the case in an interview. Interview schedules often include instructions for the interviewer, such as "Now ask . . . ," which must be separated from the questions that are read to the respondent. Such distinctions are not made in questionnaires. Although many of the differences are relatively minor, the draft of a questionnaire can look quite different from the draft of an interview schedule on the same topic.

3. *Length.* The length of a survey research instrument is a function of the range and depth of topics to be covered, the resources available to the study, and the tolerance level of the potential respondents. If the researcher wishes to include measures of 200 different concepts, it is foolish to consider making the instrument only four pages long. Similarly, if the researcher believes that potential respondents would be willing to devote only thirty minutes to a particular project, it makes little sense to construct an instrument that would take ninety minutes to complete. Finally, if the resources available to the project only allow for the reproduction and mailing of a six-page questionnaire, it is a waste of time to develop a twenty-four-page one. Generally, if the instrument the researcher wants to develop is much longer than what is economically feasible, it is wiser to reconceptualize the research problem and reduce its scope than to waste time developing the instrument.

The Content of the Instrument

Once the researcher has established general limits of the instrument, he or she faces the question of what specific measures to use. The execution of the project in a meaningful way requires that each of the important concepts be measured in some manner. The researcher may elect to develop his or her own measures of the relevant concepts using the procedures outlined in the previous chapter. As an alternative, the researcher may elect to use measures of the relevant concepts that others have developed. Of course, the most prevalent pattern is to use a combination of these two approaches. Some measures are developed based on the specifics of the research situation, whereas others are taken intact (or with some modification) from other studies.

One part of measuring each concept is deciding whether the questions will be open- or closed-ended. *Open-ended items* are questions that allow respondents to create their own answers. For example, a researcher who is interested in determining which special categories of individuals (if any) people think should receive government-funded services and benefits might ask, "What types of people, if any, do you think should be eligible for government help?" This question might, if warranted by the situation, be followed by probes such as, "What about people who can't help themselves?" Open-ended questions usually produce more complete answers in an interview than in a questionnaire situation. This is largely because the interviewer is in a position to stimulate a comprehensive answer. Although there are exceptions, open-ended questions are not typically used in questionnaires. Their use is largely limited to situations in which the researcher is uncertain about what people think about an issue. Because of the variety of answers, there is also a problem in tabulating answers.

Closed-ended items are questions for which the respondent selects the "best" answer from a set of choices provided by the researcher. One approach to determining which special categories of individuals (if any) people think should receive government-funded services and benefits using closed-ended questions is illustrated in Figure 6-3. Closed-ended questions can be used in either the interview or the questionnaire situation. The main limitation to this approach to questioning, however, is that the researcher receives an answer only to the specific question asked; there is no mechanism for explaining or expanding on the answer. If, for example, people were willing to use tax money to provide benefits to older people only if the older people also had low incomes, this would not be detected by the close-ended question approach in the illustration, because this category was not included. On the other hand, closed-ended questions are usually easier for respondents to answer and much easier for the researcher to code. The researcher must carefully consider the strengths and weaknesses

---

Figure 6-3   Sample of the closed-ended question approach

Federal, state, and local governments often use tax dollars to provide low-cost or free services and benefits to special groups of individuals. We have listed ten of these groups who can legally receive tax-supported services and benefits today. We would like to know whether you think it is a good use of our tax dollars to provide low-cost or free services and benefits to people *simply* because they are a member of one of these groups. To answer this question, simply check the category that is closest to what you think.

VG: Very good idea to use tax money this way
G: Good idea to use tax money this way
U: Uncertain whether it is a good or a bad idea
B: Bad idea to use tax money this way
VB: Very bad idea to use tax money this way

	VG	G	U	B	VB
1. Sixty or older	[ ]	[ ]	[ ]	[ ]	[ ]
2. Veteran	[ ]	[ ]	[ ]	[ ]	[ ]
3. Blind	[ ]	[ ]	[ ]	[ ]	[ ]
4. Poor health	[ ]	[ ]	[ ]	[ ]	[ ]
5. Physical disability	[ ]	[ ]	[ ]	[ ]	[ ]
6. Low income	[ ]	[ ]	[ ]	[ ]	[ ]
7. Unemployed	[ ]	[ ]	[ ]	[ ]	[ ]
8. Children and students under seventeen	[ ]	[ ]	[ ]	[ ]	[ ]
9. Victim of a natural disaster	[ ]	[ ]	[ ]	[ ]	[ ]
10. Member of a minority group	[ ]	[ ]	[ ]	[ ]	[ ]

---

of each approach to questioning in light of the objectives of the research project prior to selecting which method to use.

The Draft of the Instrument

The third step in creating a survey-research instrument is writing the initial draft of the instrument. This usually occurs in two stages:

1. *The development of an outline of the instrument.* This is similar to an outline for a paper or a speech. The researcher should give particular attention to the ordering of the topics, because the topics covered initially define the context within which all other topics will be considered. Often, researchers use a strategy of beginning with general topics (for example, What do you believe the role of government should be in providing assistance to disadvantaged persons?) and ending with specific topics

(for example, Do you believe that government should provide the frail elderly with help in paying their energy bills?)

Two other common organizing principles are *similarity of content* and *similarity of format*. Questions focusing on similar content typically appear in the same section of the instrument, as do questions that have a similar format. This reduces the need for repeating instructions each time the question format changes and makes it easier for the respondent to complete the instrument.

One additional organizing principle deserves some comment. Although the researcher would like each respondent to complete the instrument in its entirety, respondents often do not do so, particularly if the instrument is long. Because, in most studies, some variables are more important than others, the researcher usually tries to place the measures of the most important variables near the beginning of the instrument. This practice has the effect of maximizing the number of usable responses that the researcher obtains in any study.

2. *The actual writing of a draft of the instrument.* Because it is almost impossible to assess the adequacy of a schedule unless it is complete in every detail, researchers should make every effort to write each draft of the instrument as if it were the final draft. This means that every draft should be complete and should include:

1. any instructions to the respondent that are a part of the instrument;
2. any transition statements that facilitate respondents' adjustment to new tasks that are part of the instrument;
3. the specific questions in the order that they will appear in the instrument, including the response categories as they will appear if the questions are closed-ended; and
4. if the instrument is to be precoded, the coding information that will appear. (See Chapter 10.)

The more complete a draft of an instrument is, the easier it is to judge how adequate the instrument is for its intended task.

Five pages of an instrument used to assess public support for governments providing benefits for older persons and correlates thereof are reproduced in Figure 6-4 to illustrate the elements of instrument construction. In examining this instrument, note the following:

1. The use of section headings to orient the respondent to the general content of the section (for example, Part A, Feelings About Life).
2. Instructions to respondents concerning how they are to respond to each question, including the meaning of each response.
3. Placement of the response categories on the right-hand side of the page

whenever feasible. (This format makes it easier for the respondents to answer the questions.)

4. The use of brackets to denote different response categories. This format is generally superior to using numbers or symbols to denote different response categories, because it leads respondents to check one and *only* one category for each question. The format used in Figure 6-4 is generally superior to other formats, such as (using question 11 as an example):

11. What happens to me is my own doing.   1   2   3   4   5

or:

11. What happens to me is my own doing.   SA   A   U   D   SD

or:

11. What happens to me is my own doing.   —   —   —   —   —

5. The mixing of items from different but related measures in a single section. For example, items 1–12 of Figure 6-4, Part A, include measures of intolerance of ambiguity (items 5 and 9), authoritarianism (items 2, 7, and 12), fatalism (items 1, 3, 6, and 10), and personal control (items 4, 8, and 11). This coupled with wording some questions negatively and others positively, tends to reduce response bias.

The Review Draft

The fourth step in constructing an instrument of observation is to examine it according to the following six criteria:

1. *Completeness.* The primary purpose of this review is to ensure that all of the variables to be included in the study are measured in the instrument. If measures that have been developed by others are included in the instrument, it is also wise to make sure that all of the items in the measure are included in the instrument. In particular, this can be a problem if the items are interspersed with other, similar items, as is the case in Figure 6-4, Part A.

2. *Clarity.* The researcher, at this point, examines the instructions and questions in an effort to be certain they are unambiguous. A review of each question to determine if it is double-barreled or ambiguous is helpful. Examining the questions in terms of whether they are actually measuring what they are intended to measure can be helpful. Clear, concise instructions make it easier for respondents to understand what is expected of them, and such instructions result in higher response rates than do ambiguous instructions.

Figure 6-4   Illustration of a questionnaire

PART A.   FEELINGS ABOUT LIFE

This first section consists of a series of statements about life in general and about government. Please indicate the degree to which you agree or disagree with each of these statements by checking the category which comes closest to your opinion. Remember, there are no right or wrong answers; we are interested only in your opinions.

SA: Strongly agree with statement
A: Agree with statement
U: Uncertain whether agree or disagree with statement
D: Disagree with statement
SD: Strongly disagree with statement

		SA	A	U	D	SD
1.	How many friends you have depends on how nice a person you are.	[ ]	[ ]	[ ]	[ ]	[ ]
2.	What young people need most of all is strict discipline by their parents.	[ ]	[ ]	[ ]	[ ]	[ ]
3.	Without the right breaks one cannot be an effective leader.	[ ]	[ ]	[ ]	[ ]	[ ]
4.	I have often found that what is going to happen will happen.	[ ]	[ ]	[ ]	[ ]	[ ]
5.	There are only two kinds of persons in the world: the weak and the strong.	[ ]	[ ]	[ ]	[ ]	[ ]
6.	Knowing the right people is important in deciding whether a person will get ahead.	[ ]	[ ]	[ ]	[ ]	[ ]
7.	A few strong leaders could make this country better than all the laws and talk.	[ ]	[ ]	[ ]	[ ]	[ ]
8.	Many times I feel that I have little influence over things that happen to me.	[ ]	[ ]	[ ]	[ ]	[ ]
9.	You can classify almost all people as crooked or honest.	[ ]	[ ]	[ ]	[ ]	[ ]
10.	Who gets to be boss depends on who has the skill and ability; luck has little or nothing to do with it.	[ ]	[ ]	[ ]	[ ]	[ ]
11.	What happens to me is my own doing.	[ ]	[ ]	[ ]	[ ]	[ ]
12.	Most people who don't get ahead just don't have enough will power.	[ ]	[ ]	[ ]	[ ]	[ ]

Source: The extracts from a questionnaire on pp. 98–102 are reprinted by courtesy of the Center for the Study of Aging, University of Alabama.

Figure 6-4 *(cont.)*

PART C.   KNOWLEDGE AND FEELINGS ABOUT OLDER PEOPLE

In this section, we are interested in finding out what you know about older
people in general, how you feel about older people, and what you think about
growing older. In the following questions, please check <u>true</u> if you think
the statement is generally true and <u>false</u> if you think the statement is
generally false.

		TRUE	FALSE
1.	The majority of old people (past age 65) are senile (i.e., defective memory, disoriented, or severely disturbed).	[ ]	[ ]
2.	All five senses tend to decline in old age.	[ ]	[ ]
3.	Most old people have no interest in, or capacity for, sexual relations.	[ ]	[ ]
4.	Lung capacity tends to decline in old age.	[ ]	[ ]
5.	The majority of old people feel miserable most of the time.	[ ]	[ ]
6.	Physical strength tends to decline in old age.	[ ]	[ ]
7.	At least one-tenth of the aged are living in long-stay institutions (i.e., nursing homes, mental hospitals, homes for the aged, etc.).	[ ]	[ ]
8.	Aged drivers have fewer accidents per person than drivers under age 65.	[ ]	[ ]
9.	Most older workers cannot work as effectively as younger workers.	[ ]	[ ]
10.	About 80% of the aged are healthy enough to carry out their normal activities.	[ ]	[ ]
11.	Most old people are set in their ways and unable to change.	[ ]	[ ]
12.	Old people usually take longer to learn something new.	[ ]	[ ]
13.	It is almost impossible for most old people to learn something new.	[ ]	[ ]
14.	The reaction time of most old people tends to be slower than the reaction time of younger persons.	[ ]	[ ]
15.	In general, most old people are pretty much alike.	[ ]	[ ]
16.	The majority of old people are seldom bored.	[ ]	[ ]
17.	The majority of old people are socially isolated and lonely.	[ ]	[ ]
18.	Older workers have fewer accidents than younger workers.	[ ]	[ ]

Source: Items 1–25 are from Erdman Palmore, "Facts on Aging—A Short Quiz." Reprinted
by permission of *The Gerontologist*, Vol. 17, pp. 315–320 (1977).

Figure 6-4 *(cont.)*

19. Over 15% of the U.S. population are now age 65 or over.   [ ]   [ ]

20. Most medical practitioners tend to give low priority to the   [ ]   [ ]
    aged.

21. The majority of older people have incomes below the poverty   [ ]   [ ]
    level (as defined by the Federal Government).

22. The majority of old people are working or would like to have   [ ]   [ ]
    some kind of work to do (including housework and volunteer
    work).

23. Older people tend to become more religious with age.   [ ]   [ ]

24. The majority of old people are seldom irritated or angry.   [ ]   [ ]

25. The health and socioeconomic status of older people (compared   [ ]   [ ]
    to younger people) in the year 2000 will probably be about the
    same as now.

Below are 15 pairs of words that can be used to describe older people in general.
For each pair of words, we would like you to circle the number which comes
closest to your feelings about older people. For example, if you feel that
older people are more busy than idle, circle a number closer to busy. The
closer the number you circle is to busy, the more busy and less idle you feel
older people in general to be. Continue with each of the pairs.

IDLE	1	2	3	4	5	6	7	BUSY
STRONG	1	2	3	4	5	6	7	WEAK
PASSIVE	1	2	3	4	5	6	7	ACTIVE
HEALTHY	1	2	3	4	5	6	7	UNHEALTHY
UNPRODUCTIVE	1	2	3	4	5	6	7	PRODUCTIVE
RICH	1	2	3	4	5	6	7	POOR
DISSATISFIED	1	2	3	4	5	6	7	SATISFIED
ORGANIZED	1	2	3	4	5	6	7	DISORGANIZED
UNCERTAIN	1	2	3	4	5	6	7	CERTAIN
DECISIVE	1	2	3	4	5	6	7	INDECISIVE
SELFISH	1	2	3	4	5	6	7	GENEROUS
HANDSOME	1	2	3	4	5	6	7	UGLY
RIGID	1	2	3	4	5	6	7	FLEXIBLE
HAPPY	1	2	3	4	5	6	7	SAD
UNPLEASANT	1	2	3	4	5	6	7	PLEASANT

Source: The fifteen pairs of words above are from H. A. Rosencranz and T. E. McNevin,
"A Factor Analysis of Attitudes Toward the Aged." Reprinted by permission of *The
Gerontologist*, Vol. 9, p. 58 (February, 1969).

Figure 6-4 *(cont.)*

Below is a list of six different ways that people make their wishes known to governments. Please indicate how regularly you think you engage in each of these activities. Just check the category which comes closest to your opinion.

	REG: regularly	SEL: seldom
	FAI: fairly often	NEV: never

	REG	FAI	SEL	NEV
1. Participate in a political party between elections as well as at election time.	[ ]	[ ]	[ ]	[ ]
2. Send messages of support to political leaders when they are doing well.	[ ]	[ ]	[ ]	[ ]
3. Take an active part in political campaigns.	[ ]	[ ]	[ ]	[ ]
4. Engage in political discussions.	[ ]	[ ]	[ ]	[ ]
5. Inform others in my community about politics.	[ ]	[ ]	[ ]	[ ]
6. Send protest messages to political leaders when they are doing badly.	[ ]	[ ]	[ ]	[ ]

****

The final set of questions in this section concerns how you feel about growing older, how government can best help older people, and about planning for the future. Please indicate the degree to which you agree with each of these statements by marking the category which comes closest to what you think. Remember, there are no right or wrong answers. We are only interested in your opinion.

	SA: Strongly agree	SD: Strongly disagree
	A: Agree	D: Disagree
	U: Uncertain	

	SA	A	U	D	SD
1. I worry that I will be poor when I am old.	[ ]	[ ]	[ ]	[ ]	[ ]
2. Government should help older people by making sure they have enough income to live comfortably.	[ ]	[ ]	[ ]	[ ]	[ ]
3. People should be able to save for retirement themselves instead of contributing to Social Security.	[ ]	[ ]	[ ]	[ ]	[ ]
4. Family and friends should provide financial support for older people when they are no longer working.	[ ]	[ ]	[ ]	[ ]	[ ]
5. I feel that people will ignore me when I am old.	[ ]	[ ]	[ ]	[ ]	[ ]
6. Government should help older people by paying the bills for necessities like food and medical care.	[ ]	[ ]	[ ]	!]	l]
7. I believe the Social Security system will be bankrupt before I die.	[ ]	[ ]	[ ]	[ ]	[ ]

Figure 6-4 *(cont.)*

PART D.   ABOUT YOU AND YOUR FAMILY

In the final section of the questionnaire, we are interested in finding out a little about you and your family.

1. How old were you on your last birthday?   _____YEARS

2. How long have you lived in Alabama?   _____YEARS

3. How many years of school have you completed?   _____YEARS

4. What is your sex?   [ ] Male   [ ]Female

5. What is your race?   [ ] White   [ ]Black   [ ] Other

6. What is your current marital status?

    [ ] Single, never married   [ ] Divorced   [ ] Married

    [ ] Widowed   [ ] Separated   [ ] Remarried

7. Are your parents living? [ ] YES, BOTH   [ ] ONLY ONE   [ ] NEITHER

8. Please check the category below that best describes your total family income (before taxes) last year.

    [ ]$ 0 - 4,999   [ ]$15,000 - 19,999   [ ] $30,000 - 34,999

    [ ]$ 5,000 - 9,999   [ ]$20,000 - 24,999   [ ] $35,000 or more

    [ ]$10,000 - 14,999   [ ]$25,000 - 29,999

9. How adequate do you feel that your family income is in terms of meeting your family's needs?

    [ ] Very adequate   [ ] Barely adequate   [ ] Generally inadequate

    [ ] Generally adequate   [ ] Barely inadequate   [ ] Very inadequate

10. Which of the following best describes your primary activity?

    [ ] Working - blue collar occupation   [ ] Homemaker   [ ] Retired

    [ ] Working - white collar occupation   [ ] Student

11. Do you have any children?   [ ] YES   [ ] NO

    11a. If YES, how many children do you have?   _____CHILDREN

12. How many people (including yourself) live in your home?   _____PEOPLE

13. Do you own or rent your home?   [ ] OWN   [ ] RENT

3. *Difficulty level.* The researcher should review the questionnaire in terms of the abilities of the population to be studied. Some of the factors to be considered in this phase of the review are the degree to which potential respondents are familiar with the vocabulary used, the degree of experience they may have with the different question formats employed, and the nature of the responses that are expected. It is possible to use an instrument with a higher level of difficulty with test-wise professionals than with the general population. Professionals would be expected to have larger working vocabularies, to be familiar with a wider range of question formats, and to be capable of more complicated responses than those in the general population.

4. *Length.* Although increasing the length of an instrument tends to reduce response rates, crowding pages to reduce the number of pages in the instrument can have a more devastating effect on the response rate. It is usually better practice to increase the length of the instrument to provide the respondents with ample room to answer questions than it is to crowd pages with questions. Because length does affect response rates, the researcher should ordinarily emphasize conciseness and clarity in an effort to keep the instrument short. However, respondents can often answer a well-designed, six-page instrument more quickly and with less frustration than a poorly designed two-page one.

5. *Appearance.* Professional printing of the instrument is best. Doing so not only improves the quality of the appearance but also communicates a sense of professionalism to both respondents and interviewers. This should result in both higher response rates and higher-quality, more carefully considered responses. In the case of mailed questionnaires, it can reduce costs by reducing the postage costs and eliminating the need for envelopes.

6. *"Flow."* The intent of this final review is to obtain an overall impression of the instrument similar to that which a respondent might have. At this point, the researcher is interested in determining whether the ordering of questions and topics is natural or forced and whether the overall tone of the instrument is positive or negative. For example, although questions with a similar format are usually grouped together, this can result in a long section that may be boring to the respondent. The researcher, in reviewing the instrument, may discover this and divide the section into two parts separated by questions with a different format.

Pretesting the Draft

The final step in constructing the instrument is to pretest the draft with individuals who are similar to those in the population to be studied. For example, the target population for the instrument excerpted in Figure 6-4 was adult residents of Alabama. In the pretest of the instrument, the author sought input from individuals who differed in age, sex, ethnicity, marital status, income, educational attainment, and length of residence in the state. The objective, at this point, was to administer the instrument to as diverse a group of people as the target population of the instrument when the study was actually conducted. The intent of this step was to determine what difficulties, if any, the respondents might have with the instrument.

Some of the questions that the researcher would like a pretest of the instrument to answer are:

1. Do respondents interpret the questions in the way that the researcher intended?
2. How do people feel about completing the instrument?
3. What problems do people have in completing the instrument?
4. Are the instructions easily understood?
5. How long does it take to complete the instrument?

Usually, it is helpful to have a debriefing session with those who complete the instrument during the pretest stage. In addition to obtaining information on the mechanics of the instrument (for example, "Page 4 is confusing; it took me forty-five minutes to finish it."), the researcher should obtain as much information as possible on how the respondents interpreted the questions and what problems they had in determining what the questions meant. If respondents in the pretest have difficulty with some parts of the instrument, it is almost certain that respondents in the full study will also have difficulty with the same parts. Pretesting gives the researcher the opportunity to identify potential problems and rectify them prior to conducting the actual study.

Pretesting also enables the researcher to test coding and scoring procedures (Chapter 10) with actual data. In this phase of the pretest, the researcher treats the data-collection instrument just as if it were part of the study to be conducted. Items are scored, indexes are computed, and the data are analyzed just as they are to be scored, computed, and analyzed when the study is conducted. This process, in conjunction with pretest respondent comments, often reveals unanticipated problems, such as ambiguity in items.

As should be apparent by this point, the construction of a survey-research instrument is a long process filled with difficulties. For example, the instrument illustrated in Figure 6-4 required over two hundred hours and fourteen different revisions to complete. Even though this much time and effort was invested, the page focusing on demographic characteristics (Part D) is not well designed; the response categories for items vary in location, and the page itself looks cluttered and confusing. Although the time required to develop an instrument can be expected to grow shorter as a function of experience, a well-designed survey-research instrument usually reflects a major effort.

Data-Collection Methods

Once the researcher has developed and pretested the research instrument and has decided on a sampling frame (see Chapter 9 for a discussion of this phase of the research process), he or she is prepared to consider the task of actually gathering data. Even if the researcher identifies the "ideal" sampling frame for the study and develops the "perfect" data-collection instrument, the results of the study can be invalidated by poor data-collection procedures. Obviously, if data are gathered from a nonrepresentative segment of the intended population, the validity of the results of the study will be questionable. Similarly, if the respondents believe that giving truthful answers to the questions in the data-collection instrument will cause them harm, the study results will be suspect.

Although many other factors are involved, preparation is the key to gathering survey data successfully. In general, the more time and effort the researcher devotes to preparing for collecting data, the more likely it is that the data-collection process will yield valid, useful data.

Organizing a Survey

Prior to any attempts at gathering data, the researcher must establish clear, precise procedures to be followed during the data-collection phase of the project and communicate these to all who may be assisting in the collection of data. Some of the issues that should be addressed by the statement of operating procedures are:

1. From whom specifically will data be collected?
2. What procedures will be used to identify potential respondents?
3. How will these individuals be contacted?
4. How many attempts will be made to contact an individual?
5. How will an "attempt to contact" be defined?
6. How will it be validated that a contact was made?
7. What will constitute a completed instrument?

The end products of the preparation phase should be (1) a statement of what specific activities should occur during each step of the data-collection process and (2) a system for monitoring whether these activities are being carried out as specified.

Collecting data can be, as should be evident, a complicated process. It is extremely difficult to remember the myriad details that are involved in all but the simplest of data-collection procedures. In a large project, it is helpful to develop a manual of procedures describing each stage of the data-collection process in detail. Not only is such a manual useful in reminding the researcher of what has to be done, but it is also invaluable when the researcher writes the "research procedures" section of the study report. In addition to detailed descriptions of the procedures to be used in the study, the manual should include copies of all forms that are to be used.

One tool that is helpful in monitoring the progress of data collection is a data-collection summary form. This form simply summarizes all of the relevant data-collection information for a potential respondent. (See Figure 6-5 for an illustration of such a form for a mailed questionnaire survey.) Because forms of this type fit into a notebook easily, the researcher can maintain separate notebooks for each of the major phases of the data-collection process. By transferring forms from one notebook to another, the researcher can determine quickly the status of the data-collection process. Such a system also serves to help identify where problems are occurring, because the number of pages in that notebook becomes very large. Naturally, this system is of little utility unless the forms are kept up to date on a regular (preferably daily) basis.

The collection of data involves making decisions continuously. One of the major reasons for advanced planning is to make sure that the decision-making process is uniform. The researcher attempts to anticipate every contingency prior to initiating the data-collection process. Nevertheless, data are rarely collected without some unanticipated event occurring. In an effort to guarantee that similar decisions are made when similar situations occur, it is best to record in the manual of procedures both a description of the situation and the decision made.

One final consideration in conducting a survey bears some mention. One factor that can contaminate the results of a study is a *period effect*—that is, the occurrence of an event that changes how people think about an issue. For example, public support for governments providing assistance with home cooling costs would probably be higher immediately after a heat wave that resulted in the deaths of some individuals than before such an event. A study on energy assistance conducted during this period could yield biased results, because public opinion would change during the data-collection phase. Those responding at the beginning of the study would base their responses on one set of facts, whereas those responding later would base their responses on a different set of facts. To minimize the chance that period effects will occur, survey researchers try to minimize the time that they are in the field gathering data.

Figure 6-5 Sample of a data-collection summary form for a mailed questionnaire

NAME:_____ ID #:_____

ADDRESS:_____

_____

DATE RETURNED:_____/_____
             Month   Day

DISPOSITION:

___Valid Return   Coded _____/_____
                               Month   Day
___Invalid Return   Punched _____/_____
___Incomplete   Month   Day
___Ineligible   Verified _____/_____
                               Month   Day
___Refusal   Merged _____/_____
___Bad Address   Month   Day
___Not Locatable

___Remailed (Date:_____)

Mailed Questionnaires

The use of a mailed-questionnaire approach to data collection requires the following:

1. *A current list of names and addresses of those in the sample.* Creating such a list requires defining the population and, if appropriate, a sample of that population. The methods for obtaining such lists are described in detail in Chapter 9, "Population and Sampling," and will not be considered further here.
2. *A literate population.* This requirement is central to the choice of an appropriate data-collection procedure, to be discussed in a later section.
3. *A carefully considered approach to stimulating responses.* We will address this requirement now. First, we will consider the factors that have been shown to be related to the response rate for mailed ques-

tionnaires, and then we will show how these factors can be combined into an effective data-collection strategy.

Previous research on the topic suggests that ten factors are related to the response rate obtained with a mailed questionnaire. Eight of these are more or less under the control of the researcher: the length of the questionnaire, the use of incentives, the type of postage used, the number of contacts, personalization, the appearance of the questionnaire, the ease of return, and the time of year. Two other factors are part of the research design: the salience of the topic and the characteristics of the population studied. Changes in these latter two elements involve changes in the research purpose and problem. Thus, although salience of the topic and characteristics of the population to be studied influence response rates, they are not factors that the researcher can easily manipulate. The effects of each of these ten factors are summarized in Figure 6-6.

An Example of the Mailed-Survey Procedure

One common mailing strategy is a four-wave approach. This strategy involves mailing respondents a questionnaire, a postcard reminder, a second copy of the questionnaire, and a reminder letter, in that order. Typically, the last two mailings are sent only to those who have not yet responded; and, if the researcher has sufficient resources, the second questionnaire is mailed using certified mail. Although the schedule varies from study to study, a seven-to-ten-day delay between mailings is quite common. There are four basic steps in the mailed-survey procedure:

Step 1. Organize the mailing list. Names can be ordered by zip code (helpful with bulk-rate mailings) or alphabetically, making it easier to identify who has returned a questionnaire. Frequently, a data-summary sheet similar to that in Figure 6-5 is used to help organize the list.

Step 2. Gather together all of the materials needed for each mailing. Although it increases expenses somewhat, it is helpful to construct a packet for each respondent. The packets, which include all of the materials needed for each wave of mailing to the respondents, are then addressed prior to the first mailing. In this approach, the packet is removed when an individual responds, so only those who have not yet responded are left in this file. This greatly simplifies the process of deciding which potential respondents should receive any mailing.

When the researcher includes a return envelope with the questionnaire, it is important to have some means of identifying who has responded. Often the researcher records an identification number on the questionnaire for this purpose. Sometimes, when anonymity is important,

Figure 6-6   Factors affecting response rates to mailed questionnaires

Incentives: The use of incentives with a questionnaire (such as including a quarter) increases response rates. This method works only if the incentive is presented as a gift with the questionnaire. Use of a nominal sum as a reward (promising to mail the respondent a quarter when the questionnaire is returned) is ineffective.

Postage: Using more expensive postage increases response rates. Response rates are higher with certified than first-class mail and lowest for bulk-rate mail.

Number of Contacts: The more times a respondent is contacted, the more likely that individual is to respond. A third contact, preferably by telephone or certified mail, appears to be particularly helpful in raising response rates.

Personalization: Some evidence suggests that personally signing the cover letter and using an inside address with the name of the respondent increase the response rate, whereas using mailing labels decreases it.

Appearance: The response rate is higher for a neat, professional-looking, easy-to-answer questionnaire than it is for one that does not have these characteristics. Although the format of the questionnaire is more important, printing has some advantage over mimeographing.

Ease of Return: The response rate is higher for questionnaires that are easy to return than it is for those that are difficult or costly to return. Including an already-addressed envelope with prepaid postage for returning the questionnaire increases the response rate substantially.

Time of Year: It is difficult to conduct a mailed survey during Christmas or other holiday seasons. The deadline for filing income-tax returns is also not an optimum time to begin a mailed survey. Other bad times to conduct a mailed survey depend on the population being studied—for example, final-examination time for students.

Length: Increasing the length of a questionnaire decreases the response rate slightly. The effect of this factor is usually minimal except for extremely long (over thirty pages) questionnaires.

Salience: The more salient a topic is to potential respondents, the higher the response rate will be.

Population: Response rates are higher for captive populations, such as employees, than they are for samples of the general population.

the researcher includes a postcard with the identification number and asks the respondent to return this separately when he or she returns the questionnaire. Because no identification number is placed on either the questionnaire or the return envelope, respondent anonymity is guaranteed.

An alternative to the use of envelopes is the self-contained questionnaire. In this approach, the researcher uses a booklet with a foldout flap on the inside back cover. The respondent, upon completing the questionnaire, simply folds the flap over the outside cover and tapes it down. The return address is printed on this flap, so the questionnaire is ready for return. This approach has these advantages over using return envelopes:

1. If the researcher must purchase all materials, it is less expensive. Although printing costs are higher, the researcher saves both on postage (the packet is considerably lighter) and on the cost of envelopes.
2. Because the initial mailing address is intact, identification numbers are unnecessary. This simplifies the mailing process, because there is no need to verify a match between the identification number and the person to whom the questionnaire is addressed.
3. The questionnaire is easier to return. Respondents do not have to put the questionnaire into an envelope, a difficult process for some (especially elderly) respondents.
4. The researcher does not have to worry about respondents misplacing the return envelope.

Step 3. Bring bundles to the post office on the appropriate day. (As you can see, the actual mailing process is only a small part of conducting a mailed survey.)

Step 4. Read the mail to identify who has responded.

Neither of these last two is very time consuming, so the researcher can devote most of his or her time to the next phase of research—processing the data obtained.

Interviewing

The personal interview and the mailed questionnaire are the two most common methods of gathering survey data. The personal interview is similar in many respects to interviewing for information at a social service agency. Also, the principles of interviewing learned in courses in social work practice generally apply to conducting a survey interview. On the other hand, survey interviewing differs from most of the interviewing done by social workers in some important ways.

How Survey Interviews Differ from Other Types of Interviews

A survey interview differs from the type of interview typically conducted by a social worker in several major ways:

1. *The definition of the situation.* In a survey interview, the interviewer seeks out the potential respondent and asks for a favor. This is far different from a potential client seeking the services of a social worker. The potential respondent retains the right to terminate the interview at any point, and it is the obligation of the interviewer to obtain the informed consent of the respondent prior to beginning the interview. Thus, the respondent retains ultimate control of the interviewing situation.

2. *The emphasis typically placed on standardization.* Although there are exceptions, it is usually important to ask the questions in a survey instrument exactly as they are worded and in the order in which they appear. Survey instruments are usually constructed using a stimulus-response logic. With this approach, it is important that each respondent be exposed to the same stimulus situation. Altering either the wording of a question or the order in which questions are posed potentially destroys the validity of the interview. Similarly, the interviewer usually receives explicit information on which questions, if any, may be explained and how they are to be explained. When interviewing for information, by contrast, the social worker usually has greater flexibility in the interview process than this.

3. *The objective of the interview.* In a survey, interviews are typically conducted with the intent of discovering something about the characteristics of a population. Although the unit of analysis is the individual, the characteristics of the individual are unimportant (from the perspective of the research objectives) except as they help to describe what is true of the individuals in the population. Data are gathered from individuals for the purpose of comparison with other individuals. The focal point of the typical interview conducted by a social worker in a nonresearch setting, on the other hand, is the individual. The intent of a diagnostic interview, for example, is to determine the nature of a specific individual's presenting problems, not to determine the prevalence of these problems in a given population.

Gaining Respondent Cooperation

A primary problem in using personal interviews as a data-collection procedure in survey research is gaining entry. This is particularly true when special populations—such as the poor, minorities, and the elderly—are the targets. Because the members of these populations are often considered to be at risk, the ethics of research dictate that special efforts must be made to guarantee that they are fully informed of their right to nonparticipation prior to gathering data. The interviewer is specifically enjoined from placing undue pressure on individuals to obtain their permission to participate in a research project. Nevertheless, the response rate (the proportion of individuals who agree to participate in the study) for personal interview surveys can be quite high. There appear to be four main keys to gaining entry:

1. *Positive attitude.* The interviewer must believe both that the project itself is of value and that the responses of the potential respondent are worth knowing. Interviewers who believe that what they are doing is worthwhile and who also recognize that the potential respondent is doing them a favor by granting the interview have little difficulty in adopting a positive, friendly, supportive attitude toward the potential respondent.

2. *Appearance.* The interviewer's physical appearance, including dress, is often translated into perceptions of how threatening the individual is and thus affect his or her ability to gain respondent cooperation. The interviewer's objective is to appear as nonthreatening as possible. It is possible to dress too formally as well as too informally. Often someone who is familiar with the habits, customs, and dress of the target population can help determine the most appropriate mode of dress for interviewers.

3. *Identification.* An interviewer should always carry identification that introduces him or her to the subject, describes the research project and its sponsor, and provides some means for verification (for example, the name of an organization listed in the telephone directory that can be called). The researcher usually has available several other methods of establishing the legitimacy of the project to respondents. For example, prior to interviewing residents of a housing project, it is wise to post a notice explaining the research on a bulletin board and to inform the manager of the housing project of the study. An article in the local newspaper explaining the project and listing the interviewers' names can be helpful in gaining entry when interviewing a sample of the general population. If the names, addresses, and telephone numbers of the potential respondents are known in advance, a letter, followed by a telephone call for an appointment, can be helpful with some types of populations.

4. *Advance preparation.* The interviewer must know what he or she is going to say to the potential respondent at all times. Interviewers must

be prepared to answer questions about the study purpose, the method of selecting potential respondents, the importance of participating in the study, and the expected length of the interview. Furthermore, the explanations to these questions must be stated in language appropriate to the respondent. An interviewer's inability to address these issues clearly and concisely can suggest that he or she is being evasive and can interfere with establishing rapport with the respondent.

Conducting an Interview

There are relatively few principles involved in conducting a survey interview. First, and most important, the interviewer must always remember that the purpose for the interview is to determine the attitudes and opinions of the potential respondent. This means that the interviewer should maintain a value-neutral position toward the opinions expressed by the respondent. If the respondent wishes to discuss the answers given, it is usually permissible to do so at the conclusion of the interview.

There are several other factors that the interviewer should remember when conducting an interview. Some of these fall into the class of good manners and need little further comment. Very simply, the interviewer is a guest in the respondent's home and should behave appropriately. Other factors are more closely related to the interview situation. For example, many respondents typically do not think in terms of the categories commonly used in closed-ended, attitude questions. Often the respondent gives an answer that is not one of those listed. The interviewer, rather than guessing which category is closest to the respondent's intent, usually obtains better results by repeating the response and asking which category the respondent believes is most appropriate. When the interviewer uses this procedure, respondents usually learn quickly to frame their answers in terms of the response categories.

Sometimes respondents wish to provide the interviewer with information that is tangential to the purpose of the research. These comments should be recorded as accurately as possible, but it is usually important to keep the interview focused. The failure to do so can convert what is normally a thirty-minute interview into an hour-long one.

As we indicated earlier, most survey interviewing requires that the interviewer ask specific questions in a given order. It is very easy for an interviewer who is unfamiliar with the instrument to omit a question inadvertently or to change the wording of a question. Also, an interviewer who is not familiar with an instrument will need to devote a substantial amount of attention to it. This detracts from the relationship that the interviewer is attempting to establish with the respondent. Therefore, it is almost mandatory that interviewers become very familiar with the interview instrument being used.

Other Survey Data-Collection Techniques

Although the mailed questionnaire and the personal interview are the two most common survey data-collection procedures in use today, other procedures are also sometimes useful:

1. *The drop-off questionnaire.* The drop-off questionnaire procedure begins like an interview, with the interviewer establishing rapport with the respondent. Rather than conducting an interview, however, the interviewer leaves a questionnaire to be completed at the respondent's convenience. Depending on the procedure preferred by the researcher, either the respondent returns the questionnaire in a postage-paid, preaddressed envelope provided for this purpose, or the interviewer returns at a later time to get the completed instrument.

2. *The group-administered questionnaire.* A researcher might, for example, have a place on the program of a public-housing tenants' meeting. Depending on the time limitation, the researcher can either ask all members of the audience to complete the questionnaire at that time or provide members with a copy of the questionnaire to be returned at a later date. In either case, the researcher has the opportunity to explain the project to the audience personally.

3. *The telephone interview.* Telephone interviewing is, not surprisingly, quite similar to personal interviewing. The primary differences between the two approaches are that the telephone interview tends to be shorter and less complicated. Whereas researchers can use visual aids to facilitate understanding with the other data-collection techniques (including the personal interview), this is not possible with telephone interviews. Therefore, the question format in telephone interviews tends to be simpler than that used with other data-collection procedures.

Selecting a Survey Data-Collection Procedure

The researcher usually considers five factors when selecting a data-collection procedure: cost, response rate, the topic of the study, the characteristics of the population to be studied, and the need for a uniform stimulus.

Usually the mailed questionnaire is the least expensive of the data-collection options available to the researcher, and the personal interview is the most expensive. If the study is to be conducted within narrow geographic boundaries such as a community, however, either a drop-off questionnaire or a telephone interview may be the least expensive option.

Group-administered questionnaires are, of course, very inexpensive but not often a viable option.

Although mailed questionnaires are less expensive than personal interviews, the response rate to a mailed questionnaire is considerably lower. This is particularly true with low-income, less-well-educated individuals, who are often the clientele of social service agencies. On occasion, drop-off questionnaire return rates approximate those obtained by personal interviewing, making this the approach of choice if other factors are equal.

The personal interview is the optimum method of data collection when the questions to be asked are complicated and require extensive explanation. At the same time, the presence of an interviewer can, in some situations, bias the results. For example, it is unlikely the respondents will answer questions about embarrassing or illegal activities truthfully in a personal interview. In such a situation, either a drop-off questionnaire with a mail-back collection procedure or a group-administered questionnaire would probably give more valid results than would a personal interview. In general, if the topic of the study is a sensitive one, data-collection strategies that guarantee respondent anonymity are preferred.

The characteristics of the population under study should play a major role in the decision concerning the optimum data-collection strategy. As we indicated earlier, mailed questionnaires are ineffective with low-income and less-well-educated persons. These individuals are not only less likely to *respond* to a mailed questionnaire but also, because of mobility patterns, less likely than others even to *receive* the questionnaire. Similarly, telephone interviews are ineffective with such individuals, leaving the researcher with little choice but to use personal interviews.

On the other hand, some categories of individuals can be reached effectively with questionnaires and telephone interviews. Attorneys, physicians, and public officials are accustomed to using the telephone for business purposes. Often it is possible to conduct an extensive telephone interview with individuals of this type. In fact, many times the telephone interview is the most efficient data-collection strategy to use with professionals.

A final factor to consider in selecting a data-collection procedure is the stress to be placed on the uniformity of the stimulus. Obviously, the stimuli (questions) are uniform in questionnaires. This is not necessarily the case in interviews. The interviewer does not read questions in a monotone. Changing inflection can, on occasion, change the meaning of questions. Furthermore, a question concerning racial prejudice asked by a black interviewer may well not be interpreted in the same way as that same question asked by a white interviewer. Interviews are inherently less standardized than are questionnaires. If standardization is extremely critical to the study, one of the questionnaire approaches to data collection is usually preferable to interviewing.

Key Terms

survey instrument	personal interview
questionnaire	mailed questionnaire
interview schedule	group-administered questionnaire
open-ended question	drop-off questionnaire
closed-ended question	telephone interview
response rate	

Questions for Discussion

1. What are the relative merits of open-ended and closed-ended questions? What are their limitations?
2. Should slang or local idioms be used in developing a survey instrument?
3. How do the characteristics of a population influence the selection of the optimum data-collection strategy? Illustrate your answer.

Exercise

Suppose that you are interested in what service recipients think about a local mental health center.

   a. Develop a survey instrument (not to exceed three pages) to collect data on this problem.
   b. Suppose that you have $1,000 for data collection. How will you use these funds? Please be specific.

For Further Reading

Thomas A. Heberlein and Robert Baumgartner. "Factors Affecting Response Rates to Mailed Questionnaires: A Quantitative Analysis of the Published Literature." *American Sociological Review* 43 (1978), pp. 447–467. This comprehensive review of what affects response rates includes an equation for estimating the return rate for a study.

Arnold S. Linsky. "Stimulating Responses to Mailed Questionnaires: A Review." *Public Opinion Quarterly* 38 (1975), pp. 82–101. This is an excellent review of the factors that affect response rates to mailed questionnaires.

Survey Research Center. *Interviewer's Manual,* rev. ed. Ann Arbor, Michigan: The Institute for Social Research, 1976. This practical guide to interviewing includes sections on respondent selection.

7

Observational Methods

As a general rule, science uses the word *observation* to denote any act of measurement. That is, every time a researcher measures some attribute of a subject, he or she is making an observation. In this chapter, however, *observation* will be used in a more limited sense. It will be used to mean the researcher actually watching the subject.

Anthropologists, sociologists, psychologists, and social psychologists frequently use direct observation in their research. Although social workers do a great deal of observation in clinical settings, most of it is for diagnostic purposes rather than for research. Social workers could do more research using observational methods. Their clinical skills actually give them an advantage over many other social scientists, in that they are already sensitive to many subtleties of behavior. Unfortunately, social workers have not always chosen to capitalize on their advantage but have tended to depend on questionnaires and attitude scales as primary modes of data collection.

The Use of Direct Observation

Many people tend to equate social research in general with the use of the questionnaire. Chapter 2 discussed a number of ways of gathering data; it is now time to expand that discussion. Each data-gathering technique has its advantages in certain situations. Questionnaires are very useful in a number of research applications. However, the questionnaire is not the best approach in all situations. Suppose that one is interested in doing research on some aspect of infant behavior. It would not make sense to consider gathering data with a questionnaire. A more rational approach would be to observe infant behavior directly and to draw conclusions from that. Observational methods are also appropriate for doing research in nonverbal behaviors, public behavior, client behavior, and even the therapeutic behaviors of social workers. In short, any time a researcher is interested in actual behavior, observational methods are to be preferred.

The Advantages and Disadvantages of Observation

Observational research methods have two major advantages:

1. Observations gather the data fresh from the subject right at the time the behavior occurs. Most other forms of research lack this kind of immediacy.
2. A researcher can usually establish the validity of the data-gathering process in a straightforward manner. Behaviors either occur or they do not. Because behavior is visible, it is much easier to establish the claim that one is measuring what one intends to measure. When measuring attitudes or beliefs, validity is harder to establish.

On the other hand, there are certain disadvantages to observational methods:

1. One may have to wait some time for the desired behavior to occur. If one has the resources, of course, it is possible to record subjects on film or videotape. Still, one might have to wade through an enormous amount of unimportant behavior in order to get to the relevant parts.
2. Some behaviors are difficult or inconvenient to observe. It is probably easier to ask people about courtship behavior than to observe it. (It is also much less *dangerous* to ask!) With some kinds of personal behavior (for example, criminal behavior), an observer runs the risk of being driven off or even attacked, particularly among remote and unsophisticated people. A researcher who plans to do research must weigh these and other factors in making the decision to gather data in this manner.

Unstructured Observation

There are two broad categories of approach to observational data collection. The difference between them lies in the relative formality of the data-collection process. A researcher doing *unstructured* observation brings little or no structure to the observational task. Generally, he or she will watch the flow of events and will attempt to record or summarize them for later analysis. Sometimes researchers will observe events, keeping a narrative recording of behavior. Social workers who have observed a children's play group and written a narrative for diagnostic purposes have engaged in a similar activity. Often it is impractical to record a narrative, usually because the researcher believes that the act of recording will inhibit behavior. In those cases, the observer may write a summary after the observational period. Obviously, the sooner one can do the recording, the fresher the material will be. This is analogous to the social worker who, anticipating the client's discomfort, postpones recording until after an interview. Bear in mind that this is only an analogy, because a researcher will likely be recording observed behavior not the conversation of an interview.

Although it is possible to do unstructured observations in a laboratory, they are generally carried out "in the field." This use of the word *field* means the setting in which the subject's behavior normally takes place. The major rationale for doing unstructured observation is the need for or interest in describing some behavior or set of behaviors. Thus most studies using observational data-gathering techniques are *descriptive* studies. It is possible to measure the results of an experiment with unstructured observations, but because this is a very narrow application, we will not deal with it here.

As an example of the very best kind of unstructured observation, we refer you to the work of anthropologists Margaret Mead and Oscar Lewis. Mead spent a good deal of her long career in observing the people of the South Pacific. Her studies of social behavior there have shed light on the nature of human behavior in all cultures. In *Male and Female,* Mead clearly shows that "masculine" and "feminine" traits are largely unrelated to secondary sex characteristics but instead depend heavily upon social role definitions.[1] Oscar Lewis's *Five Families* is a study of five families in twentieth-century Mexico.[2] It dramatically shows the differences in life-style by social class and the impact of industrialization on a society that was largely rural in origin. These two studies are examples of a kind of unstructured observation known as *participant observation*. This term is a bit misleading, in that Mead and Lewis did not actually take part in the subjects' lives as would a regular family member. Instead, they observed as unobtrusively as they could, asking questions for clarification from time to time, but interfering as little as possible.

Not all unstructured research follows the same data-collection pattern. A continuum of activity may be observed in the actual behavior of observers. In a section on field research entitled "Watching as Active Presence," Schatzman and Strauss identify the following roles for observers that extend from a passive to an active stance:[3]

1. Watching from the outside—in which the researcher is concealed from the subjects.

2. Passive presence—in which the researcher is present in the observed situation but remains passive.
3. Limited interaction—in which the researcher may ask questions but does not influence the behavior of the subjects.
4. Active control—in which the researcher controls the interaction in order to gain specific information. (Schatzman and Strauss say that the archetype of this is really the interview. Clearly one could control a strictly observational situation, too.)
5. The observer as participant—in which the observer is a full participant whose identity as a researcher is known. (Schatzman and Strauss admit that this is a difficult and therefore rare role to carry off.)
6. Participation with hidden identity—in which the researcher becomes a full and active participant while keeping his or her identity unknown.

To this list, Leonard Bickman, a social psychologist, would add one more role—that of *provocateur*.[4] Bickman suggests that there are times when a researcher may add some modification of the observational conditions that will not totally change the naturalness of the situation. As an example, Bickman suggests introducing a worker of the other sex into a telephone repair crew. This role apparently differs from Schatzman and Strauss's "active control" category in that the provocateur does not actually control the entire situation but merely introduces one new element into it. Some of these roles raise some challenging procedural and ethical questions, which we will discuss later in the chapter, because the issues also apply to structured observations.

Unstructured observation is a fine and useful approach for a great deal of field research. Social work researchers have not even begun to exhaust the possibilities for its use in the description of "natural" behaviors, cultural factors, or the development of clinical concepts. However, unstructured observation is limited to fairly broad patterns of behavior.

Structured Observation

When a researcher wishes to focus on specific behaviors, it is often more effective to use a structured approach. (You must remember that the terms *structured* and *unstructured* refer to the researcher's approach, not to the action of the subjects. You could, for example, use a structured approach in a field study of children on a playground. Alternatively, you could use the unstructured approach in observing people on a hospital ward—a highly structured *situation*—particularly if you were interested in, say, the informal social structure of the ward.)

Structured observation differs from unstructured observation in that the observer brings a good deal of structure to the observational situation. This means that the observer is looking at certain behaviors and recording them on an instrument designed for the purpose. It is not the behavior of the *observed* that is unstructured or structured; rather it is the behavior of the *observer*. One could do either structured or unstructured observation of the same group depending on the kind of tool one chooses to use. Both kinds of observation can be done either in the field or in a laboratory setting. For example, one might be interested in studying something about the play behavior of schizophrenic children. The researcher could, depending on the nature of the research question, observe children on a playground in a more-or-less natural setting; or the researcher could observe the same children in a laboratory using one of the instruments described later in the chapter. The point is that whether an observation is structured or unstructured depends on the structure (or lack of it) in the data-gathering approach.

When a researcher does structured observation, he or she is looking for specific behaviors or events according to a fairly formal research plan. The formal plan might include counting the frequency of occurrence of a symptom, tabulating a checklist of behaviors, timing an activity or behavior, using rating scales, or looking at a number of behaviors and classifying them into concepts.

This list may sound more formidable than it really is. The following series of examples shows how these techniques can be used. You can easily see that one might do research on some specific behavior simply by counting the number of times the behavior occurs under a given set of conditions or in a given situation. Suppose that a social work researcher was interested in the effect of table games on noncommunicative group members. Suppose further that the researcher designs a simple before/after study (or, using Campbell and Stanley's terms, the pretest/posttest control-group design) for exploratory purposes. The researcher would first observe the number of times that the members of the group spoke to each other during a half-hour of normal group activity. The researcher then might introduce the group to a table game of the kind that requires communication. This might be a commercially produced game like "Clue" or "Risk" (assuming that the group can learn to play this kind of game), or it could be a simple card game like "Hearts." Following the game, the researcher might again count the number of times that members of the group exchanged words during a half-hour of group activity. An increase in verbal interaction would provide some support (but certainly not final proof) for a future experiment that would involve a more complex design, a firmer hypothesis, and random sampling of subjects.

The point of the example is that the researcher would have used a structured approach to data collection. It would move the question of the effectiveness of group games on social interaction out of the realm of impressionistic data and in the direction of a scientific approach to evaluating the effectiveness of a technique to increase social interaction in groups. Incidentally, we should point out that this kind of study could be done either in a laboratory or in a field setting—for example, a hospital ward or a group meeting in a youth-serving agency. It is the kind of research that a practitioner could do, because the means are readily available and projects of this nature do not require vast amounts of money or equipment. Over a period of time, social workers could explore a whole variety of techniques using simple studies of this type. Those techniques that show promise during such exploratory studies could then be subjected to more formal tests and experiments. Over time, social work researchers could accumulate a usable body of literature on a variety of techniques on which therapists could base more effective practice operations.

You can easily see that a similar kind of study might be done with timing substituted for counting. That is, a researcher might be interested in observing the effect of an X upon a Y in terms of minutes, hours, or even days, rather than in counting the number of occurrences.

Further, it is not hard to extend this kind of an approach to the use of rating scales. A researcher could have judges (discussed later in this chapter) rate the severity of a group of patients' hostility on a scale of 1 to 10 prior to the introduction of a technique designed to lower hostility. Following treatment, the judges could rate the members of the group again, and the researchers could calculate the effects using one of the techniques described in later chapters.

So far, we have described the use of structured observation in terms that are quite everyday and familiar. The technique can get more complicated. A number of fairly sophisticated data-gathering techniques have been developed for use in observational studies. These techniques require the use of qualitative concepts, but they still permit quantification of behaviors. Those reviewed in the next few pages have been in use for some time and are fairly widely known.

The Critical-Incident Technique

Some years ago, John C. Flanagan devised a technique that has been used quite extensively in a number of applications.[5] This approach to collecting observational data emerged from the Aviation Psychology Program during World War II. The technique grew out of the need to be able to define the behavioral components of crucial roles—for example, the nature of "combat leadership." The idea is to identify those behaviors that are identified with a specific role or status so that one can decide whether a subject is behaving in ways consistent with the role. In other words, one should be able to tell whether a wing commander is effective if he or she performs in ways that get the job done. In using this procedure, one first needs to determine the goal of the role behavior. Second, one has to develop some kind of formal data-collection procedure to identify the crucial components of the behavior under study. Flanagan cites a useful application. Often, he says, it is difficult to clearly establish improvement in psychotherapy. Therapists are often guided by vague overall clinical impressions that the patient has developed insight. The critical-incident technique focuses on collecting factual incidents that indicate actual behaviors that answer the question, "What did the patient do that indicates improvement?" The key thing is that behaviors are identified only when they are critical parts of the activity under study. One might, for example, note that after a certain amount of treatment, a formerly withdrawn patient was (1) paying more attention to his or her appearance, as evidenced by wearing a clean shirt or blouse; (2) eating with more enthusiasm than before, as evidenced by observing the quantity of food eaten; and (3) engaging in group activity with other patients on the ward, as evidenced by an observation of actual time of participation. Given that a goal with such a patient might be an increased sense of self-worth, a collection of behaviors of this sort could lead to a more objective assessment of improved functioning. This procedure documents improvement in functioning and removes it from the realm of subjective impression.

The Potential for Social Work Research.   The critical-incident technique has been used successfully in social work research. Psychologist Carroll A. Whitmer and social worker C. Glenn Conover studied the critical incidents that resulted in the hospitalization of the mentally ill.[6] The results are fascinating. Whitmer and Conover found that people did not seek hospitalization for their relatives because they recognized the symptoms of mental illness. Rather, people sought hospitalization when behavior occurred that they were not able to manage. Apparently the subjects in this study exhibited mental symptoms, sometimes for many years, that did not alarm anybody. Help was sought mainly when their behavior became intolerable for those around the patient.

The authors of this article recognize that their data is not conclusive. However, the study is certainly suggestive. Obviously, further research on this topic can lead to an entirely different focus for intervention. The authors conclude:

> It would seem logical that, since behavioral problems are significant to the members of a family and to the general public, concentration upon the recognition of early aberrant behavior and seeking understanding of that behavior might lead to more effective treatment of mental illness in the formative phase.[7]

Although this research did not cause a complete turnaround in mental health philosophy, its conclusion was consistent with other research.

It is fair to say that it is now generally recognized that early treatment of difficult behavior will, in many cases, eliminate the need for long-term hospitalization.

The Bales Interaction-Process Analysis.   Robert F. Bales, a social psychologist, has developed an observational approach that is used for research in social interaction.[8] In an early version of this approach, researchers observe group interaction and record what happens using a coding system. The coding system classifies all kinds of interactive behaviors into categories. For example, the category "shows tension" includes behavior, facial expression, body language, and verbal expressions. Generally, tabulations can be made of different kinds of interactions. Bales and his associates have found that different groups show measurably different kinds of interaction.

This kind of an approach can be of great use in group-work research, particularly when one is interested in testing therapeutic techniques that are designed to affect group interactions. A practitioner wishing to evaluate the effectiveness of a technique might select enough subjects to form two groups, an experimental group and a control group. Both groups would be observed using the Bales technique. The researcher would then give the experimental group the treatment that was to be evaluated and would give the control group a series of activities that would constitute a harmless placebo. Following the treatment, the practitioner could observe both groups again and identify differences in interaction patterns. If interaction patterns are changed (assuming that changing the interaction is the goal of treatment), then the results would lend support to the belief that the treatment was effective. Bales's work has changed over the years; the potential user should consult his various writings for the technique appropriate to a specific research problem.

The Flanders Interaction Analysis.   Ned Flanders, an educational psychologist, has devised an approach similar to what Bales has done but with some important differences.[9] Flanders developed his system for measuring interaction between pupils and teacher in the classroom. The general notion underlying this approach is that the kind of interaction that occurs has an important bearing on learning. Flanders classifies classroom interaction into ten categories. These ten categories include both teacher behaviors and student behaviors. Teacher behaviors are further subdivided into direct and indirect behaviors. Direct behaviors are those in which the teacher plays a fairly authoritative role—lecturing, giving directions, and criticizing. Indirect behaviors are more enabling and accepting behaviors. Only periods of teacher-pupil interaction (not periods of quiet study) are subject to analysis. In the Flanders approach, the observer does not keep track of individual behavior. Instead, the observer writes down the appropriate code number (from 1 to 10) of the behavior that is going on at the time. The observer records a number every three seconds. For instance, a lengthy set of instructions from the teacher might result in a long string of 5's (5 means "teacher gives direction"). It is not profitable (nor possible) to record a whole classroom day. A researcher using this technique samples periodically during the day. Processing the data involves calculating the percentages of time consumed by the various forms of teacher or pupil behavior.

The Potential for Social Work Research.   The same kind of experiment that was used with the Bales technique can be used. Obviously, some changes would be necessary in the observational instrument, because the Flanders technique is designed primarily for classroom behavior. For example, the category "teacher lectures" might become "therapist offers direct advice." Educational research using the Flanders technique has suggested that more learning is likely to occur when indirect teaching methods are used.[10] Perhaps the use of an adaptation of the Flanders technique would shed some light on the use of direct versus indirect therapeutic methods. At least, the Flanders technique is a basis on which comparison might be made.

Why do we have two techniques that seem so similar? The Bales and the Flanders techniques focus on different things. The Bales technique looks at the behavior of peers in peer situations. The Flanders technique looks at interaction in situations in which differential statuses are the norm. Bales's technique appears to be quite feeling-oriented, whereas Flanders's approach is more task-oriented. A researcher might choose between these two techniques, depending on the focus of the research. Actually, there are a great many observational techniques. The Lofland volume listed in the For Further Reading section at the end of the chapter contains a great deal of information about various classification systems. Readers wishing to develop structured observations will find Lofland extremely helpful.

The Use of Judges

Frequently, when researchers employ a structured observational technique, they will use a number of judges to fill out the observation schedule, or to count or time the behavior being studied. Bales recommends at least two when using his approach. Obviously, if several people agree on what happened to the subjects, the researcher can have a stronger claim that the research has internal validity. The problem is in getting agreement. Probably the best-known use of judges in observational applications is in certain athletic events. In diving, for example, the score is determined by several judges. First, each judge makes an individual assessment. The scores are averaged (sometimes the highest score and the lowest score are discarded), and the average becomes the individual's score. This analogy is not quite exact, because judges in international diving competition actually begin with a score of 10 and then take off fractional amounts when the dive does not meet the perfection required for a 10. Despite the differences between athletics and research, the similarity is close enough to pursue this example a bit further. It is obvious that the judging of athletic competition is not a haphazard exercise. Unless there are political overtones, as there were in the 1968 Summer Olympics, the judges are very close in their judgments. For example, seven judges who were observing a world-class diver might record scores of 9.7, 9.9, 9.6, 9.7, 9.5, 9.7, and 9.8. How can people watching someone dive into a pool agree to within one or two tenths of a point in their assessments of the quality of a performance? The answer lies in the conventions by which these judgments are made. First of all, none of the divers in world-class competition are likely to be scored a 2 or even an 8. Those have all been eliminated along the way. Only a handful of very good performers remain. A judge does not have to distinguish between poor and near-perfect performances—a judgment that would be very easy, anyway. The judge makes judgments based on very subtle yet clearly defined behavioral cues. For instance, the diver's hands must be together when the diver enters the water. The feet must be together, and the back must be straight. All this must be seen in just a second or two, but it can be done because *the judges have all been trained to look for the very same cues.* Further, the judges have had a great deal of practice in making judgments using the same criteria. The Chapter 2 discussion on rating scales included a very commonplace example. Among several friends discussing a movie, one may rate the film an 8, whereas another may rate it a 4. Yet another may say that the film was a 6. There is apt to be very little agreement. This is because these people are looking at the film with greatly varying standards of judgment. It could be said that there was very little interjudge reliability. Recall that the discussion on reliability in Chapter 2 said that a reliable measuring instrument should give the same results when repeatedly measuring the same thing. The friends who are discussing the movie are unreliable judges simply because they are not using the same measuring device. To the rater who gave the film an 8, *plot* was important, and the movie had a plot that was appealing to the rater. To the rater who gave the film a 4, *action* was a primary value, and the film lacked the kind of action that the rater liked to see in a movie. The judges who scored the diving, on the other hand, were all using the same standards of judgment. They had reached prior agreement on what was good diving.

The Applications for Social Work Research.   Trained judges can be used in social work research in a number of ways. One of the more obvious ones is in research on case movement. Another is in research designed to test the teaching of a technique. Yet a third use lies in evaluational studies. To illustrate the use of judges in case movement, consider a group of patients on a hospital ward. Assume that a social work researcher is trying to test a new therapeutic technique that is supposed to decrease hostile behavior patterns. The researcher must first decide (or, using research language, *operationalize*) what is meant by "hostile behavior." The more clearly hostile behavior can be defined, the easier it will be for judges to agree on what it is when it occurs. Next, judges should receive some training in recognizing the hostile behavior and should be given plenty of opportunity for practice. For practice purposes, other staff might engage in role playing. When all the judges have learned the same definition of hostility as the researcher has operationally defined it, they are ready to perform as a measuring instrument. If all goes well, there should be pretty fair agreement when the actual judging takes place.

Objectivity in Observational Research

The preceding discussion focused on the need for judges to have the same general frame of reference when rating, counting, or classifying behavior. A researcher using, say, the Flanders technique is well advised to have more than one person writing down the codes at three-second intervals. It is permissible to average the judges' observations in the same way that the ratings of judges in Olympic events are averaged. The use of several observers acts as a check on the objectivity of any one observer. The question of objectivity is especially crucial in observational research—much more crucial than in research in which mechanical measuring devices are used. Generally, the more mechanical the measuring device, the more objective the measurement. For instance, it is much easier to get an objective measure of a client's weight or height than it is to get an objective measure of his or her anxiety. Constructs such as anxiety, guilt, hostility, and maturity, which are important to social workers, are simply harder to measure because of the element of human judgment that is involved. The state of the art does not provide for a mechanical measure of guilt. It must be judged by one or more human observers. Unless this process can be operationalized in some fairly simple way, one rater's "guilt" may be someone else's "anxiety."

Behavioristic psychologists have tended to gloss over this problem by taking the position that if behavior is not overt, then it cannot be measured. We believe that this is a "cop-out" and that researchers are justified in trying to measure crucial constructs.

All researchers recognize that making judgments in the observation process is risky and imperfect. The reliability of observations is certainly open to challenge. Clearly, observers are products of their backgrounds and will not be totally free of biases of race, sex, age, education, social class, and other such factors. However, if researchers who are doing observational studies reach agreement on the behavioral cues or critical incidents that constitute the operational definitions of their concepts, then useful observational research can be done on the kinds of constructs most useful to social workers. It is true that this research will not be perfect. It is unlikely that research on constructs will ever be reduced to the same kind of objective process as is possible with measures of height and weight. However, by using several observers, teaching them what to look for, and providing them with a good deal of practice, the observational study of constructs can be improved.

Ethical and Procedural Questions

Reliability and validity are not the only pertinent issues in observational research. Some observational studies may raise specific ethical and procedural questions. Some observational studies are done without the subject's awareness of being a subject. This can happen in many structured observations, but it is most crucial in participant observation. This is not to say that similar questions do not arise in other kinds of research. It is to say that observation is especially vulnerable to problems. Most (but not all) of the other data-collection procedures reveal themselves to a degree. People who are interviewed by other people bearing pencils and clipboards invariably know that they are research subjects. Mailed questionnaires reveal their intent pretty clearly. In behavioral experiments, it is possible to deceive subjects about the nature of the research, but it is pretty clear to the subjects that they are being used as the source for data, because such experiments usually involve a laboratory of sorts, some apparatus, and some kind of measurement. In participant observation, however, it is often possible for people to be subjects and not know it. An ethical dilemma therefore arises.

In general, research ethics require the researcher to tell the subjects that they are research subjects. Researchers should also tell subjects the nature of the research and assure them that their identities will be concealed. Subjects in research should ordinarily become sources of data only when they have given their informed consent. (The phrase *informed consent* means that a subject has to know the nature of the research and that he or she can refuse to participate.) Although this principle was designed to apply primarily to participation in medical and psychological experiments, it also applies to data gathered in field observation when the subject is in any way exposed to social or psychological risk. Federal guidelines have been established for all research done by a facility or institution using federal funds for any kind of research.[11] These guidelines are now under review, but the current statement embodies a very strict policy on informed consent and the safeguards necessary when research is conducted. Even though these guidelines cover only research done in organizations receiving federal funds, they obviously influence all social research. Even if the federal government had no regulations, ethical researchers would not want to endanger the physical health, psychological condition, or social status of research subjects. Social work researchers need to be especially careful when gathering data from clients. Most client groups are composed of persons who are operating at some disadvantage compared to the rest of society. Social work researchers, therefore, should guard carefully their subjects' rights and privacy.

In some fields, social researchers have disagreed with the federal position. The counterargument that is usually made applies primarily to participant observation, but it is also extended to certain other types of studies. The argument claims that if subjects must give their informed consent to all studies, then it will not be possible to research a number of very interesting social phenomena. It would not be possible, for instance, to study public behavior in public places. If informed consent is necessary, people would have to be told the nature of the research. This knowledge, coupled with the awareness that they were being observed, might cause people to behave differently. This would defeat the whole purpose of the research. After all, a number of well-known studies in sociology and social psychology have been done by researchers who concealed their purposes. Over twenty years ago, three social psychologists joined a religious cult that believed that a tidal wave would engulf a large part of the United States.[12] The researchers were interested in what happens to social organizations that lose their reason for being. Had they approached the group openly and revealed their purpose, it is possible that the group would have refused to allow the researchers the privilege of observing what happened to the group when the prophecy failed to come true. The researchers, by pretending to be true believers, were able to follow the development of the group and, more importantly, were able to conclude that human organizations, when deprived of their purpose, do not dissolve but instead tend to redefine their mission and continue to operate. This study could not have been done at all under the current federal guidelines. One can easily defend this kind of observational research when it is done with "normal" subjects—that is, subjects who are not members of captive populations and who are pursuing everyday behavior. It is much harder to defend in the case of client groups who may be at considerable risk.

The federal guidelines are currently under challenge, because they severely limit social research. Few people would challenge the importance of strict regulation over biomedical research. Certain kinds of psychological research also present a clear threat to the well-being of the subjects. However, there is little or no evidence that sociological or social work researchers have actually violated the privacy or endangered the social status of subjects. As of this writing, the ethical questions remain unresolved. No researcher intends harm to subjects, but there is no clear agreement on what is harmful.

Even if doing observational data gathering posed no ethical problems, it would still present some procedural problems. The chief question is, "How much can a researcher participate?" Earlier in this chapter, we noted that the observational researcher's role can range from that of a concealed, passive watcher to that of provocateur. Some who have written on this subject take the position that the researcher should never influence the behavior that is to be observed. They see this as an ethical question. We disagree; we think that the ethical question is not whether the researcher is influencing the behavior being observed but rather whether any harm is being done to the subjects. If there is no harm, and if subjects are informed well enough to give legitimate consent, the ethical question is satisfied. Whether the researcher is concealed or openly visible, passive or active, now depends on the aims of the research.

But would people give their consent to being observed from a concealed watching place? Would they consent to being placed in situations in which a provocateur will attempt to stimulate behavior? Will their behavior differ radically when they know they are being watched? Most of the time the answer is "yes" to the first two questions and "no" to the third. Once subjects get comfortable with a situation, they tend to behave in ways that appear to be consistent with the ways they would behave if they were not research subjects. This is simply because human behavior is consistent. Sinners cannot suddenly act like saints—at least not for long. Hostile people cannot continue to masquerade as gentle folk indefinitely. This kind of logic challenges the notion that subjects behave differently when they know they are subjects. Also for this reason, experiments and even some descriptive studies need control groups, so that any effects of knowing that one's group are subjects would occur in both groups.

As a general rule (assuming that the question of harm or damage has been satisfactorily resolved), the nature of the research will dictate the posture of the researcher. The activity or passivity of the researcher depends upon whether the aims of the research are served.

Some Concluding Remarks

Good observational data collection can be of more use in social work research than is now the case. Social work research has a place for ethnographic studies. Good participant observation could tell social workers a good deal more about client groups than is currently known. If you examine the literature on poverty, child neglect, mental illness, and other areas of concern, you will be struck with how little is really known about the daily life of the people behind the demographic figures and the lists of symptoms.

Structured observations could be used in studies of both program and clinical evaluation. Too often, evaluation in these areas has rested on questionnaires and attitude surveys. Clearly, social work research could be greatly enriched by giving more attention to observational methods of data collection.

Key Terms

direct observation

structured observation

unstructured observation

field

participant observation

critical-incident technique

interaction-process analysis

informed consent

References

1. Margaret Mead, *Male and Female* (New York: William Morrow & Company, 1949).
2. Oscar Lewis, *Five Families* (New York: Basic Books, 1959).
3. Leonard Schatzman and Anselm L. Strauss, *Field Research* (Englewood Cliffs, New Jersey: Prentice-Hall, 1973), pp. 58–63.
4. Leonard Bickman, "Data Collection I: Observational Methods," in Claire Selltiz, Lawrence S. Wrightsman, and Stuart W. Cook, *Research Methods in Social Relations*, 3rd ed. (New York: Holt, Rinehart and Winston, 1976), p. 253.
5. John C. Flanagan, "The Critical Incident Technique," *Psychological Bulletin* 51, no. 4 (July 1954), pp. 327–358.
6. Carroll A. Whitmer and C. Glenn Conover, "A Study of Critical Incidents in the Hospitalization of the Mentally Ill," *Social Work* 4, no. 1 (January 1959), pp. 89–94.
7. *Loc. cit.,* p. 94.
8. Robert F. Bales, *Interaction Process Analysis: A Method for the Study of Small Groups* (Reading, Massachusetts: Addison Wesley, 1950).
9. Ned Flanders, *Interaction Analysis in the Classroom—A Manual for Observers* (Ann Arbor, Michigan: University of Michigan Press, 1965).
10. James Reed Campbell and Cyrus W. Barnes, "Interaction Analysis— A Breakthrough?" *Phi Delta Kappan* 1, no. 10 (June 1969), pp. 587–590.
11. *Federal Register,* 43, no. 231: 56174–56198.

12. Leon Festinger, Henry Riecken, Jr., and Stanley Schacter, *When Prophecy Fails* (Minneapolis: University of Minnesota Press, 1956).

Questions for Discussion

1. Why is direct observation better than a questionnaire for studying overt behavior?
2. List the advantages and disadvantages of observing as a way of collecting data.
3. Which approach is better for gathering data about group solidarity: structured or unstructured observation?
4. What problems would there be in doing a participant-observation study of criminal behavior?
5. Should researchers who are doing participant observation actually participate in the events that they are observing?
6. Is it ethical to be a provocateur when one wants to do participant observation?
7. Do you think that structured observation can really work? That is, do subjects really behave as they would if they were not being observed in a structured measurement situation?

Exercises

1. Design and carry out a simple participant-observation study that can be carried out in the classroom or the student lounge. You might, for example, look at anxiety symptoms before an examination. Begin observing a half-hour before the test, and watch the development of anxiety in one subject or a small group of subjects. Write a narrative describing the experience.

2. Do an exploratory study using the critical-incident technique. A good exercise would be to attend a party and select the critical incidents that lead to the breakup of the party. Ideally, then, you would be able to develop a rough scale that would allow the prediction of the end of any given party when certain critical incidents appear. Remember that designing an instrument is a valid use of the exploratory study.

3. Design a simple experiment in which the data will be collected by means of a structured observation. The following is a simple model:

    Suppose that a researcher wanted to study the effect of music on human behavior. He or she would draw two (or more) random groups. One group would be seated in a room where a record of one of Sousa's marches would be played. A control group would be seated in another room and would listen to a different kind of music. The researcher would count the number of people who responded to each rhythm by tapping their feet in time with the music. Is there a difference in the number of people who are affected by a march as opposed to, say, folk ballads?

(*Note:* The preceding examples are purposefully innocuous. They serve as simple exercises that do not put subjects at significant risk. You will have to decide whether or not it is ethical to inform the subjects of the research before or after the experiment. We advise persons wishing to do observational data collection to try out the techniques involved in very simple ways in order to get comfortable with them. We do not advise students to observe an adolescent gang or a therapeutic group as an exercise.

4. Design, but do not carry out unless the proper permissions are given, a study of group interaction using either Bales's interaction-process analysis or a variation of Flanders's interaction analysis. Of course, students wishing to do this will need to consult works by Bales and Flanders (see References above) before proceeding. This might be a good group project, if one is required in the course.

For Further Reading

Leonard Bickman. "Data Collection I: Observational Methods." In Claire Selltiz, Lawrence S. Wrightsman, and Stuart W. Cook, *Research Methods in Social Relations,* 3rd ed. New York: Holt, Rinehart and Winston, 1976. Chapter 8. This selection contains a strong discussion of observational methods and is aimed primarily at sociologists and social psychologists.

Leonard Schatzman and Anselm L. Strauss. *Field Research.* Englewood Cliffs, New Jersey: Prentice-Hall, 1973. This invaluable handbook to doing field research includes observational studies. It offers an excellent description of the entire field-research process including interviewing the field.

John Lofland. *Analyzing Social Settings.* Belmont, California: Wadsworth Publishing Company, 1971. This book focuses on qualitative analysis and is aimed primarily at sociologists. It is especially good on what to observe and how to classify observations.

Margaret Mead. *Male and Female.* New York: William Morrow and Company, 1949. Oscar Lewis. *Five Families.* New York: Basic Books, 1959. These are two examples of participant observation at its best. Social workers can learn a great deal about the conceptualization of research and how to use research results from these two writers.

8

Some Specialized Data-Gathering Procedures

This chapter introduces several specialized research techniques and data-collection procedures. It will lay a foundation for future study for students who decide to do advanced work. We include sufficient detail here to suggest beginning uses of these techniques and to enable you to be a critical consumer of research articles. Some of the discussion will actually have as much relevance to practice as it has to research. Content analysis, projective testing, unobtrusive measures, and situational tests are included in the discussion. The length of the treatment given to each approach varies according to our perceptions of their usefulness in social work research.

Content Analysis

Content analysis is not as clearly defined in the literature as are other forms of research. In this discussion, we define *content analysis* as the *study of the meaning of verbal communication*. The material studied may be either written or spoken. Generally, the researcher studies written or recorded material as a matter of convenience, but one could study speeches or conversations as they occur if accuracy could be maintained. Some definitions do not restrict content analysis to verbal material but include the analysis of some kinds of nonverbal data. We will not discuss nonverbal material, because we believe that it can best be handled by observational or unobtrusive approaches (see Unobtrusive Measures further on in this chapter).

Essentially, the researcher who selects content analysis as the mode of data collection does so because it fits the research question and the kind of data that is available. Generally, in these cases, a researcher will be concerned with ideas or attitudes rather than with knowledge, performance, behaviors, or mental states. Suppose that a researcher is interested in the attitudes of legislators toward public-welfare legislation. One way of proceeding would be for the researcher to ask the legislators about their attitudes using a questionnaire. The researcher might also consider doing in-depth interviews with the legislators. Suppose, however, that the researcher has reason to question the efficacy of these approaches. For instance, the researcher might believe that the legislators in his state are being very careful in what they say in interviews in an election year, or suppose that the researcher has found out that it is the custom of a number of legislators have assistants reply to written inquiries. Therefore, the researcher cannot be sure that the legislators will even be the ones who respond. In such circumstances, the researcher may conclude that some other way is needed to try to discover what the legislators think about pending welfare legislation. If it is possible to obtain copies of the legislators' speeches on a variety of occasions, then content analysis offers an alternative data-gathering approach. Actually, there are a number of ways in which the researcher might proceed to do content analysis of the legislators' speeches. The choice of approaches will be dictated by the way the research question is stated.

First, if the researcher wants to measure whether the legislators are hostile to public welfare, it would be appropriate to simply count the number of times that hostile words are used in describing public welfare. Of course, the researcher must specify in advance what he or she is looking for and what constitutes hostile language. The assumption here is that the higher the count of hostile words, the more hostile the legislator. Of course, hostility is probably relative to events going on in the world. A given set of legislators may be more hostile at one time than another. If a researcher had counted the use of hostile words from a sample of speeches for several years and then compared the level of hostility with the size of appropriations for public welfare, it might be possible to see a relationship between the two. That is, if the higher the hostility the lower the appropriation, then the researcher could make some predictions about the likelihood of the passage of a particular appropriation by sampling the number of hostile symbols used in the current legislative session. If content analysis of the speeches suggested to consumers of this research that a given year would be a bad one, they might delay the introduction of legislation until the climate was more conducive to its passage.

Content analysis is not always a simple matter of making a count of the occurrence of certain words. It is also possible to count ideas, regardless of the actual words used. Again, the careful researcher specifies in advance the rules of the game. A researcher might want to know the attitudes of, for example, newspaper editors on mental health legislation. Therefore, the researcher would look at appropriate editorials to see how frequently positive ideas toward mental health are expressed. It is not necessary that the editor use the same words all of the time, but it is essential to set up rules in the research plan about what a "positive idea" would be.

It is further possible to code statements in some kind of systematic approach. For example, a researcher might devise a very simple ordinal scale:

1 = ignorant of mental health issues
2 = slightly knowledgeable about mental health
3 = fairly knowledgeable about mental health
4 = sophisticated about mental health

The researcher might then read a number of statements made by public figures in a community and use this kind of rating scale either to compare the knowledge level of mental health in one set of people to another or to compare one set of people over time, taking sample measurements over a period of months or even years. Again, it should be clear that the researcher is obliged to define these categories operationally in a way that allows classification. Certain operational cues need to be developed—for example, to differentiate between "slightly knowledgeable" and "fairly knowledgeable."

In addition to a simple count of words or ideas, then, coding schemes (not unlike those used in observational data gathering) can be developed that may or may not use rating scales. The object of these kinds of exercises is to extract the ideas and attitudes of a person (or a group of people) by sorting and evaluating the verbal symbols that they use to express themselves. Social workers should not find this research technique difficult to understand, because it is analogous to the diagnostic analysis of a client's statements for their symbolic meaning. The difference is that content analysis is a more formalized approach, usually involving the statements of many people over time. The problem is similar: What do people really mean by what they say (or write), and what attitudes are revealed by the symbols they use?

The sociologists have probably done the most with this technique. The classic study that first gave stature (though not without controversy) to content analysis was W. I. Thomas and Florian Znaniecki's *The Polish Peasant in Europe and America,* which was published right after World War I. Thomas and Znaniecki studied the adaptation of rural farm people to modern industrial urban society by analyzing the letters and diaries of Polish immigrants. Letters and diaries are not public statements and are not generally available to social work researchers. Further, permission to use materials must be obtained in order to avoid an unwarranted invasion of privacy. An example of the use of content analysis in social work is found in Merlin Taber and Iris Shapiro's study of a few years ago.[1] Taber and Shapiro looked at the professional literature in social work in an attempt to see if a distinct knowledge base was forming that had more empirical content than was true of early articles, which were more personal and anecdotal in their content. In other words, the question at issue was whether social work was developing conceptual and verifiable knowledge or merely gathering the practice wisdom of a few experienced practitioners. They used a systematic sample of some ingenuity. They first selected the first article of the first issue of the first year of publication in a given journal. They next selected the second article of the second issue of the second year, the third article of the third issue of the third year, and so on. When they got to the last article in a given issue, they started over. They surveyed three journals and amassed 124 articles over a fifty-year period. Then they measured the content of the articles by counting the amount of column-inches devoted to empirical material. They defined *empirical material* as "statements based on experience of observation or data pertaining to or founded on experiment." Excluded were statements of belief, as well as recommendations to take some kind of action. The researchers also counted and classified the types of references used in the articles. Taber and Shapiro found an increase in material that was verifiable and an increase in the development of generalized concepts, and they discovered a decrease in the kind of personalized, anecdotal material that had characterized earlier articles. The researchers concluded that social work was developing more of an empirical knowledge base and was depending less on isolated and nongeneralizable bits of practice wisdom.

Occasionally, researchers make studies of case records using content analysis. Unfortunately, these are usually done for teaching purposes and are seldom published. Theoretically, though, social work researchers could do more of these studies than they do. There are, of course, some ethical issues involved. The use of material from case records must be handled in such a way that the privacy of the client is fully protected. Some agencies ask clients to release information in their case records for research purposes as a matter of routine. Of course, the agency guarantees anonymity to the clients.

Agency records can be a fruitful source of data. If there is anything that a social agency has in abundance, it is records! It is easy for researchers to use them because they do not have to travel around interviewing individuals. Further, a researcher can usually gain access to agency records easier than he or she could solicit the cooperation of a large number of clients. Most agencies will allow bona fide researchers to use their records as long as there is no risk to the clientele. Large agencies that receive federal funds for any kind of research have review processes that guard against the misuse of information.

Although there are advantages to using agency records, there are dis-advantages, too. First of all, most agencies' records are collected for clin-ical or administrative use. Consequently, they may not have the data that a researcher would want. The researcher may have to strike some compro-mise with accuracy and may have to do some guesswork about what really occurred. A researcher may, for example, be interested in the content of a record with relevance to the words used to describe a particular symp-tom. The person who did the recording ten years ago would have had no idea that someone would be looking for a specific idea or phrase ten years later. Consequently, the researcher is left with the task of trying to under-stand a definition of a situation that may or may not fall into the research frame of reference. Further, records may have gaps; whole years have been missing in some agency records. A researcher faced with this problem may find it difficult to collect a genuinely representative sample and may have to settle for what is available, weakening the validity of the research.

Despite these problems, social workers can glean a good bit from agency records, if they will bring some wit and imagination to the research task. Because content analysis is, frankly, a little "dirty" (imprecise and relatively poorly structured), it probably is limited to exploratory studies, although some good descriptive studies ought to be possible.

Other Agency Records

Researchers can also do studies using other kinds of agency records. Al-though these studies are not necessarily examples of content analysis, we include them here as a matter of convenience. For example, one might study the funding pattern of an agency using old financial statements. Suppose that one was interested in the changing pattern of United Way support over time. He or she might study the percentage of the budget from United Way sources (as compared with endowments, contributions, and fees) at, say, ten-year intervals. Again, such research has the same strengths and weaknesses noted above in the discussion of case records. The clever researcher may, with the use of flair and imagination, produce useful studies using the various kinds of records and papers that are avail-able. The suggested readings at the end of this chapter include some resources that one might use in studies of this sort.

Projective Tests

Few social work researchers use projective tests. Most of them have been developed by psychologists and social psychologists. Projective testing is based on the notion that what a subject does with test materials reveals something about the subject independent of his or her willingness to reveal it. Generally, these tests are designed to reveal attitudes, beliefs, opinions, psychological states, or traits. The tests with which social workers are most familiar are those aimed at psychological states and traits. They are used for diagnostic purposes in medical, mental health, and child development settings and are generally administered and interpreted by clinical psychologists. Although many of these tests have been developed for diagnostic purposes, a good number of them are used in psychological or social psychological research. Other projective tests have their primary use in product research.

Projective tests generally do not have a great deal of structure. That is, they usually contain no set questions, no "correct" answers, and no one way of doing the tasks that are to be performed. Instead, the person administering the test is interested in the structure that the subject brings to the test situation. The idea is that the subject will project his or her feelings or attitudes into the test situation. In theory, the purpose of the test is concealed from the subject. In practice, however, many (if not most) people have heard just enough about the common projective tests to arrive at the conclusion that they are being given the test to find out whether they are "crazy." Experts are of a mixed mind about whether the general knowledge of such tests is enough to invalidate their use. It is common for examiners to ascribe a purpose to the test other than the true one in order to disguise the purpose, but this will not always work today.

The Rorschach Inkblot Test is probably the most familiar projective test. The Rorschach turns up on television and in motion pictures with enough frequency that it is fair to say that most people have a vague notion of what it is designed to do. The test consists of ten cards with highly colorful patterns that look like someone has done a design on one half of the card in wet ink and then folded it in half, thus creating a mirror image on the other half of the card. The subject is asked to identify what he or she sees in the "inkblot." Over time, researchers have gathered responses from enough people to provide norms to which any given subject may be compared. Interpretation of the responses is a highly complex task, and it is clearly not for the beginner. A description of the technical aspects of this approach is not necessary in a beginning research text. Those who wish to explore the Rorschach further may want to consult the Cronbach reference given at the end of the chapter.

Another test that has historically been used in mental health settings is the Thematic Apperception Test (TAT), which consists of twenty pictures. The subject is asked to tell a story about each picture used. (It is not necessary to use them all.) This test is so wide open that the subject may explore almost anything through the medium of the test. The test requires two one-hour sessions, and the examiner may use the cards selectively.

Cronbach notes that the Rorschach is a *stylistic* test, whereas the TAT is a *thematic* test.[2] A stylistic test is supposed to reveal the subject's style of handling a problem, whereas a thematic test concentrates on the contents of the subject's thoughts and emotions. Cronbach also classifies sentence-completion tests (such as, "The thing I like best about myself is ——.") and doll play as thematic tests. Social workers are usually not trained in the use of these (or other) personality tests. Even in the hands of experts, no projective test is a foolproof diagnostic tool. It is possible for a person who is operating well in everyday life to look like a psychological "mess" on a projective test. It is also possible to fail to pick up persons with real psychological problems using these tests. This does not mean that the tests are useless; it *does* mean that they must be interpreted by highly skilled people who will exercise caution in their use. Results also must be checked by clinical observation. Projective tests may be best used as part of an overall workup—the basis for a working hypothesis about a patient.

Although social workers are unlikely to administer the tests used most frequently by psychologists in the clinic or laboratory, they may use projective techniques in some applications. Two students of one of the authors of this book once did an exploratory study that dealt with the question of whether or not social workers were less inclined than others to stereotype the mentally ill. They selected eight pictures. Four of the pictures were of people who had been diagnosed as mentally ill, but who looked quite ordinary in the picture. The other four pictures were of people who had never been diagnosed as mentally ill, but who did look unusual or even bizarre in these particular pictures. They showed the pictures to social work students and to a comparison group of arts-and-sciences students. They told the subjects that this test measured their ability to identify symptoms from nonverbal stimuli. This gave the test some semblance of logic, and the statement was not that far from the truth. Fortunately for the egos of the researchers (who had hypothesized that social work students would not stereotype), the arts-and-sciences students identified those who looked unusual as the mentally ill more often than did the social work students.

No great psychological theory was being tested here, nor could the results be regarded as anything but suggestive. However, the example shows that projective methods are useful in exploring attitudes and values.

As we mentioned earlier, some product research also uses a projective approach. A researcher might ask, "Describe the kind of person who enjoys X brand instant coffee." The point is to find out if the advertising has created a certain image in the minds of the consumer. If the subject describes the kind of consumer that the advertising is aiming at, the agency will believe that its sales campaign is effective. If a respondent answers that drinking X brand coffee is a lot like kissing a relative, then the manufacturer may conclude that the coffee advertising is projecting a dull and unexciting image.

As one might suspect, the validity of projective tests is very hard to establish. Possibly, the best method is to compare the conclusions reached by the interpreter with the reality of the subject's life. After all, this approach to data gathering is extremely wide open and allows the subject a great deal of freedom to roam. Interpretation is highly complex for most projective tests, and examiners often disagree on the meaning of a given subject's responses. Further, projective tests, despite their wide use, are not as good as clinical interviews in determining whether or not a person needs treatment. Why then should anyone bother to keep working with them? There are three fairly persuasive reasons for trying to develop valid and reliable projective tests:[3]

1. The very fact that these tests are wide open can be an advantage in that subjects may reveal more on such a test than they would or could in responses to predetermined questions.
2. Some subjects may not be able to reveal their feelings and attitudes directly because they are not aware of them. If the projective technique worked, it would allow a researcher to find out a subject's attitude when the even subject didn't know what it was (even if he or she were willing to reveal it).
3. Some kinds of attitudes may be upsetting to the subject. Consequently, the subject may find it simply too difficult to discuss some material. A good projective test would make it easier for such a subject to respond, because there would be no direct reference to painful material.

Although there are problems in using projective techniques, social work researchers should continue to try to devise useful ones, at least for exploratory studies. The potential, as indicated in the previous paragraph, makes the attempt worthwhile. The researcher does need to be aware of the ethical issues in using projective tests. By their very nature, deception is usually involved. Further, there is something of "Big Brother" in the notion that one's thoughts or mental states might be revealed whether or not one cares to reveal them. The ethics of the situation require that subjects be told as much as possible about the nature and purpose of the test. When it is fairly clear that such briefing in advance would materially affect the test, it is incumbent on the researcher to debrief the subject following the test. Again, we must emphasize the tentative nature of projective testing and the need for caution in using this approach.

Unobtrusive Measures

The discussion of research design in Chapter 4 made the point that data collection may be confounded by reactivity (the effect of the testing itself on the subject). Because of this possibility, many researchers have tried to use unobtrusive data-gathering approaches—that is, tests that do not intrude on the subject's awareness. Eugene J. Webb and his associates have made a convincing—and a highly interesting—case for using nonreactive approaches in a book that is regarded as a classic on the subject.[4] Actually, we have already discussed an unobtrusive or nonreactive technique in this chapter. Content analysis is an unobtrusive technique. It is useful, however, to add some direct comments and a few fresh points about the unobtrusive approach.

Webb and his associates make a number of important points about the reactivity of questionnaires and interviews. They point out that questionnaires and interviews create an artificial situation, which may reduce the dependability of the data. After all, most people go about their business without reflecting, in response to a researcher, on what they do. When human activity is being examined, it may well change. Further, Webb and his associates say most interviews and questionnaires are used alone. They argue that interviews and questionnaires are not infallible and that it would be better if multiple attempts were made at measurement: "If a proposition can survive the onslaught of a series of imperfect measures, with all their irrelevant error, confidence should be placed in it."[5] Or, to put it another way, if there is no one "clean" (fully valid and reliable) measure, then it is more convincing if there is agreement among several "dirty" (imperfect) measures. Webb and his associates suggest that researchers support data gained from the more traditional measures with content analysis of records, tabulations of figures gleaned from actuarial material (birth, marriage, and death records), studies of political and judicial material (voting records, court decisions), content analysis of mass-media publications and personal documents, concealed observations, and several other unusual approaches to idiosyncratic records. As an illustration of what Webb and his associates are advocating, consider a researcher who is interested in the general question of respect for authority. Because this is a complicated question, the researcher recognizes the need to start with a fairly specific and straightforward example. If this study shows promise, the researcher will move on to more complex situations. The researcher decides to approach the question specifically by studying the attitudes of college students toward university parking regulations. The researcher might construct a questionnaire that asks a series of questions designed to reveal how students regard the parking situation and the rules that govern parking. This is an imperfect approach. Students may tell the researcher just what he or she wants to hear. Or they may state extreme attitudes that do not reflect their real tendencies to act. The researcher who takes Webb and his associates' advice to heart will not stop at this point but will seek additional evidence. For example, the researcher may gain access to the records of parking violations in order to look at enforcement patterns. Further, the researcher may do a content analysis of editorials and letters to the editor in the university newspaper that concern parking rules. Still further, the researcher may spend several days observing where students actually leave their cars. Having done all of this, the researcher will look for coherence among all these various data-gathering approaches. If, for instance, it turns out that the questionnaire suggests that students are extremely hostile toward the regulations, the arrest records show frequent and repeated violations, the newspaper material regularly uses perjorative words to describe the parking situation, and students actually park in defiance of the regulations, the researcher may conclude that students do not automatically respect authority but, instead, challenge it openly when it conflicts with certain other values. From this study and others done in different situations, a researcher might make a contribution to some theory on the limits of authority or a related topic.

Social work researchers, as well as sociologists and psychologists, should seriously consider the use of a multiple approach to data gathering. Webb and his associates published their book over fifteen years ago. Still, most research studies in the social sciences use only one measure of the characteristic or attribute under study.

One aspect of Webb and his associates' work was not covered in the discussion above. This aspect has proven to be extremely novel and provocative in social science, and it may be especially profitable for social work researchers. This is what Webb and his associates call "physical traces." A good bit of archaeological research is done by analyzing artifacts —what people have left behind them. The same idea is employed here, although the time lapse is usually different. Webb and his associates cite a number of examples from general social science. A library that wishes to know how popular certain titles are might check the number of times that they have been checked out. However, because a book can be checked out without being read, this is an imperfect measure. Therefore, a researcher might verify the impression gained from this measure by actually checking the condition of the books being studied. If the books are checked out *and* well used, the library has a better case that they have been read.

Suppose that a social work researcher is interested in the attitudes of a group of clients toward group treatment. One approach would obviously be to design an interview guide or a questionnaire that contains items designed to elicit the clients' attitudes. As a further check, the researcher might look at a trace measure. For instance, how do the clients treat the group meeting room? Do they throw cigarette butts on the floor? Do they leave sandwich wrappers behind? Or do they take pride in the appearance of the room and clean up carefully after themselves? A case can be made for the notion that creating a mess in the therapy room suggests a negative attitude toward the therapeutic situation. Of course, a clinician might suggest other unobtrusive measures—observation of the group by judges, keeping track of attendance (frequent absence would suggest a negative attitude), or counting the total number of minutes group members are late for group meetings (based on the notion that lateness indicates a negative attitude toward the therapeutic situation).

Some unobtrusive measures have ethical dimensions, as we have discussed. The concealed-observer situation and the use of case records are good examples. The trace measure presents few ethical questions. Some researchers have done very novel trace studies. Several studies have been done on garbage. For instance, students at the University of Arizona have been studying the eating habits of Americans by keeping track of what people throw away.[6] The researchers, who are students in anthropology, have found that about 15 percent of all food purchased is wasted, that the mix of foods eaten is similar for people from all income levels, and that the consumption of convenience foods is increasing despite their higher cost. The most interesting finding is that sorting out the garbage proved to be more reliable than personal interviews in finding the consumption levels of various products. The reader should note here that the students used two measures—interviews and a trace measure. Certainly the inventive and creative social work researcher should be alert to the novel possibilities available for data collection using unobtrusive measures. Such measures can support—or challenge—the more traditional approaches.

Situational Tests

The situational test involves the use of a simulated situation to provide the occasion to gather data. The subject is generally asked to demonstrate a skill or to reveal an attitude in a lifelike situation. This is basically an observational approach to data gathering. We give it separate discussion (as was true of the unobtrusive measures) for emphasis. Although social work researchers have made sparing use of this technique, other social researchers have done some very interesting things with it. Some have suggested to us that the field experience course is a kind of situational test. This is really not so. Field experience is best seen as an apprenticeship-like situation or as experiential learning. It is not primarily a test situation. Further, the clients are real clients. A situational test uses a simulated situation using lifelike elements under the control of the researcher. The behavior of real clients is not standardized and is clearly not under anyone's control.

The lack of use of situational testing is somewhat amazing, given that social workers learn a great many skills that would seem to call for such an approach. It seems reasonable to assume that if one is being trained in the use of a skill, then a controlled test of that skill ought to be a good evaluative tool. Despite the logic of this argument, most social work treatment courses use paper-and-pencil tests as the final examination. Even in research applications, the behavior of the social worker is seldom an issue; it is more usual to look at client behavior. On the assumption that more knowledge will encourage the use of situational testing in both research and evaluation, some special treatment needs to be given this approach to data collection.

Early forerunners of the situational test were constructed during World War II as a means of judging the competence of espionage agents of the Office of Strategic Services, the predecessor of the CIA.[7] The men and women who had been chosen to serve in the OSS came from a variety of backgrounds. The job of the testing staff was to estimate how well they would do the various jobs to which they might be assigned by OSS. Although some women were recruited, apparently it was only the men who were sent overseas. There is no mention of any women in the description of the test situations.

To start with, none of the psychologists, sociologists, and psychiatrists who were to do the testing had extensive knowledge of the work the candidates really had to do in Europe. Few of the testing staff had been under fire, and none had been in espionage work themselves. Yet they had to assess the fitness of about 300 men and women a month to perform assignments, the exact natures of which were not very clear to anybody.

To carry out this difficult task, the testing staff used situational tests that *appeared* to them to be indicative of *some* skills that they *assumed* to be of use in various tasks having something to do with espionage. The vagueness of this last statement is intended to convey the vagueness of the problem!

The staff, although they were from diverse theoretical backgrounds, followed a *Gestalt,* or holistic, approach to assessment. This meant that the staff tried to arrive at conclusions about the candidates' personalities as a whole by putting together a variety of measures and impressions. The staff evolved a number of steps for the evaluational process. First, they analyzed the job that each candidate was expected to do. Second, they listed all the personality characteristics identified with success or failure and then selected the personality variables that could be measured. Next, they designed rating scales of each personality variable and an overall rating scale that encompassed all the personality ratings. Then, the assessment staff designed or selected a variety of assessment procedures. These procedures included interviews, observations, questionnaires, and individual and group situational tests. Again, note the use of multiple measures. The testers made a personality formulation of each candidate, based on a three-and-one-half-day testing period. This material was then incorporated into a nontechnical sketch of each candidate that could be understood by the military. Each candidate was then "staffed" by the evaluators as a final check. The staff also constantly reviewed their own appraisal system, recognizing its imperfections.

Several of the situational tests have acquired a certain amount of fame and have appeared in a number of books on testing. Probably the most famous—or infamous—is the "construction problem," used at the main testing site in Virginia. The candidate would be given two "helpers" who were in fact stooges who would show no initiative and who played definitely unhelpful roles. The point was to see if the candidate would assume leadership, remain emotionally stable, control his frustration, and show energy and initiative. The ability to get along with coworkers was also rated. The candidate was told that he was to act as foreman and to direct the helpers, but he was *not* told that the helpers had stylized obstructionist roles to play. One helper was a passive, unimaginative worker, whereas the other was an aggressive, impractical "wise guy." The helpers were instructed to follow all explicit directions, but they were also instructed to be critical, hypersensitive, and generally annoying. The testers wanted the candidate to lead the men calmly by explaining what he wanted done, delegating specific tasks, and treating the helpers with dignity while tolerating their harassment. The key desired behavior was identified as "controlled and sensible action." This was made extremely difficult by the helpers' behavior, and on one occasion, one of the candidates actually hit one of the helpers!

When all of the projective tests, questionnaires, interviews, and observations were completed, the candidates were rated on all of the variables that the staff had determined were important. Of course, as we pointed out above, the staff really could not be sure precisely what behavior was really important, because they had little first-hand knowledge or experience to guide them in what qualities or behavior made for a good espionage agent. Although a great deal of fiction had been written about spies, hard data on real spying was not readily available. The staff had to go pretty much on common sense. They looked for physically and mentally healthy people who were adaptable, creative, sensitive, and able to operate independently. They also looked for people who demonstrated certain skills believed to be useful—map reading, propaganda skills, leadership, interviewing skills, and the like.

How effective was the assessment? The answers the OSS staff found are mixed. Overseas staff and commanders in the field rated the actual effectiveness of the candidates. There was also some appraisal of returnees. These techniques had a number of shortcomings, a fact noted by the OSS assessment staff. Further, a number of men did not come back. The men appraised exhibited low correlations between the initial assessments and the appraisals made of their actual task performance. However, despite the somewhat disappointing results, the staff felt that their system was better than the one it replaced and that it held promise. Probably the most hopeful note is that the staff believed that if they had known in advance the descriptions of actual jobs in detail and the kind of personnel that were required, realistic assessment would have been possible, given time and the staff to do the task. Actually, too, the war ended just as the staff had ironed out the major "bugs."

Unfortunately, situational testing has not been as fruitfully pursued as it might have been. Cronbach concludes that for the most part, situational techniques have been converted from *testing* procedures to *training* procedures, generally taking the form of simulations or games.[8] In the general social welfare area, for example, there is the "Hampshire 'In'-Basket Test." [9] In this simulation, the trainee assumes the role of a director of a community center. Sufficient background information permits the individual to get the feel of the role. The participant is then given the contents of a hypothetical "in" basket. The ten items in the basket include a request from the police chief to allow the use of an undercover officer as a plant in the youth program so that he can spot drug pushers, a letter from the mayor asking if his wife can be put on the advisory board, and a letter from a woman who is angry because her granddaughter has been impregnated by a member of the staff. The participant is given 90 minutes to respond to the ten items. The object is to examine the management principles embodied in the ten issues represented by the items. Following the test, discussions are held with the participants. These discussions are primarily aimed at connecting the exercises to management problems in the participants' home agencies.

Although simulations are popular training tools, it is unfortunate that the research possibilities of situational testing have been largely overlooked. Perhaps in the near future, an enterprising social work researcher will take a fresh look at this approach, particularly as it pertains to research in the use of certain skills. Ethical problems are minimized, because the test situation is usually an obvious simulation. Of course, subjects would have to give their informed consent and, if there were deceptions, would have to be debriefed.

Key Terms

content analysis	multiple measures
"dirty" versus "clean" measures	trace measures
projective test	situational test
unobtrusive measures	reactivity

References

1. Merlin Taber and Iris Shapiro, "Social Work and its Knowledge Base: A Content Analysis of the Periodical Literature." *Social Work* 10, no. 4 (October 1965), pp. 100–106.
2. Lee J. Cronbach, *Essentials of Psychological Testing*, 3rd ed. (New York: Harper & Row, 1970), p. 651.
3. Claire Selltiz, Lawrence S. Wrightsman, and Stuart W. Cook, *Research Methods in Social Relations*, 3rd ed. (New York: Holt, Rinehart and Winston, 1976), pp. 337–338.
4. Eugene J. Webb and others, *Unobtrusive Measures: Nonreactive Research in the Social Sciences* (Chicago: Rand McNally & Co., 1966).
5. Ibid., p. 3.
6. Reported in *Parade,* September 9, 1979.
7. The OSS Assessment Staff, *Assessment of Men* (New York: Rinehart & Company, 1948).
8. Cronbach, *op. cit.,* p. 644.
9. J. William Pfeiffer and John E. Jones, eds., *A Handbook of Structured Experiences for Human Relations Training*, vol. 2, rev. ed. (San Diego: University Associates, 1974), pp. 41–57.

Questions for Discussion

1. Explore the similarities and differences between content analysis and diagnostic study.
2. Name two social work uses of content analysis not mentioned in this chapter.
3. Summarize the strengths and weaknesses of the projective test.
4. Should a person be treated for problems that are indicated by a projective test when there are no clinical symptoms?
5. What are the advantages of multiple measurements in data collection?
6. List some examples of social work research in which an unobtrusive approach might work best.
7. Give additional examples of the trace measure.
8. Do you agree with the authors' contention that situational testing could be very valuable in social work? What problems would need attention in using a situational test?

Exercises

1. Devise a simple plan for the content analysis of a series of editorials in your college newspaper. It is easiest if you choose editorials on some controversial issue.

2. Discuss with a clinical psychologist the use of projective tests. Does he or she use the tests for research as well as diagnosis? How accurate does the psychologist find the tests in diagnosing patients?

3. Construct a simple unobtrusive study of some behavior in your student union or residence hall. Observe the proper ethical constraints.

4. Design a situational test that will measure interviewing skills.

5. Organize a group discussion of the ethical problems presented by the data-collection procedures discussed in this chapter.

For Further Reading

Morton L. Arkava and Mark Snow. *Psychological Tests and Social Work Practice*. Springfield, Illinois: Charles C. Thomas, 1978. This brief but useful survey of the common psychological tests likely to be encountered by the social worker is especially useful for those who work in hospitals, clinics, schools, and child welfare.

John Markoff, Gilbert Shapiro, and Sasha R. Weitman. "Toward the Integration of Content Analysis." In David R. Heise, ed., *Sociological Methodology 1975*. San Francisco: Jossey-Bass, 1974. This is a very useful discussion of content analysis and the variety of applications that are possible.

Eugene J. Webb, Donald T. Campbell, Richard D. Schwarts, and Lee Sechrest. *Unobtrusive Measures: Nonreactive Research in the Social Sciences*. Chicago: Rand McNally & Company, 1966. This delightful yet profound book discusses a whole range of non-reactive measures and should be a part of any serious researcher's library.

Lee J. Cronbach. *Essentials of Psychological Testing*, 3rd ed. New York: Harper & Row, 1970. Cronbach's invaluable guide to psychological testing includes the discussion of projective, situational, and performance tests.

9

Sampling

Broadly conceived, the research process involves (1) the systematic description of the characteristics and behaviors of people or things and (2) the use of the information obtained to predict future characteristics and behaviors. The researcher selects the time period within which a study will occur, the variables or dimensions upon which observations will be made, and the subjects who will be observed. *Sampling,* or selecting a part of a whole, is involved in each of these decisions. The researcher, guided by the principles of research design, selects some of all possible time periods within which to make observations. Similarly, the researcher, guided by a conceptual framework, selects some of all possible variables to use in a given study. Finally, the researcher, again guided by the conceptual framework, selects only some of all possible subjects to observe.

Although sampling is inextricably intertwined with all phases of the research process, the use of this term is typically restricted to the processes involved in selecting subjects to observe. We will follow this convention in this text, but you should remember that many of the principles presented in this chapter have applicability to other components of the research process.

An integral part of the research design of any study is the specification of the appropriate unit of analysis. Does the research project focus on studying communities, agencies, clients, schools, families, or some other type of unit? Having specified the unit of analysis, the researcher must consider two other issues: How many units should be studied, and how should these units be selected? The answer to these two questions involves the definition of the population of concern, deciding whether it is necessary to study a part of that population or the entire population, and if the decision is to select a part, deciding how to select that part. The purpose of this chapter is to develop guidelines to aid the researcher in answering these questions.

The Unit of Analysis

The unit of analysis for a research project is that object or unit with the characteristics, attributes, or properties that are of primary concern. Within the context of a specific study, the unit of analysis is the answer to the question, "Who or what has the characteristics to be studied?" For example, in studying the effects of a natural disaster on community solidarity, the unit of analysis is "community." In this case, "natural disaster" and "solidarity" are variables used to describe communities. If, however, the purpose of the study is to determine the effects of a natural disaster on family solidarity, the unit of analysis is "family." Now, the variables "natural disaster" and "solidarity" are used to describe families.

Obviously, these two studies are different. In the first example, the effects of a natural disaster on community solidarity, the population of concern is the set of all communities, including both those that have and those that have not experienced natural disasters. (See Chapter 4 for a discussion of the use of control or contrast groups.) In the second example, the effects of a natural disaster on family solidarity, the population of concern is not the set of all communities, but rather the set of all families. Now the researcher's task is to identify all possible families, some of which have and others of which have not experienced a natural disaster. Thus, although the general topic of both studies is the same, the studies are very different. Further, the results of one of these studies may have no relationship to the results of the other.

As may be apparent from these examples, selecting the appropriate unit of analysis for a study is the same as specifying the type of unit *that should be studied*. Simply put, if the objective of a research project is to study the characteristics of clients, the researcher must gather information about clients, not communities, families, or some other objects. If, on the other hand, the purpose of a study is to examine the characteristics of social service agencies, the researcher must gather information about social service agencies, not communities or clients.

Although the principle that a study of a specific type of unit must involve gathering information about that unit may seem trivial, changing or confusing units of analysis is a common problem in research. In fact, the problem of inferring that the characteristics of a collective apply as well to the elements of the collective is so common that it has been given a special name, the *ecological fallacy*. The following two examples illustrate some of the problems encountered when the unit of analysis changes.

Suppose that a state welfare agency is evaluating the efficiency of county welfare offices. To accomplish this, the research team plans to rate each of three different components of each office on a scale from 1 to 3 (in which 1 means high and 3 means low efficiency). Hypothetical ratings for four different county welfare offices are presented in Table 9-1. These data indicate that the average evaluation for office A is superior to that of the remaining three offices. At the same time, the rating of at least one component of each of the other three offices is better than that of office A. Thus, if the evaluation of offices had been conducted in terms of one of the office components, office A would not have been rated first. These data illustrate a point more fully discussed in Chapter 11: The arithmetic mean does not provide information on the variability of scores.

The discrepancy in the results, depending on the unit of analysis selected, is even more apparent in the second example. Suppose that a state mental-health agency wishes to determine the availability of mental-health services throughout the state. One approach to this problem is to determine whether mental-health services are available within each county. On the basis of the data presented in Table 9-2, mental-health services are available in only 50 percent of the counties of the state. A second approach to this problem is to determine how many people live in counties in which mental-health services are available.

The data in Table 9-2 present a very different picture. Although mental-health services are available in only 50 percent of the counties, such services are placed in population centers so that 98.6 percent of the population (411,009 of 416,798) live in counties served by a mental-health center. Yet another approach to this problem would be to determine the ratio of the number of people in the entire state receiving mental-health services to the number desiring such services. The data from Table 9-2 show that 80.1 percent (3,929 of 4,907) of those seeking services within the state receive them. Thus, depending on the unit of analysis selected, we can estimate the coverage of the state in terms of the availability of mental

Table 9-1   Evaluation scores for four county welfare offices

| | County Welfare Offices | | | |
Unit Evaluated	A	B	C	D
Administration	2	1	3	3
Child Services	2	3	1	3
Adult Services	2	3	3	1
Total	6	7	7	7
Arithmetic Mean	2	2.3	2.3	2.3

**Table 9-2 Availability and demand for mental-health services
in four counties**

County	Service Available	Population	Number Desiring Service	Number Receiving Service
1	Yes	157,862	1,815	1,512
2	Yes	253,147	2,723	2,417
3	No	2,615	157	0
4	No	3,174	212	0
Total	2	416,798	4,907	3,929

health services to be 50 percent, 80.1 percent, or 98.6 percent. Clearly, depending on the unit of analysis selected, the results can vary substantially.

Populations

Although the unit of analysis serves to specify the type of unit that a given project will study, researchers further limit the objects or cases to be considered. For example, the researcher interested in studying clients does not attempt to study all clients of all agencies worldwide at all possible times. Rather, each study is limited to clients who possess other characteristics, such as residence in a particular community or association with a specific agency or type of agency during a given time period. Such restrictions serve to define the population of the study.

The population (some writers use the word *universe*) for a study refers to all of the subjects to which the results of a study are expected to apply. The term *population* in this context refers to two distinct but related concepts. In the narrow sense of the term, a population is defined by a rule or set of rules that allows the researcher to decide whether a given subject should be observed. This is similar to an operational definition of a concept. Given its similarity to operational definitions of concepts, we will call this method of defining a population the *operational definition of the population*.

The second meaning of the term *population* is much broader in scope, as is illustrated by the following example: Suppose that a researcher is interested in studying the types of information requested by clients of family-planning agencies. The researcher could limit the study to all of the clients of all of the family-planning agencies in a given state but believe that the results of the study would apply to clients of family-planning agencies in other states (see Figure 9-1). Thus, the population of concern is the set of clients of family-planning agencies, whereas the operational definition of the population is restricted to family-planning clients within a particular state. To distinguish it from the operational definition of the population, this second meaning of the term will be called the *conceptual definition of the population.*

It is important for the researcher and the reader of a research report to clearly distinguish between these two definitions of population. Strictly speaking, the results of a research project apply only to the subjects actually studied at the time they were studied. Although scientists hope that the results of a study done today will apply tomorrow, this will not necessarily be the case. In this case, for example, the development and popularization of a new method of birth control could make the study results obsolete very quickly. Without a thorough understanding of who or what was studied under what conditions, it is difficult to generalize to other subjects.

The Need for Sampling

Having conceptual and operational definitions of the population of the study, the researcher is now prepared to decide if it will be possible to study all elements in the population. Essentially, this decision is a question of economics. The researcher must decide what resources will be required to observe all of the population and then determine if sufficient resources are available to complete the task. *A researcher never considers*

Figure 9-1   **Relationship among unit of analysis, conceptual population, and operational population**

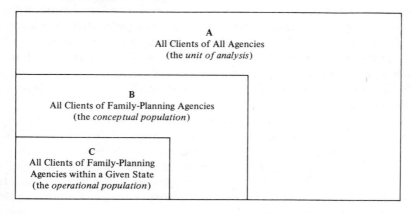

studying only a part of the population unless the costs of studying the entire population prohibit that option. Obviously, the best way to understand some attribute is to study everyone who possesses it. This is almost never possible.

Although the primary reason for not studying an entire population is the cost associated with such a project, costs appear in different forms. The following are some of the cost-related reasons that a researcher might use for not studying an entire population:

1. *Lack of time.* Suppose that a large organization, such as the National Retired Teacher's Association–American Association of Retired Persons, an organization with over 10 million members, learned that Congress was going to vote on changing Social Security retirement benefits in two weeks. Although the leadership of the organization might like to poll their membership on what the organization's position with respect to this legislation should be, there is not sufficient time to conduct such a poll, given the available staff.

2. *Lack of qualified observers.* Gathering information requires people who have the requisite skills to observe competently. Just as the chemist, physicist, and biologist employ trained observers in the laboratory to assist in observations, so do social scientists. Although, in some cases, many people might have most of the skills necessary to observe competently, in other types of projects this might not be the case. If, for example, a researcher were interested in classifying children in terms of speech defects, skilled observers would be needed. Further, as the number of observers required to complete a project increases, the complexity and size of the organization structure required to supervise the observation process also increase. It is possible for a researcher to monitor five observers in one locality, but a researcher who attempts to monitor fifty observers in twenty-six states with no assistance is either a fool or a glutton for punishment. In most organizational settings, the paperwork involved in documenting task performance and paying fifty qualified observers approaches a full-time job.

3. *Return for the effort is small.* In exploratory research (see Chapter 3), for example, the researcher may have only a vague expectation of what to anticipate. In such circumstances, it is difficult to justify the costs involved in studying the entire population.

The researcher who decides that it is not economically feasible or practical to study the entire population must then decide whether studying only part of the population will yield results that are worth the effort. The answer to this question is usually yes. However, in some situations (particularly if there is reason to believe that only one point of view will be presented), the response is no. If, for example, officials of a job-training program in a prison are interested in evaluating their program but were willing to allow the researcher to interview only "successful" prisoners, the results of the study would be extremely suspect. In this case, the researcher might well refuse to conduct the study. Further, if the researcher did conduct the study he or she would be ethically bound to indicate the nature of the restrictions placed on the data-collection effort.

What Is a Good Sample?

As defined at the beginning of this chapter, sampling refers to the process of observing only some of the subjects of a larger group of subjects. Usually, however, the researcher is less interested in the characteristics of the sample actually observed than in what can be learned about the whole population based on sample information. If, for example, a person is making soup and would like to know what it tastes like, the typical procedure is to sample. Based on the information obtained from the sample (perception of the soup's taste) the person may choose to add additional herbs and seasonings. This action assumes that the sample of the soup represents the whole pot. Thus, if the cook believes that the sample of soup needs salt, he or she will probably believe that the entire pot of soup also needs salt and will take remedial action.

As suggested by the preceding example, one basis for judging how good a sample is is to determine how well the sample represents the population from which it was selected. Samples vary in the degree to which they represent a population. Those that are very similar to the population from which they were selected are called *representative* samples, whereas those that differ substantially from the population from which they were selected are called *biased* samples.

Although researchers usually want samples that are representative of populations, using the criterion of representativeness for assessing how good a sample is leads to some interesting problems. The only way to determine if a sample truly represents a population is to know the characteristics of the population from which it was drawn. For example, in the case of the soup, the only way to determine if all of the soup needs salt (in which case we would say that the sample is representative) is to taste all of the soup. At the end of this process, the researcher can definitively indicate the degree to which the sample was representative of the population, but the question is moot because the soup is gone. If, as in this case, sampling involves destroying the product, but the only way to know whether the sample represents the population is to study the population, then the researcher has a dilemma. Essentially, although the researcher in this case would like to know how representative a sample is, he or she has no meaningful way of making such a determination.

Situations in which the subject is destroyed by the observation process do not occur in social research. This does not mean, however, that the researcher will have an easy time demonstrating that the sample selected is representative of the population from which it was chosen. Suppose, for example, that a state welfare office decided to determine the nutritional status of all clients receiving services from all of the local agencies under its jurisdiction. Because the cost and time involved in studying all clients are prohibitive, the agency decides to sample clients. After completing the data-collection phase of the project, the investigators decide that they would like to see how representative their sample is. Unfortunately, to determine the representativeness of the sample, the researchers need to know about the state of nutrition in the population from which they were sampling, the very information that was too costly and time-consuming to gather in the first place. Suppose, on the other hand, they know the nutritional status of all clients in their population from another study. Now, although it is possible to determine if the sample is representative, one must wonder why they conducted the study. If the nutritional status of clients is already known, it is somewhat silly to determine the nutritional status of a sample of clients. Consequently, although a "good" sample is one that is representative of the population from which it is selected, there is usually no meaningful way of determining whether a sample is actually representative of a population.

A second basis for judging how good a sample is is its size. A sample large enough that the researcher can conduct the study is called an *adequate sample*. To determine if a sample of a specific size will be adequate can be a complicated process involving a knowledge of statistics. The factors influencing this decision, however, are relatively simple:

1. *The homogeneity of the population.* Returning to the case of the soup tester, we might note that (after stirring) the soup is considered to be homogeneous. Because each spoonful of soup is expected to be the same as any other spoonful, a very small sample, such as one spoonful, may be adequate. If, on the other hand, the population is not homogeneous, the sample must be much larger before it is considered adequate. Although people are not soup, the same principle applies. The researcher desiring to study clients of social service agencies is interested in a population more diverse than is the researcher desiring to study clients of family-planning clinics. Thus, the researcher in the first study will probably want a larger sample than the researcher in the second study.

2. *The study design.* If a researcher is interested in simultaneously determining the effects of sex, marital status, ethnicity, and family size on
clients' rating of the services of a family-planning clinic, the sample
should probably be larger than if the researcher is interested in determining only the effects of marital status on such a rating. This factor is similar
to the first, but there is an important difference. In this case, the researcher
creates diversity in the population by selecting many variables to study.
On the other hand, the researcher who chooses to focus on only selected
attributes (for example, only females with exactly one child) can make
the population more homogeneous.

3. *The types of conclusions that the researcher would like to draw.*
In general, the more precise researchers desire to be in the statements they
make about a population, the larger their sample must be. If, for example,
a researcher is interested in whether males differ from females in their
propensity to seek treatment for venereal disease, the sample need not be
very large. If, on the other hand, the researcher would like to estimate the
exact differences in the likelihood that males and females would seek treatment, the sample size must be much larger.

4. *The size of the population itself.* A sample of ten from a population of twenty cases is large, whereas a sample of ten from a population of
200,000 cases is small. In general, the larger the population is, the larger
the sample must be before it is considered adequate.

Although it is easy to list the factors that must be considered in deciding how large a sample should be, it is difficult to answer the specific question, "How large should the sample be?" The best answer (and perhaps the
only relevant answer) is that a sample should be large enough to convince
others that it is adequate. This, of course, is not a good answer unless the
researcher knows both who is going to read the project report and how
they think sample size influences study results. A second answer, one that
is also not very helpful, is "As large as possible." A third answer, the one
usually presented in texts devoted solely to the topic of sampling, involves
the process of making statistical inferences. Although this final answer is
mathematically elegant, it is actually of quite limited utility, a point that
we develop in the next section of this chapter.

Sampling Procedures

Researchers, having reached the decision that they cannot study the entire
population, are ready to consider the bewildering array of sampling procedures that they can use. As with all other phases of the research process,

a thorough understanding of the objectives of the study will be helpful in the process of selecting an appropriate sampling procedure. Also, because the costs associated with different sampling procedures vary, a knowledge of the resources available for selecting a sample is important. Finally, a knowledge of statistics can be helpful in making some decisions.

In general, sampling procedures or processes are divided into two types: probability sampling methods and nonprobability sampling methods. A *probability sampling method* is so named because the researcher using this general method will be able to calculate the chance that any given case will be selected prior to beginning the sampling process. Suppose, for example, each of ten people writes his or her name on a 3″ x 5″ card, and all ten cards are shuffled. In this case, the chance that any given person's name will be on the first card chosen is one in ten. Thus, prior to selecting a sample of one from these ten people, the researcher knows that the probability of selecting any specific individual is one in ten. A *nonprobability sample* is one in which such prior calculations are not possible.

Researchers usually prefer probability sampling methods to nonprobability sampling methods for the following reasons:

1. Because the chance of being selected to participate in a study is determined by an impersonal process, most readers of the research report would accept that the researcher did not attempt to influence the results by selecting only those cases that were favorable to the hypotheses being tested. This is less clear with nonprobability samples in which the researcher often has discretion in who will be selected.
2. A probability sample of a given size is usually more representative of the population than a nonprobability sample of the same size.
3. With probability samples it is possible to estimate how likely it is that a sample is biased by using statistics, something that is not possible with nonprobability samples. These final two reasons are important, however, only when the operational and conceptual definitions of the population of concern are the same.

Nonprobability samples are used instead of probability samples for the following reasons:

1. It is usually less expensive to use nonprobability sampling procedures than probability sampling procedures. If the researcher has an extremely small budget, reducing the costs of data collection by selecting a nonprobability sampling method can be a very attractive alternative.
2. The purpose of a study sometimes dictates that a nonprobability sample would be more appropriate. Someone interested in understanding the decision-making process of a community would, in all likelihood, reach his or her objectives more quickly by interviewing key leaders

than by interviewing a probability sample of community residents. Similarly, the researcher who wants to understand the characteristics of a specific neighborhood might benefit from questioning long-term residents, rather than a probability sample of residents.

Figure 9-2 summarizes the common sampling methods used in social research today. The remainder of this chapter is devoted to a brief discussion of each of the sampling strategies listed.

Probability Sampling Methods

Simple Random Sampling

Although rarely used in social research, the simple random sample is the prototype for all sampling methods and is the basis for most inferential statistics. A simple random sample is a sample in which the chance, or probability, of selecting each and every case is the same. There are two basic methods of selecting a simple random sample:

1. *Sampling with replacement.* Suppose, for example, that a probation officer in an experimental program had a caseload of sixty clients. The officer would like to try a new method of monitoring clients. Before using this new method with all her clients, the probation officer decides to try it out with a sample. Knowing that probability sampling is a better method

Figure 9-2   Galtung's typology of sampling procedures

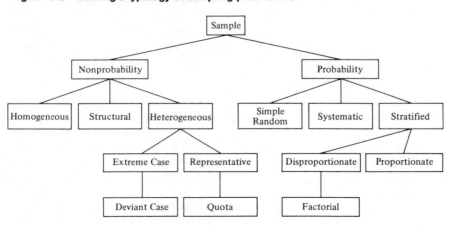

Source: Adapted from Johan Galtung, *Theory and Methods of Social Research* (New York: Columbia University Press, 1967), p. 56. Reprinted by permission of the publisher.

for selecting cases than choosing only those in which you are sure that the new method will work, the probation officer decides to select a simple random sample of her case load. To do this, the probation officer puts the name of each client on a separate piece of paper and shuffles the papers thoroughly. Then, she places all of the names in a container and selects one name. Clearly, the chance of any particular person's name being selected at that point is one out of sixty. Note, however, that unless the officer puts the name that was selected first back into the container and reshuffles the names, there will be only fifty-nine names in the container when the second name is selected. This means that the chance of selecting a particular second name would be one out of fifty-nine, not one out of sixty. Because simple random sampling requires that the chance of selecting each case be the same for all cases, the researcher using this approach must put the name first selected back into the container. Now, because the size of the population is the same each time a name is selected (sixty cases in this example), the chance of selecting a given name is the same on each separate draw. The sampling-with-replacement process can be used with any population to guarantee that the sample selected is a simple random sample. Although the same case may be selected two or more times, the researcher handles this problem either by recording the scores for that case two or more times or by replacing the name and drawing a new one.

2. *Using a table of random numbers* (see Table B-1 in Appendix B). A table of random numbers is, in itself, a simple random sample. The only difference is that such a table represents a sample of *numbers* rather than a sample of *cases*. The primary reason for using a table of random numbers is convenience. Suppose, for example, that a county welfare office serves 10,000 clients in a given year. The director of the agency decides to determine how satisfied the clients are with the services they have received. The director decides that it would be too expensive to study the population of all clients receiving services and, therefore, decides to sample clients. Clearly, the process of writing 10,000 names on separate sheets of paper and shuffling them is itself a major task. To avoid this time-consuming clerical task, the agency director decides to use a table of random numbers to select the cases to include in the study.

To use a table of random numbers, the researcher normally assigns each case in the population a code or identification number. Next, the researcher decides which direction to read the numbers in the random number table (up or down the columns, right or left across the rows). It does not matter which direction is chosen. Then, the researcher decides where to start reading the table (which column and which row). The researcher then reads a number and finds the case with the matching identification number. This case represents the first case in the sample. The researcher then continues to read the numbers in the same line until the full sample is selected.

Suppose that a mental-health worker has eight clients and wishes to select a simple random sample of four clients using a table of random numbers. Figure 9-3 illustrates the process of obtaining this sample. In the first step, the researcher assigns each of the clients an identification number. Second, the researcher decides which direction to read the table of random numbers. This researcher decided to read up the columns going from right to left. Third, the researcher decides where to begin reading numbers. This researcher selected the number in the fourth row of the eighth column. The first digit is 5, which is the identification number for Joel. The second number, reading up the column, is 9. Because no case has the identification number 9, the researcher moves to the third number, a 6, the identification number for David, who becomes the second case in the sample. The next number is 2, the identification number for Charles. There are no numbers above the 2, so the researcher moves to the bottom number of the next column to the left (row 5 of column 7). The digit is a 5, the identification number for Joel. Therefore, the final sam-

---

Figure 9-3   Using a table of random numbers

										Population of Eight Cases with Identification Numbers[2]	
4	2	6	1	4	2	9	2	9	7	1–John	5–Joel
9	9	3	8	5	4	1	6	0	0	2–Charles	6–David
4	8	5	0	9	2	3	9	2	9	3–Britta	7–Lucinda
7	3	7	8	8	0	6	5	3	3	4–Petra	8–Laurel
6	0	5	3	0	4	5	1	2	8		

Starting Point

Two numbers (0 and 9) are not used, because there are no cases with these identification numbers. Although not too much of a problem in this situation, the failure to be able to use numbers drawn can add substantially to the length of time that it takes to obtain a sample. If, for example, there had been twenty names on the list, the researcher probably would have assigned the identification numbers 01, 02, 03, 04, 05, 06, 07, 08, 09, 10, 11, 12, 13, 14, 15, 16, 17, 18, 19, and 20 to the cases. The researcher would not use the numbers 00 and 21–99. This would mean that, on the average, the researcher would select five numbers before finding one that was usable. One method that researchers sometimes use to reduce the waste is to divide the number selected by 20 and then use the remainder as the identification number. Thus, if the random number were 37, the researcher would select case 17 (37 divided by 20 is 1 with a remainder of 17). This process is defined as the "modulo" function.

ple consists of Joel, David, Charles, and Joel again. This means that information on Joel will be entered into the data matrix twice unless the researcher chooses to replace Joel and select again. Note, also, that although there are four females in the population, none was selected in this sample. This omission is deliberate in order to make a point. If the researcher believed that sex of the client was an important variable in the study, a different sampling procedure—one guaranteeing that females would have been represented—should have been used. (See the section on stratified sampling for an alternative method of selecting cases.

Although the primary emphasis of this section has been on sampling with replacement, researchers frequently use sampling without replacement if the population is large (say, 10,000 cases or more) and the size of the sample to be selected is small (less than 1 percent of the population). This procedure may bias the results some, but the size of the bias is very small. For example, in selecting a sample of fifty cases from a population of 10,000 cases without replacement, the chance of selecting the first case is 1 out of 10,000, whereas the chance of selecting the last case is 1 out of 9,950. This is a very small difference. Therefore, it is probably reasonable for the researcher to assume that sampling without replacement will not bias the study results significantly, if at all.

Systematic Sampling

Sometimes the process of drawing a simple random sample can become a relatively expensive process. One method of reducing the costs is to use a systematic sampling procedure. In this procedure, as with simple random sampling, the researcher needs a list of all the cases in the population. In selecting cases, however, the researcher uses a rule, such as "Select every tenth case" or "Select the third case from the bottom of each page of a book listing all cases," to choose the sample. By using such a rule, the researcher can avoid the time-consuming step of assigning each case an identification number, thereby reducing the costs of selecting the sample.

The rule that the researcher uses to select cases in systematic sampling normally depends on how the cases to be sampled are organized. Suppose, for example, a researcher wishes to sample 50 cases from a population of 5,000 cases. One approach to this problem would be to determine a sampling interval by dividing 50 into 5,000. The result is 100, so the researcher wants to select every 100th case. Typically, in this process, the researcher would consult a table of random numbers to select the first case. If, for example, the random number selected were 47, then the researcher would select the 47th, the 147th, the 247th, and so on to the 4,947th case, as the sample for the study.

Sometimes the list of cases in the population is organized in such a way that an even less expensive alternative to selecting cases is possible.

Suppose, for example, that the cases were listed in a book much like a telephone directory. The researcher might note that there are approximately 200 names listed on each page. If there were 5,000 names in all (a twenty-five-page directory), and if the researcher wanted a sample of 50 names, this would suggest selecting 2 names from each page. To determine which names to select from each page, the researcher would consult a table of random numbers. In this case, the rule for selection might be "Select the tenth name from the top of column one and the third name from the bottom of column two" on each page of the directory.

Although systematic sampling is usually less expensive than simple random sampling, the chance that the researcher will select a biased or nonrepresentative sample is increased. The problem that arises is that lists are usually organized in some fashion. Suppose, for example, that a researcher is sampling employees of county welfare agencies. Suppose also that each county agency has twenty-five employees and uses the organization chart shown in Figure 9-4. The directory of all of the employees of all of the county welfare agencies for the state could well be organized by county. The first entry in the directory for each county might be the agency director, and subordinate to this person's name could be the names of the four supervisors. The remaining twenty employees could be listed by area of specialization. The researcher using an interval sample selecting the twenty-fourth name from each agency from this list would obtain a sample that included workers in only the fourth area of specialization. Obviously, the resulting sample would be biased, and the results of the study questionable. The problem involved with using an interval or systematic sample in this situation is obvious. Moreover, it illustrates the importance of the researcher's understanding the way in which the list of cases in the population is organized prior to developing a sampling plan. Failing to understand (or neglecting to find out) how the organization of a list relates to the sampling procedure to be used increases the chances of biasing the results of the study.

Figure 9-4   Organizational chart for a county welfare agency

Agency Director

Supervisor	Supervisor	Supervisor	Supervisor
Employee A	Employee A	Employee A	Employee A
Employee B	Employee B	Employee B	Employee B
Employee C	Employee C	Employee C	Employee C
Employee D	Employee D	Employee D	Employee D
Employee E	Employee E	Employee E	Employee E

Stratified Sampling

When a researcher knows that a particular variable is important to a study, using a stratified sampling procedure can help to ensure that all values on that variable are adequately represented in the sample. In a stratified sample, the researcher first divides the population into categories based on the values of a stratification variable. For example, a researcher interested in ethnicity might divide the population into whites, blacks, Chicanos, and others. The researcher then selects a sample from each category using either a simple-random- or an interval-sampling approach. By using this process, the researcher is certain that whites, blacks, Chicanos, and others will be adequately represented in the sample.

When using stratified sampling, the researcher must decide whether the sample size for each category of the stratification variable should be *proportionate* or *disproportionate* to the number of cases in the categories in the population. Which of these two approaches will be most appropriate depends on the purpose of the study. Suppose, for example, that a county welfare agency director is interested in client satisfaction with services received. After some thought, the director decides that the basis of eligibility for services is an important factor in determining client satisfaction. The director, after reviewing the files, divides clients into three types: AFDC recipients, SSI recipients, and other eligible recipients (see Table 9-3). If the agency director is interested in estimating the overall satisfaction of clients, a proportionate sample would be most appropriate. In proportionate sampling, the researcher selects the same proportion or percentage of cases for each category of the stratification variable. If, for example, the agency director decided to select a 10 percent sample, the agency would select 10 percent of the "AFDC," "SSI," and "Other" eligibility categories respectively (see column 2 of Table 9-3). Because the proportions of AFDC, SSI, and Other eligibility cases in the sample are the same as their proportions in the population, the estimate of satisfaction

Table 9-3   Samples of clients of a county welfare agency, by eligibility

	Number of Cases	Samples		
		Proportionate	Factorial	Disproportionate
AFDC Eligibility	950	95	50	95
SSI Eligibility	450	45	50	45
Other Eligibility	200	20	50	40
Total	1,500	150	150	170

based on these cases should be a good estimate of satisfaction in the population.

Suppose, however, that the agency director was very interested in the opinions of the "Other" category. To get a better estimate of how people in this category rated services received, the agency director decides to double the sample size in this category, taking 20 percent rather than 10 percent. Now the sample is *disproportionate,* in that the size of the "Other" category relative to that of the "AFDC" and "SSI" categories is larger in the sample than in the population. This is the same as saying that the "Other" category is *oversampled.* The sample, by definition, is not representative of the population because there are proportionately twice as many "Others" in the sample as in the population. However, by increasing the size of the "Other" category sample, the agency director is better able to estimate how individuals in this category feel about and evaluate the services they receive.

A *factorial* sample is a special case of a disproportionate sample. In a factorial sample, the researcher selects the same number of cases in each category of the stratification variable. For example, if the county welfare agency director in the preceding example wanted a total sample of 150 clients, he or she would select 50 from each of the eligibility categories (see Table 9-3, column 3). The advantage of this type of sampling is that it facilitates making comparisons among groups. If the agency director were primarily interested in determining whether AFDC eligibility clients, SSI eligibility clients, and clients whose eligibility for services was based on other criteria differed in satisfaction with services received, a factorial sample would be the preferred method of selecting cases.

Although this example describes a two-stage sampling process (taking a sample of a sample), the process is not limited to two stages. Researchers interested in studying general populations often use three- or four- (or more) stage sampling plans. For example, a researcher interested in studying the public's image of a community mental health center may begin by dividing the city served into areas and sampling only some areas. In the second stage, the areas may be divided into blocks and blocks sampled. A third stage would involve sampling houses within blocks, and the final stage might be sampling people within houses.

Nonprobability Sampling

Purposive Sampling Methods

The process of selecting a probability sample from a given population requires that the researcher be able, at least in theory, to list all of the cases in that population. Many times, the cost of developing such a list is prohibitive. For example, although it may be possible to develop a list of all of the male residents of a medium-size city, a researcher would probably have difficulty in defending the expense of doing so. In such situations, the researcher may decide to use a purposive, rather than a probability, sampling method.

Usually, a purposive sample (sometimes called a *convenience* sample) is less expensive to obtain than a probability sample. However, because the relationship of a purposive sample to the population from which it is selected is unknown, the accuracy of estimates about what might be true in the population based on such a sample is also unknown. At the same time, a purposive sample may be the optimum choice in exploratory or hypothesis-generating research. Suppose, for example, that someone develops a new method of working with hyperactive children. A researcher interested in the effectiveness of the new method compared with more traditional methods would probably have difficulty in justifying the costs of drawing a random sample of all hyperactive children. The same researcher, however, may not encounter such difficulties in getting access to all of the children in a particular school system who have been classified as hyperactive. This sample would be adequate for examining the potential of the new method of treatment. If the results of the study using a purposive sample are positive, the researcher is justified in trying to replicate the study with a probability sample. The point of doing this is that the researcher can identify those variables or treatments that may be important using purposive samples. The researcher would probably like to replicate the study with a probability sample; the results of the first study provide an empirical basis for including variables in that replication.

The Homogeneous Sample

A homogeneous sample, as the name implies, is one in which all of the cases are similar to one another in some way. Suppose, for example, a researcher is interested in how depressed people respond to a particular treatment. One approach to obtaining a sample would be to give all people who came to a community mental-health center a test for depression. The sample would consist of all people who, on the basis of the test results (or some other measure), are classified as depressives. Because the sample consists only of those who scored high on a measure of depression, the sample is homogeneous on this variable. The relationship of this sample to the population of individuals who are depressed is unknown. Therefore, as is the case with all nonprobability samples, it is impossible to specify how the results found in the sample apply to the population in general.

The Structural Sample

A structural sample is one in which cases are selected because of their relationship to other cases. Suppose, for example, that an agency director is interested in how supervisory style affects employee morale. One approach to studying this problem would be to sample supervisors *and their employees*. The employees included in this study are selected because their supervisor is chosen. Although it would be possible to sample supervisors using one of the probability sampling methods, employees would not be sampled in this fashion, because the focus of the study is on how the supervisors relate to their employees. Thus, it is important that the agency director study the morale of the employees whose supervisors are included in the study, not the morale of a probability sample of all employees.

"Snowball" Sampling

On occasion, a researcher will select a sample and then allow those who were sampled to specify who else should be studied. Suppose that a researcher is interested in who is influential in helping a dying patient to decide whether die at home or in an institutional setting. The researcher might begin this study by asking patients with whom they discussed this decision. The second phase of the study might then involve interviewing the people whom the patient identifies. One of the questions that the researcher might ask this second set of people is with whom *they* discussed this situation. Because the researcher gathers samples progressively in this way, this technique is sometimes called "snowball" sampling. The researcher continues this pattern of questioning until he or she is satisfied that the social support network for the decision has been identified. As with the previous example, the researcher may select terminally ill individuals by a probability sampling method. After this initial selection, however, the researcher selects the remaining individuals because of their relationship to the terminally ill individual.

The Heterogeneous Sample

Homogeneous and structural samples are appropriate for certain types of research problems. However, research is usually based on heterogeneous samples—that is, samples in which cases differ from one another on one or more variables. For example, the researcher interested in parental discipline of hyperactive children might well want to study a sample of nonhyperactive children for comparison purposes. The total sample would be heterogeneous in that it would include parents of both hyperactive and nonhyperactive children. Any purposive sample in which the researcher selects cases in such a way as to ensure that the cases differ from one another on one or more variables is labeled a heterogeneous sample.

An *extreme-case sample* is one type of heterogeneous sample. In this type of sample, the researcher selects cases so that extreme values on a variable are overrepresented. For example, the researcher interested in the relationship of chronological age to life satisfaction might choose to oversample the very old—say, people seventy-five or older. Because attainment of age seventy-five represents an extreme value on the variable age, such a sample would be an extreme-case sample. Similarly, studies that oversample the very rich and the very poor are extreme-case samples of the variable "family income."

A *deviant-case sample* is similar to an extreme-case sample in that it involves oversampling of particular values of a variable. Now, however, the focus is on oversampling those values of the variable in question that have low frequencies in the population. If, for example, a researcher were interested in comparing black/white, rural/urban, or married/single differences in the tendency to seek social services, the researcher might oversample blacks, rural residents, and single people. This is because he or she knows there are more whites, urban dwellers, and married people in the total population. A deviant-case sample is similar in design to a disproportionate, or factorial, stratified sampling plan. The difference between the two designs is that the researcher does not use a probability sampling method in selecting the cases in the deviant-case sample. The use of the word *deviant* should not be understood as a perjorative word; it simply means *different* from the usual.

In extreme-case and deviant-case samples, the researcher does not necessarily attempt to select middle-range values on a variable. The researcher interested in sampling on the basis of family income using an extreme-case or deviant-case sample approach would oversample the very rich and the very poor. If the researcher sampled those with middle incomes as well, the sample would be called *representative* (because all values on the income variable would be represented in the population). If the researcher also sampled people in income categories proportionate to their occurrence in the population, the resulting sample would be called a *quota sample*. Thus, a quota sample is similar to a proportionate, stratified sample except that the cases are not selected on a probability basis. Usually in quota sampling the person actually doing the data collection (often an interviewer hired by the director of the research project) is asked to find a specified number of people with different characteristics living in a given area. For example, an interviewer might be asked to interview one black male, two black females, two white males, and four white females age sixty-five or older in a given community. In quota sampling, finding individuals who meet these qualifications is the interviewer's problem. He or she is usually instructed simply to locate the desired number and types of people. It is, of course, impossible to generalize to a wider population using nonprobability samples, but these approaches will do for special purposes (as described) or in exploratory studies, in which probability sampling is not absolutely required.

Some Practical Issues

The discussion of sampling to this point has been based on the assumption that the researcher lives in a near-perfect world. This, of course, is not the case. The research process involves compromises between the optimal and the practical. The process of identifying real people to study, like other aspects of the research process, involves compromise. We have already discussed one of these compromises: the amount of effort the researcher is willing to devote to identifying a sample given the resources available and the information return expected. In this section, we will describe some of the other problems in obtaining an ideal sample.

Perhaps the most common problem in sampling is *nonresponse*. In this situation, the researcher is able to identify who is to be studied, but some of the potential respondents choose not to participate in the study. Although the researcher can use certain strategies to minimize this problem (see Chapter 7), it does not disappear. The failure of some to participate in the study is particularly important with probability samples, because nonresponse potentially destroys the representativeness of the sample.

Although there is no simple correction for sampling bias due to nonresponse, sometimes it is possible to obtain an estimate of the size of the bias. For example, suppose that the researcher were studying the population of individuals sixty-five or older who resided in a given state. The researcher can determine the age, sex, educational attainment, income, race, and marital-status distributions of this population on the basis of records such as the United States Census Reports. Investigators can then compare the distribution of these variables in the population with the distribution of the same variables in the sample using some of the statistical techniques to be described in Chapter 13. Differences between the two distributions suggest potential sources of bias in the sample.

A second common problem in designing a sampling procedure is the *inaccessibility of lists*. Not surprisingly, social work research often focuses on specialized populations that are frequently defined as "at risk." Populations of this type include clients of a comprehensive mental-health center, recipients of welfare payments, the unemployed, hospital patients, and parolees. The agencies with primary responsibility for working with such individuals clearly have lists of clients that would facilitate the drawing of a sample. At the same time, agencies often have a responsibility to protect the identities of their clients. Therefore, obtaining access to such lists, assuming that it is legally possible, requires that the researcher enter into negotiations with the agencies in question.

The content of the negotiations between the researcher and the agency will vary depending on (1) the nature of the relationship of the researcher to the agency (for example, employee or consultant) and (2) agency regulations. The researcher seeking access to client lists should be prepared to provide the cooperating agency with at least the following information:

1. A statement of the purpose of the study.
2. A description of the study that includes a copy of the measurement instrument.
3. A succinct statement of the benefits of the study to the agency providing the list.
4. An analysis of the costs and benefits to the potential respondents of participating in the study.
5. A description of the procedures to be used in obtaining informed consent (see Chapter 6).
6. A description of the methods to be used to protect the identity of respondents.

On the basis of the information provided, agencies frequently will request changes in the procedures to be used and the questions to be asked. The researcher must weigh these changes in terms of the integrity of the study, recognizing that failure to comply may well result in a denial of access to the names needed.

Agencies frequently request that a signed consent form be used to guarantee that informed consent is obtained from each respondent. Sometimes, an agency will itself seek to obtain the permission of the potential respondents to release their names. If this activity is part of the agency's policy, it will weigh permission to do the study very carefully, because such a process is time consuming for the agency staff. Occasionally, if the data are to be collected using a mailed questionnaire, the agency will conduct the mailing itself. The advantage of this procedure, from the perspective of the agency, is that the researcher need never see the list of clients involved in the study. Agencies do not, however, elect this strategy unless they believe that conducting the study is in their own best interests.

By now, it should be apparent that obtaining a sample from agency lists can be a difficult, time-consuming process. The researcher cannot be certain that the efforts to obtain such a sample will be successful until the data have actually been collected. There are no guarantees that agencies will view a particular study as important or, even if they do, that they will grant the researcher access to the necessary information.

This discussion of the difficulties in obtaining access to agency records is not meant to discourage researchers from making every effort possible to obtain an optimal sample. It should suggest, however, that negotiations can be quite lengthy: often two to three months pass from the time the agency initially receives a request for a list until it makes names available. This discussion should also suggest the necessity of developing an alternative strategy for obtaining a sample in case negotiations with agencies should prove fruitless.

A third problem in sampling occurs when the *target population* is a category of individuals that *occurs only rarely in the general population* (for example, noninstitutionalized, never-married individuals who are at least forty-five years of age, or noninstitutionalized, frail elderly who reside in large metropolitan areas). Such individuals are often isolated from the rest of society, and thus the problems of location are made even more difficult. The researcher interested in studying such groups almost always selects a nonprobability sampling design. Often the researcher uses a combination of approaches, such as referral (that is, asking individuals if they know anyone who belongs to the target population) with snowball sampling (that is, having identified certain members of the target population, the researcher asks them if they know of any others). Even then, the nature of the population suggests that it will take a major effort to identify an adequate sample. Because of the effort required simply to find individuals in populations of this type, the researcher usually focuses attention on sample size, ignoring the issue of representativeness.

A fourth problem in sampling involves situations in which the researcher does not have *access to the population* being studied. For example, the researcher wishing to study closed ethnic communities (for example, Chinese communities in New York and San Francisco, Chicano communities in Texas and California, rural black communities in the South) of which he or she is not a member may have problems of access. Similarly, the researcher wishing to study deviant subgroups (for example, drug abusers, homosexuals, gangs) can anticipate problems of access. Several strategies are available to the researcher under these circumstances. The researcher can, for example, collaborate with others who *do* have access to the population in question. Alternatively, the researcher can employ informants who have such access. Still another possibility is to use some of the participant-observation techniques described in Chapter 7. As is the case with extreme-case samples, however, the researcher typically attends more to the issue of sample size than to the issue of sample representativeness when studying inaccessible populations.

Key Terms

unit of analysis	sample
ecological fallacy	adequacy
population	probability sample

nonprobability sample   structural sample
simple random sample   heterogeneous sample
stratified sample   homogeneous sample
systematic sample   snowball sampling technique
proportionate sample   extreme-case sample
disproportionate sample   deviant-case sample
factorial sample   quota sample
purposive sample

Questions for Discussion

1. How does a researcher avoid problems in specifying the appropriate unit of analysis?
2. Why might a researcher argue that very small, purposive samples are adequate for exploratory research?
3. How do the research problems and design influence the sampling plan a researcher selects?

Exercise

Below is a list of thirty-two subjects' names. The subjects have been divided into categories by sex and ethnicity.

a. Select a simple random sample (with replacement) of size four from this list using the Table of Random Numbers in Appendix A. Be sure to list all of the steps in this process.
b. Select a stratified, factorial sample of total size eight using sex and ethnicity as the stratification variables.

White Male	White Female	Black Male	Black Female
Charles	Alice	Aaron	Alicia
David	Britta	Alex	Barbara
Joel	Cindy	Bob	Cynthia
John	Edith	Carl	Delores
Kenneth	Laurel	Earl	Enid
Matt	Petra	Fred	Frances
Raymond	Rose	George	Helen
Thomas	Virginia	Sam	Janice

For Further Reading

Morris James Slonim. *Sampling: A Quick, Reliable Guide to Practical Statistics.* New York: Simon and Schuster, 1960. Here is an easy-to-read explanation of sampling procedures and problems in sampling.

Leslie Kish. *Survey Sampling.* New York: John Wiley and Sons, 1965. Kish provides a comprehensive discussion of sampling procedures for students with some background in statistics.

PART III

Part II dealt with some of the different strategies that researchers use to make observations. Part III focuses on how researchers use statistics to summarize the observations that they have made.

Chapter 10, "Processing Data," is divided into three sections. The first section reviews some of the procedures used for assigning numbers to responses (see Chapters 2, 3, 5, and 6). The second section describes some of the ways that researchers organize data (observations) to facilitate statistical summarization. Particular attention is given to data organization formats that are compatible with using computers to perform such summarizations. The third section is a nontechnical discussion of computers and their operation.

Chapters 11, 12, and 13 describe some of the more common statistical tools that researchers use to summarize their data. As will soon become obvious, one task facing the researcher is choosing which statistics to use. Chapters 11 and 12 in particular give considerable attention to the criteria researchers use in deciding which statistics are most appropriate in a given situation. A second point of emphasis in these chapters is the interpretation of statistics. Although we present formulas that can be used to calculate specific statistics, our focal point remains interpretation.

These chapters are not intended as a substitute for a course in statistics, in which students may well be expected to develop calculational proficiency. Rather, they are included to introduce you to statistics and to illustrate how statistics can be used in the research enterprise. Furthermore, they are written with the recognition that most researchers use computers to calculate statistics. Thus, the tasks of the researcher are to select which statistics should be calculated and to interpret the results obtained.

Chapter 11, "Single-Variable Descriptive Statistics," illustrates how statistics are used to describe a variable and presents both graphic and numerical summarization techniques. These procedures are particularly helpful to researchers in their efforts to inform others about the characteristics of the subjects.

Whether the research undertaken is exploratory, descriptive, experimental, or evaluative in purpose and form, the researcher is usually more interested in the relationships among variables than in how individuals score on a single variable. Chapter 12, "Measures of Association and Their Interpretation," approaches the question of association among variables from a descriptive perspective. It gives primary attention to the more common tools that researchers use in measuring how closely variables are associated with each other in a given data set.

Chapter 13, "Statistical Inference and Hypothesis Testing," expands on the question of how researchers assess the relationships among variables. This chapter's focus is on how information based on a sample can be used to discuss what might be true in a population. It emphasizes statistical techniques that researchers use to determine the likelihood of their results being a function of chance or random factors. The procedures described in this chapter are typically combined with those in Chapter 12, so that the researcher presents both a description of how closely variables are associated with each other and information on the likelihood of those relationships occurring by chance alone.

10

Processing Data

Although there are exceptions, most social work research involves using statistics to summarize observations. The purpose of this chapter is to illustrate how researchers process their data to make using statistics easier. Initially, we approach this task from the perspective that the researcher will be computing summary statistics by hand. Because computers are widely used in the process of analyzing data, the approach to processing that is recommended is one that is easily adapted to preparing data for use with a computer. The final section of this chapter is a brief, nontechnical discussion of computers and their operation. It is included to introduce students to some of the things that a computer can do and to the types of information that a computer needs to do its job.

Preparing data so that it can be summarized statistically involves two major steps:

1. Convert observations into a form (usually a number) that can be manipulated mathematically. This conversion is called *coding*.
2. Transfer the scores that each subject or unit receives to forms that make statistical summaries easier to compute. This transfer involves creating what is called a *data matrix*.

The amount of information to be processed in preparing data for statistical summary tends to be quite large. Even a small study, such as making 10 observations on each of 20 subjects, results in 200 observations. Thus, it is important that the researcher be well organized prior to any attempts to code and transfer data. This means that the researcher, in addition to developing plans for coding and transferring data, should develop a system for monitoring these procedures.

Finally, as with the other steps in the research process, researchers must take care to ensure that their observations are coded and transferred accurately. High-quality observation coupled with low-quality coding results in a poor-quality study just as surely as will an excellent design coupled with poor observation. Therefore, we cannot overemphasize the importance of continuous checking to ensure the accuracy of coding and transferring data.

The next two sections of this chapter include detailed discussions on the coding and transferring of data. The importance of planning and checking accuracy are emphasized repeatedly in both of these sections. The major issues addressed in the sections are summarized in Figure 10-1, an outline of questions the researcher should answer before processing data. Although many of the procedures that are recommended may seem cumbersome with small data sets, we have had too many students report that a respondent has completed sixty-eight years of school to recommend simpler, less exhaustive procedures. Furthermore, strategies such as those proposed are absolutely necessary with large data sets (for example, 100 observations on each of 500 subjects or 50,000 observations in all).

Coding Observations

The process of coding observations involves three steps. The researcher must:

1. *develop an operational definition* (see Chapter 3) or rule for assigning numbers to responses for each variable,

---

Figure 10-1   Planning checklist for processing data

  A. Organizational Plan
    1. How will the researcher know what units have been observed at any point in time?
    2. How will the researcher know which observations have been coded at any point in time?
    3. How will the researcher know which observations will be ready for analysis at any point in time?
    4. Where will the data be stored?
    5. How will the researcher protect the identities of respondents during the coding process?
    6. How will coders be trained?
  B. Coding Plan
    1. What are the operational definitions of each of the variables?
    2. Where are the variables to be coded?
    3. How will the accuracy of the coding be determined?
  C. Data-Transfer Plan
    1. What will the form of the data matrix be?
    2. How will the data be transferred to the forms?
    3. How will the accuracy of the transfer be determined?

---

2. *code the observations* made on each variable, and
3. *check the accuracy of the coding,* correcting errors where detected.

Operational Definitions Revisited

As we indicated earlier, an operational definition of a concept is a rule for assigning numbers to observations. The rule can be simple (for example, assign the number that the respondent gives to the question, "How old were you on your last birthday?") or it may be quite complex (see Chapter 5 for some examples of complex operational definitions). The researcher must, however, associate an operational definition with each variable on which observations are to be made.

Several principles guide the researcher in developing operational definitions. First, an operational definition should be *as simple as possible.* Generally, the more complex the rule is, the more likely the researcher will be to make an error when applying the rule to code data. The process of doing research is already filled with problems; the researcher hardly needs errors in coding to compound them.

Occasionally, a researcher can divide a complex operational definition into a series of steps, each of which is simple. For example, suppose that a researcher who wanted to develop a measure of personal concern about growing older used the following three Likert format items:[1]

1. I worry that I will be in poor
   health when I am older.   SA   A   U   D   SD

2. I expect that I will enjoy life more
   than I do now when I am older.   SA   A   U   D   SD

3. I am concerned that I will be poor
   when I am older.   SA   A   U   D   SD

An operational definition for an index based on responses to these three items could involve three steps. The researcher would:

1. score each item using the rule SA (strongly agree) = 1, A (agree) = 2, U (uncertain) = 3, D (disagree) = 4, and SD (strongly disagree) = 5.
2. because question 2 is worded positively whereas questions 1 and 3 are worded negatively, reverse the coding of this item (that is, change 5 to 1, 4 to 2, 2 to 4, and 1 to 5). Now, a low score on each item means that the respondent is expressing concern about growing older.
3. compute an index by adding the respondent's scores on each of the items (variables) together.

There are at least three advantages to dividing complex operational definitions into simple steps:

1. Because each operation is simple, the chance of making a mistake when coding the data is reduced.

2. It is easier to check that the coding was done correctly at each step using this approach. Thus, even if errors in coding occur, they are easier to detect and correct.

3. The computer can often be used to do some of the work. For example, in the example given, the computer can be used to do the second and third steps. Because the computer does not make arithmetical mistakes, the accuracy of the coding is improved. Also, using the computer to do these steps can reduce the amount of labor needed for coding data, particularly if the researcher has gathered data on a large number of cases and wishes to construct several indexes.

A second principle in developing an operational definition is that *each different response should be given a different number.* This is simple with closed-ended questions (see Chapters 5 and 6), because the researcher provides the respondent with a set of mutually exclusive and totally exhaustive categories. The principle is satisfied if the researcher assigns a different number to each of the possible response categories. The only thing that the researcher must remember is to assign a different number (often zero) to respondents who fail to answer the question.

Assigning numbers to responses to open-ended questions can be more difficult, particularly if the researcher has no preconceived system for categorizing responses. One approach to developing an operational definition to responses to open-ended questions that we have found useful is:

1. *Write* each response *verbatim* on an index card.
2. *Sort* the cards on the basis of similarity of content into different categories, a process similar to content analysis, as described in Chapter 8.
3. *Assign* each category a different number.

This strategy can be modified any number of ways, depending on the nature of the open-ended questions. For example, suppose that a researcher asked respondents what they believed their major problems or difficulties to be. Content analysis might suggest that the problems mentioned could be divided into four categories—social functioning, economic resources, physical functioning, and other. Depending on the purpose of the study, several different operational definitions could be constructed. One approach would be to assign a single number to each respondent, depending on what the single most important problem appeared to be. An alternative approach would be to assign four different numbers, one for each category of problem. This number could reflect either whether or not the respondent mentioned the problem or the number of times the respondent mentioned the problem.

A third principle in developing an operational definition is that *numbers assigned to categories should reflect the level of measurement attained* (see Chapter 2). For nominal variables, order is not important. Therefore, the only critical point is to assign each number a different category. For example, study the coding systems associated with the nominal variable "marital status" in Figure 10-2. Each system is equally appropriate. The researcher, however, would probably select system A or system D as the operational definition, because they are simpler. If, on the other hand, the variable were assumed to be measured on the ordinal level, only coding systems A, D, and E would be appropriate for an operational definition. Finally, if the variable were assumed to be measured on the interval level, only coding systems A and D would be appropriate for an operational definition.

The Coding Process

Coding data is usually a simple but time-consuming process. If the researcher has constructed the operational definitions of each variable carefully, there is rarely any question about what score or number should be assigned to any specific observation. Problems in coding tend to be a function more of poor organization, coder fatigue, and a lack of checking than anything else. Good coding, on the other hand, is the result of careful planning and continual checking to detect errors.

There are two steps in coding observations:

Step 1. Assign each case or subject an identification number. Normally, the identification number assigned to the subject during the data-collection phase of the project (see Chapter 6) is used as the coding identification number as well. If the instrument of observation is more than one page long, the identification number should appear on each page. Then, if the pages become scattered (not an uncommon experience when the instruments are being handled frequently), it is possible to put the instrument back together again.

There are several advantages to using identification numbers, particu-

Figure 10-2 Coding systems for the variable "Marital Status"

	Coding Systems				
	A	B	C	D	E
Never married	1	3	8	5	1
Separated	2	2	4	4	3
Divorced	3	1	6	3	6
Widowed	4	4	2	2	7
Currently married	5	5	9	1	9

larly if the researcher stores the observation instruments sequentially according to the identification number:

1. It is possible to check a random sample (see Chapter 8) of the instruments for accuracy in coding. Because the instruments are stored sequentially by identification number, it is easy to locate those that are to be checked.

2. If the researcher should identify an unusual score in the later phases of the data-processing procedures, it is a relatively simple matter to verify the accuracy of the score. Because the relevant instrument is easily located, the researcher need only see how the respondent answered the question to determine the accuracy of the score.

3. Because respondent names are not as a rule connected with identification numbers, the respondents have some guarantee of anonymity.

Step 2. Assign numbers to observations. With questionnaires and interview schedules, we prefer to code the numbers on the schedule directly.[2] The primary advantage to this approach is that it makes checking the accuracy of the coding easy. The simplest approach is to place the numbers in the right-hand margin of each page of the instrument next to the variables being coded. With interview schedules, it is possible to preprint lines on the schedule for coding (see Figure 10-3). However, such lines detract from the appearance of a questionnaire and can puzzle respondents. Thus, they should probably not be included if the respondent is to complete the instrument.

There are certain principles to remember when coding observations:

1. Perhaps most important, *do not guess* as to what a respondent might have meant by a particular response. If the respondent's writing is illegible, or if the respondent clearly did not follow instructions, it is usually better to discard the questionnaire as uncodable.

Figure 10-3 Edge coding using a preprinted coding line

	SA	A	U	D	SD	
1. I worry that I will be in poor health when I am older.	[ ]	[ ]	[ ]	[X]	[ ]	4
2. I expect that I will enjoy life more than I do now when I am older.	[X]	[ ]	[ ]	[ ]	[ ]	1
3. I am concerned that I will be poor when I am older.	[ ]	[ ]	[X]	[ ]	[ ]	3
4. I feel that people will ignore me when I am older.	[ ]	[X]	[ ]	[ ]	[ ]	2

2. *Assign a number* for each variable for each case. Although it is not normally a problem, researchers must exercise care in coding contingency questions (see Chapter 6). (Contingency questions are items that respondents may not be expected to answer, depending on how they have answered previous questions.) In this case, use a separate code for "Does Not Apply" (see Figure 10-4).

The researcher must also consider two organizational issues before beginning the coding process:

1. Decide *whether to code each instrument in its entirety* before proceeding to the next *or* code instruments *one section at a time*. Generally, if the coding system is complex, it is better to code the instruments one section at a time. This allows the coders the opportunity to become profi-

---

Figure 10-4   Illustration of a codebook

What is your current marital
status?

- (0) No response
- (1) Never married
- (2) Separated
- (3) Divorced
- (4) Widowed
- (5) Currently married

How many years of school has
your husband/wife completed?
(asked only of those who
were currently married)

   a. Code years directly or if category given
   b. Use following codes

- (00) No response
- (12) High school graduate
- (16) College graduate
- (18) Master's degree
- (20) Doctorate or more
- (99) Not currently married,
  does not apply

How many years of school have
you completed?

   a. Code years directly or if category given
   b. Use following codes

- (00) No response
- (12) High school graduate
- (16) College graduate
- (18) Master's degree
- (20) Doctorate or more

---

cient with the coding system for that section, thereby reducing the error rate. In most other circumstances, an instrument should be coded in its entirety before proceeding to the next.

2. Consider *how to inform the coders of the operational definition of each variable.* The tool most commonly used in this process is a codebook, which is excerpted in Figure 10-4. The primary advantage to this approach is that all of the information concerning how to convert the observations into numbers is located in one place. Also, a codebook is of immense value to researchers when they begin to write a description of how the research project was conducted. The codebook includes a complete description of how variables were measured. Information about this process is, as might be expected, integral to the research report (see Chapter 14).

The Accuracy of Coding

The researcher should monitor the coding process carefully, spot-checking the coding on a regular basis. It is dismaying to discover that one or more variables have been miscoded on all of the instruments. Researchers may avoid this experience if they give particular attention to screening carefully the first instruments that are coded. Even after coders (or the researcher) have become familiar with the coding process, regular checks for accuracy can be beneficial. Frequently, it is possible to establish a "buddy system," in which one coder checks the work of another and vice versa.

After all of the data have been coded, the researcher should conduct a formal test of the accuracy of the coding. One approach to this is to select a random sample of observation instruments and compare what *is* coded with what *should* have been coded for each variable. The researcher should record not only the total number of errors detected but also the variables (and the coder, if more than one individual did the coding) involved. If the researcher detects a pattern to the errors, the variables (or the coders) involved should be examined more carefully. All errors detected should, of course, be corrected. Finally, assuming there are no systematic errors, the researcher should compute an error rate. This is done by dividing the number of errors detected by the total number of observations checked. For example, the researcher might have checked ten instruments, each of which contained twenty observations, and detected one error. The error rate in this case would be .005 (1 divided by 200), or one-half of one percent. This would mean that the researcher would expect that .5 percent of the numbers that were coded would be in error.

Obviously, the researcher desires that the error rate for coding be as low as possible. At the same time, reducing the number of coding errors is costly. Thus, the researcher must balance the resources available to the study against the costs of minimizing coding errors. Often this means that the researcher will accept an error rate above zero. How large an error rate is acceptable, however, depends on the purpose of the research and, to a lesser extent, on the size of the data set.

Transferring Data

Although the researcher can use the coded observation instruments as the basis for statistical summaries of the data, this approach to analysis is inefficient and likely to lead to errors. For example, if a researcher wanted to know how many respondents supported the establishment of a halfway house for delinquent children, he or she would have to sort through all of the observation instruments to obtain the answer. If that researcher then wanted to determine how many of these respondents were willing to have the halfway house located in their neighborhood, this would require re-sorting all of the observation instruments. A more efficient approach, and one that most researchers adopt, is to transfer all of the numbers from each observation instrument to a separate piece of paper (or form). In addition to increasing efficiency (counting a column of numbers is quicker and easier than sorting through a stack of questionnaires), the approach facilitates the researcher's checking his or her work. Furthermore, because computers cannot read questionnaires, the researcher who wishes to use a computer during the analysis phase must transfer the data to a format that can be read by the computer.

This section of the chapter is divided into three parts. The first part deals with the general process of developing what is called a data matrix. Researchers who expect to calculate summary statistics by hand will find that creating such a matrix simplifies this task. The second outlines the additional restrictions that the researcher faces when preparing a data matrix for use with a computer. The final part of this section outlines some of the procedures that the researcher can use in checking to see if the data have been transferred accurately.

The Data Matrix

As we indicated earlier, researchers can be more efficient in summarizing data statistically when they arrange the data so that all of the scores that subjects receive on all of the variables can be examined simultaneously. The most common approach to this task is to create a data matrix. A *data matrix* is simply *a list of all of the scores for each subject on each variable included in the study.* Usually, each column of the matrix refers to a specific variable. Each row, on the other hand, refers to a specific case or subject. Finally, a cell in the matrix contains a number that is the coded score of the case or subject for the row in which the cell is located on the variable of the column in which the cell is located.

The elements in a data matrix may be made clearer by the following example. Suppose that a researcher gathered three pieces of information (marital status, race, and age) from each of four respondents. The researcher coded these variables as follows:

Marital status: married = 1, not married = 2
Race: white = 1, nonwhite = 2
Age: number of years

After coding the data, the researcher records the information in the data matrix shown in Table 10-1. According to the information in the data matrix, the respondent with identification number 1 is a married, non-white, twenty-seven-year-old person. The respondent with identification number 4, on the other hand, is a married, white, twenty-eight-year-old person.

The steps used in creating a data matrix are simple. The researcher:

1. writes the names of the variables across the top of a page.
2. finds the observation instrument with the smallest identification number.
3. *records* the score that that case received on each variable underneath the variable name.
4. *repeats* this process until he or she has recorded the scores for the case with the highest identification number. At this point, the researcher has created a data matrix.

Several features of a data matrix bear comment:

1. It is impossible to interpret a data matrix without knowing how the variables are coded. A score of 2 on the variable "marital status," for example, has meaning only when the researcher knows that a 2 means

Table 10-1   A data matrix of four cases with three variables

	Variables		
	Marital Status	Race	Age
Identification Number of Case	1 = married 2 = not married	1 = white 2 = nonwhite	Coded in years
1	1	2	27
2	2	1	36
3	2	2	24
4	1	1	28

that the respondent is not married. Thus, the codebook that the researcher developed during the coding process is an invaluable tool in the interpretation of the information contained within the data matrix.

2. To determine how respondents scored on a given variable, it is necessary to examine only the column associated with that variable. For example, to determine how many of the respondents were nonwhite in the matrix in Table 10-1, the researcher would examine the column associated with race. In this example, two of the respondents were nonwhite (cases 1 and 3).

3. As we noted earlier, all of the information for a given case is on the line or row associated with that case. Thus, if the researcher wanted to know the age of case 2 in the example in Table 10-1, he or she would look on line 2 under age and find that the respondent was thirty-six years old.

The Computer Data Matrix

The data matrix used by a computer is, for all practical purposes, identical to the data matrix a researcher writes on a piece of paper.[3] In fact, many times a researcher first prepares a data matrix on paper and then transfers it to a form that can be read by the computer. Furthermore, the process of creating a data matrix for use with a computer is similar to the one that a researcher uses when creating a data matrix on paper. In fact, the process of creating a data matrix for a computer is almost identical to the process a researcher would follow if a typewriter were used to write the numbers for a data matrix.

As we have indicated, the primary difference between creating a data matrix for a computer and one for hand use is in the way that the numbers are written. In creating a data matrix for use with a computer, the researcher uses a special machine to write numbers in a form that a computer can read. Normally, the machine used is either a keypunch or a terminal. Both of these machines have keyboards similar to a typewriter's, and both operate in a fashion similar to that of a typewriter. The primary difference between the two is that the keypunch punches holes in a card, which can then be read by a computer, whereas the terminal can be connected directly to the computer.

Certain problems emerge when the researcher uses a typewriter (and thus a keypunch or terminal) to create a data matrix. The first of these is that the number of numbers that can be written on a single line with a typewriter is limited. The same is true of a keypunch.[4] A card has eighty spaces, which means that the researcher cannot write more than eighty one-digit numbers on a single card. The researcher using a typewriter who has more numbers than will fit on a single line solves the problem by using a second page and taping it to the first. The researcher using a keypunch solves the problem by adding a second card. The primary advantage for a researcher using a keypunch is that the second card can and should be typed immediately. The computer can then be used to extend the length of the "line" or row of the data matrix. The major problem with this approach is that cards (like pages) can get out of order. A researcher at a typewriter solves this potential problem by numbering the pages so that they can be put into the correct order. A researcher at a keypunch does much the same, usually using a code for each card, which specifies which card of which case is entered (for example, card 4 of case 10).

A second problem in using a typewriter to write a data matrix is "lining up" variables. In writing a data matrix by hand, the researcher simply looks at the top of the page to find out what variable is to be coded in a given space. Usually, researchers try to keep the columns straight (and separate from each other) so that the information is easy to read. A researcher at a typewriter does the same thing by specifying in advance in what column (or space) certain information will be typed. For example, the researcher may decide to type the value for marital status in column (space) 5 and the value for number of children in column 6. The researcher using a keypunch does exactly the same thing—that is, decides in advance in which space(s) a variable will be punched.[5]

Careful prior planning concerning the identification of the exact spaces (columns) in which a variable will be punched is extremely important. A researcher who plans to punch the number of children a person has in a single column only to discover one or more respondents have ten or more children has a problem. A researcher writing the number by hand can simply write smaller. Unfortunately, it is not possible to punch smaller holes or type smaller numbers and thereby insert an extra digit. Thus, the researcher is faced with two choices. Either recode the variable so that it fits into a single column (for example, $9 =$ nine or more children), or change the plan for which variable goes in which column. If the latter option is chosen, the researcher must discard all of the data that have already been transferred, and begin anew.

There is a second, even more important, reason for carefully planning which variable will be in which column. As we indicated earlier, a data matrix is simply row upon row of numbers. To know what a 5 in column 7 means, the researcher must know both what variable is coded in that column and how that variable is coded. This, of course, is possible only if the researcher in fact knows which variable was punched (typed) in the column in question.

Because of the crucial importance of being able to identify where in the data matrix a particular variable is located, this information is usually included in the codebook. For example, the entry in a codebook for the variable "marital status," which the researcher wishes to punch in column

10 of the second card, is illustrated in Table 10-2. Often, because a code-book can be extremely bulky, a researcher will construct a summary sheet, which simply lists the variables and their locations as a supplement to the codebook. Such a summary can be very helpful both in identifying where in the codebook a variable is described and in using a computer to help with the analysis of the data.

There are two fundamental points about the way that computers read that makes it different from the way that we read. Both are a result of computers being unable to *interpret* data based on logic derived from previous experience, as we do:

1. *Position.* Suppose, for example, that a researcher typing (punching) the number of children a person has had allowed two columns (spaces) for this variable. For example, we would read each of the following numbers as 2:

2

2

02

A computer, however, would not. A computer would read the top number as the number 20 and the middle and bottom cases as the number 2. This, of course, is a problem only if the researcher is using more than one column to punch (type) a score on a variable. To avoid problems of this form, it is best to punch a number in each space, filling in zeroes wherever they are appropriate. Thus, of the three ways of punching the number 2 above, the form 02 is superior. This practice reduces ambiguity about what number should have been punched in the columns and guarantees that the computer will read the number correctly.

2. *Number or letter?* For computer reading, letters and numbers are not interchangeable. Often, people typing use the capital form of the letter

---

Table 10-2   Sample of a full codebook entry for a single variable

Variable Abbreviation	Variable Name	Coding	Location Card	Location Column
MS	Marital Status	(0) No response (1) Never married (2) Separated (3) Divorced (4) Widowed (5) Currently married	2	7

o as a zero. They also use the lower-case form of the letter *L* as a one. Neither of these transformations is possible with a computer. A computer always reads a letter as a letter and a number as a number. Therefore, a researcher who punches the letter instead of the number will always get an error message from the computer.

Data-Matrix Accuracy

Researchers check the accuracy of a data matrix in much the same way that they check the accuracy of their coding. They simply compare the values on the variables reported in the data matrix with those that were originally coded for the variables. Because of the way that a data matrix is organized, however, certain screening checks are easy to do with the data matrix. For example, the researcher knows how long each row should be. It is possible to check whether columns have inadvertently been added, or variables accidentally excluded, by checking the length of each row. This is particularly easy to do if the data have been prepared for use with a computer. A second simple check is on the values of each variable. Because the researcher knows where each variable is located, and what the possible values on each variable are, it is possible to inspect each column to determine whether the values that are reported represent legitimate scores. This type of check is easily done by computer. Researchers should use both of these checks (that is, length of row and values on variables) as supplements to, not replacements of, more comprehensive checks of the accuracy of the data matrix.

Computers and Their Operation

Perhaps the single most important stimulus to the expansion of large-scale survey research has been the wide accessibility of computers. Prior to the availability of computers, a research team could spend years doing statistical summaries of data that can now be done in a matter of minutes with the assistance of a computer. Sophisticated statistical analyses of data are possible for even the most statistically naive of researchers. A researcher who has access to a computer, and who is willing to convert his or her data into a format that can be read by a computer, can use any of a bewildering array of statistical techniques to analyze that data. Computers have largely eliminated the need to know how to calculate a particular statistic, because the computer does the calculations. The researcher need only know how to ask the computer to calculate the statistic in question and then allow the computer to do the rest.

The advantages of computers—their ability to process large amounts of data quickly and accurately and their ability to do complex computations quickly and accurately—may also be their disadvantages. Without computers, the addition of each measure to a study increased the time involved in calculations exponentially. Therefore, the researcher considered carefully whether it was necessary to add each separate measure. With computers, the addition of another measure does not pose any particular calculational problems. Thus, one of the restraints that used to cause researchers to consider carefully what to include in a study has been removed. This has resulted in a tendency for researchers to include variables simply because they may be interesting, rather than because there are sound theoretical or practical reasons for their inclusion. This tendency poses substantial problems for researchers, particularly in hypothesis-testing research, because the relationship of such variables to the hypotheses in question is not known.

Although a computer puts sophisticated statistical analyses within the reach of all, it does *not:*

1. *decide* which analyses are appropriate for a given data set,
2. *choose* which variables should be included in the analysis, or
3. *interpret* the results obtained.

These issues are the responsibility of the researcher. If the researcher chooses to use religious affiliation as an interval rather than a nominal variable, the computer will operate as if the scores were interval in nature. If the researcher chooses to conceive of chronological age as being caused by marital status, the computer will process the data in this fashion. The computer simply takes numbers that the researcher has provided and processes them according to procedures that the researcher has specified. A computer has no way of knowing whether the researcher understands the statistical tools to be used or whether the researcher can interpret the results obtained.

Because of the speed with which data are processed, it is possible to generate volumes of summary information using a computer. Even with a relatively small data matrix, a researcher can generate a hundred or more pages of statistical summaries of the data. This can result in an information overload for the researcher. Unless he or she has a clear understanding of why each analysis was conducted and what the results of each analysis are expected to show, the researcher is quickly lost in a morass of paper. Efficient use of the computer requires that researchers be able to answer the following questions before attempting any analysis:

1. What question will be answered by the analysis?
2. What variables are involved in the analysis?
3. What is the appropriate statistical tool to answer the question?
4. How will the results obtained be analyzed?

These questions (and their answers) flow from the research design and serve to remind the researcher that research is a systematic process for answering questions.

The Parts of a Computer

We can think of computers, broadly speaking, as consisting of three parts:

1. *Input devices.* Obviously, to use a computer, there must be some way of providing the computer with information. This is done through the use of input devices, the two most common of which are the card reader and the terminal.
2. *Processor.* The processor, as the name implies, is the part of the computer that processes information. It is the part of the computer that performs the calculations the researcher has requested.
3. *Output devices.* The most common of these is the printer. A printer simply prints the results of the calculations of the processor so that the researcher can read the results.

Researchers should be aware of other input-output devices. The researcher working with a terminal who must enter the data matrix each time he or she wishes to use the computer faces a time-consuming task. Similarly, cards tear and wear out, and the process of repunching all of the cards associated with a data matrix is time-consuming. Therefore, most computers have ways of saving information so that it need not be reentered by the card reader or terminal. The most common storage methods involve the use of tapes or disks. Tapes are simply recording tapes similar to those used by tape recorders. The researcher uses the computer to write information on the tape, which can then be used as input at a later time. A disk is similar to a phonograph record. Again, the researcher uses the computer to write information on the disk for use at a later time.

Using Computers

Actually, using a computer involves a series of steps that provide the computer with information about what is to be done (see Figure 10-5):

1. *Gain access to the machine.* This always involves identifying who will pay for using the computer. Although the way this is done varies from computer to computer (and computer site to computer site), it is always among the first things a computer needs to know. Therefore, the first step in using a computer is learning how to tell the computer who is going to pay the bill.

2. *Inform it about what is to be done.* Computers operate using sets of instructions called programs. Although researchers can provide their

---

Figure 10-5 Steps in using a computer for statistical analysis of a data matrix

1. Gain access to the computer
2. Specify the program to be used
3. Describe the data matrix
   1. Identify each variable
   2. Specify the location of each variable
   3. Count the number of cases
4. Modify the data as necessary
5. Specify the statistical analyses to be done
6. Enter the data matrix
7. Terminate use of the computer

---

own programs, most statistical analysis involves using programs written by others. Two of the most widely available sets of programs for doing statistical analysis are SPSS and BIOMED.[6] Regardless of who developed the program, the second step in using a computer is to specify which program is going to be used.

3. Describe the data matrix to be analyzed. This description is comprised of three substeps:

1. *Identify the variables* in the data matrix. With the first approach, the researcher simply specifies the number of variables, and the program generates a name for each. With the second approach, the researcher provides the names for the variables directly. The advantage of the second approach is that the researcher can assign a meaningful name to the variable (for example, Sex for the variable associated with the sexual identification of the respondent). In either case, variables are named in order of their appearance from left to right across the data matrix.

2. *Specify the location of each variable* in the data matrix. This is usually done with what is called a format statement. Format statements specify the column location of variables in the same order that they are named (that is, in order of appearance from left to right across the data matrix).

   For most purposes, variable names are arbitrary. A name for a variable is simply a convenient way of referring to the scores that are located in a particular column of a data matrix. For example, suppose that a researcher coded information on the sex of respondents in column 5 of a data matrix. Further suppose that the researcher became confused and named the variable in column 5, Race. Every time the researcher asked the program to do statistical summaries using the variable Race, the information in column 5 (that is, sexual identification) would be used. As far as the computer is concerned, the variable name Race has no meaning except as a way of specifying that the researcher wishes to examine the information in column 5 of the data matrix. As long as each variable has a unique name, the computer is satisfied. It is the researcher, not the computer, who expects names to have meaning beyond merely specifying a column in a data matrix.

3. *Count the number of cases in the matrix.* Computer programs vary in the way counting is done. In some, the researcher must count the number of cases prior to entering the data into the computer. In others, the researcher can give special instructions to the computer (either by a card or through a terminal command) and the counting is done by the computer.

4. *Modify the data when necessary.* There are a number of situations that frequently are the occasions for data modification. Two are especially common. First, suppose that a researcher has asked a large sample of subjects to state their age in response to a questionnaire item. If the researcher wants the computer to tabulate the ages of all the subjects, the resulting table is apt to be unwieldy, particularly if the subjects range widely in age. In order to simplify the data, the researcher would probably ask the computer to generate a table that shows the ages of the subjects by decade. This would be done by instructing the computer to recode subjects aged 0–9 as a 1, 10–19 as a 2, 20–29 as a 3, and so on. The result will be a very simple tabulation that will be manageable in any matrix that one wishes to construct.

The second frequently encountered type of data transformation involves the creation of a new variable. Suppose that a researcher's preliminary work has suggested that the older a person is, the lower his or her income and educational level will be, and the more likely it is that the person will become psychologically dependent. The researcher might want to combine the individual variables age, income, and education into a new variable called "psychological dependency index" for the purpose of making some further comparison. The computer can be instructed to make the necessary calculations to accomplish this task prior to using the new variable in any matrix.

5. *Specify the analyses to be done* and the variables that are to be included in each analysis. Some programs are highly specialized and do only a single type of statistical analysis. In such situations, the researcher, by selecting the program to use, has already completed this step. Often, however, the program used provides the researcher with a variety of statistical procedures that can be used. In this case, the researcher must specify which procedures to use and which variables to employ in each analysis.

6. *Enter the data matrix* to be analyzed. Obviously, unless the data are entered into the machine, the program cannot analyze them.

7. *Inform the computer that its work is finished.* Sometimes, this step involves both informing the program that the researcher has no further analyses to be done and informing the computer that there are no more programs to be used. Other times, only the final step is necessary.

Computers do not, as should be apparent, represent the solution to all of the researcher's problems. A computer is a tool that, like any other tool, can be misused as well as used. Researchers must take extreme care in preparing the data matrix for use with a computer and in describing that matrix to the computer. The quality of the statistical analysis performed by the computer is never better than the quality of the information provided. If the researcher miscodes variables or misspecifies variables, the resulting analysis will be meaningless. People, not computers, make errors, but computers rarely detect these errors. The user of a computer must understand the data set, be certain that the data matrix is accurate, and know what the computer can and cannot do.

Key Terms

coding	codebook	processor
data matrix	keypunch	output device
data transfer	terminal	program
edge coding	input device	

References

1. The items in this index are adapted from a measure developed by D. L. Klemmack and L. L. Roff, *An Analysis of Public Support for Programs and Benefits for Older People,* Project Report to NRTA-AARP Andrus Foundation, January, 1980.
2. Coding numbers directly on the instrument of observation eliminates one step in the data-transfer process if the data are to be used by the computer. Keypunchers can punch information directly from the instrument. This system works well with nonprofessional keypunchers. If professional keypunchers are to be used, however, they may insist that the data be transferred to special forms prior to keypunching.
3. A complete discussion of the way in which numbers are stored in a computer is beyond the scope of this text. For most purposes, how-

ever, conceiving of numbers being stored in the form of a data matrix is sufficiently accurate.

4. Although there are differences between keypunches and terminals, most of what applies to keypunches also applies to terminals. The remainder of this discussion will be based on the assumption that the researcher is using a keypunch to prepare data for use with a computer.

5. Usually, in keypunching, researchers do not leave extra spaces between columns as one does when writing a data matrix by hand. This means that extra care must be taken in identifying which variables will be punched in which columns.

6. SPSS refers to the Statistical Package for the Social Sciences, and BIOMED refers to Biomedical Statistical Package.

Questions for Discussion

1. Why are operational definitions of variables important in research?
2. Why would a researcher want to construct more than one operational definition from the same set of responses to a single question?
3. Why is accuracy so important in coding and transferring observations?
4. Many individuals talk about computer error, but this text stresses human error. How do people cause "computer error"?

Exercises

1. Construct a codebook for the questionnaire shown in Figure 6-4 (pages 98–102). Be sure to include information about the columns in which information will be punched.

2. Create a data matrix based on the following information:
   a. A white male who is 37 and has 2 children wishes that the local community mental health center had evening hours.
   b. A white female who is 24 and has no children wishes that the local community mental health center had evening hours.
   c. A black female who is 35 and has 8 children wishes that the local community mental health center had evening hours.
   d. A black female who is 26 and has 4 children does not care if the local community mental health center has evening hours.
   e. A white female who is 35 and has 4 children does not care if the local community mental health center has evening hours.

3. Punch (or type) the data matrix from question 2, and check it for accuracy.

For Further Reading

Johan Galtung. *Theory and Methods of Social Research.* New York: Columbia University Press, 1967. See Chapter 1 for an extensive discussion of data matrixes and their construction.

Earl R. Babbie. *The Practice of Social Research.* Belmont, California: Wadsworth, 1979. See Chapter 13 for a discussion of coding and transferring data for use with a computer.

William R. Klecka, Norman H. Nie, and C. Hadlai Hull. *SPSS Primer.* New York: McGraw-Hill, 1975. This excellent description of computers and their operation is also an introduction to one of the most widely available statistical packages for computer analysis.

11

Single-Variable Descriptive Statistics

The field of statistics provides a set of tools for describing and explaining many aspects of the empirical world. Students, when asked how well they are doing in school, report their grade averages. Baseball fans learn the batting averages of their favorite players. Polling agencies calculate the percentage of people who favor a particular presidential candidate. The government reports unemployment rates, birth rates, cost-of-living indexes, and inflation indexes in terms of percentages and percentage increases or decreases. The word *statistics,* in this text, refers to numbers that summarize features of data. We also use the term *statistics* to refer to a branch of mathematics that involves studying different ways of summarizing data. These different meanings of the word *statistics* can be confusing at times; we will use only the first of these meanings in this chapter.

The focus of this chapter is on using statistics to describe a single variable or scale. More specifically, the concepts of frequency distribution, percentage distribution, measure of location, and measure of variability are introduced and illustrated. Later chapters will consider the use of statistics to describe the relationships among variables and the use of statistics in making inferences. This chapter and later chapters on statistics are not intended as a substitute for a statistics course. They do, however, introduce and illustrate how statistics can be used in the research enterprise.

Uses of Statistics

Statistical procedures are tools to help people in their efforts to learn about the world. They suggest ways that information can be summarized. Further, when used with caution, they can be powerful tools in helping to communicate what the researcher has learned. At the same time, statistical procedures are not magical tools that, when applied to a given data set, make everything turn out acceptably. A poorly designed study that fails to answer the researcher's questions remains a poorly designed study no matter how well statistics are used.

As we noted in Chapter 10, the data matrix associated with most studies contains many entries. The researcher, when asked what the study findings are, could present the questioner with a copy of the data matrix (plus information on the codebook and how the data were gathered). This is usually not very helpful. A data matrix typically includes more information than people can readily assimilate. The problem facing the researcher is to reduce the complexity of the data matrix so that the relevant information it contains can be effectively communicated to others.

Although it is usually necessary to summarize the information contained in a data matrix in some way, the researcher must remember that summarizing always means losing information. To report the number or percentage of people studied who are satisfied with a program, for example, means reducing an entire column of a data matrix to a single number. This number, though informative, does not include information about which specific individuals were or were not satisfied with the program. Further, this number provides no clues about how those who liked (or disliked) the program scored on other variables. Using statistics to summarize information requires a trade-off between communicating results simply and losing some of the information contained in the original data matrix. The objective of summarizing data through statistics is to maximize communication while minimizing information loss.

Tools for Summarizing Single Variables

The remainder of this chapter focuses on different methods of summarizing how subjects score on a single scale, variable, or measure. Essentially, each of the methods to be discussed involves simplifying one column of a data matrix. All of the methods involve summarizing in such a way that information about specific individuals is lost. Also, all of the methods to be presented involve losing information about the relationship between scores on one variable with scores on the remaining variables. Each of the tools, however, has the advantage of providing a general indication of how subjects scored on a given variable.

Although a variety of statistical tools describe how subjects score on a single variable, the two most common are (1) the frequency distribution and (2) the measure of central tendency, with an associated measure of dispersion or variability. We will focus first on using frequency distributions to describe how subjects score on a particular variable or measure. Second, we will discuss measures of central tendency, or procedures for selecting a single value as the typical score on the variable. Finally, we will consider the companion problem of variation, or how to select a number that reflects how much the scores or values differ from one another.

Frequency Distributions

Of all of the methods of summarizing how subjects score on a single measure or variable, the one that gives the most complete information is the frequency distribution. Basically, the process of calculating a frequency distribution for a given variable is easy: One simply counts the number of subjects who have a specific value on the variable of concern and repeats this process for each and every possible value of the variable. For example, consider the variable "marital status." One might use as responses to the question "What is your marital status?" the answers "never married," "divorced," "widowed," and "married." To obtain a frequency distribution of this variable, one simply counts how many people are never married, divorced, widowed, or married.

Although it is easy to compute a frequency distribution, the researcher must make at least three different decisions about how to present the resulting summary data. These include:

1. whether the data should be grouped or collapsed prior to developing the frequency distribution;
2. whether relative or absolute frequencies should be presented; and
3. whether the data should be presented in a tabular or in a graphic form.

Grouping.   One method of reducing the complexity of the data to be presented in a frequency distribution is to reduce the number of distinct categories or values on the variable by combining similar or like categories. Age, for example, might be grouped into five- or ten-year intervals. Thus, rather than reporting that three individuals are thirty years old, four are thirty-one, and so forth, the researcher could report that there are fifteen individuals 30–34 years old. Although grouping can be an effective way to summarize information, the information loss from grouping can be substantial. Thus, the decision to group values of a variable when constructing a frequency distribution requires careful attention.

Although there are many exceptions to these rules, the researcher usually decides to group values of a variable (1) if there are too many values or (2) if there are too few cases. Common variables for which the researcher often decides there are too many values to present easily include age, years of school completed, and income. Often, if a variable has more than ten categories (values), the researcher will decide that at least some should be combined before constructing the final frequency distribution.

As is the case with the question of how many are "too many" values on a variable, the question of how few are "too few" subjects in a specific category is not easily answered. Usually, the researcher uses one of two rules:

1. If the total number of subjects is small (no larger than 100), the researcher should consider combining categories with fewer than five subjects with other categories.
2. If the total number of subjects is large (at least 500), researchers tend to combine categories that have fewer than 1 percent of the subjects with other categories.

Again, however, the researcher must never lose sight of the objective of communicating clearly to readers. If combining categories appears to interfere with effective communication, the researcher should always decide not to combine.

If the researcher decides that combining categories will improve communication, he or she faces the issue of which categories to combine. Normally, a frequency distribution is divided at meaningful points. For example, an individual's status with respect to the legal system changes at particular ages. A researcher might divide an elderly population into those 60 or older (the age of entitlement to benefits under the Older Americans Act) and those under 60. Alternative points for dividing an elderly population could be 62 (the youngest age for receiving a Social Security retirement pension), 65 (the traditional age for retirement), or 70 (the mandatory age of retirement). A younger population might be divided into those 16 or older (the minimum legal age to drive a car in many states) and those under 16. Depending on study purposes and applicable state laws, alternative division points might be ages 14, 18, 19, or 21. The principle underlying how to decide which categories to combine is always the same: Attempt to combine categories so that the result is meaningful.

Sometimes the researcher decides that collapsing categories on a frequency distribution would help in communication of information, but for some reason cannot use the principle of meaningful groupings. This problem often occurs when using attitude scales. Suppose, for example, a researcher is using an ordinal measure of how religious people are, in which the scores go from 0 (low religiosity) to 100 (high religiosity). If the measure is valid and reliable, those with higher scores are more religious than those with lower scores. At the same time, a person with a score of 50 is not necessarily twice as religious as an individual with a score of 25 (see Chapter 2). Because a "rubber yardstick" is being used to measure how religious people are, it is difficult to apply the principle of meaningful groupings. In this case, the researcher usually turns to a second rule, the rule of naturally occurring groupings.

Suppose that the researcher examining the degree of religiosity noted that 33 percent of the subjects had scores between 55 and 60 on the measure of religiosity, 27 percent of the subjects had scores between 75 and 77, and 35 percent of the subjects had scores between 91 and 94. This suggests that these data could be divided into three relatively homogeneous categories. The first category would include those scoring between 55 and 60 on the measure. People who scored in that range might be labeled "low" in religiosity. The second category would include those who score between 75 and 77 (labeled "medium" in religiosity), and the third category would include those scoring between 91 and 94 (labeled "high" in religiosity). This method of grouping subjects uses the rule of collapsing the frequency distribution into naturally occurring groupings.

Unfortunately, people answering questions posed by researchers occasionally resist being classified. Sometimes the researcher, in order to simplify a frequency distribution, wishes to combine categories on a variable but is unable to use either the principle of meaningful groupings or the method of naturally occurring groupings. The researcher then turns to a third method of accomplishing the objective: combining categories of the variable so that there are approximately the same number of subjects in each of the groupings. This method of reducing the number of categories or values to be reported in a frequency distribution is the least acceptable approach and should be used only when there is no better alternative.

Absolute and Relative Frequencies.   The second issue the researcher must address in presenting a frequency distribution is whether to report the *actual number* of subjects with each value on the variable (absolute frequency) or the *percentage* of the subjects with each value (relative frequency). Researchers usually prefer reporting percentages to actual numbers, because percentages (1) are easily understood by most consumers of research and (2) make comparisons easier. A percentage distribution, however can be deceiving if the total number of cases is small. Often researchers avoid this issue by presenting both percentages and actual numbers.

Methods of Presentation.   The final issue the researcher must consider when constructing a frequency distribution is the selection of an appropriate presentation format. Should the researcher present the frequency distribution in the form of a numerical table or in the form of a pictorial representation, such as a bar or circle graph? Professional journals usually prefer that data be presented in tabular form to minimize printing costs, whereas other types of publications (such as annual reports) often make extensive use of pictorial forms of data presentation. Generally, the researcher selects the mode of presentation that most simply conveys the information contained in the frequency distribution to the intended audience.

Regardless of the method of presentation selected, an informative frequency distribution always includes certain elements:

1. A frequency distribution must always *make explicit the specific variable or measure being discussed.* Most researchers use the title of the table or graph to present this information (see Figures 11-1 through 11-3).
2. The values or scores on the variable *must be labeled.* Without this type of information, the interpretation of the frequency distribution of scores is extremely difficult, if not impossible.
3. It is essential that the numbers be labeled so that the reader knows *whether frequencies or percentages (relative frequencies) are being presented.*
4. It is helpful to *present the total number of cases on which the frequency distribution is based,* particularly when using percentages.

Examples.   Table 11-1 and Figures 11-1 through 11-3 illustrate four different ways of presenting a frequency distribution. In each example, the title includes the variable being examined. Also, when appropriate, both the absolute and the relative frequencies are presented.

Table 11-1 illustrates a *tabular presentation* of a frequency distribution on the degree of agreement with the statement, "Government should help older people by making sure they have enough income to live comfortably." According to the table, respondents indicated their degree of agreement with the statement using one of five categories: strongly agree, agree, uncertain, disagree, or strongly disagree. Because the table shows both the absolute and the relative frequencies, the reader knows that 27.2 percent, or 258 of 947 respondents, indicated that they strongly agreed with the statement. Almost three-fourths of the respondents (72.5 percent or 687 of 947) agreed or strongly agreed with the statement.

The values of the variable presented in Table 11.1 are ordered, and thus the variable itself is ordinal in nature. When variables are other than nominal in nature, the order of presentation of values or categories in the frequency distribution becomes important. If the categories in Table 11-1 had been presented in the order "strongly disagree," "uncertain," "disagree," "agree," "strongly agree," interpretation of the table would have been more difficult. Because the purpose of constructing the table in the first place is to communicate results, usually frequency distributions of ordinal, interval, and ratio variables are presented so that a logical ordering of the values is maintained. This practice has the added advantage of making possible the meaningful computation of the cumulative frequency, or percentile distribution, of a variable.

Table 11-1   Degree of agreement with the statement, "Government should help older people by making sure they have enough income to live comfortably."

	Frequency	Percentage
Strongly agree	258	27.2
Agree	429	45.3
Uncertain	142	15.0
Disagree	100	10.6
Strongly disagree	18	1.9
Total	947	100.0

The *cumulative frequency,* or *percentile distribution,* of a variable is a variant of the frequency or percentage distributions. It is used to communicate where an individual ranks compared with others on a given variable or characteristic. Developing and using a percentile distribution are demonstrated using the following example: Suppose that a mental-health center has developed a measure of the severity of enuresis in young children. Their measure involves asking parents ten yes-or-no questions. The scores range from 0 to 10, in which 0 means the problem is not very severe, and 10 means that the problem is extremely severe. Suppose also that the center has been using this measure for five years and has gathered data on 1,000 children. To summarize these data, the researcher constructs a frequency distribution (see Table 11-2). Although the center staff know

Table 11-2   Frequency distribution on a measure of severity of enuresis for mental-health center clients

Score	Frequency	Percentage	Percentile
0	51	5.1	5.1
1	43	4.3	9.4
2	27	2.7	12.1
3	31	3.1	15.2
4	37	3.7	18.9
5	25	2.5	21.4
6	34	3.4	24.8
7	112	11.2	36.0
8	348	34.8	70.8
9	137	13.7	84.5
10	155	15.5	100.0
Total	1,000	100.0	——

that children with higher scores have more severe problems than do children with lower scores, they might also like to know how severe a particular child's problem is compared with all other children who have been evaluated at that center. To do this, they calculate a percentile distribution by determining what percentage of the cases occur at or below a given score (see Table 11-2). Thus, for example, 18.9 percent of the children treated at the center have a "severity of problem" score of 4 or less. Most of the cases handled by the center, on the other hand, have a "severity of problem" score of 8 or more (74.0 percent = 100.0 − 36.0). If parents of a child with a severity of problem score of 9 asked how severe their child's problem was, the center staff could indicate that 70.8 percent of the children seen by the center in the last five years had a less severe problem than that child does or that 84.5 percent of the children seen by the center in the last five years had a problem as severe or less so. In either case, the information presented provides an indication of where the child ranks compared with others seen by the center and thus provides more information than the "severity of problem" score alone.

Figure 11-1 illustrates a graphic mode of presenting a frequency distribution, the *bar graph*. This method of presenting data is particularly useful when the variable is measured at the nominal level. Suppose, for example, that a mental-health agency director supervises five satellite centers and wishes to compare the number of clients served in a given month by each of the satellite centers. A bar graph of these data would provide an easily interpreted display of the information. From the example presented in Figure 11-1, it is easy to see that satellite center D serves many more clients than the other centers and that satellite center C serves far fewer clients. Although the information portrayed in this bar graph could be presented in a table, the large differences in clients served by the various centers is probably best emphasized by this graphic display.

Bar graphs are constructed by converting the length of a line (or the area of a bar) into a number. The researcher could, for example, indicate that a bar ½ inch long represents 25 cases. Then, a bar 1 inch would represent 50 cases, and a 2-inch bar would represent 100 cases. So as not to confuse the reader, the base or width of the bar is the same for each satellite center. In this way, both the length and the area of each bar of the bar are proportional to the number of cases it represents. Finally, for the reader's convenience, both the number and the percentage of the clients served by a satellite center are reported above the bar for that center.

Bar graphs constructed when the variable is measured on the ordinal, interval, or ratio level are called *histograms*. The primary difference between a bar graph for a nominal variable and a histogram is that the ordering and the width of the bars is important in a histogram but not in a bar graph. In the example of the bar graph in Figure 11-1, it does not make any difference which satellite center is presented first. As long as each center has a unique name, the reader should have no difficulty in

**Figure 11-1   Bar graph of clients served by five satellite centers
of a mental-health agency for one month**

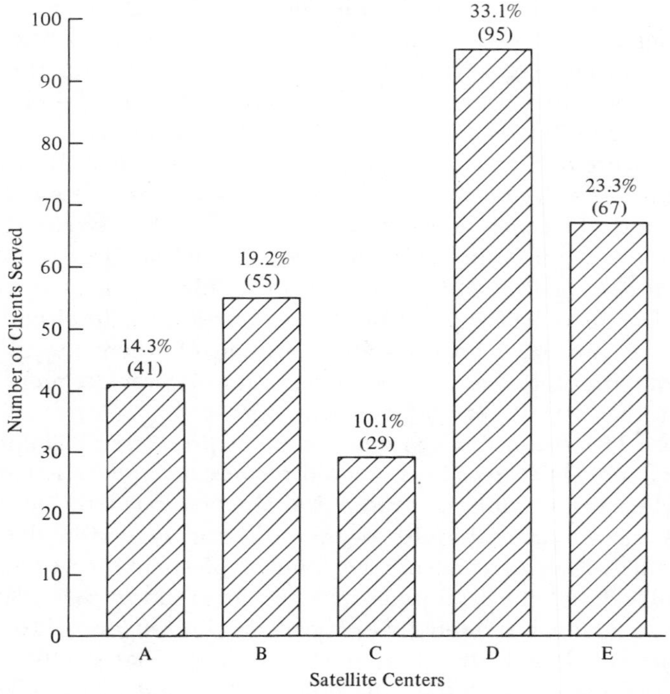

interpreting the graph. Further, although it is less confusing to the reader if the bars for each center are the same width, the width of the bar has no meaning. This is not the case with a histogram. Both the order in which bars appear and their width are important, particularly when the variable is measured at the interval or ratio level. The following example illustrates the importance of this distinction:

Suppose that the director of a home-health agency wanted to demonstrate growth in the number of clients served by the agency over time. Looking over past records of the agency, the director finds the data reported in Table 11-3. The problem with these data should be immediately obvious. The director knows the actual number of cases served in 1980, but the only data for 1960 through 1979 are grouped in five-year periods. To rectify this problem, the director decides to report the average number of cases seen each year for the periods 1960–64, 1965–69, 1970–74, and 1975–79. Because the latest time period includes only a single year, the

Table 11-3   Clients served by a home-health agency

Time Period	Number of Clients Served
1960–64	321
1965–69	436
1970–74	501
1975–79	686
1980	158

director decides to make the width of the histogram bar for this time period one-fifth as wide as those for the other four periods (see Figure 11-2). This is because data for only one-fifth of a five-year interval are available. Thus, the height of the bar is proportionate to the number of cases seen in a given year, the width of the bar is proportionate to the number of years included in the interval, and the area of the bar (height times width) is proportionate to the total number of cases seen in the time period represented by the bar. Also, because the values on the variable are ordered, it is important to present the information in order. Presenting the data for the time period 1970–74 prior to those for 1965–69, for example, would serve only to confuse the reader and make examination of the trend suggested by the data more difficult.

Yet another method of presenting relative frequencies, or percentages of a total, is the *circle graph*. A circle graph is constructed by converting a proportion or percentage into area. A full circle is considered to be 100 percent. Half of a circle then represents 50 percent, and one-fourth of a circle represents 25 percent. Although useful for demonstrating how large the different parts of any whole are, the circle graph is most frequently used to portray budgets by category of expenditure. Suppose, for example, the accountant for a family agency is preparing a report on the agency's operation to present to the business leaders of the community in which the agency operates. As a first step in preparing the report, the accountant develops the information reported in Table 11-4. To portray this information more graphically, the accountant decides to construct a circle graph (see Figure 11-3). This mode of presentation emphasizes the large proportion of the agency's budget that goes to employee salaries.

To summarize briefly, frequency distributions are one way that the researcher can summarize how subjects score on a given measure or variable. The researcher may group the data by combining similar categories if even further summarization is necessary. Either absolute or relative frequencies, or both, may be reported. Finally, the researcher may use any one of several different formats for presenting the information contained

Figure 11-2   Histogram of clients served by a home-health agency

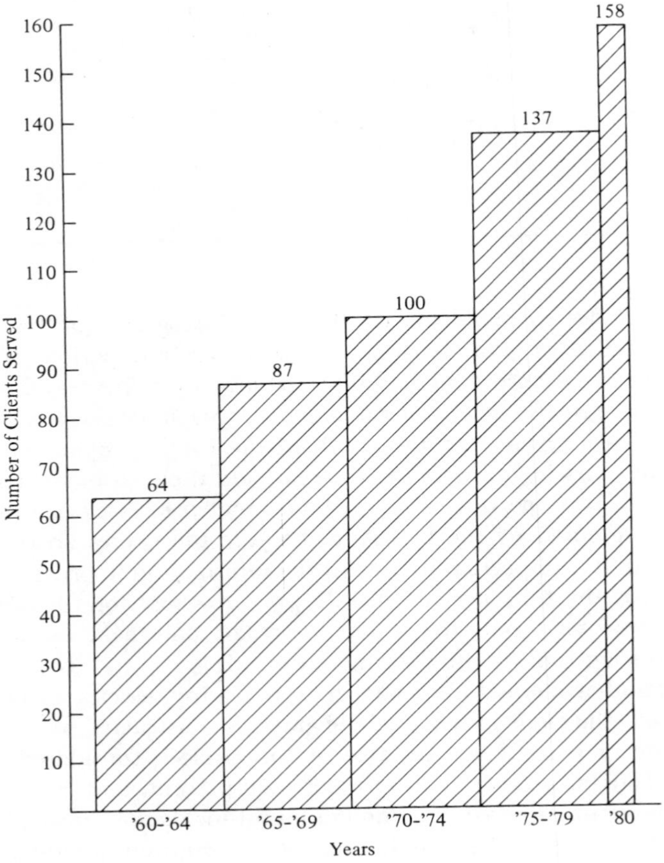

Note: Figures for five-year periods are averages; actual figures are reported for 1980 only.

in a frequency distribution. The choices include, but are not limited to, tables, bar graphs, and circle graphs.

Measures of Location

Although a frequency distribution summarizes how subjects score on a variable, sometimes even a frequency distribution presents more information than readers can readily assimilate. Two social workers discussing their jobs might well compare how "heavy" their caseloads were. One way of

Table 11-4   Summary of the budget for a family-service agency

Category	Dollars	Percentage
Salaries	$240,000	60.0
Employee benefits	60,000	15.0
Operating expenses, including rent, utilities, supplies, office equipment, and postage	60,000	15.0
Travel and conference expenses, including workshops	40,000	10.0
Total	$400,000	100.0

comparing would be to indicate the number of clients seen each day for the previous week. Although this approach is probably superior to listing each and every case seen, the ideal answer to the question would probably be a number that represented the typical number of clients seen on a typical day. A number that represents the typical score on a variable (the number of clients seen each day, in this example) is called a *measure of location,* or a *measure of central tendency.* The three common measures of location or central tendency in social research are the *mode,* the *median,* and the *arithmetic mean.*

The Mode. The *mode* is defined as *the most frequently occurring value of a variable.* The mode for the data presented in Table 11-1 is the cate-

Figure 11-3   A circle graph depicting the budget of a family-service agency

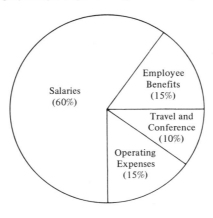

gory "agree." Slightly over 45 percent of the respondents "agree" with the statement that government should help older people by making sure they have enough income to live comfortably, whereas only 27.2 percent of the respondents "strongly agree" with this statement. The modal score on the measure of severity of enuresis reported in Table 11-2 is 8, and satellite center D is the modal category for the data reported in Figure 11-2.

The mode is the only appropriate measure of location if the variable is measured at the nominal level. It is a particularly useful measure of the typical score when the majority of the cases fall into one category on the variable. For example, the most common health problem seen in an elementary school clinic is the common cold. This malady could well account for as many as 70 percent of the cases seen by a school nurse and thus represents the mode. Similarly, if the majority of adolescents assigned to a probation officer working with the juvenile court are labeled as "incorrigible," the typical or most common case for such an officer would be the "incorrigible" adolescent.

Although the mode is the only measure of location that can be used with nominal variables, it is not a very useful measure of the typical score when no category on a variable has many cases. The following illustration may make this clearer: Suppose that a social worker working in a family-service agency has been conducting divorce counseling with couples for one year. He or she decides to determine how many therapy sessions the typical couple using this service attend prior to termination and gathers the data shown in Table 11-5. The mode for these data is five sessions, but if there were one fewer five-session couple and one more one-session couple, the mode would be one session. Further, although the mode is five sessions, 65.1 percent of the couples attend four or fewer sessions. Obviously, in this case, the mode is not a very good description of the typical number of therapy sessions for the average couple.

Table 11-5   Number of sessions before termination in divorce counseling

Number of Sessions	Frequency	Percentage
1	27	17.4
2	23	14.8
3	26	16.8
4	25	16.1
5	28	18.1
6 or more	26	16.8
Total	155	100.0

The Median.   If the variable is measured at the ordinal, interval, or ratio levels, the researcher may use the median as a measure of location or central tendency. The *median* is defined as *the point at which one-half of the scores in the distribution are higher and one-half of the scores are lower than all the other scores in the distribution.* For example, the median for the ranks (1), (2), (3), (4), and (5) is 3, and the median for the ranks (1), (2), (3), and (4) is usually defined as 2.5. Note that the median can assume a value that does not occur in the data. This occasionally leads to bizarre statements—for example, that the median family size in a particular community is 3.4 people. Although the researcher and the reader know that no family has 3.4 members, expressing the median in this way facilitates comparing results from one study to the next.

The definition of the median is simple. However, the calculation of the value of the median often requires some care. The problem involved in calculating an exact value for the median is illustrated by the data in Table 11-5. Although 51.0 percent of the cases have a score of 4 or larger (attended four or more sessions), 65.1 percent of the cases have a score of 4 or lower. Although category "4" surely includes the median, it is equally apparent that the median is not 4. Actually, to compute the exact value of the median requires a little fancy footwork:

1. Define category 4 as including all of the real numbers from 3.5 through 4.5. Note that this is the same as saying that the data are measured at the interval level for that category even if the data are clearly measured at the ordinal level. Without this assumption, however, precise determination of the median is not possible. Note also that the center of this interval is 4, the number assigned to the category.

2. Determine the proportion of the cases lying below the category including the median (17.4 + 14.8 + 16.8 = 49.0 percent, in this example).

3. Determine the number of additional cases needed to reach 50 percent, or the median. (Here, $50\% - 49\% = 1\%$, so 1.55 cases—1 percent of 155—are needed).

4. Assume that the cases included in the category that includes the median are distributed evenly across the interval associated with the category. Thus, because there are twenty-five cases in the interval including the median in this example, 2.5 cases lie between 3.5 and 3.6.

5. Determine the length of the interval associated with the number of cases needed by:

1. determining the proportion of cases from the interval needed (1.55/25 = .062, in this example), and

2. multiplying the result by the length of the interval ($0.062 \times 1 = .062$, in this example).

6. Calculate the median by adding the result from step 5 to the lower boundary of the interval determined in step 1. Thus, the median here = $3.5 + .062 = 3.562$).

These operations are summarized by the following formula:

$$\text{Median} = LL + \frac{N_1}{N_2} \times I$$

in which LL is the lower limit of the interval including the median, N_1 is the number of additional cases needed to reach 50 percent of the cases, N_2 is the number of cases in the interval that includes the median, and I is the size of the interval including the median.

The median would appear to be a better measure of location to use with the data presented in Table 11-5 than the mode is. It seems more reasonable to indicate that the typical clients of the divorce-counseling service attend 3.6 (3.562) sessions (the value of the median) rather than 5 sessions (the value of the mode). In general, when the variable is measured at the ordinal level or above and the cases are distributed approximately evenly across the values of the variable, the median is superior to the mode as a measure of location. If, however, the majority of the cases fall into a single category, it is good practice to report both the median and the mode.

Occasionally, the mode provides a better description of how the typical subject scores than does the median. This usually occurs when the frequency distribution of scores assumes an unusual form, such as occurs in a *bimodal distribution*. Suppose, for example, that mental-health counselors working at a mental-health center believed that their clients were not members of voluntary associations in the community. As a first step in a research project to determine the validity of this assertion, they ask their clients about the number of voluntary association memberships they have and obtain the data reported in Table 11-6. Using the formula presented earlier, the median for these is 2.5 ($1.5 + 1/1 \times 1 = 2.5$), whereas the mode is 4. Neither of these choices provides a good description of the number of memberships held by the typical client of the center. If the researcher is willing to stretch the definition of the mode slightly, however, it is possible to make a statement that does describe these data quite well. Most of the clients of the mental-health center either belong to no voluntary associations (46.3 percent) or belong to at least four such associations (47.5 percent). Presenting both modes is clearly superior to presenting the median when describing data such as these.

The Arithmetic Mean.   If the variable is measured at the interval or ratio level, the researcher can use a third measure of location, the arithmetic

Table 11-6   Bimodal distribution of voluntary association memberships of clients at a mental-health center

Number of Memberships	Frequency	Percentage
0	37	46.3
1	2	2.5
2	1	1.2
3	2	2.5
4 or more	38	47.5
Total	80	100.0

mean. When people refer to the "average score," they usually mean the arithmetic mean. This measure of location is the one most commonly used in research and the one most frequently reported in research reports. The *arithmetic mean* is defined as *the sum of the scores on the measure divided by the number of subjects being measured.* This definition is usually represented by the following formula:

$$\bar{x} = \frac{\Sigma X_i}{N}$$

in which X_i is the score of one of the subjects on the measure—that is, X_1 is the score for the first subject, X_7 is the score for the seventh subject, and in general, X_i is the score for the ith subject; N is the number of subjects; Σ means add scores together; and $\bar{X}$ is the arithmetic mean.

The computation of the mean is simple but can become tedious if the number of subjects is large. To illustrate this, suppose that the data matrix for the first five clients for the study summarized in Table 11-6 is reported in Table 11-7. The arithmetic mean for these five cases would be 1.6 ($0 + 0 + 1 + 3 + 4 = 8$ divided by $5 = 1.6$). Assuming that no one belonged to more than four voluntary associations, the arithmetic mean for the data presented in Table 11-6 would be 2.025 ($162/80 = 2.025$).

Unless the researcher has a good reason not to use the arithmetic mean, it is the preferred measure of location for several reasons:

1. The calculation of the arithmetic mean involves using the value of each score. Consequently, changing any score in the distribution will result in a change in the value of the arithmetic mean. This is not necessarily the case with either the median or the mode.
2. As we will demonstrate in later chapters, the arithmetic mean is more useful in calculating other statistics than are either the median or the mode.

Table 11-7   An abbreviated data matrix for computing the arithmetic mean

Client	Number of Memberships
1	0
2	0
3	1
4	3
5	4

3. Most people expect that the average score means the arithmetic mean. Thus, using this measure reduces potential confusion among readers.

Although the arithmetic mean is superior to the median and the mode as a measure of location, it does have limitations:

1. The arithmetic mean is used appropriately only with interval and ratio levels of measurement. If the data to be summarized are nominal or ordinal in nature, use of the arithmetic mean as a measure of location is inappropriate.
2. The arithmetic mean is sensitive to extreme values. Suppose, for example, that a researcher gathered monthly income data from ten individuals. Of the ten, nine had incomes of $1,000 a month, and one had an income of $3,000 a month. The mode, the median, and arithmetic mean for these data are $1,000, $1,055, and $1,200, respectively. If the income of the tenth person were $10,000 rather than $3,000 a month, however, the mode and median would be unchanged, but the arithmetic mean would be $1,900. Thus, a single extreme score can drastically change the value of the arithmetic mean. As a consequence, the median is generally considered to be superior to the arithmetic mean as a measure of location when there are extreme scores in the distribution.

Measures of Dispersion

Suppose a caseworker for a family-service agency is approached by a client who has a developmentally disabled child. The parent wants to enroll the child in a special school but does not know which of two schools in the community offering special education classes would be best. The caseworker is not familiar with either of the two schools but does know that the child will progress most rapidly in a class where the student-teacher ratio is low. Bearing this in mind, the caseworker calls both schools and asks about average class size. School A reports an average class size of 8, whereas School B reports an average class size of 8.5. On the basis of this information, the caseworker recommends that the parent enroll the child in School A. At their next meeting, the parent complains that the child would have been placed in a class with only four other children if School B had been selected. The caseworker calls the schools again and obtains the information reported in Table 11-8. School B had recently hired an additional teacher and started a new class. Thus, the child would have been placed in the smallest class if he or she had enrolled in School B rather than School A, even though the average class size was slightly larger at School B. The caseworker in this situation failed to realize that the arithmetic mean does not provide information on the variability of scores. Because class size was more variable at School B than at School A, the child could have been placed in a smaller class at School B. An adequate description of a distribution requires information about both the typical score (measures of location) and variability among scores.

A *measure of dispersion,* like a measure of location, describes a characteristic of the distribution of a set of scores. Whereas measures of location describe the typical score in a distribution, *measures of dispersion describe how the scores in a distribution differ from one another.* Like measures of location, measures of dispersion are related to the level of measurement used. Although the mode is a measure of location for nominal variables, there is no measure of dispersion for variables that are measured at the nominal level. If the level of measurement is ordinal, interval, or ratio, the researcher may use either the *range* or the *interquartile range* as a measure of dispersion. If the level of measurement is interval or ratio, the researcher may use the *standard deviation* as a measure of the dispersion of scores.

The Range.   The *range* is the simplest of the measures of dispersion and is defined as *the highest score on the variable minus the lowest score on*

Table 11-8   Class size for two schools for developmentally disabled children

School A		School B	
Class	Size	Class	Size
1	8	1	4
2	8	2	10
3	8	3	10
4	8	4	10
$\bar{X} = 8.0$		$\bar{X} = 8.5$	

the variable. If, for example, three people belonged to 3, 5, and 7 voluntary associations respectively, the range of voluntary association memberships held would be 4 (7 − 3 = 4).

The range is sensitive to extreme scores and should not be used when there is only one extreme score. Suppose, for example, a researcher counted the number of voluntary-association memberships for 100 people and found that 50 people had no such memberships, 49 people had only one such membership, and 1 person had 100 memberships. The range would be 100 (100 − 0 = 100), a number that does not really reflect the average or typical variability of scores among these people.

The Interquartile Range. To solve the problem of a few extreme scores drastically affecting the value of the range, an alternative measure, the interquartile range, is often used. The *interquartile range* is defined as *the difference in the points between which the middle 50 percent of the scores lie.* If, for example, a researcher observed the scores 1, 2, 4, and 5 on an ordinal variable, the interquartile range would be 2 (4 − 2 = 2), because 25 percent of the scores lie below 2 and 25 percent of the scores lie above 4. The calculation of the interquartile range, like the calculation of the median, poses some problems if the data are not distributed perfectly. The interquartile range is calculated in exactly the same way the median except that the researcher is looking for the points at which 25 percent of the cases and 75 percent of the cases lie rather than the point at which 50 percent of the cases lie. The following example illustrates this principle:

Suppose that a social service agency wishes to determine whether the number of presenting problems a new client has at intake is related to the length of time that the client's case is open. As a first step in the study, the agency develops a problem checklist, which it administers to each client during the intake interview. The frequency distribution of the number of problems for each new client seen during one month is reported in Table 11-9.

In summarizing the data presented in Table 11-9, the agency staff note that the values of the median and the arithmetic mean are the same, 3.5. Thus, clients coming to the agency for the first time generally have an average of 3.5 presenting problems each. The range in the number of problems at entry is 7 (7 − 0 = 7), but this number does not reflect the bunching of the scores from 2 to 5. Therefore, the agency decides to calculate the interquartile range for these data as well.

To obtain the interquartile range, the agency staff must identify the points at which 25 percent and 75 percent of the cases lie. The first of these lies in the interval associated with the value 2, whereas the second lies in the interval associated with the value 5. To estimate the exact points, they use the formula for calculating the median, except that they are seeking

Table 11-9 Distribution of presenting problems per client for clients approaching a social service agency for the first time

Number of Problems	Frequency	Percentage	Cumulative Percentage
0	10	5.0	5.0
1	15	7.5	12.5
2	27	13.5	26.0
3	48	24.0	50.0
4	48	24.0	74.0
5	27	13.5	88.5
6	15	7.5	95.0
7	10	5.0	100.0
Total	200	100.0	

the points at which 25 percent and 75 percent of the cases lie rather than the point at which 50 percent of the cases lie:

$$Q_{25} = 1.5 + \frac{25}{27} \times 1 = 2.43$$

$$Q_{75} = 4.5 + \frac{2}{27} \times 1 = 4.57$$

As the equations above illustrate, Q_{25} (the point at which 25 percent of the cases lie) is 2.43, and Q_{75} (the point at which 75 percent of the cases lie) is 4.57. Therefore, the interquartile range is 2.14 ($4.57 - 2.43 = 2.14$).

Having developed these summary statistics, the agency now has a choice in what information it will present to others. One choice, of course, is simply to present the frequency distribution reported in Table 11-9. A second choice is to describe the distribution in terms of the mean, median, range, and interquartile range. If the staff choose this latter alternative, they might describe the distribution as follows: "The scores on this measure ranged from 0 to 7, with the median and mean number of problems being 3.5. Twenty-five percent of the scores were below 2.43, and 25 percent were above 4.57. Thus, the interquartile range was 2.14." Finally, the agency staff could present both the frequency distribution and the other summary statistics they had developed.

The Standard Deviation. If a variable is measured at the interval or ratio level, the researcher may choose to use the standard deviation in addition to or in place of the interquartile range as a measure of dispersion. The meaning of the *standard deviation* is best understood in the context of pre-diction, in which the researcher uses the arithmetic mean as the "best guess" of what the value of any single score will be. The standard deviation refers to *how far scores are, on the average, from the arithmetic mean.* If the value of the standard deviation is large, the distance between the arithmetic mean and the scores is, on the average, large. If the value of the standard deviation is small, then the scores, on the average, are clustered close to the arithmetic mean.

The procedures for computing the values needed to calculate the value of the standard deviation are as follows (summarized in Table 11-10):

1. Define how far each score is from the arithmetic mean. This is done by simply subtracting the arithmetic mean from each score (see column 3 of Table 11-10).
2. Obtain a measure of the total amount of deviation from the arithmetic mean for all of the scores combined. Unfortunately, simply adding the deviation scores together does not work, because scores for which the arithmetic mean was a low guess cancel out scores for which the arith-metic mean was a high guess. Thus, the sum of the deviations is always zero. The statistician's solution to getting rid of the negative numbers in the deviation column is to square each deviation before adding the deviation scores (see column 4 of Table 11-10). The sum that results from adding the squared deviations together is called the *variation* in

---

Table 11-10   The steps in computing the standard deviation

1. Values

Score	Arithmetic Mean	Deviation	Squared Deviation
X	$\bar{X}$	$(X - \bar{X})$	$(X - \bar{X})^2$
3	5	−2	+4
4	5	−1	+1
5	5	0	0
6	5	+1	+1
7	5	+2	+4
Total 25	25	0	10

2. Formula for variation $= \Sigma(X - \bar{X})^2$

3. Formula for average squared deviation (in this case, $4 + 1 + 0 + 1 + 4 = 10$) = $\dfrac{\Sigma(X - \bar{X})^2}{N} = \dfrac{10}{5} = 2)$

4. Formula for standard deviation $= \sqrt{\dfrac{\Sigma(X - \bar{X})^2}{N}}$

(in this case, $\sqrt{\dfrac{10}{5}} = \sqrt{2} = 1.44)$

---

the data. The amount of variation in a frequency distribution is an important statistical characteristic that is used in other data-summary procedures.

3. Obtain the average squared deviation by dividing the variation by the number of cases (see step 3 in Table 11-10). This is analogous to obtaining the arithmetic mean by summing scores and dividing by the number of scores. This statistic is known as the *variance* of the data.

4. The standard deviation is defined as the square root of the variance, or the square root of the average squared deviation of a set of scores.

The standard deviation is the preferred measure of dispersion, or variability, among scores for two of the same reasons that the arithmetic mean is the preferred measure of location:

1. The calculation of the standard deviation uses the value of each score. Consequently, changing any one score will result in changing the standard deviation, but it will not necessarily result in changing either the range or the interquartile range of the scores.

2. The standard deviation is more useful in calculating other statistics than are the range and interquartile range. At the same time, the standard deviation, like the arithmetic mean, requires that the data be measured at the interval or ratio level of measurement. Further, as is the case with the arithmetic mean, an extreme score will drastically alter the value of the standard deviation.

Key Terms

statistics	mode
frequency distribution	median
relative frequency	arithmetic mean
absolute frequency	measure of dispersion
bar graph	range
circle graph	interquartile range
cumulative frequency	standard deviation
histogram	variation
measure of location	variance

Questions for Discussion

1. How can statistics be helpful to caseworkers in improving their job performance?

2. How may statistics be helpful to an agency administrator in evaluating organizational performance?
3. Under what conditions are statistics misleading?
4. List the advantages and disadvantages of each of three different ways of portraying a frequency distribution.

Exercise

A child welfare worker gives a ten-item, true-false test designed to measure degree of knowledge about nutrition to 25 AFDC mothers and obtains the following scores: 8, 6, 5, 6, 4, 7, 3, 5, 6, 7, 0, 2, 3, 5, 6, 7, 7, 9, 6, 6, 4, 8, 4, 6, 6.

a. Construct a frequency distribution for this measure for these data.
b. Determine the mode, median, and arithmetic mean for the data.
c. Calculate the range, interquartile range, and standard deviation for these data.
d. Write a brief paragraph describing how people scored on this measure.

For Further Reading

Darrell Huff. *How to Lie with Statistics.* New York: W. W. Norton and Company, 1954. This brief, entertaining book illustrates how statistics may be misleading. The chapters on averages and graphs are particularly interesting.

Abraham N. Franzblau. *A Primer of Statistics for Non-Statisticians.* New York: Harcourt, Brace and World, Inc., 1958. As implied in the title, this short text is designed to introduce statistics to the nonstatistician.

Marty J. Schmidt. *Understanding and Using Statistics: Basic Concepts,* 2nd ed. Lexington, Massachusetts: D. C. Heath and Company, 1979. Schmidt provides an excellent, comprehensive discussion of the statistical concepts included in this chapter.

12

Measures of Association and Their Interpretation

Almost without exception, empirical research centers on comparisons among scores on variables. Obviously, the heart of explanation involves comparing different groups (the independent variable values) on outcome scores (the dependent variable values). Thus, for example, the school social worker who is experimenting with different ways of dealing with hyperactive children is interested in comparing outcome scores for different treatments to determine which approaches are most effective. Although it may not be as apparent as in the case of experimentation, hypotheses that state that two variables are related also involve comparisons. The hypothesis that the level of family income is related to feelings of well-being, for example, involves comparing scores on a measure of "level of family income" with scores on a measure of "well-being." In fact, any time a researcher wishes to test a hypothesis that one variable is associated with or related to another variable, he or she wishes to compare scores on one of the variables with scores on the other of the variables. The primary purpose of this chapter is to introduce some of the more common ways in which we make comparisons between scores on two variables.

There are many similarities between the procedures used to describe the relationship between scores on two variables and those used to describe scores on a single variable (discussed in the previous chapter). For example, the first step in comparing scores between two variables is often the construction of a *bivariate frequency-distribution, or cross-tabulation, table*. This is very similar to the construction of a frequency-distribution table for a single variable. Further, researchers construct a bivariate frequency-distribution table for the same reason that they construct a frequency-distribution table for a single variable: to summarize information so that the data can be better understood.

A second point of similarity between the procedures used to compare scores on two variables and those used to describe scores on a single variable is the use of statistics to summarize the information in a frequency distribution. Now, however, rather than using measures of location or central tendency to describe a frequency distribution, researchers use *measures of association or correlation* to describe a bivariate frequency distribution. Measures of association, however, are actually more similar to measures of dispersion or variability than they are to measures of central tendency or location.

A third point of similarity between the procedures used to compare scores on two variables and those used to describe scores on a single variable involves the criteria used in selecting appropriate measures. Just as the selection of the most descriptive measure of central tendency (or dispersion) involves the level of measurement of the variable and the form of the distribution, the selection of an appropriate measure of association involves these same factors. Naturally, the decision is somewhat more complicated, because there are two variables, rather than only one, to consider.

Although there are many parallels between single-variable frequency-distribution tables and bivariate frequency-distribution tables, there are some important differences as well. For example, in some situations, particularly in experimentation, independent and dependent variables are clear. In such a situation, the researcher is interested in comparing dependent variable scores for the different independent variable scores, but not the reverse. In situations in which there are no clear independent and dependent variables, the researcher is interested in comparing scores on one variable with scores on the other, but the order of the variables is not important. In the first of these situations, the relationship of interest is *asymmetric,* and in the second it is *symmetric.* Nor surprisingly, some measures of association are asymmetric and are appropriate only when there are clear independent and dependent variables, whereas other measures of association are symmetric and may be used in any situation. Thus, in selecting a measure of association, the researcher must know not only the level of measurement with which the variables are measured and the form of the bivariate frequency distribution, but also whether the variables are independent or dependent.

This chapter begins with an examination of the procedures used to construct a bivariate frequency-distribution table. Next, we examine statistical independence in terms of its relationship to various measures of association. Then, the chapter concludes with an examination of selected measures of association. For each measure presented, we discuss the computations involved, the interpretation of the data, and practical applications of what the data show.

Bivariate Frequency-Distribution Tables

A basic bivariate frequency-distribution table is organized in the following fashion: The rows of the table refer to scores or values on one of the variables; the columns of the table refer to scores or values on the second of the variables; and the cells within the table present the number of respondents who have both (1) the score associated with the row within which the cell occurs on the first variable and (2) the score associated with the column within which the cell occurs on the second variable. Thus, to decide where to count a particular respondent, the researcher must know both the respondent's score on the first variable and that same respondent's score on the second variable. To construct a bivariate frequency-distribution table of sex and membership in the National Association of Social Workers (NASW), for example, the researcher must know both whether the respondent is (1) a male or female and (2) a member of NASW or not. The tasks in this example are to place respondents into one of four categories—male member, male nonmember, female member, female nonmember—and to count how many are in each category.

There are a variety of procedures for actually constructing a bivariate frequency-distribution table. The most direct approach is to classify each respondent into the appropriate cell and then count the number of respondents in each cell. An alternative strategy, one that simplifies the counting task, is illustrated in Table 12-1. In the first step in this process, respondents are reordered according to their scores on the first variable (sex in this example). Next, the males and the females are reordered separately on the second variable (membership in NASW in this example). Finally, the number of respondents in each bivariate category are counted, and the number is recorded in the appropriate cell of the table.

The cell values in a bivariate frequency distribution, like those in a simple frequency distribution, may be reported either in terms of actual numbers or in terms of percentages. If the choice is percentages, however, a problem arises: There are three different ways in which percentages can be computed. The researcher may choose to base the percentages on the row totals, the column totals, or the total number of respondents. Usually, one of these methods is superior to the others in terms of the purpose of the study, and this is the approach selected. Before examining the basis for selecting which approach to use in any given study, it is helpful to examine how to compute each of the different percentages.

Suppose that researchers drew a random sample of 150 adults who were at least sixty years of age and obtained information on their sex and their awareness of a senior center. These data could be summarized in a bivariate frequency-distribution table similar to Table 12-2a. As the table shows, there are 50 males, of whom 30 are aware of the center, and 100

Table 12-1 Constructing a bivariate frequency-distribution table

| | Original Data | | | Step 1 Organize on First Variable | | | Step 2 Organize on Second Variable | | |
| | | | | | Reordered Data | | | Reordered Data | |
Respondent	Sex	Member		Respondent	Sex	Member		Respondent	Sex	Member
1	M	Y		1	M	Y		1	M	Y
2	F	Y		4	M	N		5	M	Y
3	F	N		5	M	Y		9	M	Y
4	M	N		9	M	Y		4	M	N
5	M	Y		10	M	N		10	M	N
6	F	Y		2	F	Y		3	F	Y
7	F	N		3	F	Y		6	F	Y
8	F	N		6	F	N		2	F	N
9	M	Y		7	F	Y		7	F	N
10	M	N		8	F	N		8	F	N

M = male; F = female; Y = member of NASW; N = not a member.

Table 12-1 *(cont.)*

Step 3
Count Number in Each Category

Sex	Member	Frequency
M	Y	3
M	N	2
F	Y	2
F	N	3

Step 4
Create Table

Member

Sex	Y	N	
M	3	2	5
F	2	3	5
	5	5	10

females, of whom 30 are aware of the center in this sample. The first way
to compute percentages is to base the percents on the *row totals*. To do
this, the males are examined first (first row in the table). Note that 30 of
50 males (or 60 percent of the males) are aware of the center, and 20 of 50
(or 40 percent) are not aware. These percentages are recorded for the first
row of the table (see Table 12-2b). Now, the females are examined (second
row in the table). Note that 30 of 100 females (or 30 percent) are aware
of the center, and 70 percent are not aware. These percentages are recorded
in the second row of the table, and because there are no more rows in the
table, the task is complete.

Table 12-2   Computing cell values in a bivariate frequency distribution

a. Bivariate frequency distribution with cell counts

	Aware of Center		
Sex	Yes	No	Total
Male	30	20	50
Female	30	70	100
Total	60	90	150

b. Cell percentages based on row totals

	Aware of Center		
Sex	Yes	No	Total
Male	60.0%	40.0%	100.0%
Female	30.0%	70.0%	100.0%

c. Cell percentages based on column totals

	Aware of Center	
Sex	Yes	No
Male	50.0%	22.2%
Female	50.0%	77.8%
Total	100.0%	100.0%

d. Cell percentages based on total number of respondents

	Aware of Center		
Sex	Yes	No	Total
Male	20.0%	13.3%	33.3%
Female	20.0%	46.7%	66.7%
Total	40.0%	60.0%	100.0%

The second way to compute percentages in a bivariate frequency-distribution table is to base them on the *column totals*. In Table 12-2a, note that 60 individuals are aware of the senior center (column 1 of the data). Of these, 50 percent are male and 50 percent are female. These values are recorded in the first column of Table 12-2c. Next, note that 90 respondents are not aware of the center, and that of these, 20 (or 22.2 percent) are males. Because any respondent is either male or female, this means that the 77.8 percent of the respondents who are unaware of the center are female. These numbers are recorded in the second column, and because there are no more columns, the task is complete.

The final way to compute percentages in such a table is to base them on the *total number of respondents*. Returning to Table 12-2a note that thirty males are aware of the center. This is 20 percent of 150, the total number of respondents, and this number is recorded in Table 12-2d. This process is repeated for the other three cells in the table, completing the task.

Which of these three methods of computing percentages should be used in a given study? The answer, of course, depends on the purpose of the study. If a researcher is interested in comparing males with females, he or she would probably base the percentages on the row totals. In this case, 60 percent of the males, but only 30 percent of the females, are aware of the center (see Table 12-2b). If, on the other hand, one is interested in comparing respondents who are aware of the center with those who are not, he or she would base the percentages on the column totals. In this case, we note that 50 percent of those who are aware, but only 22.2 percent of those who are unaware, of the center are males. Finally, if a researcher is not interested in either of these comparisons, he or she might, particularly if the numbers are very large or very small, choose to report percentages based on the total number of respondents. This final approach, however, is rarely employed.

Actually, the rule for deciding how to compute percentages (based on row totals or based on column totals) is simple if you remember that researchers compute percentages to facilitate comparisons. *The way in which percentages facilitate comparisons is to treat the groups to be compared as if they were the same size.* Therefore, the sum of the percentages for each group or category to be compared should equal 100.0 percent. If this is the case, then the percentages have been computed correctly, and comparisons between the categories are easier.

Statistical Independence

In statistics, the task of comparing how respondents score on one variable with how they score on another is related to the search for *statistical inde-*

pendence and *statistical dependence*. Bivariate measures of association reflect the degree to which the relationship between two variables deviates from statistical independence. Because all measures of association employ the same definition of statistical independence, the differences among the measures reflect differences in how statistical dependence is defined. Definitions of statistical dependence, in turn, reflect the types of assumptions that researchers are willing to make about their data. Before considering such assumptions, however, it is important to examine what is meant by statistical independence.

Essentially, a statistician contends that two events are independent if and only if information about the occurrence of one event provides no information about the occurrence of the other event. Suppose, for example, an individual is taking a true-false test and does not know the answer to two questions. Rather than leaving the two questions blank, the individual decides to guess according to the following rule: Count the number of words in the question, and guess true if the sum is an even number. In this situation, we do not expect that learning that the individual got the first question right will help in guessing whether he or she gets the second question right. Because knowledge about how the individual scores on one of the items does not provide any clues about how he or she scores on the other, the responses to the two items are said to be independent.

The idea of statistical independence is easily extended to a bivariate frequency-distribution table. To illustrate this extension, return to the example used in the previous section. Suppose that a researcher is interested in determining whether the sex of respondents and their awareness of a senior center are statistically independent. In other words, the researcher is interested in determining whether knowing the respondent's sex improves the ability to guess whether the respondent is aware of the senior center.[1]

Note that 50 of the 150 respondents (or 33.3 percent) are male (see Table 12-3a). Thus, we can say that the chance that any respondent is male is .333, or 1 out of 3. Note also that 60 of the 150 respondents (or 40.0 percent) are aware of the senior center. We can also say that the chance that any respondent is aware of the senior center is .400. What, then, is the chance that a respondent is both male and aware of the center? Because 40.0 percent of all of the respondents are aware of the center, it is expected that 40.0 percent of the males are aware of the center as well. But because only 33.3 percent of the respondents are male, it is expected that 13.3 percent (40.0 percent of 33.3 percent = 13.3 percent) of the sample are both male and aware of the center (see Table 12-3b). This means that if the two variables are statistically independent, it is expected that 20 respondents (13.3 percent of 150 or 40.0 percent of 50) are both male and aware of the center (see Table 12-3c). Using this same logic, the expected proportions and cell frequencies can be derived for the three remaining cases—male and unaware, female and aware, female and unaware (see Tables 12-3a–c).

The procedure that Table 12-3 illustrates can be expressed mathematically as $P(AB) = P(A) \times P(B)$. In words, statistical independence means that the chance or likelihood of a joint event $[P(AB)]$, such as a respondent being both male and aware of a senior center, is equal to the product of the chance or likelihood of each event occurring separately, such as the respondent being male $[P(A)]$ times the respondent being aware of the

Table 12-3   Computing statistical independence

a. Marginal frequencies

	Aware of Center		
Sex	Yes	No	Total
Male	—	—	50
Female	—	—	100
Total	60	90	150

b. Proportions expected if variables are statistically independent

	Aware of Center		
Sex	Yes	No	Total
Male	.333 × .400 = .133	.333 × .600 = .200	.333
Female	.667 × .400 = .267	.667 × .600 = .400	.667
Total	.400	.600	1.000

c. Frequencies expected if variables are statistically independent

	Aware of Center	
Sex	Yes	No
Male	.133 × 150 = 20	.200 × 150 = 30
Female	.267 × 150 = 40	.400 × 150 = 60

d. Frequencies actually observed and reported in table 12-2a

	Aware of Center		
Sex	Yes	No	Total
Male	30	20	50
Female	30	70	100
Total	60	90	150

senior center [P(B)]. We will consider this formulation again later in this chapter.

Finally, to complete the example, we must answer the question of whether respondent sex and awareness of the senior center are statistically independent. Because we know what the cell frequencies can be expected to be if the variables are independent, the most straightforward way to answer the question is to compare these expected cell frequencies with the cell frequencies that are actually observed (that is, compare Table 12-3c with 12-3d). Although 20 males are expected to be aware of the center, 30 actually are. There are similar differences in the other cells. It is possible to conclude that sex of respondent and awareness of the senior center are not, for these data, statistically independent. This conclusion is consistent with the earlier finding that 60 percent of the males, but only 30 percent of the females, are aware of the center.

Factors to Consider in Selecting a Measure of Association

This chapter began by suggesting that most research centers on comparing how respondents score on one measure with how they score on another. Although one approach to this task is to compare the cell frequencies or percentages with one another, the number of possible comparisons can be extremely large. Even in a simple table in which each variable has only two values, six possible comparisons between pairs of cells can be made. Using the example from the previous section to illustrate, the possible comparisons of this type include:

1. males who are aware of the center with males who are not
2. males who are aware of the center with females who also are
3. males who are aware of the center with females who are not
4. males who are unaware of the center with females who are
5. males who are unaware of the center with females who also are not
6. females who are aware of the center with females who are not

Although there are only six possible pair comparisons of cell frequencies in a four-cell table, there are fifteen in a six-cell table (one variable has three values and the other two), twenty-eight in an eight-cell table (one variable has four categories and the other two), and thirty-six in a nine-cell table (each variable has three values). Clearly, the tasks of comparing cell frequencies with one another and summarizing the results of the comparisons become unmanageable without rules for deciding which comparisons should be made and how the results should be summarized. We can think of a measure of association as a set of rules or procedures that specify:

1. which comparisons should be made,
2. how the comparisons should be made, and
3. how the comparisons should be summarized.

A measure of association has the added advantage of providing information concerning how well the set of rules works to describe the information in the bivariate frequency-distribution table.

Although it is possible to calculate any measure of association in an effort to describe a bivariate frequency distribution, doing so can lead to nonsensical results in some cases. A researcher who fails to consider the nature of the data, the question that is asked, and the way in which the measure of association operates, runs a risk of obtaining results that are meaningless. The factors that are considered in this section are important in that they help the researcher to select a measure of association that is appropriate to the question that the researcher is asking. By selecting a measure of association on the basis of these criteria, the researcher should find that the interpretation of results is straightforward.

Prior to calculating any measure of association, researchers must consider two factors in selecting the appropriate measure of association. These are:

1. whether the relationship between the variables is symmetric or asymmetric, and
2. what the level of measurement (nominal, ordinal, interval, or ratio) of each of the variables is.

Because the way in which statistical dependence will be measured depends on these factors, the researcher must consider each when choosing which measure of association to use to describe a particular bivariate frequency-distribution table.

Symmetry

The simplest of the factors affecting how a measure of association is defined is symmetry. A measure of association is asymmetric if the results change depending on which of the two variables is considered first. For example, we noted that 60 percent of the males but only 30 percent of the females were aware of a senior center (see Table 12-2b). At the same time, we noted that 50 percent of those who were aware of the center were males, and 22.2 percent of those who were unaware of the center were males (see Table 12-2c). As this example illustrates, the percentages based on row totals (Table 12-2b) are different from those based on column totals

(Table 12-2c). Thus, because the percentages change depending on whether they are based on row or column totals, this method of summarizing the data is asymmetric. In a symmetric measure of association, on the other hand, the results will be the same no matter which variable is considered first. This means that *asymmetric measures of association should be used only when the researcher has obvious independent and dependent variables and is interested in determining how the independent variable affects the dependent variable.* A symmetric measure of association, on the other hand, can be used in this situation as well as in situations in which the researcher is interested in comparing scores on two variables without regard to which variable is considered first. As was the case with measures of location and measures of dispersion, the level of measurement of the variables affects the selection of a measure of association. For example, computing a measure of association with data that are measured at the nominal level when the measure is based on the assumption that the data are measured at the interval level yields results that are meaningless. Because the objective is to describe and interpret the bivariate frequency distribution, the calculation of measures that do not further that objective is of little utility.

The Form of the Relationship

Other factors may affect the choice of a measure of association. One of the more important of these characteristics is the form of the relationship between the variables. The form of a relationship refers to the shape of the graph of the relationship between two variables. Perhaps one of the most common statements in social sciences today asserts that the relationship between two variables is *monotonic.* Statements of this type come in two forms—those asserting that the relationship between the variables is positive and those asserting that the relationship is negative. A *positive* monotonic relationship between two variables occurs when

1. individuals who score high on one of the measures also tend to score high on the other and
2. individuals who score low on one of the measures also tend to score low on the other (see Figure 12-1a, p. 234).

The statement, "The higher the level of education, the larger the number of voluntary associations to which a person belongs," indicates that there is a positive monotonic relationship between level of education and number of voluntary association memberships. The statement, "The lower the level of education, the smaller the number of voluntary associations to which a person belongs," although it may leave the reader with a different impression than the first statement does, also indicates a positive relationship between these two variables.

A *negative* monotonic relationship between two variables occurs when

1. individuals who score high on one variable score low on the other and
2. individuals who score low on one variable score high on the other (see Figure 12-1b).

The statement, "The higher the level of educational attainment, the lower the need for social services," indicates a negative relationship between level of educational attainment and need for social services. Again, the statement, "The lower the level of educational attainment, the higher the need for social services," although it might leave the reader with a different impression than the first statement does, also indicates a negative relationship between the variables.

A *linear relationship* is simply a special type of monotonic relationship. The name *linear* reflects the fact that the graph of this relationship is a straight line (see Figure 12-1c). Naturally, because it is a type of monotonic relationship, a linear relationship can be either positive or negative. Note that a linear relationship between two variables is far more precise than a relationship that is monotonic but not linear. Now, rather than arguing merely that increases in the magnitude of one variable result in increases (or decreases) in the magnitude of the other, we are claiming that the changes themselves reflect a linear function. The difference between a relationship that is simply monotonic and one that is monotonic and linear is illustrated by Table 12-4. As you can see, the values of

---

Table 12-4   Positive relationships between two variables

a. A positive linear relationship

Variable X	Variable Y
1	3
2	5
3	7
4	9
5	11

b. A positive monotonic relationship

Variable X	Variable Y
1	1
2	3
3	9
4	10
5	14

Figure 12-1   Diagrams of monotonic and nonmonotonic relationships

a. A positive monotonic relationship

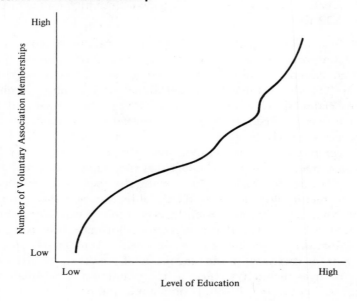

b. A negative monotonic relationship

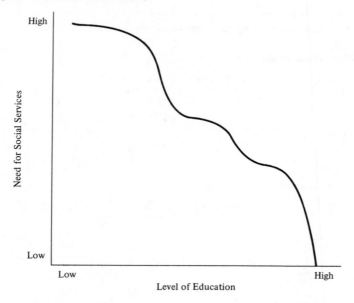

Figure 12-1 *(cont.)*

c. A negative, linear, monotonic relationship

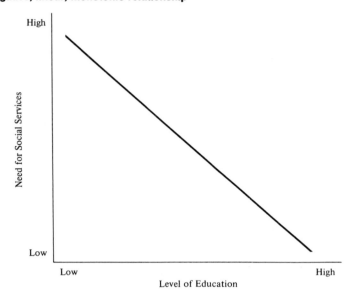

d. A nonmonotonic relationship

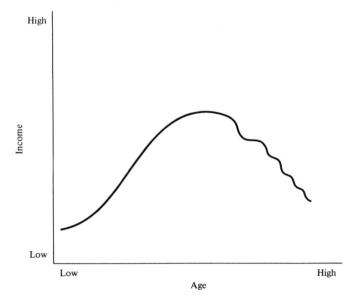

variable Y when the relationship is linear are determined by the equation $Y = 1 + 2X$. In general, when the relationship between the two variables is linear, the equation connecting values on the first variable with those on the second is of the form $Y = a + bx$. What should be equally apparent is that no simple equation connects the values of the variables when the relationship is simply monotonic.

A less common but extremely important form that a relationship between variables can take is *nonmonotonic*. A nonmonotonic relationship is one in which, for some values of the variable the relationship is positive and for others the relationship is negative (see Figure 12-1d). A good example of a nonmonotonic relationship is that between age and income. We expect that age and income will be positively related until retirement, at which time income usually drops significantly. The effect of the number of therapy sessions on client well-being may also be nonmonotonic. Although we surely expect that the more therapy sessions a client attends, the better his or her level of functioning will be, there could be a point of diminishing returns. In fact, a client who attended enough sessions could become dependent on the therapist and lose some of the ability to function that he or she had gained in earlier sessions.

Considering the possible form of the relationship between two variables when selecting a measure of association is important, because different measures of association are designed to detect different types of relationships. For example, a linear measure of association determines how well a linear rule describes the data, whereas a monotonic measure of association determines how well a monotonic rule describes the data. Thus, if the relationship between two variables is monotonic, and the researcher uses a linear measure of association to describe the data, the description of the data will not be as good as it would be had a monotonic measure of association been used instead. This is particularly important if we have hypothesized that the relationship between the variables is of a specific form. If, for example, we hypothesized that age has a nonmonotonic relationship with income, it makes no sense for us to use a linear or a monotonic measure of association to describe the data. Neither of these measures is consistent with the hypothesis, and the results we would obtain could not be interpreted in terms of the hypotheses.

Interpretating the Coefficient of Association

The final factor to consider in selecting a measure of association is how to interpret the *coefficient of association*—the number obtained when a measure of association is calculated for a specific data set. Typically, the relationship between two variables is not perfect. For example, the statement that males are more aware of a senior center than are females does not mean that knowing the sex of the respondent will allow the researcher to predict perfectly whether the respondent is aware of the senior center or not. Rather, it suggests that knowing the respondent's sex will allow one to do a better job of predicting awareness of the senior center than not knowing the respondent's sex will. The question that arises, of course, is *How much better?* The size of the coefficient of association is the answer to this question.

The size of the coefficient of association provides a measure of the *strength of the relationship* between two variables. The strength of the relationship refers simply to the degree to which knowledge of scores on one variable helps in predicting scores on the second variable. For example, if 98 percent of the males but only 2 percent of the females in a sample were aware of a senior center, knowledge of the sex of the respondent would be very helpful in predicting awareness of the senior center. In this situation, it could be said that the relationship between sex and awareness is very strong. Further, the coefficient of association would be large. If, on the other hand, 51 percent of the males and 50 percent of the females are aware of the senior center, knowledge of the respondent's sex is not very helpful in predicting awareness. In this situation, it would be said that the relationship between sex and awareness is very weak, and the coefficient of association would be small.

Although the size of the coefficient of association is always related to the strength of the relationship between two variables, this relationship is more direct and easy to interpret for some measures of association than for others. Most of the measures of association discussed in the next section have a *probable reduction in error (or PRE) interpretation*. A PRE interpretation of the coefficient of association means that the number obtained is easily converted into a number that reflects the percentage of improvement that having knowledge of scores on the first variable adds to our being able to predict scores on the second variable. For example, if the value of a PRE coefficient of association is .25, we could say that knowledge of scores on the first variable improves our ability to predict scores on the second variable by 25 percent. Using a measure of association with such an interpretation has the advantage of providing the reader of the research report with a good basis for judging how well the verbal description of the relationship fits the data. Therefore, it is recommended that researchers use measures of association that have this type of interpretation whenever possible.

Selected Measures of Association

The Percentage Difference

Perhaps the simplest measure of association is the percentage difference. It is an asymmetric measure that can be used when the variables are measured at the nominal, ordinal, interval, or ratio levels. Ideally, each of the variables should only have two values, because this facilitates the interpretation of the coefficient. If the variables are measured at the ordinal, interval, or ratio level, the sign of the coefficient reflects whether the association is positive or negative. The coefficient varies from +100 percent (a perfect positive relationship) to −100 percent (a perfect negative relationship). A coefficient of 0 percent means that there is no statistical relationship between the variables.

The computation of the percentage difference is simple, as the following example illustrates: Suppose that a school social worker is interested in determining whether a school-sponsored hot-breakfast program improves student school performance. She gathers the data summarized in Table 12-5. Because the social worker wishes to compare those who participated in the program with those who did not, the percentages are based on the row totals. The percentage difference is calculated by subtracting the percentage of those who did not participate but did improve from the percentage of those who did participate and did improve. For these data, the percentage difference is +29.1 percent (70.8 percent − 41.7 percent = +29.1 percent). This means that 29.1 percent more of those who participated in the program than those who did not, showed improvement in performance.

We could also compare program participants with nonparticipants in terms of the percentage not improving. In this case, the percentage difference is −29.1 percent (29.2 percent − 58.3 percent = −29.1 percent). This means that 29.1 percent more of those who did not participate in the program failed to show improvement in performance. This coefficient provides exactly the same information as does the first concerning the magnitude of the relationship. Its sign is different, because it focuses on failure to improve rather than on improvement. From a statistical perspective, these two measures of percentage difference are equivalent. The first was

Table 12-5   Relationship between program participation and improvement in school performance

| | Performance | | | | |
| | Improves | | Does Not Improve | | |
	Percentage	(N)	Percentage	(N)	Total
Participates in program	70.8	(85)	29.2	(35)	120
Eligible to participate but does not	41.7	(25)	58.3	(35)	60

selected simply because more people are accustomed to seeing the comparison done in that fashion. Either of these two measures, however, is appropriate.

One factor to consider in presenting percentage differences is the magnitude of the percentages themselves. There are other tables that will result in a percentage difference of +29.1 percent. For example, if 35 of the 120 program participants (29.1 percent) show improvement in performance and none of the 60 nonparticipants (0 percent) show improvement, the percentage difference is also +29.1 percent. To allow the reader to examine the basis for the percentage difference obtained, it is good practice to present the table on which the percentage difference is based. If, for some reason, this is not practical, the researcher should provide readers with sufficient information such that they can, if they desire, create the full table. For example, the results in Table 12-5 can be summarized as follows: 70.8 percent of the 120 program participants and 41.7 percent of the 60 nonparticipants, a difference of +29.1 percent, showed improvement in school performance. This statement provides more than enough information to recreate Table 12-5.

Yule's Q

Yule's Q is a symmetric measure of association that can be used when the variables are measured at the nominal, ordinal, interval, or ratio level. It may be used only when each of the variables is a dichotomy (has only two values). If the variables are measured at the ordinal, interval, or ratio level, the sign of the coefficient reflects whether the association is positive or negative. The coefficient varies from +1.00 (a perfect positive relationship) to −1.00 (a perfect negative relationship). A coefficient of 0.00 means that there is no statistical relationship between the variables.

Although Yule's Q may be used with nominal variables, it is a measure of the degree to which the relationship between two variables is positive or negative. Before examining how Q is calculated, it is worthwhile to review briefly what "positive" and "negative" relationships mean in terms of cell frequencies. Suppose, for example, we are interested in the relationship between level of educational attainment and need for social services, and we gather the data reported in Table 12-6. A *positive* relationship between these two variables means that:

1. there is a tendency for people with low levels of educational attainment to have low need for social services, and
2. there is a tendency for people with high levels of educational attainment to have high need for social services.

One measure of the tendency for the relationship to be positive is the product of the cell frequencies that are associated with a positive rela-

---

Table 12-6   Bivariate frequency distribution between level of educational attainment and need for social services

	Need for Social Services		
Education	Low	High	Total
Low	20	80	100
High	60	40	100
Total	80	120	200

---

tionship. This product, in this case, is 800 (20 × 40 = 800). A *negative* relationship between these two variables, on the other hand, means that:

1. there is a tendency for people with low levels of educational attainment to have high need for social services, and
2. there is a tendency for people with high levels of educational attainment to have low need for social services.

A measure of the tendency for the relationship to be negative is the product of the cell frequencies that are associated with a negative relationship. This product, in this case, is 4,800 (80 × 60 = 4,800).

A measure of the tendency for the relationship to be positive rather than negative is simply the difference between the measure of the tendency of the relationship to be positive and the measure of the tendency of the relationship to be negative. The value of this difference measure in this case is −4,000 (800 − 4,800 = −4,000). This difference score is itself a measure of association. The sign of the measure indicates that more respondents score in a pattern consistent with a negative relationship than score in a pattern consistent with a positive relationship. The size of the value of the coefficient, however, is partially a function of the number of cases and, thus, is difficult to interpret. Suppose, for example, we multiplied each of the cell frequencies by 10 (see Table 12-7a) or divided each of the cell frequencies by 10 (see Table 12-7b). Although the relationship between the two variables does not change, the value of this coefficient of association does. In the first of these cases, it is −40,000 [(200 × 400) − (800 × 600)] = −40,000, whereas in the second it is −40 [(2 × 4) − (8 × 6) = −40]. Thus, for this coefficient to be useful as a measure of association, some correction for the number of cases is necessary. The formula for Yule's Q includes such a correction.

Yule's Q is defined as the ratio of two values. The numerator of this ratio is the difference measure that we just discussed. The denominator of the ratio is the sum, rather than the difference, of the measures of the

---

Table 12-7   The value of the coefficient of association as a function of the number of cases

a. Cell frequencies increased by a factor of 10

	Need for Services	
Education	Low	High
Low	200	800
High	600	400

Coefficient of Association: $(200 \times 400) - (800 \times 600) = -40{,}000$

b. Cell frequencies decreased by a factor of 10

	Need for Services	
Education	Low	High
Low	2	8
High	6	4

Coefficient of Association: $(2 \times 4) - (8 \times 6) = -40$

---

tendencies toward a positive and a negative relationship. Yule's Q for the data reported in Table 12-6 is:

$$\frac{800 - 4{,}800}{800 + 4{,}800} = \frac{4{,}000}{5{,}600} = -.71$$

The value of Yule's Q for the data reported in Table 12-7 is also $-.71$. The general formula for Yule's Q is:

$$Q = \frac{AD - BC}{AD + BC}$$

in which A and D are the cell frequencies associated with a positive relationship and B and C are the cell frequencies associated with a negative relationship.

Yule's Q has a probable reduction in error interpretation. Suppose, for example, we are trying to guess whether respondents are in need of social services. Let us further assume that we know that a particular respondent has a low level of educational attainment, but that we do not know what the relationship between education and need for services is. By simply making a random guess, we can, on the average, expect to be right about 50 percent of the time. Now, suppose that we learn that the value of Q is $-.71$. The negative sign of the coefficient means that the relationship is negative. Our question is, "How much better than chance can we do if we use the rule that the relationship is negative to make our guess (that is, if education is low, guess high need; and if education is high, guess low need)?" The answer is 71 percent. The value of Q represents how much better we do when we predict according to the rule that the relationship is negative (or positive) than when we predict using random guessing. The sign of the coefficient indicates whether to use the positive-relationship or the negative-relationship rule.

The Phi Coefficient and Cramer's Statistic

Two other measures of association that can be used with variables measured at the nominal, ordinal, interval, or ratio level are Cramer's statistic and the phi coefficient. Essentially, these two measures are equivalent. The only difference is that the phi coefficient is used when there are two dichotomous variables, whereas Cramer's statistic (known as Cramer's C) is used when one of the variables has three or more values. Cramer's statistic can be used when the form of the relationship is either nonmonotonic or monotonic. The coefficient ranges from 0 (statistical independence) to 1.00 (perfect statistical dependence).

The calculation of Cramer's statistic (and the phi coefficient) involves several steps:

1. Determine what the cell frequencies would be if the two variables are independent (see the section on statistical independence in this chapter).
2. Compare the frequencies actually observed with those that we expect if the variables are statistically independent.
3. As is the case with Yule's Q, adjust the result for the number of respondents observed.

To illustrate the steps involved in calculating Cramer's statistic, examine the relationship between level of educational attainment and need for social services reported in Table 12-6. The first step in calculating Cramer's statistic is to determine what the frequencies are expected to be if the two variables are independent (see Table 12-8). These are obtained by first determining the likelihood that a case falls in a particular cell and then multiplying by the total number of respondents (see Table 12-3).

The second step in calculating Cramer's statistic is to compare the frequencies that would be expected if the variables are independent with the frequencies that are actually observed. The most straightforward way of doing this would be to subtract one from the other and then add the differences together. The problem with this approach is that the resulting sum is always zero. The problem is similar to the one encountered when calculating variation around the arithmetic mean. Positive values are counterbalanced by negative values. The solution to this problem is also

Table 12-8   Data for calculation of Cramer's statistic

a. Expected proportions if the variables are independent

	Need for Social Services		
Education	Low	High	Total
Low	.20	.30	.50
High	.20	.30	.50
Total	.40	.60	1.00

b. Expected frequencies if the variables are independent

	Need for Social Services		
Education	Low	High	Total
Low	40	60	100
High	40	60	100
Total	80	120	200

similar to that used when computing variation. The difference between the observed and the expected frequency is obtained, and then this number is squared. Now, however, before adding the results together, divide by the value of the expected frequency. To summarize the differences between the observed and the expected frequencies:

1. Compute a difference score by subtracting the expected frequency from the observed frequency;
2. square the result;
3. divide by the expected frequency; and
4. add the resulting values together.

The value obtained from this process for the data in this example is 33.33:

$$\frac{(20-40)^2}{40} + \frac{(60-40)^2}{40} + \frac{(80-60)^2}{60} + \frac{(40-60)^2}{60} = 33.33$$

This number is called Chi-square and is represented by the symbol χ^2. This measure will be discussed again in Chapter 13.

The final step in calculating Cramer's statistic is to correct the result for the size of the sample. Statisticians have determined that the largest that Chi-square can be is $N \times (L - 1)$, in which N is the number of respondents and L is the number of rows or the number of columns, whichever is smaller. If the Chi-square that is obtained from the data is divided by this number, the result varies from 1 (complete statistical dependence) to 0 (no statistical dependence). Statisticians then take the square root of this number, because the resulting statistic has a close relationship to other statistics. This means that the formula for Cramer's statistic is:

$$C = \sqrt{\frac{\chi^2}{N(L-1)}}$$

in which χ^2 is the value of Chi-square, N is the number of respondents, and L is the number of rows or the number of columns, whichever is smaller. The value of Cramer's statistic for the example is:

$$C = \sqrt{\frac{33.33}{200 \times (2-1)}} = .41$$

Cramer's statistic does not have a probable reduction in error interpretation. Zero means statistical independence, and 1 means complete statistical dependence; however, numbers between these two extremes only mean that there is some dependence. Although, for a given data set, a Cramer's statistic of .7 means that although the relationship between the two variables is stronger than does a Cramer's statistic of .4, it is not proportionately stronger. Consequently, the utility of this measure of association in describing a bivariate frequency distribution is limited. At the same time, this measure of association is the only appropriate one to use when both variables are measured at the nominal level and each variable has more than two categories.

The Gamma Coefficient

Gamma is a symmetrical measure of association that can be used when the variables are measured at the ordinal, interval, or ratio levels. The sign of the coefficient reflects whether the relationship is positive or negative. The coefficient varies from +1.00 (a perfect positive relationship) to −1.00 (a perfect negative relationship). A coefficient of 0.0 means that there is *no monotonic relationship* between the variables. When both of the variables are dichotomies, the gamma coefficient is the same as Yule's Q. The interpretation of the size of the gamma coefficient is identical to the interpretation of Yule's Q.

As is the case with Yule's Q, the gamma coefficient compares the tendency toward a positive relationship with the tendency toward a negative relationship. Now, however, because more cells are involved, the definitions of tendency toward a positive and a negative relationship are more complicated. The procedures used in calculating these tendencies are illustrated in the following example. Suppose that the school social worker who wished to examine the effect of having a hot breakfast on school performance that was used in an earlier example had somewhat more extensive data. Rather than knowing only which eligible individuals participated in the program, she knows if the individuals have breakfast regularly, occasionally, or never. Further, rather than simply knowing if the individual's school performance improves or not, she knows whether the degree of improvement is "high," "medium," or "low to none." The social worker summarizes the data in a table similar to Table 12-9.

To calculate the tendency toward a positive relationship, the school social worker begins with the cell in the upper left-hand corner. She multiplies this cell frequency by the sum of all of the cell frequencies that are to the right and below this cell frequency. For example, [30 × (30 + 20 + 20 + 30)]. The social worker repeats this process for each cell, moving from left to right and top to bottom. Next, she adds together each of these products (one for each cell that has cells to the left and below it). This sum, 5,900 in this example, is a measure of the tendency toward a positive relationship between the two variables. To calculate the tendency toward a negative relationship, the process is repeated beginning with the cell in the upper right-hand corner of the table. Now, however, the cell frequency is multiplied by the sum of all cell frequencies that are below and to the left. The sum of all of these products (2,300 in

---

Table 12-9   Calculating the gamma coefficient on the relationship between level of program participation and improvement in school performance

Program Participation	Improvement			Variable 2		Variable 1		
	High	Medium	Low to None			H	M	L–N
Regular	30	20	10	H		a	b	c
Occasional	20	30	20	M		d	e	f
Never	10	20	30	L		g	h	i

$P = 30(30 + 20 + 20 + 30) +$
$\quad 20(20 + 30) +$
$\quad 20(20 + 30) +$
$\quad 30(30)$
$\quad = 5,900$

$P = a(e + f + h + i) +$
$\quad b(f + i) +$
$\quad d(h + i) +$
$\quad e(i)$

$Q = 10(20 + 30 + 10 + 20)$
$\quad 20(20 + 10) +$
$\quad 20(10 + 20) +$
$\quad 30(10)$
$\quad = 2,300$

$Q = c(d + e + g + h) +$
$\quad b(d + g) +$
$\quad f(g + h) +$
$\quad e(g)$

$\text{Gamma} = \dfrac{5,900 - 2,300}{5,900 + 2,300} = .44$

$\text{Gamma} = \dfrac{P - Q}{P + Q}$

this example) is a measure of the tendency toward a negative relationship between the two variables.

The gamma coefficient, like Yule's Q, is defined as the ratio of two values. The numerator of this ratio is the difference between the measure of the tendency toward a positive relationship and the measure of the tendency toward a negative relationship. The denominator of this ratio is the sum of these two terms. The formula for gamma is:

$$Gamma = \frac{P - Q}{P + Q}$$

in which P is the tendency toward a positive relationship and Q is the tendency toward a negative relationship. The gamma coefficient for the data reported in Table 12-9 is:

$$\frac{5,900 - 2,300}{5,900 + 2,300} = .44$$

Because the coefficient is positive, it can be said that for these data, those who participate more actively in the hot-breakfast program perform better in school than do those who participate less actively. Further, the size of the coefficient indicates that if one attempts to predict level of school performance on the basis of level of participation in the hot-breakfast program, he or she will be 44 percent more accurate in predictions than if a random-guessing rule were used to predict level of school performance.

The Regression Coefficient

The regression coefficient is an asymmetric measure of association that can be used when the variables are measured at the interval or the ratio levels. The sign of the coefficient reflects whether the relationship is positive or negative. The coefficient can take on any value, but a coefficient of 0.0 means that there is *no linear relationship* between the two variables.

Suppose that a researcher is interested in determining whether level of educational attainment predicts how good people in a sample feel about themselves. One approach to this problem is to use a linear-prediction rule with level of educational attainment as the independent variable and how good people feel about themselves as the dependent variable. This relationship can be represented by the equation $Y_i = A + BX_i + e_i$, in which Y refers to scores on the measure of how good people feel about themselves, X refers to the respondents' levels of educational attainment, A and B are constants that have to be determined, e represents the amount of error made in prediction, and i indicates which of the respondents is being considered. In this equation, the term $A + BX_i$ represents the prediction of how good a person will feel about himself or herself based on that person's level of educational attainment.

Although any numbers can be used for A and B in this question, it makes sense to try to pick values for A and B so that the difference between the score actually observed on the measure of how good people feel about themselves (Y) and the prediction of that score based on their level of educational attainment ($A + BX$) is as small as possible. Thus, the problem becomes one of selecting a value for A and a value for B so that the errors made in predicting are at a minimum.

Although the mathematics involved are beyond the scope of this text, statisticians have shown that the errors made when using a linear-prediction rule will be smallest if the values of A and B are calculated as follows:

$$B = \frac{\sum_{i=1}^{N} (X_i - \overline{X})(Y_i - \overline{Y})}{\sum_{i=1}^{N} (X_i - \overline{X})^2}$$

$$A = \overline{Y} - B\overline{X}$$

in which $\overline{Y}$ is the arithmetic mean of the dependent variable and $\overline{X}$ is the arithmetic mean of the independent variable. In other words, to calculate B:

1. Begin by determining the arithmetic means of the independent and dependent variables.

2. Calculate the variation on the independent variable by:

1. determining how much the independent variable score for the first subject deviates from the mean of the independent variable,
2. squaring the result, and
3. adding this value to that for each of the other respondents. This sum is the denominator of the equation for B.

3. Calculate the covariation between the independent and dependent variables by:

1. determining how much the independent variable score for the first subject deviates from the mean of the independent variable,
2. determining how much the dependent variable score for the first subject deviates from the mean of the dependent variable,
3. multiplying these two values together, and
4. adding this value to that obtained by using this process for each of the other subjects. This sum is the numerator of the equation for B.

The following calculations are for the data in Table 12-10. The values for A and B in the example are -35.0 and 3.5, respectively. Therefore, the equation for predicting how good people in the sample feel about themselves, based on their level of educational attainment, is $Y = -35.0 + 3.5X$. This equation can be used to predict scores on the measure of feeling good given the individual's level of educational attainment. The predicted score for someone in the sample who has completed eleven years of school is 3.5 $(-35.0 + 3.5 \times 11 = 3.5)$. The predicted scores for people who have completed twelve and thirteen years of school are 7.0 $(-35.0 + 3.5 \times 12 = 7.0)$ and 10.5 $(-35.0 + 3.5 \times 13 = 10.5)$, respectively. Further, we can estimate the amount of error in the predictions by comparing these predicted scores with the scores actually observed on the dependent variable. In the sample data, the differences between the observed and the predicted scores are $+.5$, -1, and $-.5$ for the first, second, and third cases in the sample, respectively. The sum of these errors is 0, because overestimates (cases 1 and 3) are balanced by underestimates (case 2). To eliminate the problem of the signs, each number is squared before it is added. The sum of squared errors in this case is 1.5. This measure of error and its meaning will be discussed further in the next section on the Pearson correlation coefficient.

Pearson's Correlation Coefficient

Pearson's correlation coefficient, also known as Pearson's r, or simply r, is a symmetric measure of association that can be used when the variables are measured at the interval or ratio levels. The sign of the coefficient reflects whether the relationship is positive or negative. The coefficient varies from $+1.00$ (a perfect, positive, linear association) to -1.00 (a perfect, negative, linear association). A coefficient of 0.0 means that there is *no linear relationship* between the two variables.

Pearson's r is closely related to the regression coefficient discussed in the previous section. In fact, one formula for calculating Pearson's r is:

$$r = \frac{s_x}{s_y} B$$

in which s_x is the standard deviation of the independent variable, s_y is the standard deviation of the dependent variable, and B is the regression coefficient when one attempts to predict Y on the basis of X.

Pearson's correlation coefficient is also related to a measure of the accuracy of a regression equation in predicting dependent variable scores. As noted in the previous section, the amount of error made using a linear regression equation can be estimated by comparing observed scores with predicted scores. This can be denoted by

$$\Sigma(Y - Y')^2$$

Table 12-10 An illustration of the calculation of the regression coefficient

Respondent Number	Years of School Completed	Feeling-Good Score	$(X - \bar{X})$	$(X - \bar{X})^2$	$(Y - \bar{Y})$	$(Y - \bar{Y})^2$	$(X - \bar{X})(Y - \bar{Y})$
1	11	4	-1	$+1$	-3	$+9$	$+3$
2	12	6	0	0	-1	$+1$	0
3	13	11	$+1$	$+1$	$+4$	$+16$	$+4$
	$\bar{X} = 12$	$\bar{Y} = 7$ Totals	0	2	0	26	7

$$B = \frac{\Sigma(X - \bar{X})(Y - \bar{Y})}{\Sigma(X - \bar{X})^2} = 7/2 \text{ or } 3.5$$

$$A = \bar{Y} - B\bar{X} = 7 - (3.5)(12)$$
$$= -35$$

because each error is squared before adding to obtain the estimate. Obviously, the value of this term will be 0 if prediction is made without error. What is not as obvious is that the maximum value for error is the variation of the dependent variable about its mean. This maximum is denoted by $\Sigma(Y - \bar{Y})^2$. Now,

$$r^2 = 1 - \frac{\Sigma(Y - \bar{Y'})^2}{\Sigma(Y - \bar{Y})^2}$$

which is a measure of how much smaller, on the average, the errors are when a linear-prediction rule is used than when the prediction is based on the arithmetic mean of the dependent variable.

In this example (see Table 12-10), $r^2 = 1 - 1.5/26 = .94$, and $r = .97$. An r^2 of .94 means that, on the average, the errors are 94 percent smaller using the prediction rule from the regression equation than they are if the arithmetic mean of the dependent variable is used as the guess for each score. This is the same as saying that 94 percent of the variation in the measure of how good people feel about themselves is accounted for by knowledge of the respondents' level of educational attainment.

The Eta Coefficient

The eta coefficient is an asymmetric measure of association that may be used when the independent variable is measured at the nominal, ordinal, interval, or ratio levels and the dependent variable is measured at the interval or ratio level. It is suitable to use if the relationship between the two variables is monotonic or nonmonotonic. The coefficient varies from 0 (no statistical association between the variables) to 1 (perfect statistical association between the variables).

The eta coefficient involves comparing variations in a manner similar to that used in regression. The following example illustrates the computations involved and the interpretation of the eta coefficient. Suppose that a researcher is interested in determining whether there are differences in people's knowledge about good health practices by ethnicity. To examine this hypothesis (that there is a difference by ethnicity), the researcher gathers data from a random sample of nine individuals (three whites, three blacks, and three others who are neither white nor black). Each respondent is given a ten-question quiz on health knowledge; the results obtained are reported in Table 12-11.

Inspection of the arithmetic means suggests some differences in how well the different categories of people perform on this test. Blacks appear to do most poorly, whites score in an intermediate position, and those who are neither white nor black perform best. The question is, however, "How much does knowledge of one's ethnicity help in predicting level of health knowledge for these data?"

Table 12-11   Scores and summary information on a measure of health knowledge by ethnicity

	White	Black	Other
	4	3	5
	5	4	6
	6	5	7
$\bar{x}$	5	4	6
$\Sigma(X - X)^2$	2	2	2

To answer the question, one begins by asking how well health-knowledge scores could be predicted if a person's ethnicity were not known. If ethnicity is unknown, of course, the task is simply that of describing a single variable. The arithmetic mean for the nine scores is 5. Note that the variation in the scores is 12 and that the variance of the scores is 1.3333.

If one knows a respondent's ethnicity, however, he or she might make a different guess about level of health knowledge than the arithmetic mean for all of the data. For whites, one can guess 5; for blacks, 4; and for the residual category, 6. The variation for whites in this case is 2 (see Table 12-11), as it is for blacks and the residual category. Thus, by using the arithmetic mean for each category as a guess, the total variation is 6 (2 for each category). In general, the formula for eta² is:

$$\text{Eta}^2 = \frac{\text{sum of variation within categories}}{\text{total variation, ignoring categories}}$$

Eta², in this case, then, is 6 divided by 12, or .5. We can say that knowledge of ethnicity reduces the error in predicting health-knowledge scores by 50 percent.

Some Final Thoughts on Measuring Association

After reading this chapter, you might reach the conclusion that researchers spend their lives calculating measures of association. The formulas presented are cumbersome to use, and if the number of respondents is large, the time involved in hand calculation can be substantial. In point of fact, however, researchers rarely if ever calculate any statistics by hand. This task is done almost entirely by computers. We have presented the formulas to help you understand what is being measured by each of these different measures of association, not as an effort to convince you that you should calculate these statistics by hand. Table 12-12 summarizes the measures of association we have discussed in this chapter.

Table 12-12   Summary of the measures of association

Measure	Symmetry	Level of Measurement	Form of Relationship	Probable Reduction in Error Interpretation
Percentage Difference	Asymmetric	Nominal, ordinal, interval, ratio (dichotomies)	Does not apply	Yes
Yule's Q	Symmetric	Nominal, ordinal, interval, ratio (dichotomies)	Does not apply	Yes
Cramer's Statistic (Phi coefficient if both variables are dichotomies)	Symmetric	Nominal, ordinal, interval, ratio	Nonmonotonic or monotonic	No
Gamma (Yule's Q if both variables are dichotomies)	Symmetric	Ordinal, interval, ratio	Monotonic	Yes
Regression Coefficient	Asymmetric	Interval, ratio	Linear	No
Pearson's r	Symmetric	Interval, ratio	Linear	Yes
Eta	Asymmetric	Independent: nominal, ordinal, interval, ratio Dependent: interval, ratio	Nonmonotonic or monotonic	Yes

Note also that finding a correlation between two variables in a given data set does not mean that you have identified a causal factor. It is well known that there is a high correlation between the number of fire engines that go to a fire and the amount of damage done by the fire. One would not argue that fire engines cause damage; rather, a third factor, the size of the fire, accounts for both the amount of damage done and the number of engines that respond. The point is that the design of the research and the theory underlying the research are more important in determining causal connections than is the size of the correlation coefficient. Although the lack of association between two variables may be evidence that there is no causal connection between the variables, the presence of an association is not, by itself, evidence that there is a causal connection.

Key Terms

bivariate frequency distribution
measure of association
correlation
statistical independence
asymmetric association
symmetric association
monotonic relationship
linear relationship
nonmonotonic relationship

probable reduction in error (PRE)
percentage difference
Yule's Q
phi coefficient
Cramer's C
regression coefficient
Pearson's r
eta coefficient

Reference

1. The researcher could also be interested in determining whether awareness of the senior center helps to predict a respondent's sex. This question is of interest if one is trying to pinpoint a target audience for a media campaign to publicize the center.

Questions for Discussion

1. When variables are measured at the nominal level, the concept of the form of a relationship is not very meaningful. Why is this so?
2. Researchers, particularly since the advent of high-speed computers, often compute more than one measure of association to describe a par-

ticular data set. Do you think that this is a good practice? Why or why not?

3. We noted that the same statistic calculated in different situations may have a different name. Some examples of this are: gamma for two dichotomous variables is called Yule's Q; Cramer's statistic for two dichotomous variables is called the phi coefficient; Pearson's r calculated for two dichotomous variables is also the phi coefficient; Pearson's r calculated for a dichotomous variable and an interval variable is called a point-biserial correlation; and a Pearson's r calculated for ranked variables (ordinal variables in which no two respondents have the same rank) is called Spearman's rho. Why do you suppose that the same statistic calculated in a different situation may have a different name?

Exercises

1. A social worker for a community mental-health center wonders if rational-emotive therapy is more effective for females than for males. The social worker reviews client records at the mental-health center for the past year and finds thirty cases in which this approach to therapy was used. Using the data reported below:

   a. construct a bivariate frequency distribution,
   b. calculate the percentage difference,
   c. calculate Yule's Q, and
   d. interpret the results in terms of the social worker's question.

Case	Sex	Success	Case	Sex	Success
1	M	Yes	16	M	No
2	F	No	17	F	Yes
3	F	Yes	18	F	Yes
4	F	Yes	19	M	No
5	M	No	20	F	Yes
6	F	Yes	21	F	No
7	M	No	22	F	No
8	M	No	23	F	Yes
9	F	No	24	M	No
10	F	Yes	25	F	Yes
11	M	No	26	F	Yes
12	M	Yes	27	F	Yes
13	F	Yes	28	M	Yes
14	F	No	29	F	Yes
15	F	Yes	30	F	Yes

2. The personnel officer of a state mental hospital is concerned about staff turnover. He believes that those with greater training are leaving the hospital at higher rates than those who are less well trained. As a first step in documenting this trend, the personnel officer gathers data on level of training and time at the hospital. Using the data reported below:

   a. calculate Cramer's statistic,
   b. calculate gamma, and
   c. decide whether these data are consistent with the personnel officer's hypothesis.

	Years of Experience		
Level of Training	5 or less	6 to 10	11 or more
Technician	10	20	30
BSW	15	20	10
MSW	10	4	1

3. A social worker for a nursing home is interested in whether she should encourage visiting by relatives. The social worker decides that she can make a better case to relatives if the patient's level of mental functioning is related to the number of visits by relatives. To determine whether there is a relationship between these two variables, the social worker decides to use a pre-post design. At the beginning of the month, a test of level of functioning on a mental status questionnaire is administered to all of the patients. During the month, the social worker counts the number of times relatives come to visit each patient. At the end of the month, the test of level of functioning is administered again. The social worker's question is whether the number of visits by relatives during the month is related to changes in level of functioning. Using the data below:

   a. calculate the regression coefficient,
   b. calculate r and r^2,
   c. calculate eta and eta^2,
   d. determine the predicted change in functioning for a patient whose relatives visit two times during the month,
   e. decide whether the relationship is linear or monotonic, and
   f. answer the social worker's question.

Case	Number of Visits	Change Score
1	4	−2
2	4	−1
3	4	+1
4	4	+2
5	5	−2
6	5	0
7	5	+8
8	5	+6
9	6	+2
10	6	+8
11	6	+8
12	6	+10
13	7	+10
14	7	+8
15	7	+6
16	7	+8

For Further Reading

Hubert M. Blalock, Jr. *Social Statistics,* rev. 2nd ed. New York: McGraw-Hill, 1979. Blalock provides a comprehensive treatment of the topics included in this chapter for those who have some background in mathematics.

James A. Davis. *Elementary Survey Analysis.* Englewood Cliffs, New Jersey: Prentice-Hall, 1971. Chapters 2 and 3 of this text include very readable discussions of Yule's Q, gamma, and percentage difference.

Marty J. Schmidt. *Understanding and Using Statistics: Basic Concepts,* 2nd ed. Lexington, Massachusetts: D. C. Heath and Company, 1979. Chapters 6 and 7 of this text describe Pearson's r and the regression coefficient in detail.

13

Statistical Inference and Hypothesis Testing

The previous chapter's focus was on methods for measuring association (the strength of the relationship) between two variables. A hypothesis always specifies the expected relationship between two variables. If the researcher finds that the expected relationship is close, then a second question is: "How likely is it that the relationship occurred by chance alone?" This is the question of *statistical inference.*

Unless there is a strong association between variables in the direction that has been hypothesized, the issue of statistical inference is irrelevant. In other words, inferential statistics should not be used unless the researcher finds strong support for the hypothesis using associational methods. For a full explication of this position, consult Galtung's discussion listed among the suggestions for further reading.

The purpose of this chapter is to discuss the problem of statistical inference and its relationship to the testing of hypotheses. This discussion is not designed to replace the material that would be learned in a statistics course. It will, however, show how these statistical concepts are used in social work research. The intent is to enable readers to develop some intuitive grasp of the logic of statistical inference. This presentation will be as nonmathematical as possible. Some statistical theory will be included, but that, too, will be kept as straightforward as possible.

Chapter 9 discussed the theory of sampling. You will recall that one draws a sample not because the sample is of interest, but because he or she wants to know something about the population from which the sample is drawn. Obviously, the best way to know about the attributes of a number of people would be to assemble all the people in whom one is interested in one place at one time and measure them all. This is almost always impractical. If it could be done, however, there would be no need to worry about statistical inference. A researcher would only have to use descriptive statistics to show what was found when measuring was done. As an example, assume that a researcher wanted to know about the anxiety level of left-handed people. Suppose that an examination of the literature leads the researcher to believe that left-handed people, who live in a world primarily oriented to right-handed people, develop high levels of anxiety. To test this notion, the researcher would have to gather all the left-handed people together in one place at one time and measure their anxiety levels. Because there are millions of left-handed people in all parts of the populated world, this would be a functional impossibility. Therefore, the researcher would not be able to know the anxiety level of all left-handed people. It is possible, however, to make inferences from sample data about the anxiety level of left-handed people and to calculate the probability of arriving at a "ball park" figure. This, in essence, is the task of statistical inference. Unfortunately, it is a little more complicated than this simple example can convey.

Probability

In order to proceed, it is helpful to discuss briefly some aspects of the laws of probability. To begin with, consider a simple example. Everyone has taken a true-false test at one time or another. Consider the following item:

T   F   The Hebrew text of the St. Mark's manuscript of Isaiah, one of the Dead Sea Scrolls, is actually written in the Aramaic alphabet.

It is, of course, unlikely that social work students will encounter this item on an examination in any social work program. It is also unlikely that social work students can answer the question unless they have special knowledge not ordinarily learned in social work courses. The item is chosen for this reason. The only way of arriving at an answer (with the exception of those with special knowledge) is to guess. Clearly, there are just two possibilities. Either the statement is true or it is false. One has to proceed on the basis that there is an equal chance for either outcome. It is conventional in statistics to consider that probabilities are expressed as a decimal part of a whole 1.0. Although we are accustomed to think of this kind of choice being as a "fifty-fifty" chance or a case of "even odds," a statistician would say that one's chance of being right is a .5 probability. Equally, the chance of being wrong is also .5. You can readily see that .5 plus .5 equals 1.0. That is, all probabilities of the potential outcomes of a given event sum to 1.0.

This can, of course, get much more complicated. As the number of possible outcomes increases, the probability that any given outcome will occur decreases. Consider one of a pair of dice, a *die*. Because a die is a cube, it has six sides. They are conventionally numbered from one to six. Clearly, the chance of any one side coming up when the die is tossed is .167, or rounded for convenience's sake, .17. The total probabilities of all sides sum to a whole of 1.0, if one compensates for the rounding error.

The reason that we can count on the correctness of the probabilities in these simple examples is that we can clearly see an underlying distribution of events that accounts for all possible outcomes. The question about the Dead Sea Scrolls is either true or it is false. There are no other possible outcomes. (The item is true, incidentally, if your curiosity has been aroused.) In the case of the die, there are only six possible outcomes. There are not seven sides (or more, for that matter) on any cube.

Things are distributed in a number of ways in the world. These simple examples by no means exhaust the subject. Yet another familiar distribution will lead back to the problem of statistical inference—the normal curve.

The Normal Distribution

A number of things in the world are distributed in a way that can be described by the familiar bell-shaped curve. As students know, the grades on examinations tend to follow a curved distribution. However, the curve that actually represents the outcomes (scores on a test) is not really bell-shaped except in some very rare instances. It is more accurate to say that given an infinite number of students taking an examination, and assuming that the knowledge covered by the test is normally distributed, then the distribution of scores will be normal (that is, a graph of the scores will show the familiar bell shape). That statement is really quite complex and will take some explanation. Return to the true-false question for a minute. It was clear that there were only two possible answers, true or false. In theory, given a whole series of true-false questions, one has a .5 chance of getting each question right by guessing. Suppose that the Dead Sea Scrolls question was followed by a second question. The odds of guessing the answer are the same as they were for the first question. There is no guarantee that the answer to the second question will be the opposite of the answer to the first. That is, if the first question is true, that is no guarantee that the second question will be false. It is theoretically true that given an infinite number of true-false questions, half of the answers would be true and half would be false. No matter what the actual events in the real world, the theoretical probability underlying the whole process enables one to make predictions. In actuality, the instructor may have constructed a test in which several answers in a row are false, but for the student who is taking the exam in ignorance of the material, each question has a theoretical probability of .5 of being true or false.

In the case of the normal distribution, the underlying theoretical distribution of outcomes can be described by a perfectly symmetrical, normal (bell-shaped) curve. This theoretical distribution is based on the assumption that an infinite number of students taking the examination would have normally distributed scores. In reality, there is not an infinite number of students taking the examination, and because some students study whereas others do not, and because some students seem to have an easier time learning than others do, knowledge of the answers is not distributed by chance. Therefore, real curves do not usually reach the pictorial perfection of the normal curve. However, it is possible to understand and interpret the real distribution curves through the use of the normal curve, just as it is possible to understand that one has a .5 chance of guessing the answer to a true-false question.

In order to illustrate the above discussion concretely, consider the following example. Table 13-1 shows the distribution of grades on a hundred-item, multiple-choice examination in social policy.

Obviously, most of these students did not do well if the conventional pass level of 60 is used. The students might clamor to have the instructor "curve" the grades. This is, of course, a euphemism for "lower the requirements for passing the test," because the grades are already "curved." To understand how the idea of the curve works, it is necessary to rearrange the table. In order to make the point at issue, we will show the data as a

Table 13-1   Frequency distribution of student scores on a 100-point social-policy examination

Grades	Frequency
91–100	4
81– 90	5
71– 80	7
61– 70	9
51– 60	11
41– 50	24
31– 40	16
21– 30	13
11– 20	8
0– 10	3

Figure 13-1   Histogram of student scores on a 100-point social-policy examination

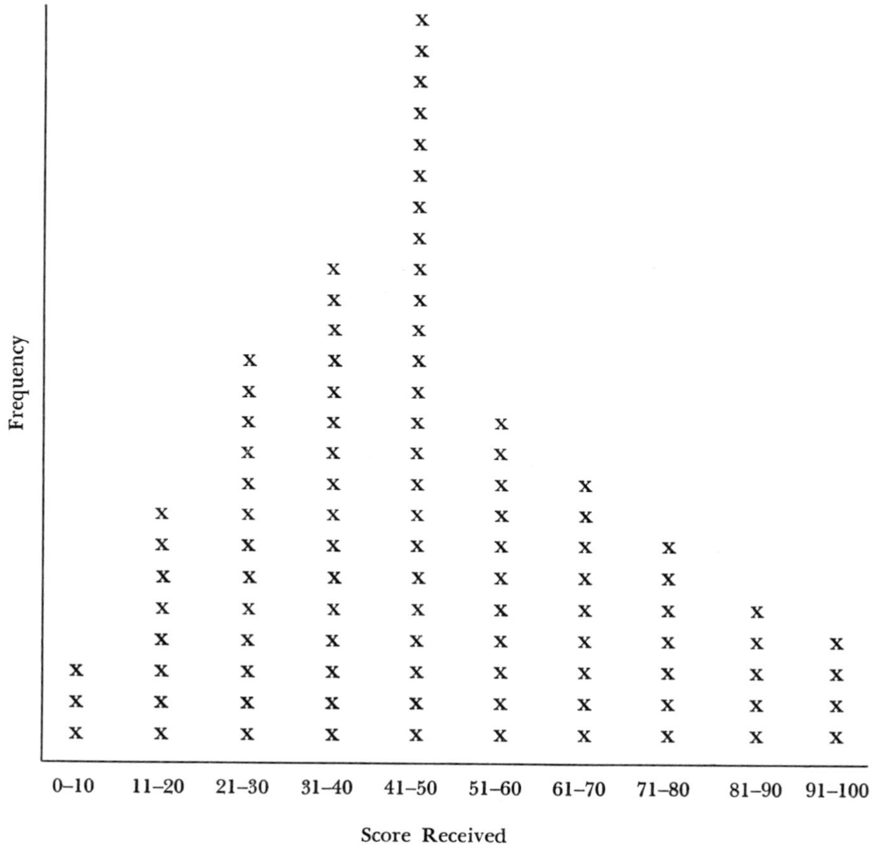

```
                                    X
                                    X
                                    X
                                    X
                                    X
                                    X
                                    X
                                    X
                          X         X
                          X         X
                          X         X
                 X        X         X
                 X        X         X
                 X        X         X    X
                 X        X         X    X
F                X        X         X    X    X
r       X        X        X         X    X    X
e       X        X        X         X    X    X    X
q       X        X        X         X    X    X    X
u       X        X        X         X    X    X    X    X
e       X        X        X         X    X    X    X    X    X
n   X   X        X        X         X    X    X    X    X    X
c   X   X        X        X         X    X    X    X    X    X
y   X   X        X        X         X    X    X    X    X    X

  0–10 11–20 21–30 31–40 41–50 51–60 61–70 71–80 81–90 91–100

                        Score  Received
```

graph (see Figure 13-1). Suppose that the instructor assembled all the students on the football field and stacked them up in piles according to grades along the sideline markers. Then, the instructor took a ribbon and draped it over the students from one goal line to the other. This admittedly ludicrous example should convey the idea that the students are now distributed under a curve represented by the length of ribbon. It should now be clear that a distribution curve is a graphic way of showing how cases are distributed along a continuum. This curve is not quite bell-shaped, but it is a fair approximation. Remember that the theoretical curve (or the theoretical distribution) that underlies the understanding of events in the real world is best understood as a continuum showing all possible scores as continuous variables for an infinite number of students continually taking this examination from now until the end of time! That is, the perfect bell-shaped curve shows what the scores would be in a mathematically perfect universe.

The mathematically perfect, theoretical curve has certain properties. Because this chapter was written with the promise that mathematics would be minimized, you will have to be content with the explanation that these properties have been worked out to be mathematically correct. Figure 13-2 shows the way in which cases are distributed with respect to the mean and standard deviations from the mean.

Because we wish to avoid lengthy mathematical explanations, we can accept the mathematician's word that the way the formula for the standard deviation works assures that the proportions shown in Figure 13-2 are constant. That is, there is always .3413 of the cases between −1 and the mean, and so on. When the formula for the standard deviation is worked using real data, the mathematics involved allow the statistician to divide up the distribution of X's under the curve in the same proportions as in the theoretical curve. The important thing about this point is that doing this allows the statistician to make comparisons involving real data based on assumptions that are theoretically true of the mathematical model. This is akin to the student's assurance of a .5 chance of getting a true-false item correct when guessing. The normal curve, then, is really a probability curve. It shows the probabilities of the ways in which scores would fall on a curve if they were normally distributed.

Figure 13-2   Distribution of cases under the normal curve

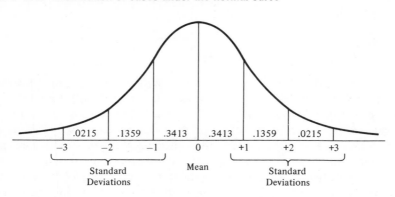

Although this discussion may seem quite esoteric, a number of practical applications of probability distributions are important in inferential statistics. The simplest of these applications is the standardized score.

Standard Scores

There are occasions when a researcher wants to know how a given subject's score relates to all other subjects' scores on a given measure. It may be practical to approach this question in familiar terms. Suppose that you meet one of your friends, who has just received an examination back. You ask her, "How did you do on the exam?" She answers, "I got a 46!" Without some frame of reference in which to understand the meaning of a score of 46, you do not know whether to say, "Congratulations!" or, "Let's go get a cup of coffee and blow off some steam!" Something more is needed in the way of information in order to make the score interpretable. The simplest way, of course, is to know that the score is a percentage of some number of points possible on the test. If your friend had told you that the examination had 50 items, you could have done a quick percentage and found that she had received a score of 92 percent on the test. Ordinarily, this would appear to be a superior grade. On the other hand, this is not a certainty. One of the authors of this book once was congratulating himself for scoring 92 percent on a test, when he found that the letter grade that he received was a C—! It turned out that the instructor in the course had been using the same examination for twenty years, and nearly everyone else in the class knew that. Consequently, the average score was a 94 and the distribution was skewed to the right!

A common way to transmit more information about the meaning of a score is to express it as a percentile rank (see Chapter 10). A more meaningful way to locate a score, however, is to calculate the standard score. In order to do this, the score must be transformed into a standard deviation unit, or z-score. This is accomplished by using the formula:

$$z = \frac{X - \bar{X}}{\sigma}$$

What this formula does is simply to convert the difference between a score and the mean score into a standard deviation unit (σ). To put it another way, the z transformation allows the researcher to compare a single score with all other scores in the entire distribution. Working through the example should make this plain. In order to keep the example simple, we will assume that the instructor in the course has figured the mean score and found it to be a 40. The instructor has also computed the standard deviation: it is 4. Substituting these values in the formula results in the following simple problem:

$$z = \frac{46 - 40}{4} = \frac{6}{4} = 1.5$$

$$z = 1.5$$

The score of 46 has been converted to a standard score of 1.5. This now allows a comparison with the other scores in the distribution. This transformation is necessary, because the other scores are part of the distribution that is displayed in standard deviation units. Remember what the curve really is: a distribution of all the cases of some x (either all known cases or all theorized cases—the reader is asked to live with an oversimplification for the time being) along both a horizontal and a vertical dimension. (Recall the stack of students on the football field.) Converting the score of 46 into a z of 1.5 allows the comparison of the student's score with the other students both in terms of their scores on the test and in the way they are distributed around the mean.

Now look at Table B-2 in Appendix B. Look for a z-score of 1.5, and find the decimal .4332 listed opposite it. Remember that the curve is thought of as a whole 1.0. The z tables used in statistics and research cover only half of the curve. That is, the table shows the z values starting from 0 (where the mean is located) to five standard deviations plus or minus the mean. In this case, the z-score of 1.5 is +.4332 of the area from the mean. If .5 of the area is to the left of the mean, then .5 and .4332 can be added together showing that the score of 46 has .9332 of the scores below it in the distribution. Therefore, .0668 of the scores are above 1.5. It can be said that approximately 93 percent of the scores are below 46 and approximately 7 percent are above 46. Your friend, then, did pretty well on the examination; only 7 percent did better.

Hypothesis Testing

A fairly simple extension of the above idea allows the researcher to test certain hypotheses. However, some preliminary theory is helpful. Again, we will keep the discussion as nontechnical as is possible, striving for an intuitive, common sense approach.

The basic task of inference is, as we have stated previously, how to use data from a sample to say something about the larger population from which it is drawn. Actually, a statistician would restate this question in a slightly different form: "When we want to generalize from statistics from a sample, how wrong will we be?" Or, to put it still another way, "When using data from a sample to infer characteristics of a population, how far off is the sample from the real world?" This is the basic question of generalizability, or external validity (see Chapter 4).

The use of random samples is essential. Generalizability is questionable using any other kind of sample. Nonrandom samples can introduce errors into the research, as we showed in Chapter 9. A researcher might generalize wrongly using random samples, but such errors would occur by chance and not as a consequence of the sampling procedure.

This next part is abstract and quite removed from practicality. However, it is a necessary part of the background. First, let us return to the notion of underlying distributions. Suppose that a researcher is interested in some population's scores on an interval scale. Obviously, if every member of the population were to fill out a questionnaire, there would be a potential of N scores. Somewhere, if it could be known, there would be an average score and a standard deviation of that score. It is conventional in statistics to let Greek cursive letters stand for the parameters of a population. The word *parameter* in this application means the figures that describe the outside limits or boundaries of the population. It is assumed, then, that the population has a mean of μ (mu) and a standard deviation of σ (sigma). For the moment, assume that μ and σ are unknowns even though in some special cases they may be known. Imagine that a huge research grant permits hiring a number of research assistants to draw R (an unknown number) random samples for several years. Suppose that the research assistants then calculated the mean of each of these random samples and then plotted all these means on a curve. This curve would then show the sampling distribution of the mean. It would be seen that the means would be normally distributed—that is, the means would "graph out" in a bell-shaped curve. This curve, however, would be much more closely compacted around the population mean, because it is composed of averages. The mean of all the means would also be the same number as the mean of the population. This relationship is shown in Figure 13-3. It may take a little time to assimilate this point. It may help to think of it this way: The average of all the averages is the same as the average of all the individual cases.

The narrower curve (which, remember, is made up of averages) has all of the properties of the curve that includes all of the individual scores. That is, it can be divided off in standard deviation units. However, these points are no longer called standard deviations. When the sampling distribution of the sample-means curve is involved, the standard deviation is called the *standard error of the mean,* or S.E.M. The actual formula for finding the standard error is:

$$\frac{\sigma}{\sqrt{N}}$$

**Figure 13-3   Sample distributions of scores and sample means based
on a given sample size**

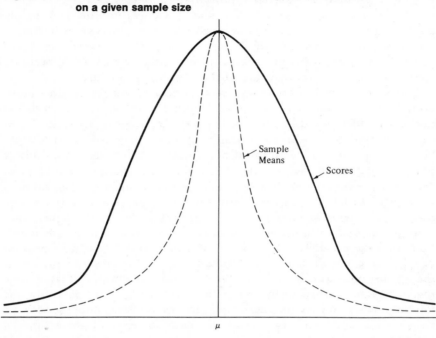

Sample
Means

Scores

μ

The interpretation is similar to that of the standard deviation. That is, the mathematics involved assures that it is probable that .6826 of the means of repeated random samples fall within an interval + or − one standard error of μ. It must be noted that a researcher may never know what μ is. What can be said is that if one hundred researchers drew the same-sized random samples from a population with a mean of μ and a standard deviation of σ, then .6826 (or a little over 68 percent) of them would lie within one standard error of μ. Where did the .6826 come from? Recall that the properties of the sampling distribution of the mean curve are the same as those of the standard normal curve. If 68 percent of the cases of x fall between +1 and −1 *standard deviations* of μ, then 68 percent of the means fall between +1 and −1 *standard errors* of μ.

Of course, in reality, no one would employ research assistants to draw an indefinitely large set of samples from any population. In reality, most researchers work with only one sample. What happens is that the standard error is calculated from the data gained from that one sample. The formula is altered to:

$$\text{S.E.M.} = \frac{s}{\sqrt{N-1}}$$

This change is necessary because σ is unknown. This formula provides an unbiased estimate of the S.E.M.

It is theoretically possible, then, to estimate a parameter by drawing a random sample from a population, calculating the sample mean and standard deviation, and calculating the standard error of the mean, which will include μ with a selected degree of probability. The way that it has been done above would allow a researcher to have the confidence to say that μ is within the standard error with a probability of about .68. Most social researchers would like to be more confident of that. Although the figures are not sacred, most social scientists conventionally assume that they want to be 95 percent, or sometimes 99 percent, confident when estimating parameters. Again, recall the characteristics of the standard normal curve. In order to be 95 percent confident that the interval around the sample mean contains the population mean, it is necessary to go 1.96 standard errors plus or minus the mean. This is because 95 percent of the area under the curve is included in an interval between $+1.96$ and -1.96 above and below the mean. To be 99 percent confident, the interval must be between 2.58 standard errors plus or minus the mean.

To illustrate the discussion so far, consider the following simple problem. A researcher has administered the Taylor Manifest Anxiety Scale to a random sample of 101 anxious people. The researcher wants to have a rough estimate of μ. This scale is an interval measure on which the score may vary from 0 to 50. The average score is 40 (in research language, $\overline{X} = 40$), and s turns out to be 5. The researcher decides that the 95 percent confidence interval is sufficient for her purposes. She therefore works the equation:

$$\text{S.E.M.} = 1.96 \times \frac{5}{\sqrt{101-1}} = .98$$

Now, by adding and subtracting .98 from the mean (40), she obtains an interval of from 39.02 to 40.98. Actually, it is not contended that μ is between 39.02 and 40.98. What can be said is that one can have confidence that, in the long run, if a large number of researchers did exactly as this one did, 95 percent of the intervals obtained would include the true parameter.

The above process is called calculating a *confidence interval*. It is unlikely that you will spend much time figuring confidence intervals. The reason for including the discussion is that it is a preliminary step to the process of hypothesis testing, and it should make that process more intelligible.

The z-Transformation

In the previous section, the z-transformation was used to compare the score of one person with the scores of a large group of people. Another form of the z-transformation allows the researcher to compare the mean of a sample with the mean of a population whose standard deviation is known. This use of the z-transformation is best explained through the use of an example. Suppose that a social work researcher is interested in testing a new technique for reducing anxiety in a certain client population. It is impractical to use the new technique on all anxious clients, so the researcher draws a sample. Fortunately for this example, the agency has routinely given a series of tests to all of their new clients for several years. Among these tests is the Client Anxiety Test, a 100-item, multiple-choice instrument especially created for this kind of work. The agency's leased-time computer firm has reported that, for all clients, the average score on the CAT is 70, and the standard deviation is 15. Given the way in which the population is defined, then, the parameters (μ and σ) are known. The researcher then proceeds to draw a random sample of one hundred from the agency's caseload. The average score ($\bar{x}$) of the sample on the CAT is 67.5. The question in the researcher's mind is, Is the sample anxious enough to be a good representation of the anxiety level of the entire caseload? The object of doing the experiment is to evaluate the potential effectiveness of a technique on all anxious clients in the caseload. Therefore, the researcher wants a sample that is a good representation of the caseload. It would not do to use a sample that was so different from the rest of the caseload that generalization would be questionable. Therefore, the question can also be interpreted as asking whether or not the sample is so different from the caseload that the experiment would be invalid.

The solution to this question is analogous to the previously discussed process of comparing a score on a test with all other scores. The difference is that, in this instance, the researcher wants to compare the mean of the sample group with the means of all other possible samples of a given size. As a result, the formula for the z-transformation differs in that the denominator includes the formula for the standard error of the mean. Here is the formula:

$$z = \frac{X - \mu}{\sigma / \sqrt{N}}$$

The difference here is that the distance between the mean of the sample is being transformed into a *standard error* unit. Comparisons of individual scores and all other scores are made on the curve of the distribution of all the x's. However, comparisons of sample means are made to the more compact curve showing the distribution of all possible means. The question is whether or not this sample mean is too different from all other possible sample means. If it is too different, it will not be a good representation of the entire caseload.

Working out the formula is not difficult:

$$z = \frac{67.5 - 70}{15/\sqrt{100}} = -1.67$$

Again, we have an answer of 1.67. However, this time it is a -1.67, so it is clear that this z falls on the left side of μ. The interpretation is the same as it was in the standard score problem—that is, approximately 93 percent of the possible *means* would fall above the one obtained in the sample. Now, can the question be answered about whether this mean is too different from the other possible means that could have occurred? Yes, with some additional information. Recall that social scientists have agreed to accept the convention that they want to be 95 percent or 99 percent confident about their results. If one wants to be 95 percent confident that the mean of the sample is close enough to μ, then it is essential that the z-score fall in an interval within which 95 percent of all the means would fall.

In doing statistics of this sort, the researcher is always testing a hypothesis. Actually, two hypotheses are involved. The first, the so-called research hypothesis, says that the mean is different from μ. The other hypothesis is called the null hypothesis. The word *null* means *negative*. In statistical language, the null hypothesis simply says that there is no difference (literally a null difference) between the sample mean and the population mean. Researchers can make two errors in judging whether a sample is sufficiently like the population. These are called Type I and Type II errors. A Type I error occurs when one rejects a null hypothesis when it is true. A Type II error occurs when one accepts a null hypothesis when the alternative is true. It turns out that using confidence levels of at least 95 percent minimizes the risk of committing a Type I error.

The procedures that most statisticians use always test null hypotheses.[1] This seems illogical, because the researcher is really interested in the research hypothesis. Without resorting to complicated mathematical explanations, the simplest way to explain this apparent contradiction is to say that the tradition of statistics that has grown up in social science in the last fifty years assumes that if all nulls are disproved, then the research hypothesis will be left and will be obviously true. Further, the way in which the mathematics of the problem work, all that can be done is to disprove the null.

Let us return to the problem. If it is essential that the z-score fall in an interval within which 95 percent of all the means would fall, then it is essential to locate a z-score that will cut off that interval.

Here, another set of conventions must be mastered. A statistical test is often facetiously referred to as an animal that sometimes has one tail and sometimes two. The key idea here is whether the researcher is interested in *any* difference between the mean and μ or in a difference *in only one direction*. In the example used for this illustration, the researcher is concerned that the sample may not be anxious enough to be used as an experimental group. Note that it would not have mattered if the sample had yielded an anxiety score higher than 70. That would have been all right, because the experimenter wants anxious people for the experiment. In this case, the only concern arises if the sample is too "nonanxious." For this reason, the researcher will employ the so-called one-tailed test. That is, the researcher will want to use a z-score for the boundary of the interval that will exclude those means of samples that would be so low as to be virtually nonanxious subjects. The region so cut off is called the *critical region*. An illustration may help you visualize this (see Figure 13-4).

In those cases when the researcher is concerned with differences in any direction—either too high or too low—a two-tailed test is used. Figure 13-5 is a picture of the two-tailed test. Remember what is being indicated here. If the z-score (which represents the difference between a sample mean

Figure 13-4   Critical region for a one-tailed test of hypothesis

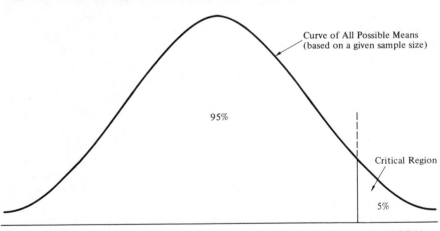

Curve of All Possible Means
(based on a given sample size)

95%

Critical Region

5%

+1.645 S.E.M.

Figure 13-5   Critical region for a two-tailed test of hypothesis

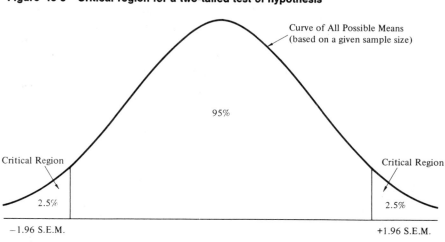

---

and the mean of the population) was so extreme as to occur out in the tail or tails of the distribution, it would be considered statistically significant. If the z-score were small enough to fall within the interval around the mean, then the statistician would not reject the null hypothesis. Effectively, this means that a small z-score indicates that there is no difference, whereas a large z-score indicates that one cannot say that there is no difference. How little is small? In the case of the z-score, the cutoff point for the critical region for a one-tailed test is 1.65. In the case of a two-tailed test, the z cutoffs are +1.96 and −1.96. Why these points? Because 1.65 cuts off 95 percent of the area in one tail. A one-tailed test takes off 5 percent all in one tail. The two-tailed test has 1.96 as a cutoff point, because the two-tailed test cuts off 2.5 percent in each tail. This can be verified by using Table B-2 in Appendix B as before.

This approach can be used only in those situations in which the standard deviation of the population is known. This is a serious limitation, because in many cases the standard deviation of the population is unknown. Census data and data on public schools are the main data sources for which the measurements are so vast that a researcher can assume that μ and σ are known. Of course, if the population of interest to the researcher is small and well defined, it is possible that sufficient data exist to allow the researcher to know the important parameters. Most of the time, however, the parameters are unknown. Researchers are interested in large groups—the poor, the mentally ill, or children, for example —for whom extensive measures simply do not exist. Fortunately, there is a remedy for this problem. This is called the t-test.

"Student's" t

When μ and σ are unknown, researchers usually turn to a procedure known as the t-test. This test was developed in the 1920s by W. S. Gosset, writing under the pen name "Student." The t-test has two main uses: (1) A single sample can be compared to a population whose parameters are unknown. (2) Two samples can be compared to see if they are statistically close to each other. An illustration of each is the simplest way to show how the t-test works.

In the first instance, suppose that a family-oriented agency has an evaluational study in process. Part of the study involves the efficiency of workers in carrying out foster-home studies. A consultant has told the agency that a perfectly good foster home study can be done in a series of 10 interviews. The agency decides to accept 10 interviews as an optimum goal for which all workers are to aim. The question is, How close are all workers to the goal? A random sample of 26 social workers is drawn from the statewide staff of the agency. The average number of home visits made prior to licensing by the workers in this sample turns out to be 13 and the standard deviation of the sample is 3. The question is, Are these workers operating efficiently? The evaluator will work the formula for t:

$$t = \frac{\overline{X} - \mu}{S/\sqrt{N-1}}$$

Recall that the opening paragraph of this section said that the t-test was used when μ and σ were unknown. Yet, here in this formula is the symbol for μ. When using the t-test, it is necessary to use an assumed (or sometimes a guessed) μ. This is an arbitrary process, admittedly, but it is the only way to proceed. Further, although the numerator of the fraction used to figure t is the same as the numerator of the fraction in the z-formula, there is a difference in the denominator. In the z-formula, σ was divided by the square root of N. Because sigma is unknown, the t-formula substitutes s (the standard deviation of the sample) and divides it by $N-1$. This is recognizable as the formula for the standard error. The use of $N-1$ makes the estimate of the standard error unbiased. Here again, because means are being compared, the comparison is done on the standard-error curve in the same way that it was done for z. Here is the substitution of numbers for symbols:

$$t = \frac{13 - 10 \text{ (the difference between the assumed } \mu \text{ and } \overline{X})}{\dfrac{3}{5} \begin{array}{l}\text{(the standard deviation of the sample)} \\ \text{(the square root of } N-1)\end{array}}$$

$$t = 5$$

Table B-3 in Appendix B at the back of the book gives the significant values of t. One additional item is needed in order to make interpretation possible. To know the significant value of t, one must look for the value given in the table by the number of *degrees of freedom* (*df*). Briefly, the idea is that within certain limits, numbers are free to vary around a fixed point. For example, consider this simple equation: $2 + 3 + \_ + \_ = 10$. This equation has one degree of freedom in that as soon as the third number is specified, the fourth is fixed. If the third number in the sequence is 4, then the last number has to be 1, because the total cannot exceed the limit of 10. In the case of the t test, there is a different distribution curve for each size of N. Therefore, there is a variation in the distribution of probabilities for each N, according to the amount of freedom there is for N to vary. For the purposes of using the table, the degrees of freedom associated with each N is equal to $N - 1$. In this example, one wishing to use the table would look up the critical value for t in the columns opposite 25.

The table shows critical values for both one-tailed and two-tailed tests. In this case, a direction is specified, because the question is whether the workers are making too many visits. Therefore, the probability of error is all on the right-hand side of the curve. The appropriate critical value is 1.708 for a one-tailed test at the .05 level of significance. Because a t of 5 was obtained, clearly there is a significant difference between the number of home visits made by the workers and the average that is desired by agency administration. It may help to remind readers of what is at issue here. Remember that it is not the sample that is the center of interest. The assumption is that, 95 times out of 100, another researcher performing the same sampling process and making the same calculation would get a similar result. Therefore, the evaluator is questioning not the number of visits made by the workers in the *sample* but the number of visits made by *all the workers in the agency*. It is that population that one would want to generalize about, not just the sample.

The second general use of the t-test is a fairly straightforward extension of this one. There are differences in the formula, but these differences are not as formidable as they appear to be. It will again be easier to approach this version of the t-test through an example.

Suppose that an agency has measured samples of two sets of clients on some instrument. This hypothetical instrument is scaled from 0 to 100. The agency wants to know which of the two populations scores higher on the instrument. Remember that this is a problem in inference. The agency people can see a difference in the scores of the samples. That is not what is important. The question is whether there is a difference between the two populations from which the samples are drawn. If there is a significant difference between the sample means, then the agency can infer that one cannot say that there is no difference. Recall the peculiar conventions of statistical significance. All that one can do is to disprove the null, because the research hypothesis cannot be directly proved. In this example, Sample

A turns out to have a mean of 80 with a standard deviation of 4, whereas Sample B has a mean of 76 with a standard deviation of 6. To complicate matters, Sample A consists of 24 clients, whereas Sample B has 28. This is not an unrealistic situation. Very often, samples are of differing sizes. There are a number of ways that this can happen. For example, the person doing the sampling might take a 10 percent sample of two populations of different sizes. The formula that will be used takes into account the possibility of different sample sizes. The formula is:

$$t = \frac{(\bar{X}_1 - \bar{X}_2) - (\mu_1 - \mu_2)}{\hat{\sigma}_{\bar{x}_1 - \bar{x}_2}} \quad \text{(a pooled estimate of the variances)}$$

To get $\hat{\sigma}_{\bar{x}_1 - \bar{x}_2}$, the following calculation is made:

$$\sigma_{\bar{x}_1 - \bar{x}_2} = \sqrt{\frac{N_1 S_1^2 + N_2 S_2^2}{N_1 + N_2 - 2}} \cdot \sqrt{\frac{N_1 + N_2}{N_1 N_2}}$$

Notice that the numerator of the fraction is similar to the one in the first use of the t-test. In this case, the researcher is interested in comparing how similar two populations are to one another. The difference between the sample means $(\bar{X}_1 - \bar{X}_2)$ is an estimate of the difference between the population means $(\mu_1 - \mu_2)$. Usually, the researcher is trying to test the hypothesis that the populations are the same $(\mu_1 = \mu_2)$, so that the numerator is even simpler. In this case, it is $\bar{X}_1 - \bar{X}_2$, because the difference between the population means is assumed to be zero.

There is considerable difference in the denominator of the fraction. This difference comes about because of the different standard deviations and the different sample sizes. The denominator thus becomes a way of pooling the differences of the two sample standard deviations and sample sizes into one estimate of the parameters of the population. In using this formula, the researcher operates on the assumption that the two samples are actually alike, but the test will reveal if there are differences.

Although, as we have said, the problem looks formidable, it is not. Substituting the quantities that have been provided, it works like this:

$$\sigma_{\bar{x}_1 - \bar{x}_2} = \sqrt{\frac{24(16) + 28(36)}{24 + 28 - 2}} \cdot \sqrt{\frac{24 + 28}{24 \times 28}}$$

Under the first radical, 24 is the first N. It is multiplied by the variance (the standard deviation squared) of Sample A. To this is added the product of the second N (28) multiplied by the variance in Sample B. The rest of the equation is self-explanatory. Proceeding, it can be seen that:

$$\hat{\sigma} = \sqrt{\frac{384 + 1008}{50}} \times \sqrt{\frac{52}{672}}$$

$$= \sqrt{27.84} \quad \times \sqrt{.077}$$

$$= \quad 5.28 \quad \times \quad .278$$

$$\hat{\sigma} = \quad 1.47$$

The figure of 1.47 can now be substituted in the formula for t:

$$t = \frac{80 - 76}{1.47}$$

$$= \frac{4}{1.47}$$

$$t = 2.72$$

A t-score of 2.72 can now be looked up in the appropriate table. The number of degrees of freedom in this case equals 50. Because there are two samples, it is necessary to add them together and subtract 2. You will recall that in the first example, the degrees of freedom were found by the simple expression $N - 1$. In the first example, there was only one sample.

The table does not show the appropriate critical value for 50 degrees of freedom. Instead, the table tends to be more general as degrees of freedom (df) increases. This example thus provides the opportunity to discuss what to do in this instance. It is necessary to interpolate the critical value by taking half the difference between the critical value for 40 and 60 degrees of freedom. A little quick work with a pencil will show that the appropriate critical value is 1.68 (rounded) at the .05 level of significance. Because the calculation of t yielded a value of 2.72, the researcher would reject the null hypothesis. That is, the results of the calculations make it clear that one cannot say that there is no difference. The sample means are too far apart on the t-curve for 50 degrees of freedom to be considered as having no difference.

In this example, it was assumed that both samples were drawn from the same population. Actually, this is not always a safe assumption; ordinarily, a researcher would test it using a simple version of what is called the F-test. In this version of the F-test, the two variances are compared in a ratio, with the larger variance always used as the numerator of the ratio fraction. In this example, the resulting fraction would be 36/15, and the ratio would then be 2.25. This ratio of one variance to another is called F. The significance of F is given in Tables B-4 and B-5 in Appendix B at the back of the book. To use these tables, it is necessary to again make use of the concept of degrees of freedom. In this case, one calculates the degrees of freedom for the numerator ($N - 1$, N being the number of cases in the sample whose variance is found in the numerator) and for the denominator (again, $N - 1$ for the number of cases in the sample whose variance constitutes the denominator). In this example, then, one looks across the table to find 27 df ($28 - 1$) and down the side to find 23 df. When neither of these is available (as is usually the case with the larger numbers), interpolation again is necessary to find the critical value. To save time, you can see that the significance level for F for either 24 or 30 df in the numerator and 23 in the denominator is exceeded by 2.25, so interpolation is not necessary. Clearly, it was not valid to do this problem on the assumption that both samples were drawn from the same population. A different formula for t should have been used! As you can guess, this has been a mildly deceptive way of approaching the point that there are two formulas for $\hat{\sigma}$. The choice depends upon the outcome of the F ratio. When the F ratio is close to 1, use the formula for $\hat{\sigma}$ on p. 274. When the F ratio changes so that the two variances of the samples are dissimilar, then use the following formula:

$$\hat{\sigma} = \sqrt{\frac{S_1^2}{N-1} + \frac{S_2^2}{N_2 - 1}}$$

This formula is somewhat simpler. It yields a value of 1.41. If this value for $\hat{\sigma}$ is used in the equation for t, a t-value of 2.84 results.

In this case, the result is the same: t is significant. The error in selecting the proper formula for $\hat{\sigma}$ turns out not to have mattered. This will not always be the case, and the careful researcher is advised to compare the two variances in the F-ratio before proceeding to calculate t.

So far, the discussion has centered on situations when a researcher is working with either one sample that is to be compared to a population or two samples that are to be compared to each other. In practical research, it is often necessary to work with more than two samples. In such cases, neither the z-transformation nor the t-test will do very much good. The next section will discuss a procedure known as the one-way analysis of variance (or ANOVA, as it is usually written).

Analysis of Variance

The ANOVA procedure can be used to test for significant differences among the means of two or more samples. Ordinarily, ANOVA is used in situations in which one wishes to look at relationships between a nominal (or higher order) scale and an interval scale. The explanation of this procedure is best approached by a simple problem. Bear in mind that the problem would ordinarily involve larger samples and more complex measurements than are being used here. This example is computationally simple in order to avoid our bogging down in the arithmetic.

Suppose that a social worker wants to test the effectiveness of three different kinds of treatment on a particular kind of client problem. Again, for simplicity, let it be stipulated that the client problem is a behavior that can be counted. This will provide a very simple interval scale. We will not detail the alternative treatments but will refer to them as treatments A, B, and C. The treatments are designed to increase some kind of behavior. A number of clients have been identified and randomly assigned to one of the three treatment groups. Preliminary study of the groups suggests that prior to the experiment there were no gross differences in the condition of any of the clients, so that there is a reasonable amount of confidence in the effectiveness of the random assignments. We can use a simple variation on the post-test-only control-group design (see Chapter 4):

$$R \quad A \quad O$$
$$R \quad B \quad O$$
$$R \quad C \quad O$$

The R's indicate random sample, whereas A, B, and C are the three treatments.

Note that there is no untreated control group in this design. It is not necessary, because in this situation the researcher wants to look at the differential effect of three treatments, not just the effect of treatment versus no treatment. In effect, each treatment uses the other two as a control.

Although it is common to refer to the clients identified as groups A, B, and C as *groups,* they are really merely *sets.* Unfortunately the word *groups* implies a relationship between clients that may or may not exist. That is, treatments A, B, and C do not have to be *group* treatments. The subjects assigned to Group A, for example, may be receiving individual problem-solving treatment, the subjects assigned to Group B may be receiving some form of drug therapy, whereas those in Group C may be receiving highly individualized relaxation therapy. It is not necessary for any of the clients to ever even see each other, let alone engage in interaction. It is not absolutely essential that the therapies be carried out at exactly the same time, although if there were large time lapses—months or years—among the use of the three approaches, this would be questionable.

Of course, if treatments A, B, and C were in fact group therapies, then the subjects would be in actual face-to-face groups. The point is that it is not necessary to be using a group therapy to use this kind of statistical approach.

To pick up the threads of the example, let us assume that three sets of clients have been randomly selected, treatments have been completed, and counts have been made of the occurrence of the behaviors that treatments A, B, and C are designed to encourage. The following results are obtained:

A	B	C
9	7	4
8	5	6
5	6	8
6	4	7
7	3	5
35	25	30
$\overline{X} = 7$	$\overline{X} = 5$	$\overline{X} = 6$

The question now is: Is there a significant difference among the three treatments? Obviously, treatment A worked best in the experiment, but remember that this is not the central question. The question is whether these results give an accurate picture of the effect of these treatments had they been used on the entire population of clients who had the particular behavioral problem that the treatments are designed to affect.

One of two things is true. Either the treatments have a differential effect on clients with this particular problem, or they do not. The statistician puts it another way, but it comes down to the same thing in practice. Either the three groups—after treatment—have a common variance, or they do not. You will recall what the variance is: the difference between the average score and each individual score, squared. Because this is an inferential problem, the researcher is interested not in the sample variance but in the variance in the population under study. Because the variance in the population is unknown, the researcher has to infer it from the data provided in the samples.

In order to be able to infer what the probability is that the effects of treatments A, B, and C would have made a difference had they been used to treat the whole population of clients, it will be necessary to form some estimate of the effects of treatments A, B, and C on the population. Actually, the statistician makes not one estimate but two. These two estimates are then compared in an F-ratio. If the resulting ratio is close to 1.0, then it is assumed that there is little difference among treatments. If the ratio exceeds a margin allowable by chance, then it is assumed that there may be a difference among treatments and the implied null hypothesis (that there is no difference) is rejected.

These two estimates of the population variance are called the *within* and the *between* estimates. The within estimate is based on the variances within each sample. The between estimate is based on the variance between each sample mean and the grand mean. The grand mean is the average of all scores in all samples. The calculation of the example will help make this clear.

Ordinarily, statisticians do not calculate the within estimate when using hand-calculation methods, because it is somewhat laborious. Therefore, in this example, we will calculate the total estimate (the sum of the between and the within estimate) and the between estimate. We will obtain the within estimate by subtracting the between estimate from the total estimate.

This is the formula for calculating the total estimate of the variation (the mathematical subscripts have been omitted for simplicity):

$$\Sigma \Sigma (X - \bar{X})^2 = \Sigma \Sigma X^2 - \frac{(\Sigma \Sigma X)^2}{N}$$

Again, this formula looks more formidable than it really is. Essentially, it is an extension of the formula used in finding the variance of a single column of figures. The summation sign (large sigma) means "the sum of." In order to find the total estimate (or the total sum of squares), one first squares all the individual scores (each score is an x). Recall that the total scores for each set of subjects and the means of each set have already been figured. It is now necessary to sum all the original scores ($35 + 25 + 30 = 90$) and to sum the squares of each column ($255 + 135 + 190 = 580$), as shown in Table 13-2. It is now a simple matter of plugging these quantities into the formula.

$$\Sigma \, \Sigma (X - \overline{X})^2 = 580 - \frac{(90)^2}{15}$$

In this case, $N = 15$, because the total sum of squares treats all three samples as one big sample. Continuing to work the problem begun above, we get:

$$= 580 - \frac{8100}{15}$$

$$= 580 - 540$$

$$\Sigma \, \Sigma (X - \overline{X})^2 = 40$$

The formula for the between estimate is:

$$\left[\frac{(\Sigma X)^2}{n} + \frac{(\Sigma X)^2}{n} + \cdots \frac{(\Sigma X)^2}{n} \right] - \frac{(\Sigma \Sigma X)^2}{N}$$

This formula, too, looks more frightening than it really is. To work it, one merely adds together the sum of each set of scores, squares each sum, divides each by the number of scores in the set, and subtracts the same quantity that was subtracted from the first term when the total sum of

---

Table 13-2   Illustration of initial calculations for analysis of variance

	A		B		C	
	X	X²	X	X²	X	X²
	9	81	7	49	4	16
	8	64	5	25	6	36
	5	25	6	36	8	64
	6	36	4	16	7	49
	7	49	3	9	5	25
Total	35	255	25	135	30	190

squares was calculated earlier. The completed calculation works as follows:

$$= \frac{(35)^2}{5} + \frac{(25)^2}{5} + \frac{(30)^2}{5} - \frac{(90)^2}{15}$$

$$= \frac{1225}{5} + \frac{625}{5} + \frac{900}{5} - 540$$

$$= 245 + 125 + 180 - 540$$

Therefore:

$$\left[\frac{(\Sigma X)^2}{n} + \frac{(\Sigma X)^2}{n} + \ldots + \frac{(\Sigma X)^2}{n} \right] - \frac{(\Sigma \Sigma X)^2}{N} = 10$$

The two quantities needed to calculate the within sum of squares are now available, 40 and 10. (Remember that the within sum is obtained by first calculating the total sum of squares, then calculating the between sum of squares, and subtracting the between from the total.) It is usual to summarize the remaining calculations in a table (see Table 13-3). Once again, the F-ratio makes use of the idea of degrees of freedom. The total df is equal to the total N minus 1. The between estimate is associated with $k - 1$, in which $k =$ the number of groups. The within estimate is equal to $N - k$ (that is, the total N minus the number of groups). The between and the within sums of squares are divided by their respective degrees of freedom in order to obtain the ratio used to calculate F. As before, the significance of F is determined from the table. In this case, the critical value for the .05 level of significance is 3.88. That is, if F had been greater than 3.88, the null hypothesis would be rejected. Because F is smaller than 3.88, it can be said that there is no basis for rejection of a statement that there is no difference among treatments for the population of clients with the particular condition under study.

Had F been significant, there would be unanswered questions. Is treatment A statistically significantly better than both treatments B *and* C? Or, are treatments A and B superior to treatment C? Advanced and complicated techniques are available for answering this question, but they are beyond the scope of this text. Some of these procedures need to be

Table 13-3   Summary table for analysis of variance

	Sums of Squares	Degree of Freedom	Estimates	F Ratio
Total	40	$N - 1 + 14$		
Between	10	$k - 1 = 2$	5	
Within	30	$N - k = 12$	2.5	2.000

planned into the data-processing routine from the beginning, whereas others can be used after the fact when a significant F has been detected. Readers wishing to explore this question are referred to the Snedecor and Cochran volume in the reading list at the end of the chapter.

Hypothesis Testing Using Chi-Square

A limited amount of hypothesis testing can be done using Chi-square, a measure of association that was discussed in Chapter 11. Ordinarily, Chi-square is most valuable as the basis for a series of associational measures. By itself, it is not a very powerful test, because it is only appropriate when using nominal scales. Further, the test is very sensitive to the size of the sample. When the sample is either small (30 or less) or fairly large (100 or more), Chi-square can be a very misleading statistic.[2]

Ordinarily in social work research, Chi-square is used to test whether the results actually obtained in a matrix differ from what would have been expected if chance alone were operating. Consider the following simple example:

> An agency has developed a policy with regard to promotion. On the surface, the policy statement seems quite fair, but the agency executive notices that in casual conversation there seems to be an increasing polarization of the men and women on the staff. The executive suspects that the policy may be subtly sexist, but because the polarization is not complete and the discomfort is only vague, no one has quite been able to put a finger on the problem. Not wishing to support a sexist policy, the executive decides to attack the apparent problem logically. She decides that the first step is to find out if, in fact, the men and women hold different attitudes toward the policy. It is possible that her impression of a genuinely significant polarization is wrong and that opposition is not on a sexual basis.
>
> As a first step, then, the executive confers with the staff individually and obtains from each worker a statement of opinion that she believes to be genuine. The executive prepares a matrix on the basis of these conversations (see Table 13-4).

The researcher set the matrix up this way because she wanted to know if there was a relationship between being female and having a negative attitude toward the policy. If the question was whether men were against the policy, then male and female would have been reversed in the table. This arrangement is customarily based on the way in which the question is asked, since the outcome is not affected by the order in which the calculations are made.

The first step in finding Chi-square is to find out the expected cell values if chance alone were operating. Although the calculation is laborious by hand, it is straightforward and easy with an electronic calculator.

Table 13-4   Relationship between sex of worker and attitude toward policy

| Sex of Worker | | Attitude Toward Policy | | |
		Against	For	Total
Female		18(a)	12(b)	30
Male		10(c)	14(d)	24
	Total	28	26	54

Note: Letters in parentheses are conventionally assigned group designations, indicating the people in that sex-and-attitude category.

To find the expected frequency for any cell, all one has to do is to multiply together the total number of cases in the row in which the cell is found and the total number of cases in the column in which that cell is found, and divide this product by the total number of cases. Each cell is lettered beginning with *a* in the upper left-hand corner and working from left to right. The task of finding the expected frequencies for the four cells in this matrix is completed in Table 13.5.

The question now is, Are the values that have been found by interviewing the staff any different from the values that might have occurred by chance?

The next step is to calculate the statistic Chi-square. This calculation is shown in Table 13-6.

Next, it is necessary to look up the critical value of Chi-square in the appropriate table in Appendix B. Again, this table requires that the degrees of freedom be known. For the Chi-square statistic, the degrees of freedom are obtained by multiplying the number of rows minus 1 times the number of columns minus 1. In the case of the 2-by-2 matrix, this is

---

Table 13-5   Calculation of expected frequencies

Cell	Row Total		Column Total		Product Divided by N
a	30	×	28	=	840/54 = 15.6
b	30	×	26	=	780/54 = 14.4
c	24	×	28	=	672/54 = 12.4
d	24	×	26	=	624/54 = 11.6

Table 13-6   Calculation of chi-square

Cell	Fo	Fe	Fo-Fe	(Fo-Fe)²	(Fo-Fe)²/Fo
a	18	15.6	2.4	5.76	.3200
b	12	14.4	—2.4	5.76	.4800
c	10	12.4	—2.4	5.76	.5760
d	14	11.6	2.4	5.76	.4114
					1.7874 Chi-square

simple because $1 \times 1 = 1$. Using a conventional level of significance (.05), you can see that Chi-square would have to exceed 3.841 in order for it to be significant.

On the basis of these data, the executive does not have clear evidence that there is a significant polarization of the staff by sex on the issue. Given that no obvious sexist bias is apparent in the policy, it may be that the opinions of the staff are divided in ways other than the female staff responding to an inarticulated sense of discrimination. The dislike of the policy may have some other basis. In any case, the polarization is not extreme at this point. The executive may want to watch attitudes of the staff over time to see if changes occur, but at this point, no clear trend over chance is obvious.

Note that the two scales used in this example are both nominal scales. If one of the scales had been ordinal (for example, a scale using the scale points "new" workers versus "old" workers), Chi-square could still be used, but there are better and more precise ways of dealing with the problem. If, in fact, there were differences noticed between persons new on the staff and persons who had been on the staff for some time, the executive could have used entirely different scaling for both variables (years of experience versus a simple preference rating scale of 1 to 5 on the policy) and handled the question as a correlation problem.

As a general rule of thumb, a researcher always prefers a higher order of scale to a lower one. Nominal scales are very imprecise unless all one needs to do is to sort. There is no choice, of course, when dealing with such simple variables as male and female. When there is a choice, it is usually proper to scale as precisely as is possible.

The use of Chi-square is not limited to 2-by-2 tables. Certain nominal variables might require very large tables. Generally, however, for a very large matrix with very many empty cells, Chi-square will be difficult to interpret. Samples with fewer than thirty usually require a correction procedure, because with such a small sample, had only one or two persons fallen in a different cell, the results would be quite different. Consider the following two matrixes:

10	5	15
5	10	15
15	15	30

11	4	15
4	11	15
15	15	30

In the first example, Chi-square is .474 and is not significant at the .05 level of probability. In the second example, Chi-square is 8.3522. Actually, this kind of a difference could come about if only one case were different on the variable being measured. In other words, a very small shift in the matrix when the total sample is small can result in significance when there is really no reasonable difference.

The same kind of misleading result can happen in the case of very large samples. Notice that in the following two matrixes the proportions are the same. The only difference is that the sample is much larger in the second example.

20	15
15	20
	70

200	150
150	200
	700

In the first example, Chi-square is 1.4584, whereas in the second, it is 14.584. In other words, significance can sometimes be obtained simply as a function of a large sample. Although this principle applies to all tests of significance, it is especially crucial in using Chi-square.

As a general rule, the researcher is best advised to use Chi-square very conservatively. We prefer to use other measures of association based on Chi-square that are described in the previous chapter when nominal or ordinal scales are involved.

A Concluding Comment

The hypothesis-testing procedures discussed in this chapter are the most common of the elementary procedures. They are useful in the kinds of situations that have been described. Of course, most researchers calculate these tests on modern electronic computers. Our major purpose in presenting the examples here has been to show the internal logic of the processes and to provide some intuitive basis for interpretation.

When association between variables suggests that relationships may be statistically significant, and when the variables are measured by ratio or interval scales, the researcher is well advised to select these more powerful tools. Chi-square can be used sparingly with nominal scales or in situations with one nominal and one simple ordinal scale, but this is not a very powerful approach. Use a higher order of scaling if possible.

Key Terms

statistical inference	null hypothesis
probability	research hypothesis
the normal distribution	Type I error
bell-shaped curve	Type II error
standard score	one-tailed test
underlying distribution	two-tailed test
parameter	critical region
sampling distribution of the mean	Student's t
standard error	ANOVA
confidence interval	Chi-square
the z-test	

References

1. There is a branch of statistics, known as Bayesian statistics, that does not operate this way. Bayesian statistics are not, however, widely used in social work research.
2. See Chapter 15 in Hubert M. Blalock, Jr., *Social Statistics,* 2nd ed. (New York: McGraw-Hill, 1972), especially the discussion on pages 285–295.

Questions for Discussion

1. If one could measure the attributes of an entire population, it would not be necessary to bother with inferential statistics. Why is this so?
2. Why is it true that as the number of possible outcomes increases, the probabilities of any one outcome decrease?

3. What is the purpose of standardizing a score?

4. If one does a z-transformation of the difference between means, a *t*-test, or an analysis of variance, and gets a significant difference, what does it mean?

Exercises

1. A client is observed as having 20 days of symptom-free behavior following a new treatment. The agency has kept records on all its clients who have exhibited similar symptoms. The average number of days of symptom-free behavior for all such clients is 25 with a standard deviation of 5 days. How does this client compare with others with the same behavior?

2. A social work researcher wants to draw a sample for an exploratory study of a proposed new service for aging clients. The researcher carefully explains the nature of the study to several groups of older clients who come to the agency for meetings. The clients agree to allow the researcher to call on them as needed for the project. Accordingly, the researcher draws a random sample of clients over 60 to use in the study. The completed sample is composed of thirty people whose average age is 65. Since the agency keeps records of all clients, the researcher is able to determine that the average age of the clients in the population that might use the service is 70. The standard deviation is 5 years. The researcher wants to be sure that the sample is not too young. What can be done to assure the worker's confidence in the sample?

3. A social work researcher has devised a new training program for foster parents. One of the features of the program is a series of sessions with a specialist in childhood development. The purpose of this part of the training program is to increase the foster parents' knowledge of human behavior on the theory that this increased knowledge will help foster parents interpret and deal more constructively with foster children. It has been possible, through the cooperation of the foster parents, to set up an experiment using a control group. A random sample of foster parents has had bona fide training sessions with the expert. A second random sample has had a series of group meetings with the expert, but these sessions have been a carefully designed placebo. In short, the foster parents have been successfully kept in the dark as to which group is the experimental and which is the control. (If the training is successful, it is hoped that the control group will be given it after the measurements are taken.) A paper-and-pencil test measures knowledge gained in the training sessions. Group A, the experimental

group, is composed of twenty foster parents. They scored an average of 90 points on the test with a standard deviation of 5. The control group, which had eighteen foster parents, averaged 75 on the test with a standard deviation of 8. Using the .05 level of significance, calculate whether the experimental training made a statistically significant difference. Does it look as if this training should be given to all the agency's foster parents?

4. In yet another experiment, a children's agency has been using three ways of encouraging assertiveness in children. The agency has decided that if one of these ways is better than the others, then it should be emphasized. On the other hand, if all three work equally well, the staff might as well use the approach that each finds most comfortable. The agency has selected three random samples of children (after obtaining permission both from the children and their parents). Each sample has been given a different method of assertiveness training. Then a situational-testing process allows the children to exhibit assertive behavior, while observers collect data. Each score represents assertive behaviors identified for each child during the testing periods. Is the method of assertiveness training crucial?

Method A	Method B	Method C
11	7	8
9	6	9
6	5	10
7	8	12
10	9	7
5	8	11
4	4	6

For Further Reading

Hubert M. Blalock, Jr. *Social Statistics,* 2nd ed. New York: McGraw-Hill Book Company, 1972. See Chapters 7, 8, 9, 11, and 16 for a fully detailed exposition of the procedures summarized in this chapter.

Marty Schmidt. *Understanding and Using Statistics,* 2nd ed. Lexington, Massachusetts: D. C. Heath and Company, 1979. This is an extremely thorough yet clear statistics text. See especially Chapters 5, 8, 10, 11, and 14 on hypothesis testing.

Johan Galtung. *Theory and Methods of Social Research.* New York: Columbia University Press, 1967. See Chapter 4 for a discussion of the relationship between association and inference.

G. W. Snedecor and W. G. Cochran. *Statistical Methods.* Ames, Iowa: The Iowa State University Press, 1967.

PART IV

In Part IV, Chapter 14 discusses the research process, from selecting a question to preparing the research report. It is intended to provide an overview of the entire content of the book. Chapter 15, the final chapter, examines some issues in social work research that we consider to be very important. It includes research ethics, the influence of funding and sponsorship on social workers who do research, and a plea for social workers to reach for higher goals in the research enterprise.

14

Doing Social Work Research

This chapter treats as a whole the process of doing research in social work. Our aim in this chapter may be understood as a final assembly line that puts together the components that we have constructed earlier. In that sense, this chapter represents a summing up of the previous chapters, with one additional element—getting started.

Getting Started in Research

In many books on research methods, this topic appears very early. Some writers postpone the discussion until they have first discussed the general topic of scientific method; but even among those who postpone the topic, it is likely to appear a good bit earlier than it does in this book. There are two reasons why we have reserved this topic until now:

1. You are in a good position to choose a research subject only after you have learned something about research. In other words, you are in a much better position to think about doing research than you were when you read Chapter 1.
2. This topic has been delayed because getting started is the most difficult part of doing research. Once the problem has been selected and refined, the rest of the process flows fairly logically. However, if you start off on the wrong problem—or start off on the correct problem wrongly—the entire research is done awkwardly at best.

Sources of Research

Selecting a question is the most creative act of the researcher. *Answering* the question is more a matter of skill than creativity, because research is a deliberate activity whose techniques and conventions are known. Knowing the techniques and procedures, however, does not make one a researcher. It is the spirit of creative inquiry that is the key factor in actually doing research, because it is the spirit of inquiry that causes the researcher to ask questions.

For social workers, there are three general sources of research topics:

1. *The work situation.* There are always a number of elements in the workplace that may start the creative process in motion. Does the program work? How well? Can the agency's goals be reached in more efficient or effective ways? *How* does the program work? Who actually benefits? Are there unanticipated outcomes of the program? Are there better therapeutic techniques? What kind of clients use the service? What is known about their problems? Are their needs being met? This list could be extended for many more lines, but you should get the idea. Many concerns about the actual job can be explored in research. One can start with exploratory research on client needs and problems. This could be followed by a descriptive study of a certain type of client who presents difficult service problems. Later, experimental or quasi-experimental studies might test new program or therapeutic ideas designed to help this particular type of client. One of the authors of this book once participated in a study of single mothers served by an agency. The study found that the agency had the wrong perception of the clients that were being served. The needs of the actual clients were different than had been assumed during planning. The agency had assumed a younger, more dependent client, seeking long-term services. In actuality, an older, more independent woman was seeking very concrete short-term service. Although this study was never published and would have been of limited interest to anyone else, it was useful in making adjustments in the agency's service policy. Many such valuable uses of research abound in daily social work practice, if one will but look for them.

2. *The professional literature.* Members of any technology, trade, or profession should take the time to read the professional literature. Aside from the benefit of keeping up on new things, the literature is a fertile source of questions that can be used in research. Sometimes one will read a paper with which he or she disagrees. This is an opportunity to do a piece of research if for no other reason than to "straighten out those misguided fools" who wrote the first paper. Sometimes, one will read of a successful program or technique that should be tested in a different location or with a different kind of client. It is important in any field to replicate successful studies—to repeat them to see if they hold up in a different situation or at a later time. The literature is full of studies that suggest future directions for research. Sometimes journals call for papers.

In a recent issue of *Social Work,* the editorial board issued a call for articles on practice and articles on minority concerns.[1] Among other topics, the board wanted articles on the description and analysis of practice, evaluations of practice approaches, and demographic information about minorities. These topics obviously lend themselves to research. In *Social Casework,* Dorothy Fahs Beck, director of research of the Family Service Association of America, discussed the ways in which universities and family agencies could cooperate in teaching research.[2] Her article listed a number of topics that are appropriate not only for students but also for practitioners who want to become involved in research. Included are client follow-up studies, time and cost studies, exploratory interviews of clients about the services they have received, and single-case designs of client progress. Both of these articles suggest more than we can list here and should be read by the student who wants a research topic. Periodically, journals will issue these calls for papers. In effect, such calls help focus the beginning researcher on what is timely and important. People who read the professional literature regularly will encounter these invitations and would do well to follow up on them. If you routinely read the journals, you should not lack for topic suggestions.

3. *Personal concerns.* A number of people become interested in research because they have a personal interest in a particular subject area. This personal interest may be a highly individual and idiosyncratic one, or it may be related to membership in a group. For example, one person may research the nature of left-handedness simply because he finds something fascinating about the phenomenon itself, whereas another might research left-handedness because she herself is left-handed and believes that more should be known generally about the left-handed. There is a certain danger in doing research in areas in which one has a personal interest, regardless of one's motive. The danger is simply that one may find his or her judgment clouded by personal concerns. This need not be the case, but it is something that the researcher must keep in mind.

This discussion raises the question of whether research with women, the aged, the disadvantaged, minorities, or other groups that have suffered discrimination must or ought to be done by persons who are members of the group. In a thoughtful paper, Neilson Smith addressed the specific question of who should do minority research.[3] His answer is applicable beyond minority research. Smith argues that research on minority groups need not be restricted to minority group members if the researcher (1) follows the objective rules of the scientific method and (2) is willing to listen to members of the group under study. It is desirable to use consultants from any population under study. Consultants ought to keep the researcher attuned to the concerns and rights of the population. Researchers should always, as a matter of ethics, respect the privacy, dignity, and worth of any subject. If the researcher cannot respect the rights of the subject, the research shall surely be flawed.

Selecting the Right Question

An inquiring look at what is happening in one's own agency, frequent reading of the literature, and a careful examination of one's interests should generate some ideas about what to research. This is, however, only part of the process of getting started. The next task is actually to settle on the exact question to be asked. The biggest danger in research, particularly for the new researcher, is the tendency to take on too much at a time. It is for this reason that the selection of the right question is so crucial. The trick is to be able to translate what may be a rather broad concern into a very concrete and specific question. Generally speaking, the more specific the question, the better the study.

Several other factors must be kept in mind almost simultaneously. These concerns are so interwoven with the task of selecting the question that, although they may look like another stage of the development of research, they are in fact an intimate part of question formulation. These factors include some very practical issues:

1. Does the proposed question have an empirical answer? That is, can a way be found to measure the concepts involved? Is the information required available?
2. Is the research feasible? That is, does the researcher have enough time and money to answer the research question? Can sufficient research subjects be conveniently found? Is a lot of extra help necessary and available?
3. Is the question important? Does anybody beyond the researcher care about the answer? Will an answer, even a negative one, be useful?
4. Is the research ethical? Is there risk? Is the risk tolerable? Will the research damage anyone's privacy, health, well-being, or dignity? Can permissions be obtained from subjects or institutions involved?

If the answers to these kinds of questions suggest that the research is beyond the capabilities of those considering the research, the proposed question should be rejected or at least modified until it is clearly manageable. Research always takes more money, time, cooperation, and work than anybody thinks it will, so errors should be made on the side of caution.

In addition to the practical factors listed above, other things can intrue into the question-selection process. Some topics are more popular than others at any given time. Outside funding may be available for some topics but not others. Some topics are more prestigious than others. One might like to think that social work researchers are above considerations like these. However, no researcher is likely to want to spend a lot of time on an untimely topic for which there is no funding and little recognition. There is no sense in expecting social work researchers to be different from other people on these issues. If the beginning researcher feels swayed by these kinds of considerations, it is certainly understandable.

Assuming a topic that is answerable, feasible, reasonably important, and ethically sound, the researcher must make some adjustments for manageability. Earlier in this discussion, we said that researchers sometimes ask too large a question. We can now say more about this issue in the light of the preceding discussion. Suppose a social worker reads an exploratory study that suggests a new conceptual framework for explaining human development. This tentative explanation, it shall be stipulated, is the result of another social worker's observations of a group of children in an institution (a captive group). The social worker, becoming intrigued with these new ideas, decides to move from the exploratory level to the descriptive study. It is not necessary for the social worker to ask whether the explanation of human development is correct in all details. It would be necessary only to ask a specific question that was crucial. Suppose that an original theoretical statement hypothesized that for the adult's psychological development it was crucial to be offered lots of citrus fruit at age two in order to provide a sound preparation for eating apples at age three and melons at age four. It would not be necessary for the researcher to wait and see how the child had developed by adulthood. It would be necessary to see only whether or not the child was able to eat apples at age three. In other words, if a crucial connection is not made between one developmental task and another, then the whole explanation is questionable and unsupported. Thus, a relatively simple research question can test, in part, a highly complex whole. Of course, this is not all there is to it. A really attractive new developmental scheme would have researchers swarming all over it, testing various propositions. It is in the accumulation of all these related bits and pieces that dependable knowledge would grow, and if there were reasonable consensus in the research, future social workers would develop increasing confidence in the explanation. Even if there were a great deal of support, however, the conceptual framework would always remain open to scientific scrutiny. It would never become sacred and unchallengeable. Science does not sanctify knowledge.

It is up to the researcher to choose the level of research at which he or she wants to work. It may be helpful for you to refer to the earlier chapters on the kinds of research questions appropriate for exploratory, descriptive, experimental, and evaluative research. Generally, we can say that the level of research that can be chosen depends somewhat on the state of the knowledge available at the present time. Some questions have already undergone a great deal of exploratory work that has paved the way for descriptive studies. Other subjects are new and may need a lot of basic work.

As a rule of thumb, the more information available, the more specific the kinds of questions that can be asked and the more precise the research can be.

After selecting a workable question and determining the level of research, it is time to return to the library.

Using the Library

The researcher may have spent some time in the library as a part of the question-selection process. On the other hand, if one has selected a question out of personal interest or from practice, he or she may have spent very little time in the library. The amount of time needed in the library will, of course, depend on how much time has already been spent there and how much material has been found.

It is important to mention that research cannot be done without knowing what has already been done. No researcher can avoid doing some kind of a search for useful literature. Science is cumulative. Somebody somewhere has done something that relates to any topic that any researcher is likely to select. It is, for all practical purposes, impossible to find a wholly new topic. It is important for the researcher to locate accounts of previous work in order to have a body of knowledge to which the new work can be related. It is also useful simply to see what other people have done. Often it is possible to find an instrument already designed that can be used "as is" or can be adapted. Sometimes one will read of attempts that did not work. It may help to know about approaches that did not work in order to avoid some problem in the present research. Perhaps another researcher will have tested a unique sampling technique or an unfamiliar statistical routine that can be helpful. All of these reasons justify the literature search.

How Does One Find Appropriate Literature?

We said earlier that someone somewhere has at some time done something on virtually every topic. The question that each new researcher formulates usually represents a variation on an existing theme. Usually, no one has asked the question in quite the same way, or of quite the same subjects, or at quite the same point in time. Occasionally, a beginning researcher will find that someone has asked exactly the same question in the same way of the very subjects that one has in mind. When this happens, the researcher may decide that the time has come to replicate the study. Alternatively, the researcher may decide to change the question in some important way and proceed. Beginners sometimes complain that they cannot find literature that bears on their question at all. Frankly, this usually means that they have not done a very good job of searching. Sometimes one has to range pretty far afield to find related literature, but it is always there.

A good place to begin is with the publication *Social Work Research and Abstracts* and its predecessor publication *Social Work Abstracts.* Over two hundred journals are abstracted on a quarterly basis. Abstracts are classified by subject. Other useful tools are *Sociological Abstracts, Psychological Abstracts,* and the *Education Index.* These can be found in the reference room of any college or university library. *Dissertation Abstracts* and the ERIC (Educational Resource Information Center) files also contain a great deal of material that often does not find its way into the periodical literature. You can usually depend on the reference librarian to assist in the location and use of these resources.

The beginning researcher may want to try using the card catalogue. Two shortcomings, however, make this procedure a limited one:

1. The card catalog is organized into such general categories that it is usually not very useful to the researcher who is usually trying to keep the subject limited in its scope.
2. The card catalog contains only the material in that particular library. On the other hand, the indexes and abstract volumes listed above are inclusive. Using them, the researcher should be able to locate articles and even fugitive materials from all important sources.

As one begins to find articles that bear upon the chosen subject, one can follow up the footnotes or references in the articles in order to find additional material. Along this same line, the beginning researcher may find an introductory social work, psychology, sociology, or social psychology textbook extremely useful. Because introductory texts, by their nature, cover the field, they will contain references to the classic studies on the most important issues. The researcher can then find and read them.

How Much Literature Is Enough?

This is a very difficult question to answer for all purposes. As a rule of thumb, the better one knows the subject area, the less literature one needs to cite. That is, an experienced person usually knows something about the subject area and knows the important writers. An inexperienced person who does not know the literature in a given area will probably need to accumulate enough notes to become reasonably conversant with the researchers who frequently publish in the area. Then, he or she will have some feel of what must be included and what can be left out.

The beginning researcher will find it extremely useful to use note cards. Virtually every college freshman is taught to use note cards, but something seems to happen to this practice somewhere in the sophomore year. Some students write papers by checking out the books currently available in the library, spreading them out on the floor, and then producing a document by going from left to right and taking juicy bits from each book. Thus, the ordinary research paper resembles an old-fashioned patchwork quilt. This is not the best strategy. There is really no effective way to avoid the hard work of taking a great many notes and then sorting them out for their value. Most researchers collect more literature than they actually can use productively. The work will go very much better, however, if you have too much material and must sort through it and eliminate some than if you have too little and must stretch it to fit.

Selecting a Research Design

Once researchers have digested the accumulated wisdom (and the data) from reading previous research, they find that they can usually make a final appraisal of the research question. These final adjustments on the research question involve reconciling the research question with the level of research (exploratory, descriptive, explanatory, or evaluative) and the design appropriate to the question. Several processes go on all at one time. What the researcher has to do is to select an appropriate design given the nature of the question and the chosen level of research. Obviously, exploratory research uses an unsophisticated approach—usually a one-shot case study or a simple before/after design. You will recall that the rules of the game are rather wide open for exploratory research. If a great deal of exploratory work has already been done by others, the researcher may want to move to a larger descriptive study in a field setting or to a study of association. These studies, too, may actually be one-shot designs.

When doing a descriptive study, researchers will try to present as clear a picture as possible of the phenomenon under study. They will focus on a more limited question (perhaps a hypothesis, as described in Chapter 3), select a probability sample, and use relatively sophisticated instrumentation.

If the phenomenon under study is ready for explanatory research, or if the researcher wants to evaluate a technique or program, he or she will select one of the explanatory designs (Chapter 4). If a standard explanatory design is not possible, a quasi-experimental design (see the reference to Campbell and Stanley at the end of Chapter 4) may be useful. Of course, the researcher will state the explanatory hypothesis clearly and define the terms carefully, both formally and operationally. Again, even the beginner will take care in the selection of the sample and will follow a formal data-collection plan.

Selecting the Proper Scale

Once the researcher has settled the question of the level of research and has selected a design, he or she will need to make a final decision on the instruments to be used in measurement. There are exceptions to this, of course, if one is doing exploratory study using unstructured observations or interviews, or a pure literature study aimed at clarifying concepts. In these studies, there will usually be no highly technical instrument because of the tentative and introductory nature of the research. However, if measurement is required, the researcher must pay considerable attention to how it is to be done. Obviously, some things are easier to measure than are others. In some cases, as we pointed out in Chapter 2, the best that can be done is to say whether a characteristic is present or absent. In other cases, fairly complex measurements can be made. Some variables can be measured only by a simple nominal scale. Others can be ranked or rated on ordinal scales. Still more complex variables require an interval or a ratio scale. The important thing is to match the scale to the level of data available. One should always use the highest order of scale available. If the data can be measured by a ratio scale, then a ratio scale should be used. There are studies (which we shall not single out here) in which the researcher has opted for a crude scale when a higher-order scale was preferable. This is not good practice.

Selecting the Data-Collection Procedure

Again, we present this task as a step (for learning purposes) when in actuality deciding on the data-collection procedure is bound up with the selection of scales and research design. The researcher will need to decide how to use the scale in the selected design. As we have outlined in previous chapters, a rational approach can be followed here. If actual behavior is to be studied, the researcher should probably select an observational approach. If one wants to study thoughts, beliefs, attitudes, or perceptions, the questionnaire or interview may be selected. Content analysis is appropriate for the study of verbal communication. A projective test might be used if the researcher thinks that the subject will have trouble putting feelings into words. If the research involves an attribute that can be captured using a trace measure, the researcher should think about using one. If professional performance is being studied, a situational test may be best. Or the researcher may want to try a series of single-case studies as a means of testing a therapeutic technique. The major point to be made here is that the data-collection approach should be the one that best lends itself to the kind of data that are to be collected.

Reporting the Research

Research reports are not the most scintillating literature in the world. There is very little room in them for wit or heady prose. They tend to follow a set pattern. The good thing about them is that the researcher never has to worry much about the outline of the report. Regardless of the field in which they are done, the major components are very much the same.

The Introduction

In the introduction to the report, the researcher should clearly state the problem that is to be investigated. There is no need to "go 'round Robin Hood's barn" in order to do this. It is best simply to begin, "This paper addresses the problem of . . . ." Nothing is more annoying than to have to read through a page or two to find the research question. The writer should also give a brief explanation of the importance of the question and state to whom the answer is important. Very little else is necessary in the introduction.

The Literature Review

In the next section, the researcher should summarize the important literature that bears upon the research problem. Assuming that the researcher has accumulated a number of studies and acquired some sophistication about the research area, it should not be hard to select the most relevant studies. As a rule of thumb, the researcher should ordinarily aim at presenting no less than eight nor more than twelve studies in this section of the report. This rule is at best a rough gauge, because there may be occasions when presenting more or fewer studies will be appropriate. One exception to this rule is the exploratory study that is composed entirely of reviewed literature as described in Chapter 3. Obviously, this kind of study report will have a unique format: It will consist of an introduction that sets out the plan, the review itself, and a conclusion.

Beginners sometimes have trouble figuring out how much to say about an article or book. Ordinarily, a piece of literature can be reviewed in two sentences. It is usually enough to say, "Smith studied the self-concept of high school students. She discovered that left-handed students had a consistently different self-concept than right-handed students." This brief format will not always work. Some studies are simply too important or too involved to summarize this briefly. When the researcher wants to say more than the above format permits, he or she should expand the review to include a summary of the research question, a concise description of the subjects, the techniques used, and the findings. Something like the following fictitious example may result:

> Smith studied the self concept of left-handed high school students as a part of a larger study of the relationship of left-handedness and character development. Using random sampling techniques, Smith obtained a stratified random sample of high school juniors in a large, urban school district. The Smith-Jones self-concept scale was administered to all students in the sample. Then, all were given a manual dexterity test. The students were asked to sort cards of various colors into piles. The left-handed students were ridiculed as they sorted their cards. Then all students were again given the Smith-Jones test. The left-handed students were then compared with the right-handed students using the Smith-Jones covariance rotation. Smith found no significant difference between left-handed and right-handed students in their self-concept despite the attempt to lower their self-confidence.

This rather long review of a piece of literature would be done in those instances when the researcher intended the following:

1. to make major use of Smith's findings;
2. to use Smith's manual-dexterity task in a different situation;
3. to use the Smith-Jones self-concept scale;
4. to apply the "Smith-Jones covariance rotation," an unusual (and, incidentally, fictitious) statistical procedure; or
5. to compare the results in a present experiment with those found by Smith.

In other words, a brief review of two or three sentences will do for most purposes, but a longer format is appropriate when a study, or something in it, is to be a major factor in the present research. Thus, the length of the individual review tends to vary with the importance of the research being reviewed. Generally, the articles or books used are reviewed in order of their publication. Another way of doing the review may be dictated by the nature of the present study; for example, one might review articles in ascending order of their importance to the present work.

Describing the Procedures

The third major section of the research report should carefully and fully set forth what the researcher did in carrying out the project. If there is a hypothesis (either descriptive or experimental), it should be stated and the terms defined. The research design should be described. The method of sampling should be clearly stated and described so that a reader can tell how the sample was selected. The researcher should also describe the sample in enough detail to enable the reader to know precisely who the subjects were. At a minimum, the researcher should include a description of the sample by age (mean, median, and standard deviation), sex (percentage of males and females), education (average years), and income (mean, median, and standard deviation), *unless these variables are unnecessary or inappropriate.* A consumer of the research ought to be able to visualize the subjects well enough to be able to accept that the sample is roughly representative of the population under study. It would be unconvincing, for example, if a sample that purported to be representative of the general public contained only men between the ages of 20 and 35 with college degrees and an average income of $30,000. Obviously, a study of infants would not be expected to report age, income, and education. A study of young women between 20 and 35 would not be expected to have men in the sample. A study of high school dropouts would not be expected to involve college graduates. Use some "horse sense" in selecting and describing the sample.

Some researchers (including some experienced ones) gather more descriptive data than is necessary. Some published studies reveal that data have been collected that the researcher had no real use for. This is an unwarranted invasion of privacy. Researchers should solicit only information for which they have a definite use.

Next, the researcher should describe exactly what was done to collect data and what scales were used. If a standardized test was used, this should be reported. Generally, it will be necessary to tell the reader a little about what the test is designed to show and how it works. It will help to provide a reference for all but the most common commercially developed tests. Should the reader want more information about the test, he or she can look up the reference.

Beginning researchers are well advised to consider using a standardized test whenever possible. This is because someone else has already worked out the "bugs" and determined the validity or reliability of the instrument. Most of the researcher-designed instruments used in theses and dissertations have serious validity and reliability problems. The beginning researcher should consult O. K. Buros's *Mental Measurement Yearbooks* (see the reference librarian again) to see if a dependable test is available. These volumes—misnamed because they are published periodically, not annually—contain a great deal of data on virtually every measurement of any consequence. Critical reviews of tests are included and periodically updated.

If the researcher cannot find a usable test, he or she will have to devise one and try to argue the case for its validity and reliability using the approaches outlined in Chapter 2. This is not easy, and it is very time-consuming. Projective tests, of course, constitute a special problem, and reliability and validity are very hard to establish. Unobtrusive trace measures and situational tests also have uncertain qualities. Questionnaires and interviews are somewhat less difficult, because there are standard procedures to follow. Observational methods are comparatively the easiest, because behavior is usually their focus and behavior either occurs or it does not.

Whatever the measurement procedure is, the researcher must explain what was done, and under what circumstances it was done, in sufficient detail so that a reader could replicate the study without guesswork.

Presenting the Results

After clearly describing the procedures, the researcher should present the results in as clear and uncomplicated a way as possible. Research reports should not obscure the subject but should clarify it. Unfortunately, researchers often get too far "inside." That is, they tend to write for other researchers. This is especially inappropriate in social work research. Clinicians and planners will use the products of research only if they can understand them. The fact that most social workers are not primarily researchers places a special burden on those who are.

In the "Results" section of the paper, the findings should be presented naked and unadorned. That is, the results should be presented without editorial comment of any kind. Comments on the meaning of the findings should be held for the final section of the report.

Exploratory studies that use quantitative data follow the same reporting conventions of more formal descriptive studies, even though the research is less stringently carried out. In both of these studies, the data will be processed by converting the raw data into descriptive statistics. The data will usually be displayed in tables and graphs. Central tendencies will be reported by the mean and the median. Both mean and median are used because each shows different things: The mean shows the arithmetical average, whereas the median is the point that divides a set of scores in half. The mean and the median are identical when the distribution is symmetrical and normally distributed. The greater the distance between the mean and the median, the less symmetrical the distribution as a rule, although there will be exceptions in the case of multimodal distributions.

In addition to showing the shape of the distribution and the central tendencies in the data, researchers doing exploratory and descriptive studies involving quantities will also show the spread of the scores. The range is useful in showing the distance from top to bottom. The standard deviation shows the spread of scores around the mean.

Relationships in two or more scales are shown by statistical approaches linked to the kind of scale in use. Relationships between two nominal scales are shown using Chi-square or those measures related to or based on Chi-square. Relationships between ordinal scales are shown using Spearman's rank-order correlation coefficient. Relationships between interval and ratio scales are shown by the application of Pearson's product-moment correlation coefficient. For more than two scales, there is a family of procedures called multivariate analyses, which are beyond the scope of this book. It is enough to say here that techniques are available for more complex comparisons. These techniques can be learned in more advanced courses.

Explanatory studies tend to use the more complex statistical routines. Researchers looking for significant differences between variables will use inferential statistical tests, such as "Student's" t, the z-transformation, or ANOVA. The more complex the data, the higher the order of scale that can be used. The higher the order of the scale, the more sophisticated the statistical test.

Regardless of the complexity of the data-processing routine, the results should be presented without explanatory comment, so that the consumer can form an independent conclusion about the meaning of the data. Only after the results have been shown may the researcher state his or her own conclusion.

Forming a Conclusion

When the results have been presented, the researcher should offer an explanation of their meaning. If the study has been an exploratory study, what do the data suggest as a next step? If the study is a descriptive study, what do the data show about a given phenomenon or state of affairs? If the research is explanatory in character, what has been explained and how well?

Conclusions must be based on the results. They do not come in out of "left field." In our roles as teachers, we have had more experience than we ever wanted with students whose conclusions were simply a statement of bias and opinion and not based on the data. The competent researcher draws a conclusion that is consistent with the results and does not argue beyond the data.

There are other important elements in this final section of the report. The study being reported must be related to the important literature on the topic. This means that the result of the study must be compared with the results of other studies, preferably those that have been discussed in the literature review. The researcher must also critique his or her own work by pointing out the limitations and problems in the study. Research reporting is the only literary form in which one is expected to pick apart the weaknesses of his or her own work. Finally, the researcher should suggest the directions that future research on the topic might take.

A Note on Writing Style

It sometimes appears that research writers strive for a ponderous, unwieldy paper that no one can understand. The idea seems to be that the fewer there are who understand the paper, the better it must be. This is wrong. The cleaner and more simple the report, the more likely it is to be read and followed. The beginning researcher will do well to write short, clean sentences. Avoid long clauses that lose the reader. Two short, clear sentences are preferable to one long, foggy one. Above all, the researcher should not use words that he or she does not completely understand. Unfortunately, a person who writes simply and clearly runs the risk of being called a popularizer. Further, it often looks as if the major rewards go to those who write as did the sociologist Talcott Parsons, who wrote in a ponderous style, in which a sentence frequently was a half-page or longer. Professor Parsons and his cohorts have set regrettable precedents that should not be allowed to affect the research report. The beginning researcher should take to heart the notion that it is better to be understood than to be "deeply profound."

References

1. Anne Minahan, "Reaching and Writing to Improve Practice," *Social Work* 25, no. 1 (January 1980).
2. Dorothy Fahs Beck, "Pattern for University-Agency Cooperation in the Teaching of Research," *Social Casework* 60, no. 6 (June 1979).
3. Neilson Smith, "Who Should Do Minority Research?" *Social Casework* 54, no. 9 (November 1973).

Questions for Discussion

1. Why is it easier to answer a research question than to ask one?
2. What are the main sources of research questions?
3. What do you think is the biggest danger for the beginning researcher? Why?
4. What are the major factors in choosing a research question?
5. Is there a way to avoid a literature search?
6. Why will a researcher who is familiar with a topic need less library work than a beginning researcher?
7. Why would a research report need a review longer than one or two sentences?
8. Why should researchers try to use standardized tests?
9. What kind of information is needed in a research report to describe the sample?
10. Why should the results of a study be presented without comment in the results section of the paper?
11. Should research reports be addressed only to other researchers?

Exercises

1. Suggest sources for research questions other than those mentioned in the chapter.

2. Write a brief proposal for an exploratory study. Select a question, review five pieces of literature, and outline the procedures to be followed. Include the sample-selection process and the data-collection method.

3. Write a brief proposal for a descriptive study. As above, select a question and do a very brief literature review of five pieces. Select a research design, a sample, and a data-gathering approach appropriate for the problem.

4. Submit a brief proposal for an explanatory or an evaluative study. As in exercises 2 and 3, select a question, a design, a sample, a procedure, and an instrument.

For Further Reading

Thelma F. Batten. *Reasoning and Research*. Boston: Little, Brown and Company, 1971. This step-by-step walk through the research process was written for sociologists but is quite useful for the beginning social work researcher.

Delbert C. Miller. *Handbook of Research Design and Social Measurement*, 2nd ed. New York: David McKay Company, 1970. This is the complete guide for the social science researcher; it includes very practical information on methods of collecting data, scale construction, and the sequencing of the research task.

O. K. Buros, ed. *Mental Measurement Yearbooks*. Highland Park, New Jersey: Gryphon Press (issued irregularly).

15

An Unscientific Postscript

We have borrowed the title of this chapter from the philosopher Sören Kirkegaard. Kirkegaard's *Unscientific Postscript* was an important theological work of the nineteenth century, and a far more important book than this one. We have presumed to borrow the title for this chapter because it expresses our intent so well. We want to share our thinking with you about some issues in social work research. Our comments will expose some of our own beliefs, feelings, and hopes for the future of research in social work. These remarks, because they are based on convictions, will not be as rational or as orderly as the material in the preceding chapters—hence the use of the word *unscientific*. Because we obviously want to leave these highlighted issues fresh in your mind as you complete the course, the remarks stand as a kind of postscript to our overall message.

We want to talk informally to you about these issues. Accordingly, we have adopted a less formal style for this chapter, so that we can discuss things as if we were speaking directly to you. There are no "Questions for Discussion," no "Exercises," no "For Further Reading" list.

Please don't think that these topics are "fillers," or "add-ons" to add bulk to the book. Rather, we want you to understand that we chose to deal with them in this way in order to emphasize them. Our fantasy is that this kind of exposure may make some contribution toward the resolution of some of the issues.

The Need for a Research Orientation

First of all, we are concerned because social work is not as research-oriented as we would like it to be. In economics, education, political science, psychology, or sociology (as examples), research is expected to be a central professional activity. Even clinical and counseling psychologists (who are primarily trained to give services) devote a good bit of their preparatory time in learning to do research. Most social workers see themselves entirely as service personnel. Only a few show any excitement for research. In our opinion, it is doubtful if social work will achieve the high goals that it has set for itself unless it places an increased emphasis on research. Practitioners who are well prepared in research are better practitioners. They will be better able to evaluate the effects of their practice and will be in a better position to test and refine innovations in both direct practice and policy. The question of whether social workers are professionals has been debated throughout most of this century. Of course, most social workers *argue* that social work is a profession. It is our conviction that if we were properly equipped to generate and evaluate knowledge, we would *be* more professional, and we would not have to debate the issue. The ability to generate and fully evaluate one's own knowledge base is, for us at least, the essence of professionalism. If we could reach the point of research-based practice and policy, other disciplines would find it easier to recognize us as professionals. As it stands, we use techniques that are developed and tested by others—primarily psychiatrists, psychologists, and management scientists. In effect, this leaves us in the position of being technicians. There is nothing wrong with being a technician. A technician, however, is not the same thing as a professional, because the technician usually applies knowledge developed by others who do the basic research in a field. We realize, of course, that many of our colleagues will not like this argument for more research training. We, however, find it convincing. Therefore, we will continue to argue for more research emphasis in social work education, because we firmly believe that this is a primary way in which knowledge building can be enhanced and the role of the social worker strengthened.

The Need for More Experimentation

One of the products of a heightened research emphasis in social work would be the expansion of explanatory research. Most published social work research is either exploratory or descriptive. These kinds of research are necessary and important. However, exploratory and descriptive research is not enough. The development of a professional knowledge base requires that attempts be made to explain the phenomena that concern the practitioners of the discipline. Social workers have shied away from experimentation. Our guess about this is that the practitioner believes that the term *experimentation* carries the connotation of irresponsible trial-and-error operation. Further, it appears that social workers are reluctant to use control groups. A number of writers have commented on this problem over the years. The crux of the problem is that some practitioners have taken the position that if a new procedure or policy has any merit at all, it should be available to everybody and not just given to the experimental subjects. It is difficult for social workers to allow controls to go untreated, even when the treatment's value is uncertain. Even when experimentation does take place, practitioners have been known to introduce a further complication. They may intervene in the sampling process in order to select the best prospects for the experimental group. Of course, although this is awkward for the researcher, it is to be expected, given the service orientation of the social worker.

We want to make it very clear that we do not condone irresponsible experimentation. In the chapters dealing with data collection, we pointed out the ethical considerations that apply to each procedure. This is an appropriate point at which to repeat some of that discussion. We do not believe that any experimental research should be done with any subject unless that subject has given his or her informed consent. Researchers should not endanger the health, emotional state, rights, or privacy of subjects, unless the subjects clearly know and accept the risk. The same principle applies to exploratory and descriptive research that carries any significant risk for the client. In exploratory or descriptive research that involves minimal risk, we would concede that it is permissible to delay a full explanation of the nature of the research until the data-collection phase is completed. However, in such cases, the subject should be thoroughly debriefed, and the data should not be used without the subject's permission. We repeat: Deception may be all right in situations in which there is *minimal risk to the subject* and explanations are provided afterward. As we have pointed out throughout the discussions on data collection, most of the data that social workers collect will be drawn from populations who are at some social disadvantage. We have no business in systematically increasing pain and suffering just to see if we have developed an interesting technique.

At the same time, we think that it is possible to do more explanatory research. Very often, when we want to test a new technique or a new policy, there is very little that is actually dangerous to those who do not get the innovative treatment, so there should be no emotional barrier to experimentation. The controls do not have to go wholly untreated, either. They can be given the best treatment that was available before the innovation was proposed. We could also consider, as an alternative to the usual experiment, a *staged-treatment design*,[1] a diagram of which is shown in Figure 15-1.

In this design, Group A receives the experimental treatment for some period of time. Group B does not. When Group A has completed the course of treatment, Group B then receives it. In other words, the experi-

Figure 15-1   The staged-treatment design

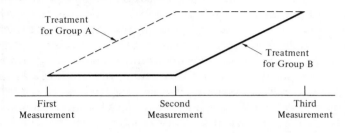

menter simply delays the innovative therapy or program for Group B and gives it at a later stage. Group A can be compared to Group B (we are assuming random selection of both groups) just prior to the introduction of the treatment to Group B. Of course, if the treatment did Group A no good, one would probably not proceed to try it on Group B. If the new procedure showed promise with Group A, then it could be offered to Group B. The main advantage of this design, obviously, is that it is intended to allow researchers to deal with the feelings of social workers who would be unable to withhold a treatment or program that rationally appeared to be beneficial. Because no one is denied the innovation, there is no question of depriving clients of services.

Doing Research with Populations at Risk

Certain human aggregates are at some minimal risk even in the most innocuous research. Many of these aggregates have suffered discrimination and unfair treatment—for example, women, members of minority religious and ethnic groups, the old, the emotionally disturbed, the medically ill, the poor, the developmentally disabled, the physically handicapped, and the very young. We have noted at appropriate points the need to be very careful in doing research involving people in these categories. We cannot overstress the need to protect their health, privacy, dignity, and life situation. True, we need more certain knowledge of their needs and difficulties. However, we should not obtain this information at the cost of grave penalties for the subjects. It is not necessary to be a member of a group or aggregate in order to do research involving the group or aggregate. It *is* necessary to be aware of the sensitivities of the population and to avoid exploitation of fellow human beings. No knowledge is worth the infliction of unnecessary pain.

Does the Research Serve the Client or the Agency?

The above discussion leads us to this important point: When social workers do research, are they serving the client, or are they serving the agency? This question needs to be "teased apart" a little bit. It appears to us that a lot of research may unintentionally have as its goal the justification of an agency policy or practice. We believe that this is an insufficient motive. In the best of all possible worlds, it can be argued, the best research is that from which the benefits for the clientele are equal to the benefits for the agency. This is not always the way it works in practice. Here is a purely hypothetical example: Agency A has a chance to receive a grant from Foundation B. Agency A certainly can find a use for the money involved in the grant. Foundation B is looking for innovative programs to fund. Agency A, therefore, undertakes to devise a research project into the effectiveness of Treatment C on the neuroses of left-handed orthopedic surgeons. Now, our question is, Whose interests are primarily being served? Does Agency A really have a concern with the neuroses of left-handed orthopedic surgeons, or does it primarily have its eye on the grant? What kind of counseling service will the surgeons get if the grant is secured? Although this example is a ludicrous one, the principle behind it is quite serious. It is our impression that in a number of cases, the principal beneficiary of research is the researcher or the employer. The client is exploited in order to rationalize the application for funding. Obviously, we do not support this kind of approach to research. We think that the client's needs should come first when there has to be a choice. We would prefer a situation in which the agency, sensing a need of the clientele, explores that need and then applies for funding in order to research a bona fide attempt to meet the need. Although it is easy for us to state a highly moral (to us) opinion, the critical state of funding for both programming and research in the human services is ultimately responsible for the scramble to get funds from any source available. We would hope that, even in extreme cases, some benefit accrues to the client, but we think frankly that many times the benefit is microscopic.

Data Gathering on the Job: Social Worker or Researcher?

We are led by the above discussion into yet another question. When social workers are gathering data on the job, what is their role? To get at this issue, let us consider another hypothetical situation. Suppose that an agency wants to evaluate its effectiveness in treating a specific kind of client. The social workers who are carrying out the treatment approach are asked to fill out an estimate of client functioning at intake. Thereafter, the estimates are made at four-week intervals. We think that this poses a dilemma for the social worker/researcher. Social workers believe in their clients' desire and ability to improve. It is therefore difficult for the worker carrying the case to evaluate improvement. In a sense, to do so is to evaluate one's own work. There is a place for self-evaluation. However, when one is conscious of the use being made of the data, the individual social worker is "over a barrel." One's objectivity is taxed to the limit. Most of us see improvement in our clients. At least, we hope for it, expect it, and even long for it. Can we admit it when there is little or no improvement? Probably some can. For others, hope may get in the way of a realistic appraisal. We are not suggesting that social workers are deliberately dishonest. We are saying that their belief in their clients and in their mission may inflate their evaluations. Therefore, we think that the only fair way to handle this problem is to have case movement and other such variables rated by an outside person. This removes the pressure of rating one's own clients.

There is yet another aspect to this problem. Suppose that two treatment approaches are being tested. In one approach, the client is seen every two weeks. In the other, the client is seen every week. Suppose that the client in the two-week treatment group has an emergency. Does the worker give the client extra time? Or does the worker hold to the experimental treatment schedule? An extra treatment will contaminate the research. Most, if not all, social workers would scrap the treatment schedule and offer an extra appointment. This is the more humane choice. It will, however, "play hob" with the scientific control of the treatment process. Probably the data gained from this subject should be discarded. It should be clear, however, that the combined role of researcher/practitioner is not without its dilemmas. Probably the best way out of the one in this example is to make a full disclosure to the client about the nature of the research and the importance of the schedule (or other experimental procedure). If the client has entered the experiment with full knowledge of the conditions, it may be easier to maintain the integrity of the experiment. Even then, some subjects may simply have to be given extra service and excluded from the experiment if continuation would be clearly harmful to their best interests. Again, our ethical stance requires us to argue that researchers scrupulously avoid any kind of unnecessary damage to client groups.

The Influence of Sponsors

There is yet another related issue. In some cases, the federal government or a private foundation sponsors social work research. Let us assume that the agency has legitimately found a need in its service area and has asked for and received a grant to study either the problem itself or an interventive policy or practice designed to deal with the problem. The issue now is whether or not the client's interest takes precedence over the sponsor's interest. This is an issue quite closely related to the previous two points. Obviously, the ethical social worker will argue that the client's interest should come first. Our intent in raising this issue is to support those social workers who would be on the client's side. We want to discuss this issue because we recognize that the worker will be under tremendous but subtle pressure to bow to the interests of sponsors, particularly if the sponsor is the federal government. It is easy to take the position that "he who pays the fiddler calls the tune." Indeed, if one accepts federal funds, he or she usually finds that the "feds" do have certain expectations. Our point is a simple one. If the clients do not need the service for which the grant is offered, it is better not to apply for it than to inflict a program on clients in order to get the money that would allow one to research the impact or effect of the program. Again, it is easy for us to say this, because no one is dangling a grant in front of us at this time.

The Need for Operational Definitions and Specific Outcome Criteria

Two related issues to doing more experimentation must be considered. First, social work researchers ought to pay more attention to operational definitions of concepts. Second, social work researchers ought to look for specific outcomes as the "payoff" of research. Let us explain these in more detail.

In Chapter 3, the operational definition was defined as the concrete operations that one had to perform in order to measure a concept. That is, a practitioner who wants to research anxiety must specify clearly the way in which anxiety is to be measured. It seems to us that, far too often, social work researchers fail to come to grips with really good operational definitions. As this is written, many social workers are concerned with the question of "burnout." There are many definitions of this term, but generally they include loss of interest in the job, ineffective performance, and even actual indifference to the plight of clients. Although we have a pretty good idea of what various writers mean *formally* by this topic, we have yet to see a really good *operational* definition. No one has yet been able to devise a scale or instrument that would help identify the "burned out." It is good to raise the issue and to try to come to a useful formal definition; however, little effective research on the problem can occur until burnout can be measured in some convincing way.

The same criticism can be made of outcome criteria. Social work research is frequently vague in its definitions of successful outcomes. This may be, in part, a result of the general vagueness of social work policy and practice outcomes. If you need some illustration of this point, we invite you to ask a dozen social workers what their goals are in treating, say, alcoholics. We will wager that you will get at least ten different answers. The same situation exists with respect to policy outcomes. Ask a local NASW chapter's social policy committee members what their aims are with respect to poverty. Again, we will wager that you will get an answer that will be hard to measure. Even if there is agreement, it will be something like "to end poverty, of course!" How will they know that they have ended it? What specifically will be true of the clientele who are no longer poor? Is additional income acceptable as the sole criterion? How much is enough?

Let us try to take some of the sting out of the above paragraph. We do not mean it as a hostile comment. We are very concerned that social work's goals may be far too nonspecific to permit a researcher to get a good hold on them. The same problem exists to an extent in any professional activity. One can get a good argument going over the question of the goals of medicine, law, or law enforcement. At the same time, *in a given case,* a physician can probably reach a pretty good conclusion about what he or she is trying to do. On the other hand, a social worker may be hard pressed to reach a firm conclusion about a given case. This lack of specificity is no problem on the broader goals of social work or any other profession; however, it is a real barrier to research on the level of specific cases. There is a school of thought within social work, for example, that takes the position that the goal of therapeutic activity in any particular case is to help the client develop insight into his or her behavior. From a research point of view, this presents a terrible problem. How can we know when another person has developed insight? How much insight is enough? Any answer to these questions is based pretty much on intuition. It is not subject to outside verification.

One of us was once talking to a social worker who worked with alcoholics. The worker took the position that his professional goal was to help the alcoholic develop insight into the reason for drinking. It was of no concern to the worker whether the drinking *behavior* was affected in any way. The worker could tell, he said, when the client had become insightful, but he could not tell anyone else how he knew this. It was simply something that one knew, based on a professional judgment. This kind of vagueness is not very helpful in doing research. It is this kind of nonspecific outcome that may have triggered the behaviorists into looking for something better. Consequently, they will consider an attribute as significant only when it is observable and countable.

We are not strict behaviorists, so we do not advocate the strict outcome limits that the behaviorists use. We do think that social work researchers can do better than they have often done. It is for this reason that we have stressed behaviors, scores on standardized tests, or the use of trained judges' evaluations as evidence of outcome in the examples in the research-design and data-collection chapters in this book. We hope that this not-so-subtle device will be imitated by users of this book when you do research! All we are arguing for, really, is for social work researchers to commit themselves to the use of as neat and clear a definition of their projected outcome as is possible, given the state of the art. If we are treating people for alcoholism, then our treatment should have some effect on drinking patterns. If we are treating people for marital discord, then our treatment should have some effect on the number of arguments that couples have. If we are testing a policy that is supposed to reduce the powerlessness of people in a neighborhood, then we should be able to locate numerical data on increased volume of municipal services or increased impact on decision making.

There are those who argue that many outcomes cannot be reduced to numbers because outcomes are too subtle. We flatly reject this contention. If a result is so subtle that it does not leave any mark on anything that can be recognized as a part of empirical reality, then it has a very precarious claim on existence. Unmeasurable outcomes are a bit too nebulous. We have a great deal of trouble taking the outcome of a social or psychological process on faith. We will continue to argue that it ought to be possible to demonstrate what we do by some empirical process. Although we have primarily been thinking about outcomes related to experiments, we can extend the need for good definitions of concepts in exploratory and descriptive research. We ought to be able to describe things in empirical ways. It is not sufficient to say simply that one has the clinical impression that anxiety or powerlessness are perceivable to those who know what to look for. This, too, sounds too much like magic that can be understood only by insiders.

The Need for More Theoretically Based Research

We have one last "hot" issue. We think that there ought to be more theory-based research. Most exploratory research is exempt from this criticism because of the nature of exploration. Evaluative research, too, is not really subject to this criticism, because this is usually a matter of practicality. However, much descriptive research, and certainly what experimentation is being done, should in our view dip more deeply into theory examination and theory testing. We will not point any accusing fingers, of course, but we can cite an example of the positive kind of thing that we like to see. Some years ago, Reid and Shyne studied the effect of short-term casework.[2] Since the publication of *Brief and Extended Casework* in 1969, a continuous line of research has amplified the theory of what has come to be called the task-centered approach to helping people. Each year, two or three articles are added to the research that supports the original formulation by William J. Reid. Clearly, this ongoing testing of theory has made task-centered practice important and useful. This is the way a knowledgeable profession grows and develops.

A Final Comment

These, then, are our "unscientific" opinions. It will obviously take more than this one argument to resolve these issues. Both of us enjoy doing research. We hope that at least some of you who have used this book will want to make research an important part of your professional career. We hope that you will enjoy doing research as much as we do.

References

1. Carol H. Weiss, *Evaluation Research* (Englewood Cliffs, New Jersey: Prentice-Hall, 1972), p. 65.
2. William J. Reid and Ann W. Shyne, *Brief and Extended Casework* (New York: Columbia University Press, 1969).

Appendix A

Protection of the Rights of Human Subjects in Research

(from the NASW Code of Ethics)

The social worker engaged in study and research should be guided by the conventions of scholarly inquiry:

1. The social worker engaged in research should consider carefully its possible consequences for human beings.
2. The social worker engaged in research should ascertain that the consent of participants in the research is voluntary and informed, without any implied deprivation or penalty for refusal to participate, and with due regard for participants' privacy and dignity.
3. The social worker engaged in research should protect participants from unwarranted physical or mental discomfort, distress, harm, danger, or deprivation.
4. The social worker who engages in the evaluation of services or cases should discuss them only for professional purposes and only with persons directly and professionally concerned with them.
5. Information obtained about participants in research should be treated as confidential.
6. The social worker should take credit only for work actually done in connection with scholarly and research endeavors and credit contributions made by others.

Source: Reprinted by permission of the National Association of Social Workers, as adopted by the 1979 NASW Delegate Assembly, effective July 1, 1980.

Appendix B Tables

Table B-1 Random numbers

10480	15011	01536	02011	81647	91646	69179	14194	62590	36207	20969	99570	91291	90700
22368	46573	25595	85393	30995	89198	27982	53402	93965	34095	52666	19174	39615	99505
24130	48360	22527	97265	76393	64809	15179	24830	49340	32081	30680	19655	63348	58629
42167	93093	06243	61680	07856	16376	39440	53537	71341	57004	00849	74917	97758	16379
37570	39975	81837	16656	06121	91782	60468	81305	49684	60672	14110	06927	01263	54613
77921	06907	11008	42751	27756	53498	18602	70659	90655	15053	21916	81825	44394	42880
99562	72905	56420	69994	98872	31016	71194	18738	44013	48840	63213	21069	10634	12952
96301	91977	05463	07972	18876	20922	94595	56869	69014	60045	18425	84903	42508	32307
89579	14342	63661	10281	17453	18103	57740	84378	25331	12566	58678	44947	05585	56941
85475	36857	43342	53988	53060	59533	38867	62300	08158	17983	16439	11458	18593	64952
28918	69578	88231	33276	70997	79936	56865	05859	90106	31595	01547	85590	91610	78188
63553	40961	48235	03427	49626	69445	18663	72695	52180	20847	12234	90511	33703	90322
09429	93969	52636	92737	88974	33488	36320	17617	30015	08272	84115	27156	30613	74952
10365	61129	87529	85689	48237	52267	67689	93394	01511	26358	85104	20285	29975	89868
07119	97336	71048	08178	77233	13916	47564	81056	97735	85977	29372	74461	28551	90707
51085	12765	51821	51259	77452	16308	60756	92144	49442	53900	70960	63990	75601	40719
02368	21382	52404	60268	89368	19885	55322	44819	01188	65255	64835	44919	05944	55157
01011	54092	33362	94904	31273	04146	18594	29852	71585	85030	51132	01915	92747	64951
52162	53916	46369	58586	23216	14513	83149	98736	23495	64350	94738	17752	35156	35749
07056	97628	33787	09998	42698	06691	76988	13602	51851	46104	88916	19509	25625	58104
48663	91245	85828	14346	09172	30168	90229	04734	59193	22178	30421	61666	99904	32812
54164	58492	22421	74103	47070	25306	76468	26384	58151	06646	21524	15227	96909	44592
32639	32363	05597	24200	13363	38005	94342	28728	35806	06912	17012	64161	18296	22851
29334	27001	87637	87308	58731	00256	45834	15398	46557	41135	10367	07684	36188	18510
02488	33062	28834	07351	19731	92420	60952	62180	50001	67658	32586	86679	50720	94953
81525	72295	04839	96423	24878	82651	66566	14778	76797	14780	13300	87074	79666	95725
29676	20591	68086	26432	46901	20849	89768	81536	86645	12659	92259	57102	80428	25280
00742	57392	39064	66432	84673	40027	32832	61362	98947	96067	64760	64584	96096	98253
05366	04213	25669	26422	44407	44048	37937	63904	45766	66134	75470	66520	34693	90449
91921	26418	64117	94305	26766	25940	39972	22209	71500	64568	91402	42416	07844	69618
00582	04711	87917	77341	42206	35126	74087	99547	81817	42607	43808	76655	62028	76630
00725	69884	62797	56170	86324	88072	76222	36086	84637	93161	76038	65855	77919	88006
69011	65797	95876	55293	18988	27354	26575	08625	40801	59920	29841	80150	12777	48501
25976	57948	29888	88604	67917	48708	18912	82271	65424	69774	33611	54262	85963	03547
09763	83473	73577	12908	30883	18317	28290	35797	05998	41688	34952	37888	38917	88050
91567	42595	27958	30134	04024	86385	29880	99730	55536	84855	29080	09250	79656	73211
17955	56349	90999	49127	20044	59931	06115	20542	18059	02008	73708	83517	36103	42791
46503	18584	18845	49618	02304	51038	20655	58727	28168	15475	56942	53389	20562	87338
92157	89634	94824	78171	84610	82834	09922	25417	44137	48413	25555	21246	35509	20468
14577	62765	35605	81263	39667	47358	56873	56307	61607	49518	89656	20103	77490	18062
98427	07523	33362	64270	01638	92477	66969	98420	04880	45585	46565	04102	46880	45709
34914	63976	88720	82765	34476	17032	87589	40836	32427	70002	70663	88863	77775	69348
70060	28277	39475	46473	23219	53416	94970	25832	69975	94884	19661	72828	00102	66794
53976	54914	06990	67245	68350	82948	11398	42878	80287	88267	47363	46634	06541	97809
76072	29515	40980	07391	58745	25774	22987	80059	39911	96189	41151	14222	60697	59583
90725	52210	83974	29992	65831	38857	50490	83765	55657	14361	31720	57375	56228	41546
64364	67412	33339	31926	14883	24413	59744	92351	97473	89286	35931	04110	23726	51900
08962	00358	31662	25388	61642	34072	81249	35648	56891	69352	48373	45578	78547	81788
95012	68379	93526	70765	10593	04542	76463	54328	02349	17247	28865	14777	62730	92277
15664	10493	20492	38391	91132	21999	59516	81652	27195	48223	46751	22923	32261	85653

Source: Reprinted by permission from W. H. Beyer (ed.), *Handbook of Tables for Probability and Statistics,* 2nd ed. (Boca Raton, Florida: CPR Press, 1968). Copyright The Chemical Rubber Co., CRC Press, Inc.

Table B-1 *(cont.)*

16408	81899	04153	53381	79401	21438	83035	92350	36693	31238	59649	91754	72772	02338
18629	81953	05520	91962	04739	13092	97662	24822	94730	06496	35090	04822	86772	98289
73115	35101	47498	87637	99016	71060	88824	71013	18735	20286	23153	72924	35165	43040
57491	16703	23167	49323	45021	33132	12544	41035	80780	45393	44812	12515	98931	91202
30405	83946	23792	14422	15059	45799	22716	19792	09983	74353	68668	30429	70735	25499
16631	35006	85900	98275	32388	52390	16815	69298	82732	38480	73817	32523	41961	44437
96773	20206	42559	78985	05300	22164	24369	54224	35083	19687	11052	91491	60383	19746
38935	64202	14349	82674	66523	44133	00697	35552	35970	19124	63318	29686	03387	59846
31624	76384	17403	53363	44167	64486	64758	75366	76554	31601	12614	33072	60332	92325
78919	19474	23632	27889	47914	02584	37680	20801	72152	39339	34806	08930	85001	87820
03931	33309	57047	74211	63445	17361	62825	39908	05607	91284	68833	25570	38818	46920
74426	33278	43972	10119	89917	15665	52872	73823	73144	88662	88970	74492	51805	99378
09066	00903	20795	95452	92648	45454	09552	88815	16553	51125	79375	97596	16296	66092
42238	12426	87025	14267	20979	04508	64535	31355	86064	29472	47689	05974	52468	16834
16153	08002	26504	41744	81959	65642	74240	56302	00033	67107	77510	70625	28725	34191
21457	40742	29820	96783	29400	21840	15035	34537	33310	06116	95240	15957	16572	06004
21581	57802	02050	89728	17937	37621	47075	42080	97403	48626	68995	43805	33386	21597
55612	78095	83197	33732	05810	24813	86902	60397	16489	03264	88525	42786	05269	92532
44657	66999	99324	51281	84463	60563	79312	93454	68876	25471	93911	25650	12682	73572
91340	84979	46949	81973	37949	61023	43997	15263	80644	43942	89203	71795	99533	50501
91227	21199	31935	27022	84067	05462	35216	14486	29891	68607	41867	14951	91696	85065
50001	38140	66321	19924	72163	09538	12151	06878	91903	18749	34405	56087	82790	70925
65390	05224	72958	28609	81406	39147	25549	48542	42627	45233	57202	94617	23772	07896
27504	96131	83944	41575	10573	08619	64482	73923	36152	05184	94142	25299	84387	34925
37169	94851	39117	89632	00959	16487	65536	49071	39782	17095	02330	74301	00275	48280
11508	70225	51111	38351	19444	66499	71945	05422	13442	78675	84081	66938	93654	59894
37449	30362	06694	54690	04052	53115	62757	95348	78662	11163	81651	50245	34971	52924
46515	70331	85922	38329	57015	15765	97161	17869	45349	61796	66345	81073	49106	79860
30986	81223	42416	58353	21532	30502	32305	86482	05174	07901	54339	58861	74818	46942
63798	64995	46583	09765	44160	78128	83991	42865	92520	83531	80377	35909	81250	54238
82486	84846	99254	67632	43218	50076	21361	64816	51202	88124	41870	52689	51275	83556
21885	32906	92431	09060	64297	51674	64126	62570	26123	05155	59194	52799	28225	85762
60336	98782	07408	53458	13564	59089	26445	29789	85205	41001	12535	12133	14645	23541
43937	46891	24010	25560	86355	33941	25786	54990	71899	15475	95434	98227	21824	19585
97656	63175	89303	16275	07100	92063	21942	18611	47348	20203	18534	03862	78095	50136
03299	01221	05418	38982	55758	92237	26759	86367	21216	98442	08303	56613	91511	75928
79626	06486	03574	17668	07785	76020	79924	25651	83325	88428	85076	72811	22717	50585
85636	68335	47539	03129	65651	11977	02510	26113	99447	68645	34327	15152	55230	93448
18039	14367	61337	06177	12143	46609	32989	74014	64708	00533	35398	58408	13261	47908
08362	15656	60627	36478	65648	16764	53412	09013	07832	41574	17639	82163	60859	75567
79556	29068	04142	16268	15387	12856	66227	38358	22478	73373	88732	09443	82558	05250
92608	82674	27072	32534	17075	27698	98204	63863	11951	34648	88022	56148	34925	57031
23982	25835	40055	67006	12293	02753	14827	22235	35071	99704	37543	11601	35503	85171
09915	96306	05908	97901	28395	14186	00821	80703	70426	75647	76310	88717	37890	40129
50937	33300	26695	62247	69927	76123	50842	43834	86654	70959	79725	93872	28117	19233
42488	78077	69882	61657	34136	79180	97526	43092	04098	73571	80799	76536	71255	64239
46764	86273	63003	93017	31204	36692	40202	35275	57306	55543	53203	18098	47625	88684
03237	45430	55417	63282	90816	17349	88298	90183	36600	78406	06216	95787	42579	90730
86591	81482	52667	61583	14972	90053	89534	76036	49199	43716	97548	04379	46370	28672
38534	01715	94964	87288	65680	43772	39560	12918	86537	62738	19636	51132	25739	56947

Table B-2 Areas under the unit normal distribution

z	Area Between Mean and z	Area Beyond z	z	Area Between Mean and z	Area Beyond z	z	Area Between Mean and z	Area Beyond z
0.00	.0000	.5000	0.45	.1736	.3264	0.90	.3159	.1841
0.01	.0040	.4960	0.46	.1772	.3228	0.91	.3186	.1814
0.02	.0080	.4920	0.47	.1808	.3192	0.92	.3212	.1788
0.03	.0120	.4880	0.48	.1844	.3156	0.93	.3238	.1762
0.04	.0160	.4840	0.49	.1879	.3121	0.94	.3264	.1736
0.05	.0199	.4801	0.50	.1915	.3085	0.95	.3289	.1711
0.06	.0239	.4761	0.51	.1950	.3050	0.96	.3315	.1685
0.07	.0279	.4721	0.52	.1985	.3015	0.97	.3340	.1660
0.08	.0319	.4681	0.53	.2019	.2981	0.98	.3365	.1635
0.09	.0359	.4641	0.54	.2054	.2946	0.99	.3389	.1611
0.10	.0398	.4602	0.55	.2088	.2912	1.00	.3413	.1587
0.11	.0438	.4562	0.56	.2123	.2877	1.01	.3438	.1562
0.12	.0478	.4522	0.57	.2157	.2843	1.02	.3461	.1539
0.13	.0517	.4483	0.58	.2190	.2810	1.03	.3485	.1515
0.14	.0557	.4443	0.59	.2224	.2776	1.04	.3508	.1492
0.15	.0596	.4404	0.60	.2257	.2743	1.05	.3531	.1469
0.16	.0636	.4364	0.61	.2291	.2709	1.06	.3554	.1446
0.17	.0675	.4325	0.62	.2324	.2676	1.07	.3577	.1423
0.18	.0714	.4286	0.63	.2357	.2643	1.08	.3599	.1401
0.19	.0753	.4247	0.64	.2389	.2611	1.09	.3621	.1379
0.20	.0793	.4207	0.65	.2422	.2578	1.10	.3643	.1357
0.21	.0832	.4168	0.66	.2454	.2546	1.11	.3665	.1335
0.22	.0871	.4129	0.67	.2486	.2514	1.12	.3686	.1314
0.23	.0910	.4090	0.68	.2517	.2483	1.13	.3708	.1292
0.24	.0948	.4052	0.69	.2549	.2451	1.14	.3729	.1271
0.25	.0987	.4013	0.70	.2580	.2420	1.15	.3749	.1251
0.26	.1026	.3974	0.71	.2611	.2389	1.16	.3770	.1230
0.27	.1064	.3936	0.72	.2642	.2358	1.17	.3790	.1210
0.28	.1103	.3897	0.73	.2673	.2327	1.18	.3810	.1190
0.29	.1141	.3859	0.74	.2704	.2296	1.19	.3830	.1170
0.30	.1179	.3821	0.75	.2734	.2266	1.20	.3849	.1151
0.31	.1217	.3783	0.76	.2764	.2236	1.21	.3869	.1131
0.32	.1255	.3745	0.77	.2794	.2206	1.22	.3888	.1112
0.33	.1293	.3707	0.78	.2823	.2177	1.23	.3907	.1093
0.34	.1331	.3669	0.79	.2852	.2148	1.24	.3925	.1075
0.35	.1368	.3632	0.80	.2881	.2119	1.25	.3944	.1056
0.36	.1406	.3594	0.81	.2910	.2090	1.26	.3962	.1038
0.37	.1443	.3557	0.82	.2939	.2061	1.27	.3980	.1020
0.38	.1480	.3520	0.83	.2967	.2033	1.28	.3997	.1003
0.39	.1517	.3483	0.84	.2995	.2005	1.29	.4015	.0985
0.40	.1554	.3446	0.85	.3023	.1977	1.30	.4032	.0968
0.41	.1591	.3409	0.86	.3051	.1949	1.31	.4049	.0951
0.42	.1628	.3372	0.87	.3078	.1922	1.32	.4066	.0934
0.43	.1664	.3336	0.88	.3106	.1894	1.33	.4082	.0918
0.44	.1700	.3300	0.89	.3133	.1867	1.34	.4099	.0901

Source: Tables B-2, B-3 and B-6 are taken from Tables II₁, III, and IV of R. Fisher and F. Yates, *Statistical Tables for Biological, Agricultural and Medical Research,* published by Longman Group Ltd., London (1974) 6th edition (previously published by Oliver & Boyd Ltd., Edinburgh) and by permission of authors and publishers.

z	Area Between Mean and z	Area Beyond z	z	Area Between Mean and z	Area Beyond z	z	Area Between Mean and z	Area Beyond z
1.35	.4115	.0885	1.90	.4713	.0287	2.45	.4929	.0071
1.36	.4131	.0869	1.91	.4719	.0281	2.46	.4931	.0069
1.37	.4147	.0853	1.92	.4726	.0274	2.47	.4932	.0068
1.38	.4162	.0838	1.93	.4732	.0268	2.48	.4934	.0066
1.39	.4177	.0823	1.94	.4738	.0262	2.49	.4936	.0064
1.40	.4192	.0808	1.95	.4744	.0256	2.50	.4938	.0062
1.41	.4207	.0793	1.96	.4750	.0250	2.51	.4940	.0060
1.42	.4222	.0778	1.97	.4756	.0244	2.52	.4941	.0059
1.43	.4236	.0764	1.98	.4761	.0239	2.53	.4943	.0057
1.44	.4251	.0749	1.99	.4767	.0233	2.54	.4945	.0055
1.45	.4265	.0735	2.00	.4772	.0228	2.55	.4946	.0054
1.46	.4279	.0721	2.01	.4778	.0222	2.56	.4948	.0052
1.47	.4292	.0708	2.02	.4783	.0217	2.57	.4949	.0051
1.48	.4306	.0694	2.03	.4788	.0212	2.576	.4950	.0050
1.49	.4319	.0681	2.04	.4793	.0207	2.58	.4951	.0049
						2.59	.4952	.0048
1.50	.4332	.0668	2.05	.4798	.0202			
1.51	.4345	.0655	2.06	.4803	.0197	2.60	.4953	.0047
1.52	.4357	.0643	2.07	.4808	.0192	2.61	.4955	.0045
1.53	.4370	.0630	2.08	.4812	.0188	2.62	.4956	.0044
1.54	.4382	.0618	2.09	.4817	.0183	2.63	.4957	.0043
						2.64	.4959	.0041
1.55	.4394	.0606	2.10	.4821	.0179			
1.56	.4406	.0594	2.11	.4826	.0174	2.65	.4960	.0040
1.57	.4418	.0582	2.12	.4830	.0170	2.66	.4961	.0039
1.58	.4429	.0571	2.13	.4834	.0166	2.67	.4962	.0038
1.59	.4441	.0559	2.14	.4838	.0162	2.68	.4963	.0037
						2.69	.4964	.0036
1.60	.4452	.0548	2.15	.4842	.0158			
1.61	.4463	.0537	2.16	.4846	.0154	2.70	.4965	.0035
1.62	.4474	.0526	2.17	.4850	.0150	2.71	.4966	.0034
1.63	.4484	.0516	2.18	.4854	.0146	2.72	.4967	.0033
1.64	.4495	.0505	2.19	.4857	.0143	2.73	.4968	.0032
1.645	.4500	.0500				2.74	.4969	.0031
			2.20	.4861	.0139			
1.65	.4505	.0495	2.21	.4864	.0136	2.75	.4970	.0030
1.66	.4515	.0485	2.22	.4868	.0132	2.76	.4971	.0029
1.67	.4525	.0475	2.23	.4871	.0129	2.77	.4972	.0028
1.68	.4535	.0465	2.24	.4875	.0125	2.78	.4973	.0027
1.69	.4545	.0455				2.79	.4974	.0026
			2.25	.4878	.0122			
1.70	.4554	.0446	2.26	.4881	.0119	2.80	.4974	.0026
1.71	.4564	.0436	2.27	.4884	.0116	2.81	.4975	.0025
1.72	.4573	.0427	2.28	.4887	.0113	2.82	.4976	.0024
1.73	.4582	.0418	2.29	.4890	.0110	2.83	.4977	.0023
1.74	.4591	.0409				2.84	.4977	.0023
			2.30	.4893	.0107			
1.75	.4599	.0401	2.31	.4896	.0104	2.85	.4978	.0022
1.76	.4608	.0392	2.32	.4898	.0102	2.86	.4979	.0021
1.77	.4616	.0384	2.326	.4900	.0100	2.87	.4979	.0021
1.78	.4625	.0375	2.33	.4901	.0099	2.88	.4980	.0020
1.79	.4633	.0367	2.34	.4904	.0096	2.89	.4981	.0019
1.80	.4641	.0359	2.35	.4906	.0094	2.90	.4981	.0019
1.81	.4649	.0351	2.36	.4909	.0091	2.91	.4982	.0018
1.82	.4656	.0344	2.37	.4911	.0089	2.92	.4982	.0018
1.83	.4664	.0336	2.38	.4913	.0087	2.93	.4983	.0017
1.84	.4671	.0329	2.39	.4916	.0084	2.94	.4984	.0016
1.85	.4678	.0322	2.40	.4918	.0082	2.95	.4984	.0016
1.86	.4686	.0314	2.41	.4920	.0080	2.96	.4985	.0015
1.87	.4693	.0307	2.42	.4922	.0078	2.97	.4985	.0015
1.88	.4699	.0301	2.43	.4925	.0075	2.98	.4986	.0014
1.89	.4706	.0294	2.44	.4927	.0073	2.99	.4986	.0014

Table B-2 *(cont.)*

z	Area Between Mean and z	Area Beyond z	z	Area Between Mean and z	Area Beyond z	z	Area Between Mean and z	Area Beyond z
3.00	.4987	.0013	3.15	.4992	.0008	3.50	.4998	.0002
3.01	.4987	.0013	3.16	.4992	.0008	3.60	.4998	.0002
3.02	.4987	.0013	3.17	.4992	.0008	3.70	.4999	.0001
3.03	.4988	.0012	3.18	.4993	.0007	3.80	.4999	.0001
3.04	.4988	.0012	3.19	.4993	.0007	3.90	.49995	.00005
3.05	.4989	.0011	3.20	.4993	.0007	4.00	.49997	.00003
3.06	.4989	.0011	3.21	.4993	.0007			
3.07	.4989	.0011	3.22	.4994	.0006			
3.08	.4990	.0010	3.23	.4994	.0006			
3.09	.4990	.0010	3.24	.4994	.0006			
3.10	.4990	.0010	3.25	.4994	.0006			
3.11	.4991	.0009	3.30	.4995	.0005			
3.12	.4991	.0009	3.35	.4996	.0004			
3.13	.4991	.0009	3.40	.4997	.0003			
3.14	.4992	.0008	3.45	.4997	.0003			

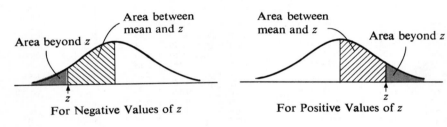

For Negative Values of z   For Positive Values of z

$$z = \frac{X - \mu}{\sigma}$$

Table B-3   Critical values of "Student's" *t*-distribution

df	Level of Significance for One-Tailed Test (α)					
	0.10	0.05	0.025	0.01	0.005	0.0005
	Level of Significance for Two-Tailed Test (α)					
	0.20	0.10	0.05	0.02	0.01	0.001
1	3.078	6.314	12.706	31.821	63.657	636.619
2	1.886	2.920	4.303	6.965	9.925	31.598
3	1.638	2.353	3.182	4.541	5.841	12.941
4	1.533	2.132	2.776	3.747	4.604	8.610
5	1.476	2.015	2.571	3.365	4.032	6.859
6	1.440	1.943	2.447	3.143	3.707	5.959
7	1.415	1.895	2.365	2.998	3.499	5.405
8	1.397	1.860	2.306	2.896	3.355	5.041
9	1.383	1.833	2.262	2.821	3.250	4.781
10	1.372	1.812	2.228	2.764	3.169	4.587
11	1.363	1.796	2.201	2.718	3.106	4.437
12	1.356	1.782	2.179	2.681	3.055	4.318
13	1.350	1.771	2.160	2.650	3.012	4.221
14	1.345	1.761	2.145	2.624	2.977	4.140
15	1.341	1.753	2.131	2.602	2.947	4.073
16	1.337	1.746	2.120	2.583	2.921	4.015
17	1.333	1.740	2.110	2.567	2.898	3.965
18	1.330	1.734	2.101	2.552	2.878	3.992
19	1.328	1.729	2.093	2.539	2.861	3.883
20	1.325	1.725	2.086	2.528	2.845	3.850
21	1.323	1.721	2.080	2.518	2.831	3.819
22	1.321	1.717	2.074	2.508	2.819	3.792
23	1.319	1.714	2.069	2.500	2.807	3.767
24	1.318	1.711	2.064	2.492	2.797	3.745
25	1.316	1.708	2.060	2.485	2.787	3.725
26	1.315	1.706	2.056	2.479	2.779	3.707
27	1.314	1.703	2.052	2.473	2.771	3.690
28	1.313	1.701	2.048	2.467	2.763	3.674
29	1.311	1.699	2.045	2.462	2.756	3.659
30	1.310	1.697	2.042	2.457	2.750	3.646
40	1.303	1.684	2.021	2.423	2.704	3.551
60	1.296	1.671	2.000	2.390	2.660	3.460
120	1.289	1.658	1.980	2.358	2.617	3.373
∞	1.282	1.645	1.960	2.326	2.576	3.291

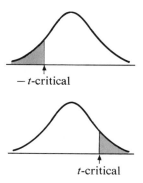

$-t$-critical

t-critical

One-Tailed Tests

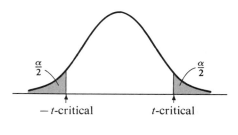

$\frac{\alpha}{2}$ $\frac{\alpha}{2}$

$-t$-critical t-critical

Two-Tailed Tests

Table B-4 Critical values of the F-distribution ($\alpha = 0.05$)

df numerator

df denominator	1	2	3	4	5	6	7	8	9	10	12	15	20	24	30	40	60	120	∞
1	161.4	199.5	215.7	224.6	230.2	234.0	236.8	238.9	240.5	241.9	243.9	245.9	248.0	249.1	250.1	251.1	252.2	253.3	254.3
2	18.51	19.00	19.16	19.25	19.30	19.33	19.35	19.37	19.38	19.40	19.41	19.43	19.45	19.45	19.46	19.47	19.48	19.49	19.50
3	10.13	9.55	9.28	9.12	9.01	8.94	8.89	8.85	8.81	8.79	8.74	8.70	8.66	8.64	8.62	8.59	8.57	8.55	8.53
4	7.71	6.94	6.59	6.39	6.26	6.16	6.09	6.04	6.00	5.96	5.91	5.86	5.80	5.77	5.75	5.72	5.69	5.66	5.63
5	6.61	5.79	5.41	5.19	5.05	4.95	4.88	4.82	4.77	4.74	4.68	4.62	4.56	4.53	4.50	4.46	4.43	4.40	4.36
6	5.99	5.14	4.76	4.53	4.39	4.28	4.21	4.15	4.10	4.06	4.00	3.94	3.87	3.84	3.81	3.77	3.74	3.70	3.67
7	5.59	4.74	4.35	4.12	3.97	3.87	3.79	3.73	3.68	3.64	3.57	3.51	3.44	3.41	3.38	3.34	3.30	3.27	3.23
8	5.32	4.46	4.07	3.84	3.69	3.58	3.50	3.44	3.39	3.35	3.28	3.22	3.15	3.12	3.08	3.04	3.01	2.97	2.93
9	5.12	4.26	3.86	3.63	3.48	3.37	3.29	3.23	3.18	3.14	3.07	3.01	2.94	2.90	2.86	2.83	2.79	2.75	2.71
10	4.96	4.10	3.71	3.48	3.33	3.22	3.14	3.07	3.02	2.98	2.91	2.85	2.77	2.74	2.70	2.66	2.62	2.58	2.54
11	4.84	3.98	3.59	3.36	3.20	3.09	3.01	2.95	2.90	2.85	2.79	2.72	2.65	2.61	2.57	2.53	2.49	2.45	2.40
12	4.75	3.89	3.49	3.26	3.11	3.00	2.91	2.85	2.80	2.75	2.69	2.62	2.54	2.51	2.47	2.43	2.38	2.34	2.30
13	4.67	3.81	3.41	3.18	3.03	2.92	2.83	2.77	2.71	2.67	2.60	2.53	2.46	2.42	2.38	2.34	2.30	2.25	2.21
14	4.60	3.74	3.34	3.11	2.96	2.85	2.76	2.70	2.65	2.60	2.53	2.46	2.39	2.35	2.31	2.27	2.22	2.18	2.13
15	4.54	3.68	3.29	3.06	2.90	2.79	2.71	2.64	2.59	2.54	2.48	2.40	2.33	2.29	2.25	2.20	2.16	2.11	2.07
16	4.49	3.63	3.24	3.01	2.85	2.74	2.66	2.59	2.54	2.49	2.42	2.35	2.28	2.24	2.19	2.15	2.11	2.06	2.01
17	4.45	3.59	3.20	2.96	2.81	2.70	2.61	2.55	2.49	2.45	2.38	2.31	2.23	2.19	2.15	2.10	2.06	2.01	1.96
18	4.41	3.55	3.16	2.93	2.77	2.66	2.58	2.51	2.46	2.41	2.34	2.27	2.19	2.15	2.11	2.06	2.02	1.97	1.92
19	4.38	3.52	3.13	2.90	2.74	2.63	2.54	2.48	2.42	2.38	2.31	2.23	2.16	2.11	2.07	2.03	1.98	1.93	1.88
20	4.35	3.49	3.10	2.87	2.71	2.60	2.51	2.45	2.39	2.35	2.28	2.20	2.12	2.08	2.04	1.99	1.95	1.90	1.84
21	4.32	3.47	3.07	2.84	2.68	2.57	2.49	2.42	2.37	2.32	2.25	2.18	2.10	2.05	2.01	1.96	1.92	1.87	1.81
22	4.30	3.44	3.05	2.82	2.66	2.55	2.46	2.40	2.34	2.30	2.23	2.15	2.07	2.03	1.98	1.94	1.89	1.84	1.78
23	4.28	3.42	3.03	2.80	2.64	2.53	2.44	2.37	2.32	2.27	2.20	2.13	2.05	2.01	1.96	1.91	1.86	1.81	1.76
24	4.26	3.40	3.01	2.78	2.62	2.51	2.42	2.36	2.30	2.25	2.18	2.11	2.03	1.98	1.94	1.89	1.84	1.79	1.73
25	4.24	3.39	2.99	2.76	2.60	2.49	2.40	2.34	2.28	2.24	2.16	2.09	2.01	1.96	1.92	1.87	1.82	1.77	1.71
26	4.23	3.37	2.98	2.74	2.59	2.47	2.39	2.32	2.27	2.22	2.15	2.07	1.99	1.95	1.90	1.85	1.80	1.75	1.69
27	4.21	3.35	2.96	2.73	2.57	2.46	2.37	2.31	2.25	2.20	2.13	2.06	1.97	1.93	1.88	1.84	1.79	1.73	1.67
28	4.20	3.34	2.95	2.71	2.56	2.45	2.36	2.29	2.24	2.19	2.12	2.04	1.96	1.91	1.87	1.82	1.77	1.71	1.65
29	4.18	3.33	2.93	2.70	2.55	2.43	2.35	2.28	2.22	2.18	2.10	2.03	1.94	1.90	1.85	1.81	1.75	1.70	1.64
30	4.17	3.32	2.92	2.69	2.53	2.42	2.33	2.27	2.21	2.16	2.09	2.01	1.93	1.89	1.84	1.79	1.74	1.68	1.62
40	4.08	3.23	2.84	2.61	2.45	2.34	2.25	2.18	2.12	2.08	2.00	1.92	1.84	1.79	1.74	1.69	1.64	1.58	1.51
60	4.00	3.15	2.76	2.53	2.37	2.25	2.17	2.10	2.04	1.99	1.92	1.84	1.75	1.70	1.65	1.59	1.53	1.47	1.39
120	3.92	3.07	2.68	2.45	2.29	2.17	2.09	2.02	1.96	1.91	1.83	1.75	1.66	1.61	1.55	1.50	1.43	1.35	1.25
∞	3.84	3.00	2.60	2.37	2.21	2.10	2.01	1.94	1.88	1.83	1.75	1.67	1.57	1.52	1.46	1.39	1.32	1.22	1.00

Source: Tables B-4 and B-5 are taken from Table 18 in E. S. Pearson and H. O. Hartley (eds.), *Biometrika Tables for Statisticians*, 3rd. ed., Vol. I (Cambridge: Cambridge University Press, 1966). Reprinted by permission of the *Biometrika* Trustees.

Table B-5   Critical values of the F-distribution (α = 0.01)

df numerator

df denominator	1	2	3	4	5	6	7	8	9	10	12	15	20	24	30	40	60	120	∞
1	4052	4999.5	5403	5625	5764	5859	5928	5981	6022	6056	6106	6157	6209	6235	6261	6287	6313	6339	6366
2	98.50	99.00	99.17	99.25	99.30	99.33	99.36	99.37	99.39	99.40	99.42	99.43	99.45	99.46	99.47	99.47	99.48	99.49	99.50
3	34.12	30.82	29.46	28.71	28.24	27.91	27.67	27.49	27.35	27.23	27.05	26.87	26.69	26.60	26.50	26.41	26.32	26.22	26.13
4	21.20	18.00	16.69	15.98	15.52	15.21	14.98	14.80	14.66	14.55	14.37	14.20	14.02	13.93	13.84	13.75	13.65	13.56	13.46
5	16.26	13.27	12.06	11.39	10.97	10.67	10.46	10.29	10.16	10.05	9.89	9.72	9.55	9.47	9.38	9.29	9.20	9.11	9.02
6	13.75	10.92	9.78	9.15	8.75	8.47	8.26	8.10	7.98	7.87	7.72	7.56	7.40	7.31	7.23	7.14	7.06	6.97	6.88
7	12.25	9.55	8.45	7.85	7.46	7.19	6.99	6.84	6.72	6.62	6.47	6.31	6.16	6.07	5.99	5.91	5.82	5.74	5.65
8	11.26	8.65	7.59	7.01	6.63	6.37	6.18	6.03	5.91	5.81	5.67	5.52	5.36	5.28	5.20	5.12	5.03	4.95	4.86
9	10.56	8.02	6.99	6.42	6.06	5.80	5.61	5.47	5.35	5.26	5.11	4.96	4.81	4.73	4.65	4.57	4.48	4.40	4.31
10	10.04	7.56	6.55	5.99	5.64	5.39	5.20	5.06	4.94	4.85	4.71	4.56	4.41	4.33	4.25	4.17	4.08	4.00	3.91
11	9.65	7.21	6.22	5.67	5.32	5.07	4.89	4.74	4.63	4.54	4.40	4.25	4.10	4.02	3.94	3.86	3.78	3.69	3.60
12	9.33	6.93	5.95	5.41	5.06	4.82	4.64	4.50	4.39	4.30	4.16	4.01	3.86	3.78	3.70	3.62	3.54	3.45	3.36
13	9.07	6.70	5.74	5.21	4.86	4.62	4.44	4.30	4.19	4.10	3.96	3.82	3.66	3.59	3.51	3.43	3.34	3.25	3.17
14	8.86	6.51	5.56	5.04	4.69	4.46	4.28	4.14	4.03	3.94	3.80	3.66	3.51	3.43	3.35	3.27	3.18	3.09	3.00
15	8.68	6.36	5.42	4.89	4.56	4.32	4.14	4.00	3.89	3.80	3.67	3.52	3.37	3.29	3.21	3.13	3.05	2.96	2.87
16	8.53	6.23	5.29	4.77	4.44	4.20	4.03	3.89	3.78	3.69	3.55	3.41	3.26	3.18	3.10	3.02	2.93	2.84	2.75
17	8.40	6.11	5.18	4.67	4.34	4.10	3.93	3.79	3.68	3.59	3.46	3.31	3.16	3.08	3.00	2.92	2.83	2.75	2.65
18	8.29	6.01	5.09	4.58	4.25	4.01	3.84	3.71	3.60	3.51	3.37	3.23	3.08	3.00	2.92	2.84	2.75	2.66	2.57
19	8.18	5.93	5.01	4.50	4.17	3.94	3.77	3.63	3.52	3.43	3.30	3.15	3.00	2.92	2.84	2.76	2.67	2.58	2.49
20	8.10	5.85	4.94	4.43	4.10	3.87	3.70	3.56	3.46	3.37	3.23	3.09	2.94	2.86	2.78	2.69	2.61	2.52	2.42
21	8.02	5.78	4.87	4.37	4.04	3.81	3.64	3.51	3.40	3.31	3.17	3.03	2.88	2.80	2.72	2.64	2.55	2.46	2.36
22	7.95	5.72	4.82	4.31	3.99	3.76	3.59	3.45	3.35	3.26	3.12	2.98	2.83	2.75	2.67	2.58	2.50	2.40	2.31
23	7.88	5.66	4.76	4.26	3.94	3.71	3.54	3.41	3.30	3.21	3.07	2.93	2.78	2.70	2.62	2.54	2.45	2.35	2.26
24	7.82	5.61	4.72	4.22	3.90	3.67	3.50	3.36	3.26	3.17	3.03	2.89	2.74	2.66	2.58	2.49	2.40	2.31	2.21
25	7.77	5.57	4.68	4.18	3.85	3.63	3.46	3.32	3.22	3.13	2.99	2.85	2.70	2.62	2.54	2.45	2.36	2.27	2.17
26	7.72	5.53	4.64	4.14	3.82	3.59	3.42	3.29	3.18	3.09	2.96	2.81	2.66	2.58	2.50	2.42	2.33	2.23	2.13
27	7.68	5.49	4.60	4.11	3.78	3.56	3.39	3.26	3.15	3.06	2.93	2.78	2.63	2.55	2.47	2.38	2.29	2.20	2.10
28	7.64	5.45	4.57	4.07	3.75	3.53	3.36	3.23	3.12	3.03	2.90	2.75	2.60	2.52	2.44	2.35	2.26	2.17	2.06
29	7.60	5.42	4.54	4.04	3.73	3.50	3.33	3.20	3.09	3.00	2.87	2.73	2.57	2.49	2.41	2.33	2.23	2.14	2.03
30	7.56	5.39	4.51	4.02	3.70	3.47	3.30	3.17	3.07	2.98	2.84	2.70	2.55	2.47	2.39	2.30	2.21	2.11	2.01
40	7.31	5.18	4.31	3.83	3.51	3.29	3.12	2.99	2.89	2.80	2.66	2.52	2.37	2.29	2.20	2.11	2.02	1.92	1.80
60	7.08	4.98	4.13	3.65	3.34	3.12	2.95	2.82	2.72	2.63	2.50	2.35	2.20	2.12	2.03	1.94	1.84	1.73	1.60
120	6.85	4.79	3.95	3.48	3.17	2.96	2.79	2.66	2.56	2.47	2.34	2.19	2.03	1.95	1.86	1.76	1.66	1.53	1.38
∞	6.63	4.61	3.78	3.32	3.02	2.80	2.64	2.51	2.41	2.32	2.18	2.04	1.88	1.79	1.70	1.59	1.47	1.32	1.00

Table B-6   Chi-square probabilities

				Probability			
	0.50	0.30	0.20	0.10	0.05	0.02	0.01
1	0.455	1.074	1.642	2.706	3.841	5.412	6.635
2	1.386	2.408	3.219	4.605	5.991	7.824	9.210
3	2.366	3.665	4.642	6.251	7.815	9.837	11.341
4	3.357	4.878	5.989	7.779	9.488	11.668	13.277
5	4.351	6.064	7.289	9.236	11.070	13.388	15.086
6	5.348	7.231	8.558	10.645	12.592	15.033	16.812
7	6.346	8.383	9.803	12.017	14.067	16.622	18.475
8	7.344	9.524	11.030	13.362	15.507	18.168	20.090
9	8.343	10.656	12.242	14.684	16.919	19.679	21.666
10	9.342	11.781	13.442	15.987	18.307	21.161	23.209
11	10.341	12.899	14.631	17.275	19.675	22.618	24.725
12	11.340	14.011	15.812	18.549	21.026	24.054	26.217
13	12.340	15.119	16.985	19.812	22.362	25.472	27.688
14	13.339	16.222	18.151	21.064	23.685	26.873	29.141
15	14.339	17.322	19.311	22.307	24.996	28.259	30.578
16	15.338	18.418	20.465	23.542	26.296	29.633	32.000
17	16.338	19.511	21.615	24.769	27.587	30.995	33.409
18	17.338	20.601	22.760	25.989	28.869	32.346	34.805
19	18.338	21.689	23.900	27.204	30.144	33.687	36.191
20	19.337	22.775	25.038	28.412	31.410	35.020	37.566
21	20.337	23.858	26.171	29.615	32.671	36.343	38.932
22	21.337	24.939	27.301	30.813	33.924	37.659	40.289
23	22.337	26.018	28.429	32.007	35.172	38.968	41.638
24	23.337	27.096	29.553	33.196	36.415	40.270	42.980
25	24.337	28.172	30.675	34.382	37.652	41.566	44.314
26	25.336	29.246	31.795	35.563	38.885	42.856	45.642
27	26.336	30.319	32.912	36.741	40.113	44.140	46.963
28	27.336	31.391	34.027	37.916	41.337	45.419	48.278
29	28.336	32.461	35.139	39.087	42.557	46.693	49.588
30	29.336	33.530	36.250	40.256	43.773	47.962	50.892

Degrees of Freedom

The probability that an obtained chi-square equals or exceeds the tabled values is shown at the top of each column. With $df = 16$, for instance, the probability that χ^2-observed ≥ 26.296 is 0.05, when H_0 is true.

Index